INDIA AND INTERNATIONAL LAW

INDIA
AND
INTERNATIONAL LAW

Edited by

BIMAL N. PATEL

MARTINUS NIJHOFF PUBLISHERS
LEIDEN / BOSTON

A C.I.P. Catalogue record for this book is available from the Library of Congress.

Printed on acid-free paper

ISBN 90-04-14519-2

Koninklijke Brill NV incorporates the imprints Brill Academic Publishers,
Martinus Nijhoff Publishers and VSP.
http://www.brill.nl

Printed in the Netherlands

Table of Contents

ACKNOWLEDGMENTS

It has been my immense pleasure and honour to edit this volume *India and International Law*. This project received inspiration and continuous assistance from Mr Jayaraj, Secretary-General of the Indian Society of International Law, which made my tasks much easier.

I felt that there was a need to put in a single place and to the extent possible contribution of India to the codification and the progressive development of international law. While there are number of general works dealing with the impact of India, this work is first of its kind which provides detailed analysis and insights in this respect into each of the important areas of international law. To achieve this aim, the authors have undertaken major exercise to historically analyze all developments, which enables the readers to see how India has acted or reacted with the changing global affairs and what one can reasonably expect in the future based on their analysis. Several officers of the Ministry of External Affairs of the Government of India have contributed to this work although in their personal capacity, thus enriching the overall substance of the work.

It is hoped that each essay will inspire interest among scholars, academicians and policy-makers to pursue further research for academic and policy purposes. Furthermore, it is also hoped that *India and International Law* will become a useful reference tool for those who are seeking practical expertise on India's policy and practical approach to international law. Some chapters provide excellent reference to the case laws of the Supreme Court and the High Courts of India whereby these courts have made important pronouncements on the implementation of international law in the domestic setting. This volume also provides readers with useful information on India's position as of 31 December 2004 on the Multilateral Treaties deposited with the UN Secretary-General.

It is a matter of great appreciation that all contributors despite their busy professional occupations, showed interest into the project and ensured its timely completion. I would like to express my profound gratitude to all authors for their team spirit and commitment.

On behalf of all authors and on my own behalf, I would like to thank Mr Ram Niwas Mirdha, President, Indian Society of International Law, for writing an inspiring and meaningful foreword for this book. The efforts of the Indian Society of International Law in the dissemination of international law in India and many developing countries deserve great appreciation (www.isil-aca.org). We would like to thank Ms Annebeth Rosenboom, Brill Academic Publishers for securing the publication of this work, who in this way makes an important contribution for the spread of knowledge of international law in the world. I would like to express my gratitude to Mr Shikhar Ranjan, Afro-Asian Legal Consultative Committee (AALCO) for his assistance. I am beholden to my family, especially my wife, for her interest and support throughout the project. The views are expressed in the personal capacity of the authors. I gladly accept the responsibility for any editorial error or omission. I look forward to receiving suggestions from the readers of this work, which has not been subsidized by any governmental or private source (bimalrupal@hotmail.com).

Bimal N. Patel
The Hague, June 2005

FOREWORD

India is one of the few countries in the world, which has been constitutionally ordained to foster respect for international law, enter into just and honourble relations with other nations and to honour the treaty obligations. India has been in the forefront of nations to promote multilateralism and international law in order to secure a peaceful world with economic justice to all peoples. It has contributed to the struggles against apartheid, colonialism and economic inequality at global level, just to name a few. India's position on these issues has contributed significantly to the formulation of progressive legal principles and normative standards in international relations. India has always endeavoured to promote a democratic multilateral legal framework where the principles of Panchsheel (five principles of co-existence) would guide international law and relations. Of course, India has taken sometimes a position that may not be in line with the expectation of some countries, as for instance, its position on the International Criminal Court and the UN reforms. This has not certainly diminished the credibility of India as a promoter of international law and of civilized behaviour between nations.

India has produced several international lawyers of repute who have been expressing their views on international law in a pronounced manner particularly after the independence of the country. The views of various experts are not available at any one single source. There has been a need to put in one place as far as possible the views of some Indian international lawyers of repute who would bring out India's contribution to the codification and progressive development of international law in various fields so that the policy-makers and scholars both in India and outside would get the assistance of a single volume which would serve the purposes of policy, research and reference. The long felt need has been fulfilled by Bimal N. Patel, a young scholar of international law energized by a combination of benign nationalism and the spirit of internationalism. In this volume, he has made an effort to bring together views of some of the knowledgeable experts regarding India's contribution to various fields of international law. Needless to say that these views are necessarily not of the government but on many important points are actually at variance to it.

I have no doubt that these essays would be of real assistance to those who wish to learn and understand India's general position on the issues that have been discussed. Thus, this attempt to serve the needs of international legal community should be highly appreciated. My ready acceptance to write foreword to this book edited by Mr Patel arises out of genuine appreciation of his pioneering and worthy efforts to fill this significant gap in world literature on international law. It is necessary for the world to acquaint itself with the thinking of Indian experts on issues of current concerns of international law.

Ram Niwas Mirdha
President
Indian Society of International Law

June 2005

ABOUT THE CONTRIBUTORS

A. David Ambrose Lecturer, Department of Legal Studies, University of Madras.

Leeladhara Bhandary M. PhD candidate, Jawaharlal Nehru University; Research Officer, Indian Society of International Law.

M. Gandhi Counsellor & Legal Adviser, Permanent Mission of India to the United Nations (New York).

Amal K. Ganguli Senior Advocate, Supreme Court of India; Regional Secretary for South West Asia, Union Internationale des Avocats; Member, Executive Council, Indian Society of International Law; Member, Executive Committee (India) International Law Association; Senior Counsel and Arbitrator in various commercial and administrative disputes in India and abroad.

C. Jayaraj Secretary General, Indian Society of International Law; Advocate, Supreme Court of India; Co-editor in Chief, ISIL Yearbook on International Humanitarian and Refugee Law.

V. G. Hegde Associate Professor of International Law, School of International Studies, Jawaharlal Nehru University, New Delhi. Formerly Senior Legal Officer, Legal and Treaties Division, Ministry of External Affairs, Government of India, New Delhi, Visiting Faculty - Indian Law Institute and the Indian Academy of International Law.

Subhash C. Kashyap *Currently*: Honorary Professor Centre for Policy Research; President Observer Research Foundation (ORF) Institute of Politics and Governance and Citizenship Development Society; Editor *South Asia Politics* (Monthly); Editor-in-Chief *Indian Social Science Review;* Advocate Supreme Court of India and Consultant in Constitutional Law; Member Board of Directors IIDEA (Stockholm). *Formerly*: Secretary-General Parliament of India (Lok Sabha); Head CIDP of IPU (Geneva), Member of the National Constitution Commission and Chairman of its Drafting Committee.

B. C. Nirmal Professor of Law, Law School, Banaras Hindu University, Varanasi.

Bimal N. Patel Staff member, Organization for the Prohibition of Chemical Weapons, The Hague, the Netherlands; Honorary Coordinator (Europe) Indian Society of International Law; Member - International Law Association, European, American, Netherlands, Australian-New Zealand Societies of International Law; Eminent Scholar and Visiting Professor Gujarat National Law University, Adjunct Professor, Sardar Patel University (e-mail: bimalrupal@hotmail.com).

Ravindra Pratap Assistant Professor, Indraprastha University School of Law, Delhi (e-mail: ravindrapratap@hotmail.com).

Pemmaraju Sreenivasa Rao Member, International Law Commission; Associate Member, Institut de Droit International. Formerly Chairman, International Law Commission (1995); President, Asian-African Legal Consultative Organization, AALCO (1998); Additional Secretary and Legal Adviser, Ministry of External Affairs of India, Co-Agent and Advocate in the *Case Concerning the Aerial Incident of 10 August 1999 (Pakistan v. India)*, International Court of Justice; have served various national, regional and international conferences and committees in various capacities; hold teaching positions in various universities such as Visiting Professor, Michigan University Law School; Senior Rockefeller Fellow, Marine Policy and Ocean Management, Woods Hole Oceanographic Institution Fellow, Woodrow Wilson International Center for Scholars, Washington.

Vishnu Dutt Sharma Legal Officer, Ministry of External Affairs, Government of India.

Manoj K. Sinha Currently Visiting Professor at Raoul Wallenberg Institute of Human Rights and Humanitarian Law, Lund Sweden; Assistant Professor (Research) Indian Academy of International Law, New Delhi.

Surinder Kaur Verma Professor of Law, University of Delhi; Formerly Director, Indian Law Institute; Dean and Head, Faculty of Law, University of Delhi; President, International Association for the Advancement of Teaching and Research in Intellectual Property (ATRIP).

INTRODUCTION

Despite the fact that international organizations, non-governmental organizations, civil society and individuals play an important role in forwarding ideas and shaping indirectly the rules, principles and concepts of international law, however, the fact remains that states are still the most fundamental actors in formulating international law. While each state attempts to play an important role in global politics to formulate rules, principles and concepts of international law that govern their relations, however, some states are able to play more prominent role due to variety of situations and factors. The history of international affairs of the last fifty years suggest that there are few states which have taken lead in ensuring that international law continue to further the goals of peace, rule of law, democracy, good governance and development. India has been undoubtedly one of these states. Its efforts to remove colonialism, apartheid, global economic inequality, etc. are the hallmarks of its contribution; currently its role in the evolving international regimes of international trade, international patents, space and maritime laws, just to name a few, is significant. On the other hand, its efforts to reform international organizations like the United Nations and to ensure permanent membership in the Security Council for countries which have made significant contributions to the realization of the purpose and principles of the United Nations indicate its commitment to work for more democratic international legal institutions.

India has been a torchbearer in enhancing the ideals and idealism of international law through variety of ways and means. To begin, India has firmly stood up to the protection of the principle of sovereign equality of states whereby despite the little prospect for all states to carry equivalent weight in international relations, it has made strenuous efforts to uphold this principle for the benefits of developing countries. India has enjoyed substantial influence in the world for its efforts to achieve, often difficult, the goals of international law. At the time of rapid globalization, India is playing unique role to eliminate the global economic inequality through legal frameworks. India has been persistent in its efforts to resolve conflicts through peaceful means, to promote disarmament, to enhance true democratic values and human rights, to open markets and create international financial stability, to raise living standards of poor countries, to protect the environment by advocating the creation of new legal mechanisms at regional and global levels.

It is against this hallmark of its contribution, the essays in this volume seek to identify and critically assess the contribution of India to the codification and progressive development of various faculties of international law. The volume also attempts to find out what are the challenges posed by the current global power structure to India and how it will respond to them in the arena of international law. Contributions to this volume have attempted to systematically respond to these questions.

Bimal N. Patel (ed.), **India and International Law, 1-8.**

Subhash C. Kashyap examines how the Indian constitution and the drafters of the Constitution have taken care of the traditional international concerns such as war and peace, peaceful settlement of international disputes, negotiations, conclusion and implementation of international agreements as well as modern international law concerns such as protection of environment and human rights. He lucidly explains the critical role of the three organs of the Indian state, the executive, the legislature and the judiciary in upholding the best principles of international law. He further illustrates and justifies his arguments through national and international case law and stipulations of all national acts, which incorporates the concerns of international law. His chapter is divided into the preamble, fundamental rights and duties, legislative jurisdiction in international law concerns, executive powers of the Union of India and international treaties. As a special service to the readers of human rights, Kashyap provides an annex stipulating human rights provisions in the UN documents and in the constitution and laws of India and a list of court cases on environmental matters. Kashyap clearly and coherently guides the readers how to understand the initiation and operation of international law in India and thus provides a sound launching pad for all other chapters.

The second essay in the first part focuses on India's position on some general principles of international law. **Pemmaraju Sreenivasa Rao** analyses an evolution of historical traditions of India and international law from ancient times to British India times through post-independence era. He provides a thorough analysis of India's position and contribution on the general principles and major issues of contemporary international law such as recognition, succession, self-determination, principles of non-use of force and non-intervention, state responsibility, prohibition of use of nuclear weapons, terrorism, legislative role of the UN Security Council, judicial review of the decisions of the UN organs, terrorism, *jus cogens* and *erga omnes* obligations, the jurisdiction of the International Criminal Court, emerging system of multilateral order and the United Nations and peaceful settlement of disputes. He convincingly argues how the consistent position of India has contributed to the promotion of rule of law in international relations during the pre-colonial era and in the post-independent phase. He shows how India defends and promotes the international community interests and strives for representative global institutions. Furthermore, Rao analyses how India has attempted to cope with violations and what are the fundamental pillars of Indian position in resolving international disputes including those disputes with its immediate neighbours.

The chapter on Trade in Services and India by **Surinder K. Verma**, provides a comprehensive overview of the regime of trade in services, its evolution, the current status and general and specific obligations for all the member States of the WTO. Verma shows why and how the concerns and interests of India in the service sector are common with other developing countries of the WTO. Verma explains India's positions and demands to the developed countries during the negotiations on GATS. Although India has taken a consistent position on various issues, Verma notes that the actual practice of implementation has remained illusory.

She concludes that the actual history of implementation since the conclusion of the Uruguay Round Agreements does not evidence the extension of favourable treatment to the developing countries. In particular, the commitments made by the developed countries in the area of temporary movement of natural persons are far from satisfactory. She suggests that an assessment by the Council for Trade in Services (CTS) under Article XIX should be mandatory before embarking on negotiating guidelines for the new round of negotiations. Such an assessment must be carried out by the CTS in collaboration with UNCTAD, which has already commenced such work. Until such an assessment is complete, both, in overall terms and sector-wise, it is very difficult to conclude that developing countries have gained much from the GATS. With regards to the temporary movement of natural persons, she advocates that there is a need for making substantially higher commitments by the developed countries in this area if the balance of benefits under GATS is to be preserved. Higher levels of commitments can be achieved on the basis of rules that are transparent; no additional tariff/tax or other regulatory restrictions on the nationals of foreign countries that do not apply to one's own nationals; no quantitative limits on temporary movement of natural persons; fees/charges applicable for providing social security nets should not apply to temporary movement of natural persons; no non-tariff barriers and no regulatory restrictions on the movement of natural persons. Verma concludes that India is negotiating all service sectors, which are open for negotiations, and has taken a cautious approach.

In his discourse on India and the International Patent System, **V. G. Hegde**, notes that India's approach towards the evolution of the international patent system is one of caution. He focuses on the role played by India, along with other developing countries, to revise the international patent system and its desire to be part of the system without compromising its basic economic and developmental objectives. His study examines the negotiating positions taken by India with a view to reduce the rigours of the international patent system not only for itself, but also for other similarly placed developing countries. He shows how the implications of various modifications, which have been undertaken by India to meet its WTO obligations, have been slowly sinking down into the Indian economic and industrial development process. While it appears that India has managed to withstand some of these changes, the precise legal and economic implications of these changes, particularly in the area of pharmaceutical and chemical sector, needs long-term review. He notes that while India is moving forward with the changes as envisaged under the WTO regime, some of these changes are likely to become new battlegrounds for a new interpretative matrix within the WTO dispute settlement system.

The Economy, Trade and Finance and international law part contains three essays. **Ravindra Pratap** in his essay on the Sovereign Economic Freedom and Interests of Other States discusses States' freedom to take economic measures to the detriment of other States' interests under modern international law. The paper gives a historical perspective of the issue at hand and discusses treaty law, resolutions of international bodies and *jus cogens*. Instead of focusing on the contribution of India in this field, Pratap has taken a different approach, namely the sovereign economic freedom professed by developing countries. He shows how the expanding domain of international law has become nothing but a measure of diminishing sovereignty and deepening dependence while allowing the states to remain sovereign and to the extent to remain independent. He identifies the major cause, which allows some states to act in disregard to the sovereignty of other states. He concludes that the sovereign equality of States and non-intervention, which lie at the core of the treaty *primus inter pares*, remain as illusory today as they were more than half a century ago.

Manoj Kumar Sinha brings out with certitude the fact that India's experience in human rights reveal that democracy, freedom and rule of law are not luxuries which only the Western societies can afford. Sinha sustains this basic argument, with the case law, practices and constitutional guarantees, throughout his discourse on the laws of human rights and the Indian constitution. After examining the constitutional regime, Sinha dwells on the directive principles of the State policy and international obligations. He succinctly summarizes the constitutional guarantees and the role of the Supreme Court of India in the upholding of the human rights during the emergency situations. He outlines in details the human rights implementation mechanisms at national levels which can enable the researchers to perform in-depth research into this subject to understand the Law and Practices of Human Rights in India. In view of the fact of the non-inclusion of certain human rights in the Indian constitution and the non-incorporation of the International Covenant on Civil and Political Rights into India's municipal laws, he explains how the Indian judiciary, in keeping pace with the contemporary developments, has rationalized the needed human rights into justiciable fundamental rights. Sinha effectively argues how the Supreme Court of India has enriched and enlarged the right of access to justice through public interest litigation and has transformed the Supreme Court into a poor man's court. In nutshell, Sinha's exposition of laws of human rights and Indian laws provides much useful critical appreciations of the situation to readers and researchers alike.

One of the most important aspects of international humanitarian law, namely, status of refugees, has been thoroughly analyzed by **B.C. Nirmal** in his contribution, *Legal Status of Refugees in India*. He examines how the issue of refugees has been dealt with since the dawn of the Indian Civilization through the 21st century. He thoroughly analyses the provisions of the Indian constitution to understand the protection of refugees and how various human rights treaties at international level and national implementation machineries at national level are rendering services to the protection of the refugees. He provides detailed inventory of statutory laws of India along with the case laws of the Supreme Court and various high courts, which guides the researchers through the emerging refugee jurisprudence in India. He shows how India can be considered a good example in hosting refugees from different countries in the past and how it has accorded humanitarian treatment and protection in the spirit of the UN Charter, human rights treaties and the cardinal principles of international refugee law. His concluding remark that India has been able to deal with the numerous refugees problems in a satisfactory manner even in the absence of a refugee specific legislation and that its human rights commissions and courts are better placed to provide needed protection to individual as well as group refugees has been well supported by facts and figures throughout the discourse. However, Nirmal takes a critical view on the existing gaps and ambiguities in the relevant laws of India, which results into a refugee policy that is beset with a lack of uniformity, predictability, accountability and transparency. He also criticizes the persistent absence of any legal process for identification of individual refugees, matters relating to admission and treatment of asylum seekers, which are handled by the administrative authorities according to certain vague and general guidelines. This practice is not in accord with the rule of law and the right to equality and non- discrimination, which the Indian Constitution pledges to secure for all citizens and non-citizens (including refugees). He strongly advocates a need for a domestic legislation to provide for the protection, rehabilitation and repatriation of refugees. In his view, the enactment of a refugee specific legislation would not only serve to codify India's international legal obligations for refugees and establish transparency, fairness, predictability and certainty in its refugee policy but it would also enhance its credibility and standing in the international community, and enable the courts and human rights institutions to protect the rights of refugees in a better way.

In International Criminal Law: Crime Prevention and Punishment, **Vishnu Dutt Sharma** explains the dire necessity for having precise definition of aggression, terrorism and drug crimes, which are acceptable to all nations. He argues that there is no denying that a lot is yet needed to be done as the process of creating preventive and combative measures always remains evolving because of changing social conditions, due to new scientific and technological developments. He is sceptical about the effectiveness of the International Criminal Court (ICC), as he identifies, certain provisions of the Statute which may result in undermining the effectiveness of the Court, such as, the consent regime for the exercise of jurisdiction by the court; "opting out" of the court's jurisdiction by states parties over war crimes for a limited period; referral of cases and deferral of proceedings by the Security Council, which may have the effect of direct interference by a political body in the functioning of a judicial body; and freedom of the Prosecutor to initiate investigation or prosecution on his own and the potential reaction of states. He advocates that if the world community is really serious in preventing and dealing effectively with the widespread criminality, it may have to put sincere efforts in having a comprehensive international extradition treaty creating explicit obligation to extradite a criminal. He concludes that the wide range international criminal justice reforms are thus required in defining the crimes, providing for more effective measures to counter them by ensuring the availability of criminals for prosecution, which could certainly help minimizing the criminal activities and could contribute to the goal of establishing international peace and security.

M. Gandhi's essay focuses on the State Responsibility and international environmental law and the contribution of India in this field. Gandhi, keeping in line with the overall approach of this volume, provides comprehensive overview of the evolution of law of state responsibility to environmental harm since Stockholm Conference and goes on to analyze the concept of state responsibility and international commons, the work of the International Law Commission (ILC) and international liability for injurious consequences arising out of acts not prohibited by international law and the status of state responsibility and liability in international environmental law. He analyses the evolution of the concept of State responsibility in international environmental law. He identifies the major weaknesses of the current rules of state responsibility in the realm of pollution and describes the role of various actors for the current state of affairs. He argues by citing the statutory mechanisms and case laws, how Indian legislature and judiciary have contributed in evolving new national standards for environmental protection. It becomes clear in his analysis that India, at international level, has played an important role by seeking a balance between the environment and development imperatives. He reveals dual approach of country like India at international and national level. At international level, India, leading the cause of developing countries has hard-bargained for softer environmental standards, in particular, when it affects the development of the developing countries. However, at the same time, at national level, India has been proactive in promulgating stringent environment laws. Gandhi advocates that this duality of approach needs to be converged. He identifies measures, which could rectify this duality, such as provision of incentives to the States, such as, setting equitable standards, on the basis of the principle of common but different obligation, for the developing countries, in vital areas of life threatening pollution such as Climate Change. Another possible way is, by a codification of law of state responsibility through integration and unification of nationally accepted environmental standards on State responsibility and liability, which by nature are more stringent, legalistic, and free from development related expression. He suggests that this could be done through a process modeled on UNCITRAL. This method could certainly help consolidation and codification of pure principles of environmental law acceptable to many developing countries as they are fit for instantaneous application.

International Environmental Law and India by **A. David Ambrose** examines India's contribution in this contemporary area of international law. He provides a comprehensive overview of the developments in international environmental law prior to and after the Stockholm Conference and analyses how India's position has been developing since the Stockholm Conference. The much debarred concept of sustainable development at national and international level remains main focus of his inquiry in the paper, which in turn, enables the readers to have a comprehensive understanding of the linkage between environment and sustainable development from an Indian point of view. He provides a thorough analysis of the role and contribution of three pillars of the Indian government, namely, the executive, judiciary and legislative, in advocating India's position at international level and in the development of environmental jurisprudence at national level. He shows how the Executive organs of India have participated in all the major international environmental negotiations and discussions from which the *opinio juris* part of customary international law can be made out and what has been the role of the Indian Legislative organ in incorporating the decisions taken at such international negotiations within municipal system. Finally, he examines the contribution of the Indian judiciary in the development of international environmental law in India.

India and the Law of Outer Space by **C. Jayraj**, seeks to locate the policy and institutional aspects of Indian space activities within the context of the existing international space laws and argues for a legally binding domestic regulatory framework in the light of its obligations under various international legal instruments. It analyzes the existing international treaty and normative framework, which internationally govern the space activities and recaptures the basic principles in this regard since they form the basis of a State Party's obligations domestically and internationally. As India has been an enthusiastic participant in the deliberations in the UNCOPUOS contributing significantly to the progressive development of international space law, an overview of the India space activities and institutions has also been discussed to show that such activities have legal consequences for India. Jayraj proposes a basic structure of a possible legal framework, which can cover all legal aspects of the space activities of India. The Indian space organizations such as Indian Space Research Organization and its scientists are enjoying enormous public esteem in view of their excellent contribution to India's reputation as a space faring nation. Under such circumstances, he advocates that India could do better if it enacts a domestic law on its space activities subject to such constitutionally permissible restrictions and national security interests. In view of the complexity of drafting a comprehensive legislation, he proposes to have a broader range of participants in drafting the text including space scientists and expert international lawyers.

The essay on the International Court of Justice and India, by **Bimal N. Patel,** examines how India has contributed to the development of jurisprudence and to the functioning of the International Court of Justice. He analyses India's contribution to advisory jurisdiction of the Court, looks at contentious cases in which India was involved as a party, and considers the general attitude of India towards the Court. Patel examines whether the contribution developed by India is an isolated product of thinking or is it inspired and influenced by contemporary theories and phenomenon elsewhere. He shows what have been the exact influence and the judicial legacy of India's contribution. Patel argues that the Indian position and attitude towards the Court is heavily guided by national interest considerations than the broader purpose of development of international law through the functioning of the ICJ. He argues that the Indian position in the advisory opinions concerning the broad issues of development or interpretation of international law shows that it has high faith in the impartiality, objectivity and capability of the ICJ. Indian position in the contentious cases does not enable to think about the futility of the judicial process because of the post-adjudicative phase uncertainty in the compliance of the judgment of the ICJ. Patel argues that the quality and quantity of reservations to the compulsory jurisdiction attached by India and many other States have reduced the usefulness of the optional clause system and thus of the Court itself. In this regard, he proposes that India should re-examine its reservations to the compulsory jurisdiction in the changed circumstances, which can set an example for other countries too. He also advocates that India, in future negotiations of the treaties, should consistently advocate attaching a jurisdictional clause to every multilateral treaty, conferring jurisdiction, at least, primarily, upon the ICJ.

The usefulness of this volume is contained in its approach, its selection of topics and its inbuilt ambition to inspire in-depth research into each of the selected topics. Along these lines, comes the much useful contribution on International Commercial Arbitration and Enforcement of Foreign Awards in India. While the volume focuses more on the topics of public international law, this essay can be much described as India's approach in the realm of international commercial dispute settlement. **Amal K. Ganguli** first makes the inquiry on the law of arbitration in India, then explains protocols on arbitration clauses and provides a detailed background on the international convention on the execution of foreign arbitral awards of 1927 (Geneva Convention of 1927). Ganguli offers in-depth insights into India's reaction to the protocol on arbitration and clauses as well as the Geneva Convention and analyses the implementation mechanism of these instruments. While examining the genesis of the New York Convention, Ganguli that the New York Convention was an attempt to rectify the weaknesses of the Geneva Convention such as clarification of the arbitration concepts and uniformity in the rules of interpretation, etc. He provides a succinct analysis of India's reaction to the New York Convention. In the limited space, Ganguli convincingly attempts to argue how India has responded to the need for speedy and effective resolution of disputes arising out of international commercial transactions and how India has respected every single united move of the world of nations being a signatory to all the international Protocol and Conventions and ratifying them at the earliest. He underlines the importance for India to adopt the UNCITRAL Model Law, namely, to bring about an uniformity in the law and practise of international commercial arbitrations and also to provide for enforcement of the foreign arbitral awards. Advocating bright future for international arbitration in India, Ganguli outlines latest measures that have been undertaken by the Government, various arbitration institutions and the Law Commission of India. These measures and resources include, excellent infrastructure provided by the Indian arbitration institutions, legislative reforms, recognition and expeditious execution of foreign awards, well-developed legal regime, jurisprudence and availability of legal and technical experts, comparable to the best in the world. In his words, *India could therefore be the natural choice for the men of commerce for the seat of international arbitrations.*

THE CONSTITUTION OF INDIA AND INTERNATIONAL LAW

Subhash C. Kashyap*

1. Introduction

There were times in ancient Indian history when the country was studded with independent republics and kingdoms with elected heads of State. There is enough evidence of the existence of codes that governed the relationship between them. Highly sophisticated rules of behaviour regulated the role of diplomatic representatives to each other's realms, conduct of negotiations, entering into agreements and treaties, war and peace. Some of the most modern concerns like those of globalisation, ecological balance, environmental health and human rights in international law occupied prominent spaces in ancient Indian literature and popular consciousness. The consciousness of human rights as a universal value goes back to centuries before the Christian era when the concept of nation states was not even born. In modern Indian history, however, it was during India's struggle for freedom from British rule and against inhuman repressive measures that the demand for human rights was forcefully raised.

Before independence, India was a part of the British Empire. It was not a sovereign state and as such could not be a member of the comity of nations in terms of international law. However, howsoever incongruous and anomalous, India was a member of the League of Nations and the International Labour Organization set up after the First World War. It signed international treaties and participated in international conferences. Notwithstanding this international status recognition, in terms of domestic polity, India continued to be denied self-determination and responsible self government and Indians had no access to basic human rights and freedoms.

There was no law guaranteeing the subjects justiciable fundamental rights and liberties. Even the little safeguards provided under some laws could be taken away. Some black laws, in fact, curtailed individual rights and liberties and did violence to basic human rights. Indians were humiliated and discriminated against in many ways,

* Honorary Research Professor Centre for Policy Research; President ORF Institute of Politics and Governance; Honorary Editor, *South Asia Politics*; Member, Board of Directors, International Institute for Democracy and Electoral Assistance (Stockholm); Advocate Supreme Court of India and consultant in Constitutional Law.

Bimal N. Patel (ed.), **India and International Law, 9-32.**

in their own country. The arbitrary acts of the British authorities in India and the inhuman repressive measures resorted to by them to silence the peaceful struggle for freedom strengthened the case for constitutional guarantees of basic human rights. From its earliest stages, the national struggle for Indian freedom, in its practical manifestation, was largely directed against racial discrimination and to securing basic human rights for all the peoples of the world at large.

As early as 1895, the Constitution of India Bill envisaged for India a constitution guaranteeing to everyone of its citizens, freedom of expression, inviolability of one's house, right to property, equality before the law and in regard to admission to public offices, right to present claims, petitions and complaints and right to personal liberty.

The Indian National Congress at its special session in Bombay in August 1918 demanded a declaration guaranteeing "equality before the law, protection in respect of liberty, life and property, freedom of speech and press, and right of association".

The Commonwealth of India Bill, finalised by the National Convention in 1925 embodied a specific "declaration of rights" visualising for every person certain fundamental rights. A resolution passed at the Madras Session of the Indian National Congress in 1927 reiterated that the basis of any future Constitution for the country must be a declaration of fundamental rights.

The Motilal Nehru Committee appointed in 1928 by the All Parties Conference declared in its Report that the first concern of the Indian people was to secure fundamental human rights that had been denied to them.

The famous Karachi Resolution of 1931 on "Fundamental Rights and Social Change" further clarified the goal and added another dimension to the demand for constitutional rights.

Following the destruction and devastation caused by the Second World War, there appeared to have dawned on the international plane a clearer realization of the importance of fundamental rights of all human beings and of the role of international organizations in upholding and enforcing them. The genesis and growth of international law of Human Rights can be traced from that point. The decades that followed would be known, among other things, for the development of the international law of human rights. From being a matter of relationship between the individual and the State, fundamental rights of the individual human being became a global concern and part of the agenda of international organizations beginning with the United Nations.

It is interesting to study how the emergence and growth of India as a new State and as a member of the comity of free nations of the world coincided with the building of the United Nations and its agencies and organs. Also, the drafting of the

Fundamental Rights in the Indian Constitution and of the Universal Declaration of Human Rights proceeded almost at the same time and on similar lines.

The process of India acquiring a real international status was accelerated with India becoming a founder member of the United Nations and a full fledged 'State' under Article 3 of the UN Charter in 1945. Notwithstanding the partition of India and creation of Pakistan in 1947, with the transfer of power to Indian hands at midnight of the 14-15 August, India became a full sovereign State and a subject of international law in its own right. It was the successor State with continued membership of the United Nations and its organs and all the rights and obligations under international law including those flowing from the past treaties and agreements.

The question of India being the successor State remained a live issue in international law circles for quite some time. Despite the Indian National Congress asking for it, the British Government did not agree to clearly provide in the Indian Independence Act that the Dominion of India will have the status of the successor State to British India and that all the external and internal treaty rights and obligations would devolve on free India. Immediately after the passing of the Indian Independence Act, the Government of India constituted Partition Council to consider *inter alia* issues connected with the succession. The Council appointed an Expert Committee to examine the juridical position. The Committee concluded that the partition did not result in the "extinction of the international personality of free India". The Steering Committee supported the view of the Expert Committee and after considering the views of the Cabinet Committee of the UK, the Foreign Office and the House of Commons concluded that the Dominion known as India will not only in name but also in fact remain identifiable with the international person known as India and all the obligations and rights of India will continue to be discharged or assisted by the Dominion of India.

But, faced with the disagreement expressed by Pakistan, the British Government referred the matter to the United Nations for its legal opinion in regard to the legal status of India and its succession rights and obligations as a successor of British India. The opinion that emerged from the Assistant Secretary-General in charge of Legal Affairs was that from the point of view of international law, the partition of India did not constitute dismemberment. It was a situation where a part of the State had broken off and become a new State. India continued its international status and retained all the rights and obligations of membership in the international organizations. The UN Security Council adopted a resolution on 21 August 1947 accepting the membership of Pakistan as a new State and thereby indirectly accepting India as the Successor State.[1]

It was against this backdrop that the founding fathers sat down to frame a constitution for independent India. The first sitting of the Constituent Assembly was

---

[1] T.S.N. Sastry, *State Succession in Indian Context* (Dominant: Delhi, 2004).

held on 9 December 1946. Only four days thereafter, the then Prime Minister Nehru moved the Objectives Resolution which pledged to make India an "independent sovereign republic" where "there would be guaranteed to all the people of India, justice, social, economic and political; equality of status, of opportunity and before the law; freedom of thought, expression, belief, faith, worship, vocation, association and action, subject to law and public morality" and "adequate safeguards would be provided for minorities, backward and tribal areas, and depressed and other backward classes".

The Resolution *inter alia* promised to maintain the integrity of the territory of India "according to justice and the law of civilized nations" so that it attains its rightful and honored place in the world and makes a full and willing contribution to the promotion of world peace and the welfare of mankind.

The fifty nations that came together to set up the United Nations Organization realized that without the recognition of human rights globally, world peace was not possible. What may be regarded in our times as the inalienable rights of all members of the human family, were crystallized in the Charter of the United Nations. The Preamble to the Charter affirmed "faith in fundamental human rights, in the dignity and worth of the human person, in the equality of men and women and of nations large and small". Under Article 1(3) of the Charter, one of the purposes of the UN was to achieve international cooperation in solving international problems of an economic, social, cultural or humanitarian character and in promoting and encouraging respect for human rights and for fundamental freedoms for all without any discrimination on grounds of race, sex, language or religion. Further, Articles 13, 55, 56, 62, 68 and 76 of the Charter provide *inter alia* for (a) UN General Assembly making recommendations for assisting the realization of human rights, (b) UN promoting universal respect for human rights and principles of equal rights and self determination of peoples, (c) responsibility of the Economic and Social Council (ECOSOC) of the UN to promote universal respect for human rights, and (d) setting up a Human Rights Commission.

The Universal Declaration of Human Rights adopted by the UN General Assembly on 10 December 1948 may be said to be almost the first ever international effort to codify the fundamental rights. The declaration was followed by a series of covenants and conventions. There have been several specific UN Treaties like (a) International Covenant on Civil and Political Rights, 1966, (b) International Covenant on Economic, Social and Cultural Rights, 1966, (c) Convention on Elimination of all Forms of Racial Discrimination, 1955, (d) Convention on Elimination of all Forms of Discrimination against Women, 1979, (e) Convention against Terror, 1985, (f) Convention on the Rights of the Child, 1989. The obligations cast binds the signatory nations. There are over one hundred covenants, declarations, treaties, conventions or other such instruments of the UN in the Human Rights area.

The basic provisions of the Constitution of India relevant to considering its interaction and inter-relationship with international law concerns are: (a) the Preamble, (b) the Fundamental Rights, (c) the Directive Principles of State Policy, (d) the Fundamental Duties of Citizens, (e) Article 73, (f) Articles 245 and 246 and the Seventh Schedule, List I, (g) Article 253, (h) Article 260, (i) Article 363 and (j) Article 372.

2. The Preamble

The Preamble to the Constitution of India, as adopted by the Constituent Assembly, which speaks of "We, the People of India", makes a solemn resolve to constitute India into a "Sovereign Democratic Republic" securing for all its citizens justice, liberty and equality, and promoting among them all fraternity. Justice is further defined as social, economic and political. Liberty includes liberty of thought, expression, belief, faith and worship, and equality means equality of status and of opportunity.

The words used in the Preamble of the Constitution are some of the noblest. They embody the highest values that human ingenuity and experience have been able to devise thus far. Professor Sir Ernest Barker of the Oxford University was so moved by the text that he quoted it as a preface to his treatise and thought that it represented the quintessence of his work. He concluded "it seemed to me, when I read it, to state in a brief and pithy form the argument of much of the book; and it may accordingly serve as a keynote".

3. Fundamental Rights (Civil and Political Rights)

Representing the crystallization of the values and concepts held dear in India's varied and rich cultural heritage, and having its roots deep in the motivational forces of the national struggle for independence, the formulation of a bill of rights was among the first tasks to which the Constituent Assembly addressed itself. A comprehensive charter of rights was soon evolved through various stages in the Assembly and its committees. Coming closely on the heels of the Universal Declaration of Human Rights, inclusion of a bill of rights in the Constitution of India accorded with the contemporary democratic and humanitarian temper and the constitutional practice in other nations of the world. It reflected in no small measure the anxiety of the founding fathers to incorporate and implement the basic principles enunciated in the Universal Declaration. Also, incorporation of a charter of fundamental rights in the Constitution became necessary in view of the special problems of minorities and the need to assure them of the fullest protection of their rights.

Part III of the Constitution which contains perhaps one of the most elaborate charters of human rights yet framed by any State, consistent with the aim of the unity of the nation and the interests of the public at large, has been described by Justice Gajendra Gadkar as the "very foundation and cornerstone of the democratic way of life ushered in this country by the Constitution".[2] These fundamental rights substantially cover all the traditional civil and political rights enumerated in Articles 2 to 21 of the Universal Declaration. According to Justice Bhagwati:

> [T]hese fundamental rights represent the basic values cherished by the people of this country since the Vedic times and they are calculated to protect the dignity of the individual and create conditions in which every human being can develop his personality to the fullest extent. They weave a 'pattern of guarantee' on the basic structure of human rights and impose negative obligations on the State not to encroach on individual liberty in its various dimensions.[3]

The fundamental rights have been guaranteed under six broad categories, namely,

a. the right to equality including equality before law and the equal protection of laws (Article 14), prohibition of discrimination on grounds of religion, race, caste, sex, or place of birth (Article 15), equality of opportunity in matters of public employment (Article 16); and abolition of untouchability and the system of titles (Articles 17 and 18);

b. the right to freedom including the right to protection of life and personal liberty (Article 21), right to freedom of speech and expression, assembly, association or union, movement and to reside and settle in any part of India, and right to practice any profession or occupation (Article 19);

c. the right against exploitation, prohibiting all forms of forced labour, child labour and traffic in human beings (Articles 23 and 24);

d. the right to freedom of conscience and free profession, practice and propagation of religion (Articles 25 to 28);

e. the right of minorities to conserve their culture, language and script and to establish and administer educational institutions of their choice (Articles 29 and 30);

f. the right to constitutional remedies for the enforcement of all these Fundamental Rights (Article 32).

Some of the fundamental rights like 'equality before law and equal protection of all laws' (Article 14), protection in respect of conviction for offences (Article 20), protection of life and personal liberty (Article 21), protection against arrest and detention in certain cases (Article 22), freedom of religion (Articles 25-28) etc. are available to all "persons".

---

[2] *Sajjan Singh vs. State of Rajasthan,* AIR 1965 SC 845.
[3] *Maneka Gandhi vs. Union of India,* AIR 1978 SC 597.

Described by Dr. S. Radhakrishnan "as a pledge to our people and a pact with the civilized world", the fundamental rights are made binding on the State, *i.e.* the executive as well as the legislature. As Patanjali Sastry, Chief Justice, said:

> [T]he whole object of Part III of the Constitution is to provide protection for the freedoms and rights mentioned therein against arbitrary invasion by the State.[4]

The Supreme Court of India has always attached the greatest importance to human rights and to UN documents like the Universal Declaration and the various covenants and treaties on human rights. Articles of the Universal Declaration and of the covenants have been relied and cited in a number of leading cases. Thus, in *People's Union for Civil Liberties vs. Union of India case*, the Court said:

> [I]nternational law today is not confined to regulating the relation between the States. Scope continues to extend. Today matters of social concerns, such as, health, education and economics apart from human rights fall within the ambit of International Regulations. International Law is more than ever aimed at individuals. It is almost [an] accepted proposition of law that the rules of customary international law which are not contrary to the municipal law shall be deemed to be incorporated in the domestic law.[5]

In a large number of cases during the last 55 years, the Supreme Court has helped to preserve, protect and enforce the basic rights and liberties of the individual against the State. As stated by Justice Sujata Manohar, Member of the National Human Rights Commission of India and a former Judge of the Supreme Court, there are two lines of reasoning used by the Indian Supreme Court in support of using international human rights norms in its domestic jurisdiction. Firstly, the fundamental rights, which are guaranteed by the Constitution, can be interpreted in the light of international human rights norms since these international human rights norms indicate the current accepted view of what is the content of the various fundamental rights which are guaranteed by the Constitution. Secondly, the Court has also said that the courts can use international conventions declaring universal fundamental rights as a legitimate guide in developing the Common Law. In the case of constitutions that are framed after 1945, the Bill of Rights contained in the Constitution (wherever present) relies largely on internationally accepted human rights norms prevalent at the time. Quite often the language of these rights contained in a constitution is also taken from such international documents or similar provisions in the constitutions of other countries.

Thus, the Supreme Court of India read into Articles 14 and 21 of the Constitution the right to travel abroad and return to one's own country in keeping with Article 13(2) of the Universal Declaration of Human Rights and Articles 12(2), (3) and (4) of the International Covenant on Civil and Political Rights (ICCPR).

---

4 *State of West Bengal vs. Subodh Gopal Bose,* AIR 1954 SC 92.

5 *People's Union for Civil Liberties vs. Union of India,* AIR 1997 SC 568.

Although India had not signed the Convention against Terror, the Supreme Court interpreted the words "life or personal liberty" in Article 21 of the Constitution to include the right to live with human dignity and against torture or assault by the State in police custody. For torture, rape and death in police custody, the Court held that it was a public wrong against a "constitutional right".[6] Any victim of unlawful detention or arrest, therefore, had an enforceable right of compensation even though while ratifying the ICCPR India had made a reservation that its legal system did not recognize a right to compensation for victims of unlawful arrest or detention. The Supreme Court held the reservation irrelevant and said compensation could be awarded for a public wrong involving infringement of a citizen's fundamental right to life. The National Commission to Review the Working of the Constitution (2002) has since recommended that the provisions of the Constitution in Article 21 be brought into conformity with Article 5 of the Universal Declaration and Articles 7 and 9(5) of ICCPR by adding the following clauses to Article 21:

> (2) No one shall be subjected to torture or to cruel, inhuman or degrading treatment or punishment.
>
> (3) Every person who has been illegally deprived of his right to life or liberty shall have an enforceable right to compensation.

The Protection of Human Rights Act, 1993, which came into force with effect from 28 September 1993, provided for the setting up of a National Human Rights Commission, State Human Rights Commissions in states and Human Rights Courts for better protection of human rights and connected matters. In addition, now there are (a) the National Commission for Women under the National Commission for Women Act, 1990, (b) the National Commission for Scheduled Castes under Article 338 as amended in 2003, (c) the National Commission for Scheduled Tribes under Article 338A as inserted in 2003 by the Eighty-ninth Amendment, (d) the National Commission for Minorities under the National Commission for Minorities Act 1992, (e) the National Commission for Backward Classes under the National Commission for Backward Classes Act 1993.

4. Directive Principles (Economic and Social Rights)

The Directive Principles of State Policy embodied in Part IV are a unique feature of India's Constitution. Article 37 declares that the Directive Principles are fundamental in the governance of the country and that it shall be the duty of the State to apply these principles in making laws. Thus, it is clear that these constitutional directives were not intended to be merely moral precepts but were to be treated as positive mandates and part and parcel of the human rights provisions of the Constitution.

---

[6] *D.K.Basu vs. State of W.B.*, 1997 (1) SCC 416; *Nilabati Behera vs. State of Orissa,* 1993 (2) SCC 746.

The Indian constitutional format in respect of human rights was remarkable as a significant and unique attempt at conflict resolution for the delicate balance it sought to achieve between political and civil rights on the one hand and social and economic rights on the other or between the individual rights and social needs. The whole scheme was based on a philosophy postulating a dialogue between individualism and social control. The Constitution-makers believed in the equal importance of the two sets of rights as a cardinal tenet of their philosophy. Human rights for them were indivisible and civil and political as well as social and economic rights had got to co-exist to make for true human happiness and lead to the fullest flowering of each human personality not only in individual but also in wider community interest.

Until the 1960s and 70s there was considerable debate in academia and among nations in regard to the primacy of civil and political rights *vs.* economic and social rights. The emergence of the third generation of environmental, cultural and developmental rights and particularly the adoption by the UN General Assembly of the Declaration of the Right to Development (1986) should set the controversy at rest. It is now globally accepted that development and human rights are interrelated and all human rights are universal, indivisible, inter-dependent and interrelated as affirmed by the Vienna Conference on Human Rights of 1993.

The decisions of the Supreme Court from the 1970s onwards have emphasized the positive aspects of the Directive Principles enshrined in the Constitution of India. These have been held to supplement fundamental rights for achieving the objective of a welfare State. Even the fundamental rights may be amended by the Parliament to implement the Directives and such legislation may be held to be valid unless it offends any of the basic features of the Constitution.

To mention two of the Directive Principles: Article 48A enjoins the State to protect and improve the environment and safeguard the forests and wildlife; Article 51 directs the State to strive for promotion of international peace and security, just and honorable relations between nations, respect for international law and treaty obligations and settlement of international disputes by arbitration.

5. Fundamental Duties (Duties to Community)

The fundamental duties enshrined in Article 51A now are in consonance with Article 29(1) of the Universal Declaration of Human Rights which says: "Everyone has duties to the community in which alone the free and full development of his personality is possible". While the Fundamental Rights provisions covered the rights of the individual and the Directive Principles the duties of the State, there were until 1976 no provisions in the Constitution of India laying down the duties of the individual even though the traditions and temper of Indian thought through the ages laid greater emphasis on duties. When Mahatma Gandhi was requested to give his thoughts on the Universal Declaration of Human Rights, he said, "the source of right is duty. If we all discharge our duties, rights will not be far to seek. If leaving duties unperformed we run after rights, they will escape us like will-o'-the-wisp, the more we pursue them, the further they will fly. I learned from my illiterate but wise mother that all rights to be deserved and preserved come from duty well done. Thus the very right to live accrues to us only when we do the duty of citizenship of the world. From this one fundamental statement, perhaps it is easy enough to define duties of man and woman and correlate every right to some corresponding duty to be first performed. Every other right can be shown to be usurpation hardly worth fighting for".

The fundamental duties of citizens enshrined in Article 51A *inter alia* included (a) renunciation of practices derogatory to the dignity of women, (b) protection and improvement of the natural environment including forests, lakes, rivers and wildlife, and to have compassion for living creatures. (this reinforces the other constitutional provision - Article 48A - under the Directive Principles which enjoins the State to protect and improve the environment and safeguard the forests and wildlife), (c) development of the scientific temper, humanism and the spirit of inquiry and reform. The Constitution ordains that science and technology must be tempered with a sense of humanism because ultimately the end of all progress is the human being and the quality of life and relationships that are developed.

The courts can certainly take fundamental duties of citizens into consideration while construing a law amenable to more than one interpretation. The Supreme Court of India has in several cases relied on Fundamental Duties contained in Article 51A to determine the duty of the State, and when necessary, given directions or framed guidelines to achieve the purpose.

The Fundamental Rights incorporated in Part III, the Directive Principles in Part IV and the Fundamental Duties in Part IVA added later, actually constitute one organic whole, which follows from the Preamble. Taken together, they really proclaim the fundamental values and constitute the foundational principles of the Constitution. Thus, the preambular assurance of the dignity of the individual, which in fact happens to be the basic principle underlying the Universal Declaration of Human Rights, is sought to be implemented through various provisions of Parts III and IV. The values of freedom and equality befitting the dignity of the human individual, made more complete and substantive by ideals of economic and social justice, so eloquently proclaimed by the Preamble, are elaborated in the Fundamental Rights and the Directive Principles.

It would be seen that the various provisions of the Fundamental Rights, Directive Principles of State Policy and Fundamental Duties of the citizens under the Constitution of India are in fulfillment of the principles in one or the other document in international law of human rights, international environmental law etc. The Table (see Annexure I at the end of the book) would show how the provisions incorporated in the Constitution of India adopted on 26 November 1949 closely resemble those embodied in the Universal Declaration of Human Rights, ICCPR and the International Covenant on Economic, Social and Cultural Rights (ICESCR).

6. International Peace and Security (Article 51)

The provision in the Constitution of India most specifically dealing with 'international peace and security', 'relations between nations', 'international law and treaty obligations' and 'settlement of international disputes' is Article 51 of the Directive Principles. It says:

> The State shall endeavour to
>
> (a) promote international peace and security;
>
> (b) maintain just and honourable relations between nations;
>
> (c) foster respect for international law and treaty obligations in the dealings of organized peoples with one another; and
>
> (d) encourage settlement of international disputes by arbitration.

Article 51 of the Constitution had its source and inspiration in the Havana Declaration of 30 November 1939. The first draft (draft Article 40) provided:

> [T]he State shall promote international peace and security by the prescription of open, just and honourable relations between nations, by the firm establishment of the understandings of international law as the actual rule of conduct among governments and by the maintenance of justice and the scrupulous respect for treaty obligations in the dealings of organised people with one another.

With the acceptance of amendments moved by Dr. Ambedkar, H.V. Kamath, Ananthasayanam Ayyangar and P. Subbarayan, draft Article 40 was adopted by the Constituent Assembly in its present form as Article 51. During the debate, all the speakers emphasized commitment of India to promoting international peace and security and adherence to principles of international law and treaty obligations. While reference to settlement of disputes through arbitration was agreed to be added by an amendment, some members expressed strong reservations in the context of the functioning of arbitrators. Obviously, the emphasis on arbitration as the preferred means for peaceful settlement of disputes was ill-concerned or misplaced. Neither India nor other countries of the world today prefer arbitration as the best for peaceful settlement of international disputes.

Article 51 has been relied upon by courts to hold that various international covenants etc. particularly those to which India is a party or signatory, become parts of national law insofar as there is no conflict between the two.[7] In *Kesavananda Bharati vs. State of Kerala* case, Chief Justice Sikri said:

---

[7] *In re. Berubari Union,* AIR 1960 SC 845; *Ali Akbar vs. U.A.R.,* AIR 1966 SC 230; *Maganbhai vs. Union of India,* AIR 1969 SC 783; *Gramophone Co. vs. Birendra,* AIR 1984 SC 667; *Varghese vs.*

> [I]n view of Article (51) of the Constitution, this Court must interpret language of the Constitution, if not intractable, which is after all a municipal law, in the light of the United Nations Charter and the solemn declaration subscribed to by India.[8]

Even though as one of the Directive Principles under Part IV of the Constitution, Article 51 is not enforceable through a court of law, Dr. Ambedkar had said in the Constituent Assembly that the intention was that the executive and legislature should not only pay lip service to these directive principles but "they should be made the basis of all executive and legislative action that may be taken hereafter in the matter of governance of the country".

7. Legislative Jurisdiction in International Law Concerns (Articles 245-246 and the Seventh Schedule)

Under Articles 245 and 246 the Parliament can make laws for the whole or any part of India within its area of competence as defined and delimited under the distribution of legislative powers between the Union and the States *vide* the Seventh Schedule. Laws made by the Parliament cannot be questioned on grounds of extra-territorial operation (Article 245). The Seventh Schedule to the Constitution embodies three lists, *viz.* the Union List, the State List and the Concurrent List consisting of 97, 66 and 47 items, respectively. In the three-fold distribution of legislative powers, residuary powers of legislation have been left with the Union (Article 248). In regard to the Union List, the jurisdiction of Parliament is exclusive. International relations, foreign affairs, international organizations and international law matters generally have been specifically assigned by the Constitution to the jurisdiction of the Union Parliament. Thus, in the Seventh Schedule, List I (Union List), the following entries are included:

a. Foreign affairs; all matters which bring the Union into relation with any foreign country (entry 10);

b. Diplomatic, consular and trade representation (entry 11);

c. United Nations Organistaion (entry 12);

d. Participation in international conferences, associations and other bodies and implementing of decisions made thereat (entry 13);

e. Entering into treaties and agreements with foreign countries and implementing of treaties, agreements and conventions with foreign countries (entry 14);

f. War and Peace (entry 15);

Bank of Cochin, AIR 1980 SC 470; *UPSE Board vs. Hari Shankar,* AIR 1979 SC 65; *Prem Shankar Shukla vs. Delhi Adm.,* AIR 1980 SC 1535; *Vishaka vs. State of Raj.* (1997) 3 SCC 433.

[8] *Kesavananda Bharati vs. State of Kerala,* AIR 1973 SC 1461.

g. Foreign jurisdiction (entry 16);

h. Citizenship, naturalization and aliens (entry 17);

i. Extradition (entry 18);

j. Admission into, and emigration and expulsion from India; passports and visas (entry 19);

k. Pilgrimages to places outside India (entry 20); and

l. Piracies and crimes committed on the high seas or in the air (entry 21).

8. Executive Power of the Union and International Treaties (Articles 73 and 253)

Under Article 73 of the Constitution, the executive power of the Union extends to all matters with respect to which Parliament may make laws and to the exercise of all powers that accrue to the Government of India from any international treaty or agreement. It is important to remember that all executive power has to be exercised in accordance with the Constitution and the laws.

Parliament has been given the power to make any law for the whole or any part of the country to give effect to any international treaty, agreement, convention or decision (Article 253). Article 253 specifically provides:

> [N]otwithstanding anything in the foregoing provisions of this Chapter, Parliament has power to make any law for the whole or any part of the territory of India for implementing any treaty, agreement or convention with any other country or countries or any decision made at any international conference, association or other body.

Implementation of treaties is in the exclusive domain of the Union under Article 253. Even though while signing and ratifying an international treaty or agreement, India commits itself to implementing it and Article 51 speaks of the State endeavor to "foster respect for international law and treaty obligations", it has to be remembered that under the scheme of the Constitution and the common law system accepted by India during the British rule and continued after the Constitution, international treaties even after being signed and ratified do not become enforceable or automatically part of national law. In order to be legally enforceable and to get implemented these have to be incorporated appropriately in enabling municipal law. If the municipal law is contrary to international law, it is the former that prevails. However, if there is no conflict with national law, the courts in India generally try to so interpret the statutes as to be in harmony with international law rules.[9]

[9] *In re Berubari Union,* AIR 1960 SC 845; *Gramophone Co. vs. Birendra,* AIR 1984 SC 667.

8.1. Treaty-making Powers

Treaties are said to be the main source of international law. In India, the Union Parliament can make laws in regard to entering into and implementing treaties etc. *vide* entry 14 of the Union List in the Seventh Schedule and thereby regulate the exercise of executive powers of the Union which are coextensive with its legislative powers and specifically extend "to the exercise of such rights, authority and jurisdiction as are exercisable by the Government of India by virtue of any treaty or agreement" (Article 73). Thus, treaty-making and implementing are basically executive functions under the scheme of Constitution of India as also under the common law. Parliament in India has no role in treaty-making or ratification processes. But, in certain matters *e.g.* those affecting the rights of the individual citizens, entailing alterations in the national laws or involving cession of the Indian territory, treaties cannot be implemented without the Parliament's approval through a law or constitutional amendment as may be necessary. Thus, an extradition treaty cannot be enforced without an Act of Parliament.[10] Also, in exercise of the inherent sovereign powers of the State, the Parliament can even enact laws for extra-territorial operation (Article 245 (2)).[11]

The single importance of putting in the Constitution Article 253 over and above the entries in List I of the Seventh Schedule was to clarify beyond doubt that for implementation of an international treaty, agreement or covenant or to give effect to a decision taken at an international forum, the Union Parliament could make any law irrespective of some items in the State List being attracted. Such law could also provide for parliamentary approval being necessary. Thus, the distribution of legislative powers between the Union and the States under the Constitution cannot come in the way of international law obligations being implemented through parliamentary law. The fact, however, is that the Parliament has not so far made any law on treaty-making powers and until that is done, the power of the executive in the matter of treaty-making shall remain unfettered.

8.2. Extra-territorial Jurisdiction (Article 260)

Under Article 260 of the Constitution read with entry 16 of the Union List in the Seventh Schedule of the Constitution, the Government of India may, by treaty or agreement with another country, exercise some extra-territorial jurisdiction in the territory of that country and "undertake any executive, legislative or judicial functions vested in the government of such territory". Article 260 clarifies that every such agreement shall be subject to and governed by any law relating to the exercise of foreign jurisdiction for the time being in force.

---

[10] *State of West Bengal vs. Jugal Kishore,* AIR 1969 SC 1171.
[11] *Bishambar vs. State of U.P.,* AIR 1982 SC 32.

8.2.a. Article 372

Article 372 continued all the pre-Constitution "laws in force" until altered, repealed or amended except that all those laws that were repugnant to any provision of the Constitution were declared to be void. The importance of this provision here lies in the fact that continuance of "laws in force" means continuance of the British common law also as that was applied by courts in India in the pre-Constitution period.[12]

8.2.b. Article 363

Article 363 bars the jurisdiction of all courts including the Supreme Court in matters arising out of "any provision of a treaty, agreement, covenant, engagement, sanad or other similar instrument" entered into by the Government of India with any princely Indian state. In the *Maharaja Pravin Chandra Bhunj Deo Kakatiya* case, it was held by the Supreme Court that any dispute arising out of the Merger Agreement, or the Instrument of Accession, was beyond the competence of the courts to enquire into.[13]

8.3. Cession of Territory

The Supreme Court in its advisory opinion under Article 143 of the Constitution in the *Berubari Case,* said that where the implementation of an agreement/treaty involved cession of Indian territory, it could not be done even by passing a law under Article 3. A Constitution Amendment Act under Article 368 was necessary. The Court was of the opinion that Article 3 applied only to a federal redistribution of territories and not to cases of cession of territory to a foreign state.[14] The opinion was followed in subsequent Supreme Court judgements in *Rama Kishore Rama Kishore Sen and Others vs. Union of India*; *Maganbhai vs. Union of India,* and *Union of India vs. Sukumarsen Gupta,* cases. [15]

8.4. Acquisition of territory

Even after India became a sovereign, democratic republic with the commencement of the Constitution on 26 January 1950, the task of achieving freedom from foreign colonial rule remained unfinished inasmuch as there still remained several pockets of Indian territories under French and Portuguese possession. Article 1 of the Constitution describing the Union and its territory says that the territory of India

---

[12] *Builders Supply Corpo. vs. Union of India,* AIR 1965 SC 1061.

[13] *Maharaja Pravin Chandra Bhunj Deo Kakatiya vs. State of Madhya Pradesh,* AIR 1961 SC 775.

[14] *In re Berubari Union and Exchange of Enclaves,* AIR 1960 SC 845.

[15] *Rama Kishore Sen and Others vs. Union of India,* AIR 1966 SC 644; *Maganbhai vs. Union of India,* AIR 1969 SC 783; *Union of India vs. Sukumarsen Gupta,* AIR 1990 SC 1962.

shall *inter alia* comprise "such other territories as may be acquired" thereby clarifying that for acquisition of territory no parliamentary approval or legislation was essential.

In accordance with the principles of international law and the Constitution of India, a negotiated settlement was reached with the French. A plebiscite was held in Chandranagore in June 1947. Following the very heavy vote in favour of merger with the Indian Union, Chandranagore was transferred to India *de facto* on 2 May 1950 and *de jure* on 9 June 1952. The *de jure* transfer came after a treaty concluded between India and France was duly ratified. The Chandranagore (Merger) Act 1954 later merged the territory in the State of West Bengal.

Administration of other French possessions in India *viz.* Pondicherry, Karaikal, Mahe and Yaman was transferred to India *de facto* under an agreement between the Governments of India and France on 21 October 1954. Later, on 28 May 1956, a treaty was signed enabling France to cede these territories to India permanently and *de jure*. The transfer was formalised on 16 August 1962 after the exchange of instruments of ratification.

The Constitution (Fourteenth Amendment) Act 1962 included these territories in the First Schedule of the Constitution as the Union territories.

Unlike the French, the Portuguese were not very responsive to the Indian aspirations and requests in regard to cession of the Indian territories of Goa, Daman and Diu and the enclaves of Dadra and Nagar Haveli in their possession. Negotiations between the Indian and Portuguese authorities failed to yield any results. The Dadra and Nagar Haveli enclaves freed themselves. The Government of India blocked the passage of Portuguese troops to the enclaves through the Indian territory. On a Portuguese complaint, the International Court of Justice held in the *Right of Passage over Indian Territory* case that the Portuguese right of passage was confined only to civilian access and that too was subject to Indian control in accordance with international law principles.[16]

On 12 June 1961, the Varisht Panchayat of free Dadra and Nagar Haveli on behalf of the people of the enclaves requested the Government of India to allow their integration into the Union of India. This was achieved through the Tenth Constitution Amendment in 1961 when Dadra and Nagar Haveli were included in the First Schedule as the Union Territories.

In December 1961, the Government of India had to take recourse to armed action to liberate the other Portuguese possessions in India *viz.* Goa, Daman and Diu. The action was swift and decisive. The Constitution (Twelfth Amendment) Act of 1962 included these territories in the First Schedule as the Union Territories. Subsequently, they became a separate State. The Supreme Court held in the *Sebastiao*

---

[16] Case concerning *Right of Passage over Indian Territory* (Merits), Judgment, ICJ Reports 1960, p. 46.

Franciso Xavier Dos Ramedios Monterio case[17] that the use of force by India did not amount to "subjugation or annexation". What was done was fully covered by the right of self-determination available to colonies under international law. In 1974 a treaty was finally signed between India and Portugal recognizing sovereignty of India over these territories.

An entirely different case was that of the merger of the State of Sikkim into the Indian Union. Sikkim was one of the princely states on the northern borders in pre-independence India. However, instead of seeking its accession to India like the other princely states, the Government of India on 5 December 1950 entered into a treaty with the Maharaja allowing Sikkim to retain its independent identity as a protectorate of India. A strong People's movement for democracy and the deteriorating law and order situation compelled the Maharaja to seek the help of Indian armed forces. In 1974, the newly elected People's Assembly of Sikkim resolved to be associated with the political and economic institutions of India. Sikkim was admitted to the Indian Union as an Associate State by the Constitution (35th Amendment) Act of 1974. In April 1975, the Sikkim Assembly passed another resolution seeking to become an integral part of India. A popular referendum also supported it. The Constitution (36th Amendment) Act of 1975 admitted Sikkim as an integral part of India and as a new State in the First Schedule.

9. International Environmental Law (Articles 47, 48, 48A, 49, 51A(g), List III (Concurrent), Entries 17A and 17B)

One of the latest branches of international law that has emerged and has been developing during recent years is environmental law. Foundations of international concern in the area were laid at the 1972 UN Conference on Human Environment at Stockholm with the then Prime Minister of India, Shrimati Indira Gandhi playing a seminal role flagging the urgent need for international cooperation to meet the burgeoning problems of environmental decay. The Stockholm Declaration highlights the action agenda that has since become more imperative. Notwithstanding the problems of national borders and sensitivities on issues of sovereignty, the declaration was based on the realization that environment and ecology were essentially global and could not be attended to within any territorial boundaries.

An eminent Indian jurist and one time President of the International Court of Justice, Dr. Nagendra Singh played a leading role in the preparation of the World Charter for Nature adopted by the UN General Assembly in 1982 and the Report of the World Commission on Environment and Development (Bruntland Commission), 1987. It was during the period Dr. Nagendra Singh was ICJ President that the ICJ declared its willingness to deal with environmental protection cases.

The Constitution of India as adopted in 1949 did not contain any specific mention of environmental protection. There were, however, some provisions which

---

[17] *Sebastiao Franciso Xavier Dos Ramedios Monterio vs. State of Goa* (1970) SCR 100.

were relevant to environmental issues as can be observed in the Directive Principles, *e.g.*

a. Article 47 (Duty of the State to raise the level of nutrition and the standard of living and to improve public health): The State shall regard the raising of the level of nutrition and the standard of living of its people and the improvement of public health as among its primary duties and, in particular, the State shall endeavour to bring about prohibition of the consumption except for medicinal purposes of intoxicating drinks and of drugs which are injurious to health.

b. Article 48 (Organization of agriculture and animal husbandry): The State shall endeavour to organize agriculture and animal husbandry on modern and scientific lines and shall, in particular, take steps for preserving and improving the breeds, and prohibiting the slaughter, of cows and calves and other milch and draught cattle.

c. Article 49 (Protection of monuments and places and objects of national importance): It shall be the obligation of the State to protect every monument or place or object of artistic or historic interest, declared by or under law made by Parliament to be of national importance, from spoliation, disfigurement, destruction, removal, disposal or export, as the case may be.

The following provisions related to environmental protection were added by the Constitution (42nd Amendment) Act 1976:

a. The State shall endeavour to protect and improve the environment and to safeguard the forests and wild life of the country (Article 48A),

b. It shall be the fundamental duty of every citizen to protect and improve the natural environment including forests, lakes, rivers and wild life and to have compassion for living creatures (Article 51A(g)).

Entries on 'forests', 'protection of wild animals and birds' and 'population control and family planning' were transferred to the Concurrent List in the Seventh Schedule thereby enabling the Union Government to exercise more meaningful and effective control and go for Union laws for the purpose.

During the debate on the above Constitution Amendment, in the Upper and Lower Houses of the Parliament, suggestions were made and amendments moved for casting a responsibility on the Government for taking adequate measures for preventing environmental pollution and conserving and developing water, soil and other natural resources. An apprehension was expressed that the endeavour to safeguard the forests and wildlife (Article 48A) might not affect adversely the tribal people. While none of the amendments was accepted, the then Prime Minister Shrimati Indira Gandhi tried to dispel the apprehension about tribal life being adversely affected. She said:

> [o]n the contrary, if forests are better looked after and wild life is preserved, there would be far greater opportunities for employment as well as a better ecological balance in the whole area which would lead to an improvement in the life of the tribal. So far, the feeling of responsibility towards nature was absent all over the world. It was not absent in our own ancient books; but came about because we adopted the western viewpoint. Now the time has come to go back to the sources of strength of the human race and to try to preserve and revitalize them.

The National Commission to Review the Working of the Constitution (2002) recommended the addition of the following new Article in Part III of the Constitution containing Fundamental Rights:

> *30D. Right to safe drinking water, prevention of pollution conservation of ecology and sustainable development –*
>
> Every person shall have the right –
>
> (a) to safe drinking water;
>
> (b) to an environment that is not harmful to one's health or well-being; and
>
> (c) to have the environment protected, for the benefit of present and future generations so as to –
>
> (i) prevent pollution and ecological degradation;
>
> (ii) promote conservation; and
>
> (iii) secure ecologically sustainable development use of natural resources while promoting justifiable economic and social development.

Under a strategic plan of action for the implementation of the Directive Principles of State Policy, the Constitution Commission has *inter alia* suggested:

a. Intensification of animal husbandry programmes and production of quality dairy products

b. Integrated Programme of intensive Aquaculture, including use of common property resources like village ponds and lakes.

c. Afforestation and Wasteland Development to bring an additional 12 million hectares under forest plantation and contribute to rural asset building activity.

d. Soil and Water Conservation to support forestation and Natural Resource Conservation towards eco-friendly agriculture.

e. Water Conservation and Tank Rehabilitation.

f. Production and use of organic manures through vermiculture and other improved techniques and production of organic health foods from them.

The Indian Parliament has enacted several laws in recent years in the area of preventing environmental pollution and preserving the ecological balance, *e.g.*

a. Water (Prevention and Control of Pollution) Act, 1974,

b. Water (Prevention and Control of Pollution) Cess Act, 1977,

c. Air (Prevention and Control of Pollution) Act, 1981,

d. Wild Life (Protection) Act, 1972,

e. Wild Life (Protection) Amendment Act, 1982,

f. Prevention of Cruelty to Animals (Amendment) Act, 1982,

g. Forest (conservation) Act, 1980,

h. Insecticides Act, 1968,

i. Environment (Protection) Act, 1986, etc.

As stated by P. Chandrasekhara Rao in the conclusion of his brilliant paper on the theme, "the Constitution of India, as amended, prescribes a flexible approach to environmental problems, an approach which shows an awareness of the stakes involved and which also permits the State to adopt an integrated and realistic solution to the problem, especially having regard to the fact that there are few, if any, activities of man which do not in one way or another relate themselves to environment…further, the present scheme of the Constitution throws open several ways and means for the enactment of Union legislation with respect to State subjects, *e.g.*, by consent of States under Article 252 as in the case of the Water Pollution Act, 1974, and by virtue of Article 253 for implementing international agreements or decisions of international bodies as in the case of the Air Pollution Act, 1981. In short, the Constitution contains a flexible structure that could serve as a spring-board for taking meaningful measures in the filed of environment".

The judiciary in India, particularly the Supreme Court, has been particularly active in the area of preventing environmental pollution as can be seen by the very large number of cases decided and directions given (Annexure II).[18]

---

[18] For a summary of the facts of the cases and decisions of the Court, see *Fundamental Duties of Citizens: Report of the Committee set up by the Government of India to operationalize the suggestions to*

In several cases relating to the preservation and conservation of environment, ecology, and prevention of degeneration of forests, wild life, flora and fauna, etc., the Supreme Court has relied upon provisions under the Fundamental Rights, the Directive Principles and the Fundamental Duties.

As the Verma Committee said "The Supreme Court of India has in several cases relied on the Fundamental Duties contained in Article 51A to determine the duty of the State, and when necessary, give directions or frame guidelines to achieve the purpose. This has been done in several cases relating to preservation and conservation of environment, ecology, and prevention of degeneration of forests, wildlife, flora and fauna, etc". The Court has observed that "the preservation of environment and maintenance of the ecological balance are the responsibility not only of the Government but also the Fundamental Duty of every citizen".[19]

The Verma Committee on the Fundamental Duties has listed and documented as many as 137 Supreme Court cases in the area of environmental protection.[20]

The Supreme Court has held that under Article 48A read with Articles 39(e) and 47, it is the duty of the State to improve public health and "protect and improve the environment"[21] to protect public health from the alarming levels of air pollution. The Supreme Court banned the plying of diesel buses in Delhi and directed the Government to change public transport from diesel to compressed natural gas.[22]

Many of the environmental pollution issues have been brought before the courts under Articles 32 or 226 by way of Public Interest Litigation. The Supreme Court has taken a very active interest in the matter. The effort has been to strike and maintain a balance between the needs of preservation of the environment and economic development of the country.[23]

---

teach Fundamental Duties to the Citizens of the Country, Government of India, Ministry of Human Resources Development, New Delhi, 1999.

[19] Report of the Justice Verma Committee on Fundamental Duties, Government of India, Ministry of Human Resources Development, New Delhi, 1999.

[20] *Buffalo Traders Welfare Asso. vs. Maneka Gandhi,* 1994 Supp (3) SCC 448 (Slaughter House Idgah, Delhi); *M.C. Mehta vs. Union of India,* 1994 Supp (3) SCC 717 (Air Polution by industries); *Vellore Citizens Welfare Forum vs. Union of India,* 1996 AIR (SC) 2715 (Right to clean environment; *M.C. Mehta vs. Union of India,* (1999) SCC 413 (Traffic Management and pollution, Delhi); *T.N.G. Thirumulkpad vs. Union of India,* (1998) 9 SCC 632 (Protection of forests); *M.C. Mehta vs. Union of India,* (1998) 9 SCC 93 (Protection of Taj Mahal), *M.C. Mehta vs. Union of India,* (1998) 8 SCC 648 (Lead-free petrol for pollution control), *M.C. Mehta vs. Union of India,* (1998) 1 SCC 363 (Removal of hoardings); *S. Jagannath vs. Union of India,* 1997 (1) JT 160 (Coastal pollution due to shrimp farming); *Indian Council for Enviro-Legal Action vs. Union of India,* AIR (SC) 1446 (Industrial Pollution).

[21] *M.C.Mehta vs. Union of India,* J T 2002 (3) SC 527.

[22] *M.C. Mehta vs. Union of India,* (2002) 4 SCC 356, 378.

[23] *Rural Litigation and Entitlement Kendra vs. State of U.P.,* AIR 1987 SC 359; *Banwasi Seva Ashram vs. State of U.P.,* AIR 1987 SC 374; *Subhash Kumar vs. State of Bihar,* AIR 1891 SC 420.

Whenever a problem of ecology is brought before the court, it is bound to keep in mind Articles 48A and 51A(g). "The least that the court may do is to examine whether appropriate considerations are borne in mind and irrelevance excluded. In appropriate cases, the Court may go further".[24]Thus, in the matter of protecting Taj Mahal from decay on account of the environmental pollution, the Supreme Court issued several directions.[25] It ordered the water polluting tanneries closed.[26]

By its creative interpretation of "right to life" in Article 21 to include the right to the quality of life which includes right to pollution free water and air – "to live with dignity" - the Supreme Court has made a significant contribution to protect "environment" from dangerous levels of pollution. For this purpose the Court has drawn support from Articles 47, 48A and 51A(g) and read them with Article 21. It has held that on the basis of Article 21, the duty under Article 48A can be enforced.[27] The Court said that:

> [R]ight to life is a fundamental right under Article 21 of the Constitution and it includes the right of enjoyment of pollution free water and air for full enjoyment of life. If anything endangers or impairs that quality of life in derogation of laws, a citizen has right to have recourse to Article 32 of the Constitution for removing the pollution of water or air which may be detrimental to the quality of life.[28]

In the *A.P. Pollution Control Board case*, the Supreme Court linked the ecological pollution issues with basic human rights and said:

> [e]nvironmental concerns arising in the Court under Article 32 or under Article 136 or under Article 226 in the High Courts are, in our view, of equal importance as Human Rights concerns. In fact, both are to be traced to Article 21, which deals with fundamental rights to life and liberty. While environmental aspects concern 'life', human rights aspects concern 'liberty'.[29]

In the *M.C. Mehta* case, the Supreme Court propounded the doctrine that natural resources like air, water, sea and soil being necessary for life and for the general use of the people are to be held by the Government in public trust.[30] These are a gift of nature and cannot be for private ownership.

---

[24] *Shri Sachidananda Pandey vs. State of West Bengal,* AIR 1987 SC 1109.
[25] *M.C. Mehta vs. Union of India,* AIR 1997 SC 734.
[26] *M.C. Mehta vs. Union of India,* AIR 1988 SC 1037; *Vellore Citizens Welfare Forum vs. Union of India,* AIR 1996 SC 2721.
[27] *Satish vs. State of U.P.,* (1992) Supp (2) SCC 94; *Tarun vs. Union of India,* (1992) Supp. 2 SCC 448; *Mehta vs. Union of India* (1992) Supp 2 SCC 85, 633, 637.
[28] *Subhash Kumar vs. State of Bihar,* AIR 1991 SC 420.
[29] *A.P. Pollution Control Board vs. M.V. Nayudu* AIR 1999 SC 825.
[30] *M.C. Mehta vs. Kamal Nath* AIR 1997 (I) SCC 388.

The Supreme Court has, with reference to Article 51A(g), issued oral orders stopping quarrying operations at certain places in Uttar Pradesh. Similarly, it has issued directions regarding declaring disputed areas as 'reserved forests' under section 20 of the Indian Forests Act of 1927.[31]

The Government of India also has been fully alive to the imperative needs of ecological and environmental protection. The Ministry of Environment and Forests through its various schemes/programmes/activities has been attempting to inculcate a sense of responsibility, love and respect among all sections of society for the natural environment including forests, lakes, rivers and wildlife and the need to protect and preserve it – for now and posterity – through non-formal methods of education. During the past 23 years of its existence, several initiatives have been taken and a variety of schemes and programmes launched to cover all sections of society, *e.g.*

a. National Environment Awareness Campaign,

b. Eco/Nature Clubs at Schools,

c. Paryavaran Vahini,

d. Commissioning the Production of Films on Various Aspects of Environment, Forests and Wild Life,

e. Centres of Excellence on Different Areas of Environment and Forests for Strengthening Awareness, Research and Training,

f. National and Regional Museums of Natural History,

g. Awards and Fellowships,

h. National Afforestation and Eco-Development Board,

i. National River Conservation Directorate,

j. Biosphere Reserves Programme, Wet Lands and Lakes Conservation, River Conservation Programme, Project Tiger, Project Elephant, and other protected areas programmes and several forestry programmes, etc.

k. In-service Training Programmes regarding Protection of Environment and Forests including Wild Life:

---

[31] *Mumbai Kamgar Sabha vs. Abdulbhai,* AIR 1976 SC 1455; *Rural Litigation and Entitlement Kendra vs. State of Uttar Pradesh,* AIR 1987 SC 2426; *Banwasi Seva Ashram vs. State of Uttar Pradesh,* AIR 1987 SC 374.

i. Indian Council of Forestry Research and Education, Dehradun, organizes several training programmes in the field of forestry education, management and research,

ii. Indira Gandhi National Forest academy, Dehradun, imparts a wide range of in-service professional training to the Indian Forest Service personnel,

iii. Directorate of Forest Education, Dehradun, provides training to State Forest Service personnel and Forest Rangers,

iv. Indian Institute of Forest Management, Bhopal, provides in-service training,

v. Wild Life Institute of India, Dehradun, imparts training to Government and Non-Government personnel on conservation and management of the wild life resources,

vi. Lal Bahadur Shastri National Academy of Administration, Mussoorie, Indian Institute of Public Administration, New Delhi, Administrative Staff College of India, Hyderabad, and Indian Institute of Management at Ahmedabad, Bangalore, Calcutta, etc. have included environment and forestry components in the existing training programmes being organized by these premier management institutions,

vii. Central and State Pollution Control Boards also organize in-service training programmes from time to time for industry personnel,

viii. Ozone Cell of the Ministry of Environment and Forests organizes specialized training programmes for personnel of industries, etc.

10. Conclusions

It would be seen that the Constitution of India has taken meticulous care of many of the traditional and modern international law concerns including war and peace, peaceful settlement of disputes, entering into agreements and treaties and their implementation, cession and acquisition of territory, international organizations, environmental protection and human rights – civil and political, economic and social. The three organs of the State – the Executive, the Legislature and the Judiciary – established by the Constitution, have also generally, among them, tried their best to jealously guard the best principles of international law through executive action, legislation and judicial interpretation in harmony with the provisions of the Constitution of the sovereign democratic republic of India.

THE INDIAN POSITION ON SOME GENERAL PRINCIPLES OF INTERNATIONAL LAW

Pemmaraju Sreenivasa Rao[*]

1. Historical Tradition of India and International law

At the very outset, it must be noted that States belonging to different regions of the world, irrespective of the cultural traditions they symbolize, subscribe to the same basic principles of international law. Referring to the relations between countries of the Orient or the East, it is observed that even before a powerful Europe existed "ancient cultures hailed basically the same principles, or perhaps rather ideas, that are purported to have been invented by the occidental world".[1] The conclusion drawn from that is that: "different systems in the world today may be based on the same theoretical foundation when we get down to the real essence of our common values in international law".[2] For instance, sophisticated rules about the sanctity of treaties[3], protection of envoys, respect for the humanitarian principles governing the law of war, protection of civilians, unarmed, injured in combat, and not using weapons causing excessive and disproportionate harm, and exchange of prisoners were developed principles of international relations in ancient India.[4] As Nagendra Singh, a former President of the ICJ, pointed out:

---

* Member, International Law Commission, Associate Member, Institut de Droit International, and former Additonal Secretary and the Legal Adviser, Ministry of External Affairs, Government of India.

[1] B. J. Theutenberg, "Different Trends of the International Legal System of Today", in *The Future of International Law in a Multicultural World*, Rene-Jean Dupuy (ed.) Workshop, The Hague, 17-19 November 1983, 261-284, at 265.

[2] *Ibid.*, 266.

[3] Treaties concluded in ancient India were not subject to the type of formalities, as we know of them today. But they are still valid treaties. See the *Case Concerning the Right of Passage over Indian Territory (Portugal v. India)*, Merits, Judgment, 12 April 1960, ICJ Reports, p. 6. Portugal had relied on the Treaty of Poona of 1779 and on *sanads* (decrees) issued by the Maratha ruler in 1783 and 1785, as having conferred on Portugal sovereignty over the enclaves with the right of passage to them; India had objected that what was alleged to be the Treaty of 1779 was not validly entered into and never became in law a treaty binding upon the Marathas. The Court, however, found that the Marathas did not at any time cast any doubt upon the validity or binding character of the Treaty. http://www/icj-cij.org.

[4] *Ibid*,; See also Nagendra Singh, "The Basic Concepts of Universality and The Development of International Law", Rene-Jean Dupuy (ed.), *supra* note 1, 239-259, at 241-249; R. P. Anand, "The Role of Asian States in the Development of International Law", *ibid.*, pp. 105-116; M. L. Sarin, "The Asian -African states and The Development of International Law", *ibid.*, pp. 117-142.

***Bimal N. Patel (ed.),* India and International Law, 33-65.**

> It would thus appear that through centuries of history relying mostly on a process of trial and error based on application of reason, retaliation and mutual self-interest coupled with the principle of reciprocity, it was possible to develop inter-State law right from ancient times to the difficult middle ages and then down to the modern world today.[5]

Several writers documented India's tradition in international law.[6] It is clear from this that it is better not to overemphasize "the particular structure of the modern Euro-centric international law".[7] The essential point is that international law, since the conclusion of the Treaty of Westphalia, began to operate on a more secular basis and natural law tradition. These practices had their impact on the mutual relations of States in other parts of the world as well over a period of time, particularly with the domination of the European powers over distant lands. As the system of sovereign States spread across the world, it is observed, so did the system of international law that was based on it.[8]

2. British India and International Law

It is well-known that British India during the colonial period was treated as a separate State, with an international legal personality of its own. It was a member of the League of Nations. It became party to the Statute of the Permanent Court of Justice and the General Act on the Pacific Settlement of Disputes of 1928 (the Act). It entered into treaties and ratified them. It had the dubious distinction of being the only country that ratified the 1937 Geneva Convention for the Prevention and Punishment of Terrorism, which the UK and other countries did not ratify.[9] British India also participated in the San Francisco Conference that led to the establishment of the United Nations.

---

5 N. Singh, *Id.* at 249.

6 C.J.Chacko, "India's Contribution to the Field of International Law Concepts", 93 *Recueil des Cours*, 117-121 (1958-I); C.H. Alexandrowicz, *An Introduction to the History of the Law of Nations in the East Indies (16th, 17th and 18th Centuries* (1967); C.H. Alexandrowicz, "The Afro-Asian World and the Law of Nations (Historical Aspects)", 123 *Recueil des Cours* 117-214 (1968-I); K.R.R.Sastry, "Hinduism and International Law", 117 *Recueil des Cours*, 503-615 (1966-I); Nagendra Singh, *India and International Law*, 1973 (vol.1, Part A); R. P. Anand, *New States and International law* (1972); R .P. Anand, *Origin and Development of the Law of the Sea: History of International Law Revisited* (1983); M.K. Nawaz, *The Changing Law of Nations: Indian Focus* (2000).

7 Theutenberg, *supra* note 1, at 276.

8 Edith Brown Weiss, "The Rise and Fall of International Law?", LXIX *Fordham Law Review* 345-372 (2000), at 347 (citing J. L. Brierly).

9 For a comment on the Convention for the Prevention and Punishment of Terrorism, 1937 see BYBIL, XIX (1938), 214-216. British India became party to the Convention obviously because of its own insecurity due to the struggle for India's independence which was in full swing at the time. For a fuller account see Geoffrey Marston, "Early Attempts to Suppress Terrorism: The Terrorism and International Criminal Court conventions of 1937", LXXIII *British Yearbook of International Law, 2002* (2003) 293-313.

3. Succession

After India gained its independence the first matter to be settled was the status of India and Pakistan in relation to British India. It is well accepted that India is the same legal entity as British India and that Pakistan is a totally new State.[10] Another question to be settled was about the succession of India and Pakistan to treaties to which British India was a party prior to the independence. Article 4 of the Indian Independence (International Arrangements) Order of 1947, dealt with the matter. It noted that:

> 4. Subject to Articles 2 and 3 of this agreement, rights and obligations under all international agreements to which India is a party immediately before the appointed day will devolve both upon the Dominion of India and upon the Dominion of Pakistan, and will, if necessary, be apportioned between the two Dominions.[11]

On the basis of this Article 4, Pakistan claimed succession to the 1928 General Act on the Pacific Settlement of Disputes in order to invoke the jurisdiction of the International Court of Justice (the Court) first in the case concerning the *Trial of the Prisoners of War* of 1973. Pakistan was seeking interim measures from the Court to restrain India from transferring 195 Pakistani Prisoners in custody of India to the custody of Bangladesh, for trial in that country on charges of genocide. This raised two questions. First, whether independent India is bound by the commitments made by British India under the 1928 General Act, which is political agreement. Second, whether Pakistan could claim succession to a political treaty, which by its very nature does not run with the land that is transferred to it as part of partition. India did not participate in the proceedings but submitted memorandums first

[10] "The Succession of States in relation to the membership in the United Nations", Memorandum prepared by the UN Secretariat, *I. L. C. Yearbook*, 1962, vol. II, p. 119; M. N. Shaw, *International Law* (5th edn, 2004) at 865. The author observed that "(I)n deciding whether continuity or succession has occurred, one has to consider the classical criteria of the creation of statehood, together with assertions as to status made by the parties directly concerned and the attitudes adopted by third states and international organizations." After examining the relevant circumstances, for example, he noted that after the dissolution of the former Soviet Union, the Russian Federation was regarded as the continuation of that State and hence was designated as the original member of the UN, with the status of a permanent member of the Security Council. The case of the Federal Republic of Yugoslavia (Serbia and Montenegro), following the dissolution of the Socialist Federal Republic of Yugoslavia (SFRY), was different. While Slovenia, Croatia and Bosnia were recognized by the members of the European Community and admitted as new members of the UN, FRY was not treated as a continuation of the SFRY. FRY maintained that it was so but had to yield and seek membership of the UN also as a new State. According to the Opinion 10 of the Arbitration Commission on Yugoslavia, former SFRY simply ceased to exist. Shaw at 866-867.

[11] For the India Independence (International Arrangements) Order of 1947, see Annex-C of the Indian Counter Memorial in the Pleadings, Memorials and Written Documents, *Aerial Incident of 10 August 1999* (Pakistan *v.* India), para. 18.

contesting the jurisdiction of the Court and second, explaining its position on the issues of succession raised by Pakistan. In that case India took the view that the 1928 General Act was a political treaty and could not be transmitted automatically to the Successor State. It also argued that the Act could not have survived the demise of the League of Nations as it was integrally linked to the same. Before filing any written pleadings, Pakistan however requested the Court to discontinue the proceedings indicating that agreement was reached with India following negotiations with that country. The Court accordingly by an Order of 15 December 1973 removed the case from its list.[12] In the event, none of the arguments India advanced came to be considered by the Court.

Later, by way of abundant caution, to foreclose any future possibility of engagement of India before the Court, on the basis of the 1928 General Act, against its consent, India sent a communication to the Secretary General of the United Nations dated 18 September of 1974. It stated that the Government of India "never regarded themselves as bound by the General Act of 1928 since her independence, whether by a succession or otherwise". Accordingly, it asserted once again that "India has never been and is not a party to the General Act of 1928 ever since her independence".[13]

Nevertheless, Article 17 of the General Act read with Article 36(1) and Article 37 of the ICJ Statute was one of the grounds again relied upon by Pakistan to establish the jurisdiction of the Court in the case concerning the *Aerial Incident of 10 August 1999*.[14] Pakistan in this case sought compensation from India claiming that it was responsible for the destruction of one of its aircrafts and for the killing of persons aboard the aircraft in violation of its obligations under the UN Charter, customary international law and relevant treaty provisions.

The claim of Pakistan that it is a co-successor to all treaties to which British India was a party including the 1928 General Act was contested by India. It also rejected the contention of Pakistan that the 1928 General Act devolved upon India. It repeated its earlier position that the General Act was not only a political treaty but also one that was integrally linked to the League of Nations and hence could not survive the demise of that institution. The Court did not find it necessary to pronounce upon the status of the 1928 General Act following the demise of the League of Nations. On the other hand, the Court found that the Indian communication to the Secretary-General of the United Nations dated 18 September 1974 had the effect of removing India beyond any doubt as a party to the 1928

---

[12] *Trial of Pakistani Prisoners of War* (Pakistan *v.* India), Order of 15 December 1973, ICJ Reports 1973, p. 347.

[13] For the full text of the Indian communication, see annex B to the Indian Counter Memorial, note 11.

[14] *Aerial Incident of 10 August 1999* (Pakistan *v.* India), (Jurisdiction), ICJ Reports 2000, para. 12

General Act as of 16 August 1979 by virtue of the operation of Article 45 of the Act.

It was sufficient for the Court to reject the contention of Pakistan on the ground that India could not be considered to be a party to the General Act as of 16 August 1979, that is, as of the date of its application in the present case. It may be noted in this connection that India is not party to the 1978 Convention of Succession of States in respect of Treaties, which is in force since 6 November 1996. Nevertheless, in so far as it is seen that some of its provisions, like Article 16 and 17, are reflective of the customary principles of international law,[15] India may be regarded as a "newly independent State", which had inherited the personality of British India.[16] Article 16 States that

> A newly independent State is not bound to maintain in force, or to become a party to, any treaty by reason of the fact that at the date of the succession of States the treaty was in force in respect of the territory to which the succession relates.[17]

Consequently, India argued, there could not be any automatic succession in respect of the 1928 General Act, even if it is regarded as in force for British India at the time of independence of India in 1947.

In any case, with respect to the political treaties, it is well-accepted in international law that they do not automatically devolve upon successor States.[18] O'Connell reviewed the question of transmissibility of certain treaties, particularly those concerning renunciation of war and pacific settlement of disputes, copyright and counterfeiting and weights and measures upon succession, and came to the conclusion that "clearly not all these treaties are transmissible". He further noted that "no state has yet acknowledged its succession to the General Act for the Pacific Settlement of International Disputes".[19] Oscar Schachter drew similar conclusions with specific reference to Article 4 of the India's Independence Order of 1947. He observed that:

> The intended effect of this provision appears to extend to Pakistan treaty rights and duties, which would not devolve upon it under the generally accepted rule of law. For it has been recognized that when a territory breaks off and becomes a state, succession takes place only `with regard to such

---

15 See ICJ Reports, 1997, p.72.

16 See the oral argument submitted by Professor Alain Pellet on behalf of India in the case concerning the *Aerial Incident of 10 August 1999*, note 14, CR.2000/2 translation-4 April 2000, p. 6 of 14.

17 Quoted by Professor Pellet, *Ibid.*, p.7 of 14.

18 See Robert Jennings and Arthur Watts (eds.), *Oppenheim's International Law*, (9th edn, vol..1, 1991), p.211; Shaw, *supra* note 10 at 874-875.

19 D. P. O'Connell, "State Succession in Municipal Law and International Law", 2 *International Relations* (1967) at 213.

> international rights and duties of the predecessor as are locally connected with the part of the territory ceded or broken off, and with regard to the fiscal property found on that part of the territory'. Conversely it has been clear that no such succession occurs in regard to rights and duties of the old state which arise from its political treaties of alliance or of pacific settlement. It has also been the view of the majority of writers that the new state does not succeed to other non-local agreements, such as treaties of commerce and extradition.[20]

Independent India and International Law

4. Recognition

At the time India became independent, a number of other countries were also getting liberated from the colonial rule. With respect to their recognition, India adopted a very pragmatic approach. To put it in doctrinal terms, the approach adopted is closer to the declaratory, as opposed to the constitutive, theory of recognition.[21] It gave recognition to a State or government as soon it has in its estimation an effective control over the territory, irrespective of the ideology or political system the country or government concerned professed. These are matters for the people and the government concerned, according to India, and not determining factors for extending recognition. It factored into this policy its own historical background and loss of true nationality under colonialism. Policy of recognition hence became a vehicle to support all nationalist forces and for expediting the end of colonialism. While most of the time it went on to establish diplomatic relations almost simultaneously with the decision of recognition, only in one case (Israel), it not only delayed its decision on recognition, but also did not establish any diplomatic relations until long after. However, there was no doubt in the minds of the authorities of India concerned that even that decision could not be postponed for too long because of the effective control of the territory by Israel. One authoritative commentator who observed the policy of recognition of India in the first 15 years of its independence summarized very accurately its position in this respect as one that respects the general practice of other States and the applicable principles of international law. Thus, "it recognized States as soon as the conditions of Statehood have been fulfilled".[22] In addition, "a substantial measure of

---

[20] Oscar Schachter, "The Development of International Law through the Legal Opinions of the United Nations Secretariat", XXV *BYIL*, 91-132 (1948) at 106.

[21] Some authors hold the view that recognition is constitutive, others as declaratory and still others as both. It is also stated that recognition is a matter of political discretion. Further, there is a wide gap between the literature and the practice. "This is a field in which", as B. S. Murty noted "decision-makers, by having recourse to the usual techniques of interpreting and distinguishing facts, subordinate the doctrine to policy so as to secure preferred decision outcomes". For a discussion of the various forms recognition and their legal consequences, B. S. Murty, *International Law of Diplomacy* (1989) at 180.

[22] K. P. Mishra, "India's Policy of Recognition of States and Governments", 55 *American Journal of International Law* 38 (1961) at 424.

effectiveness has been the guiding principle of the Government of India".[23] Further, "the principle of legitimacy, which has long been discarded by other countries, has found no sympathy in India".[24]

While this is still the general policy of India, in more recent years it did not hesitate to express its approbation by withholding its recognition of certain regime changes effected in some countries, where large sections of the population were of Indian ethnic origin. This it did by breaking off diplomatic relations or as in the case of Pakistan, by reducing the level of its diplomatic representation. In the case of Pakistan and Fiji, it also opposed their participation as members of the Commonwealth. The case of recognition of change of governments of Fiji, Afghanistan and Pakistan is relevant. It may be recalled that in the recent past in these countries there were regime changes that resulted in displacement of legitimate or duly elected governments through undemocratic means. Further, they also instituted highly discriminatory policies towards the Indian ethnic community or otherwise indulged in serious violations of human rights. Even in such cases, the Government of India revised its position and resumed normal diplomatic relations, as soon it became politically feasible.

5. Prohibition of the Use of Nuclear Weapons

Ever since the dropping of the atomic bombs on the Japanese cities of Hiroshima and Nagasaki, the debate about the legality of the use of the nuclear weapons in international law is a hotly contested one. Their testing and possession as a measure of deterrence was also questioned. International treaties to prevent proliferation of nuclear weapons and to ban the testing of these weapons in a comprehensive manner were concluded. The International Court of Justice was approached for a decision on the legality of nuclear testing and for an advisory opinion on the legality of their use. Those who defended their testing and use argued that the issues involved are matters of international disarmament negotiations and these cannot be judged on legal grounds without a treaty or customary practice explicitly prohibiting the same.

The International Court of Justice rendered its advisory opinion on the *Legality of the threat or use of Nuclear Weapons* on 8 July 1996. It generally considered such a threat or use would be "contrary to the rules of international law applicable in armed conflict, and in particular the principles and rules of humanitarian law". It left, however, the matter of legality of the threat or use of the nuclear weapons "in an extreme circumstance of self-defence, in which the very survival of a State would be at stake", as an open-ended one. In such a situation, the Court noted that it "cannot conclude definitively whether the threat or use of nuclear weapons would be lawful or unlawful, in view of the current state of international law, and of the elements of fact at its disposal". The opinion of the Court that in most cases the

---

23 *Id.*, at 423.
24 *Id.*, at 424.

threat or use of nuclear weapons would be contrary to international law is significant enough. Even under the extreme circumstances it envisaged, it did not endorse that such a threat or use would be lawful but only expressed its inability to come to any definitive conclusion. It thereby avoided answering the question in its entirety and to that extent declined to give its advisory opinion.

Whether the Court lost a historic opportunity to pronounce upon a matter that engaged the international community for so long and so intensively is worth debating. But in the context of an advisory opinion there is really no duty on the part of the Court to pronounce upon all the matters before it. It is well within its rights to use its discretion and decline to pronounce on matters on which it considered it did not have enough information.

More to the point, whether it failed to draw proper conclusions from the lack of any express prohibition in customary or conventional law of the threat or use of nuclear weapons is a much more debatable point. Georges Abi-Saab analyzed the dilemma of the Court in a most lucid manner. The Court simply contradicted itself and having stated what it said in the first paragraph of 2(E) of its *dispositif*, failed to reach the most obvious and logical answer that such a threat or use of nuclear weapons even in the extreme circumstance it envisaged was unlawful.[25]

India actively worked for the prohibition of nuclear weapons ever since it became independent. It did not sign the treaties banning tests, including the comprehensive test ban treaty and the earlier treaty banning nuclear proliferation, even though it supported that concept as part of a larger scheme of comprehensive prohibition of nuclear weapons. Its emphasis has always been on eventual elimination of nuclear weapons and general and complete disarmament.[26] It is by now well-known that the guarantees given to the non-nuclear States to eventually eliminate the nuclear weapons have become hollow. The advisory opinion of the International Court of Justice provided an important opportunity both for the nuclear weapons States and for others to declare and accept the threat or use of nuclear weapons under any circumstances would be illegal and the Court to pronounce it so.

---

[25] Georges Abi-Saab, "The Court and the Bomb: A Case of Mutual Deterrence?", 7 *Transnational Law & Contemporary Problems*, 430-457 (1997) at 456.

[26] See the Statement of Vijayalaksmi Pandit, Leader of the Indian Delegation to the Political Committee of the United Nations, 15 October 1963, welcoming the Treaty Banning Nuclear Weapons Tests in the Atmosphere, in Outer Space and Underwater, 10 October 1963 in Nagendra Singh and P. Sreenivasa Rao, Contemporary Practice of India in the Field of International Law- 1963-64, 8 *International Studies*, 457-500 (1967); The Delhi Declaration of 28 January 1985 (urging the nuclear weapon States, among other things, to agree to undertake prevention of an arms race in outer space, and a comprehensive test ban treaty with a view to ultimately to eliminate nuclear arms everywhere); B.H. Weston, R.A. Falk, A. D'Amato, *Basic Documents in International Law and World Order*, 273-274 (American Casebook Series, 2nd edition, 1990).

India submitted a memorial in which it argued that not only was such a threat or use of nuclear weapons illegal but even testing should be considered so, as testing and manufacture and maintenance of stockpiles is itself a threat to the peace and security of mankind.[27] But the nuclear weapons States argued that even the threat and use of nuclear weapons was not illegal in the absence of any express international agreement to that effect binding the nuclear weapons States. The Court's opinion having kept the possibilities open by not deciding in the issue in the limited context survival and self-defence of a State gave room for maintenance of current policies of the nuclear powers.[28]

It is not entirely coincidental that India, having argued and worked in favor of total prohibition of nuclear weapons for over 45 years since its independence, given the prevailing theories of security strategy of States in which nuclear weapons are factored prominently, decided to have its own nuclear weapons. Yashwant Sinha, the then External Affairs Minister of India, in a statement of 12 March 2004 in a statement on "Geopolitics: What it takes to be world power", explained the Indian position on the subject after it declared itself to be a nuclear power since 1998. He noted:

> In a world where weapons of mass destruction are still to be eliminated, nuclear weapons sadly remain the ultimate guarantor of a nation's security. It was the imposition of an imperfect non-proliferation order, evidence of which is all around us, that compelled us to make the transition from nuclear abstinence to that of a reluctant nuclear power. And, it was after we, as a nation, agonized over the issue for decades, that this Government finally took the plunge six years back.[29]

6. International Terrorism

International terrorism has become a universal concern since the unfortunate events of 9/11 of 2001 involving terrorist attacks on the New York World Trade Center and Washington's Pentagon. The more recent 3/11 of 2004 Madrid bombings brought that specter of global violence to Europe also. Consequently, there is less likelihood today than ever before to isolate terrorism from the political causes including exaggerated claims for self-determination. This trend commenced with the UN Declaration on Measures to Eliminate International Terrorism of 1994. It may be recalled that Declaration condemned all acts and methods and practices of

---

[27] For the text of the Indian Memorial, see P. Sreenivasa Rao, Advisory Opinion of the International Court of Justice in Legality of the Threat or Use of Nuclear Weapons: An Assessment From Indian Perspective, Annex I and II, 37 *Indian Journal of International Law,* 219-249 (1997) at 226-249.

[28] For the text of the Advisory Opinion of the ICJ, www.icj-cij.org/icjwww/idecisions. Also available at the same site are 29 written Statements, two written comments, including the Indian statement, and 21 oral statements delivered before the Court between 30 October and 15 November 1995.

[29] Available at http://meaindia.nic.in, p. 2.

terrorism. Rejecting for the first time in unequivocal terms that certain political causes justified using even terrorist acts as means to achieve them, the Declaration noted that:

> Criminal acts intended or calculated to provoke a state of terror in the general public, a group of persons or particular persons for political purposes are in any circumstances unjustifiable, whatever the considerations of a political, philosophical, ideological, racial, ethnic religious or any other nature that may be invoked to justify them.[30]

The Security Council also pronounced to the same effect. In fact it even went ahead and using its Chapter VII powers, its Resolution 1373 (2001) of 28 September 2001 obliged States to criminalize the provision of funds to terrorists, freeze the financial assets of people who commit terrorist acts and prohibit the provision of services to those who participate in terrorism. For the first time the Security Council thus imposed measures not against any State, its leaders, national or commodities, but against acts of terrorism and terrorists across the globe.[31]

This Resolution also established a Counter Terrorism Committee (CTC) as a subsidiary organ of the Security Council and is assisted by an advisory body of experts. It is mandated to receive reports from the member States on the implementation of the obligations imposed by the Security Council. It has no specific powers of sanctions but working with individual countries it could provide a substantial degree of technical assistance and cooperation to facilitate the implementation of the Resolution 1373. The UN is reviewing the work of this Committee and several proposals are under consideration to improve its focus and working methods. In addition the linkage between terrorism and organized crime, drug trafficking and illegal trade in weapons and other prohibited weapons of mass destruction is also receiving the attention of the UN.[32]

The events in Afghanistan and the activities of Al-Qaeda, Osama Bin laden and the Taliban were the subject of separate sanctions issued by the Security Council beginning with the Resolution 1267 (1999), which focused, among other things, on the freezing of financial assets of Taliban. A Sanctions Committee was established under paragraph 6 of Resolution 1373 (2001) to receive reports from States and monitor implementation of the sanctions imposed.[33]

---

[30] United Nations, *International Instruments related to the Prevention and Suppression of International Terrorism* , 230-236 (New York, 2001) at 233.
[31]Emilio J., Cardenas, *The United Nations Security Council's Quest for Effectiveness*, valedictory Statement at the Michigan Journal of International Law Seminar, 20 March 2004 on International Law, draft with the author, 1-6, at 1.
[32] For example, Report of the Policy Working Group on the United Nations and Terrorism, A/57/273-S/2002/875, 6 August 2002, 1-18, at 9-11.
[33] *Supra* note 21 at 2.

The two-track approach to deal with terrorism in general through the CTC and the specific activities of the terrorist organizations, regimes and individuals through the Sanctions Committee has imposed its own burdens on the member States. The lack of a unified and integrated approach and the inadequacy of the existing sanctions and reporting mechanisms combined with the genuine difficulty for States to separate the legal from the illegal activities are also responsible for the lack of success of the Security Council's efforts to combat terrorism merely through legislative exercises of a mandatory nature.

7. Legislative Role of the Security Council

There is also the growing apprehension that such measures, apart from their doubtful legal validity, are also without commensurate benefits to the international community. As a side effect, they could even be seen as a basis for abusing the role of the Security Council to deal with issues, which are decidedly outside the scope of its functions as strictly defined under the UN Charter.[34] This tendency became quite manifest in the case of the more recent Security Council Resolution 1540 (2004) which imposed on all States the obligation to refrain from providing any form of support to non-State actors that attempt to develop, acquire, manufacture, possess, transport, transfer or use nuclear, chemical or biological weapons and their means of delivery. While assuring States that this resolution does not create any new obligations or conflict with the obligations States assumed under other treaties in respect of non-proliferation of weapons of mass destruction, it calls upon States to cooperate in promoting more effective implementation of the prevention of proliferation of such weapons. It also established for two years a Committee of the Security Council to receive reports from States on the actions they took for implementing the obligations.

---

[34] One such unacceptable extension of the powers of the Security Council would be to use them to achieve unilateral imposition of the hegemony of nuclear powers over non-nuclear powers. For example, forcing them under threat sanctions from the Security Council to conform to the obligations of the Comprehensive Test Ban Treaty even before they or even without them accept those obligations by becoming parties to that treaty. That such proposals are not the product of a far-fetched imagination could be seen from the suggestion made by one commentator, who nevertheless understood that such powers were not granted to the Security Council under the Charter. See Paul Szasz, "The Security Council Starts Legislating" 96 *American Journal of International Law* 901-95 (2002). The author noted that during the past decade, "determined *proprio motu* the boundary between two states, and has established a highly intrusive arms control regime for a state, a claims commission, and two international criminal tribunals- all actions not explicitly provided for in the Charter. The addition of a legislative capacity would appear to be another such enhancement, the bounds of which it may be worth exploring, at least tentatively". He then suggested that "the Council could reasonably determine that, since any nuclear explosion would constitute a threat to the peace within the meaning of Charter Article 39, all such explosions would hence forth be prohibited and the control system of the Comprehensive Test Ban Treaty would be an appropriate means of ensuring compliance with the edict". Szasz at 904.

Anticipating the adoption of this resolution, India made it clear that it "is concerned at the increasing tendency of the Security Council in recent years to assume legislative and treaty-making powers on behalf of the international community, binding on all States, a function not envisaged in the United Nations Charter". It also pointed out that it cannot "accept any obligations arising from treaties that India has not signed or ratified", a position it claimed is fully consistent with the fundamental principles of international law and the law of treaties. In addition, it noted that:

> India will not accept externally prescribed norms or standards, whatever their source, on matters within the jurisdiction of its Parliament, including national legislation, regulations or arrangements which are not consistent with India's constitutional provisions and procedures, or are contrary to India's national interests, or infringe on its sovereignty.[35]

This statement of India should be viewed in the context of its general support of the role of the United Nations and the preeminent role of the Security Council in the field of maintenance of international peace and security. India, as one of the original members of the United Nations, has lived up to the obligations arising from Article 25 of the Charter. It has fully respected all its decisions and even welcomed the obligations it imposed on States in pursuance of the interests of the international community to combat the global menace of terrorism. It has the necessary domestic legislation to implement the decisions of the Security Council, which it used to implement the sanctions imposed on South Africa, Iraq, and Afghanistan and in connection with the freezing of funds likely to be used for terrorism and terrorist acts or activities.[36] It is also a party to all the international conventions including the one against the financing of international terrorism.[37]

8. Judicial Review of the Decisions of the Organs of the UN

The Indian view is then generally in consonance with the caution expressed both by States and international law experts. This is in respect of the need for the Security Council to act within the limits of the powers delegated to it by member States of the United Nations in accordance with Article 24 of the UN Charter. Article 25 itself does not impose any obligations on member States, if the decisions taken by the Security Council are not "in accordance with the present Charter". The question

---

[35] See the Letter dated April 27, 2004 addressed to the President of the Security Council expressing the position of India on the Resolution S/RES/1540 (2004), available www/un.int/India. Also see the Statement of the Permanent Representative of India to the UN, Vijaya Nambiar, at the Security Council on May 25, 2004. Available at the same website.

[36] The United Nations (Security Council) Act, 1947. See P. Chandrasekhara Rao, *The Indian Constitution and International Law* (Taxman, 1993) at 150 & 153.

[37] India became party to the International Convention for the Suppression of the Financing of Terrorism on 23 April 2004 and the Convention entered into force on 10 April 2002. International Convention for the Suppression of Terrorism Bombing (22 September 1999, entry into force of the Convention 23 May 2001).

of judicial review of the decisions of the Security Council has engaged the attention of the International Court of Justice on occasion through the medium of its advisory opinions in the *Certain Expenses* of the United Nations (1962) and the *Namibia* (1971).[38] The question also arose at the jurisdictional phase of the *Lockerbie* case involving the validity of Resolution 748 (1992) in terms of Article 25 of the UN Charter. The ICJ took the view that the decisions of the United Nations were not *prima facie* in contravention of its powers. But as Bowett noted that in the case of the Resolution 748 (1992), its validity could be examined if the matter were to go to the merits stage.[39] Brownlie comes to the conclusion that while the matter is obviously a very complex one, "the Security Council is subject to the test of legality in terms of its designated institutional competence". He noted that therefore certain basic criteria would apply. He noted further that a "determination of a threat to the peace cannot be used as a basis for action which (if the evidence so indicates) is for collateral and independent purposes, such as the overthrow of a Government or the partition of a State".[40]

Questions concerning the legislative powers of the Security Council apart, there are other valid questions about the representative nature of the Security Council to act on behalf of the international community and the play of veto in the decision-making of that body which require careful review. Moreover, the tension between the relative powers of the General Assembly and the Security Council under the UN Charter raises its own consideration. To some of them we will return below.

9. The UN *Ad Hoc* Committee and Conventions on International Terrorism

Still on the subject of combating international terrorism, while the Security Council resolutions avoided any definition, it must be noted that there have been several attempts to define international terrorism.[41] Some bilateral extradition treaties provided for that but used a list method. That is, specific acts are listed which if committed would be treated as terrorist acts. In such cases these treaties oblige the parties to extradite or prosecute the offender disregarding the plea that those

---

[38] See Ian Brownlie, "International law at the Fiftieth Anniversary of the United Nations, General Course on International Law", 255 *RdC* (1995), at 215.

[39] Quoted in Brownlie, Id., at 218.

[40] *Ibid.*

[41] The Report of the Policy Working Group on the United Nations and Terrorism, without attempting a comprehensive definition of terrorism delineated some broad characteristics of the phenomenon. According to that "(T)errorism is, in most cases, essentially a political act. It is meant to inflict dramatic and deadly injury in civilians and to create an atmosphere of fear, generally for a political or ideological (whether secular or religious) purpose. Terrorism is a criminal act, but it is more than mere criminality". It added that to overcome the problem of terrorism it is necessary to understand its political nature and as well as its basic criminality and psychology. For the text of the Report, *supra* note 32.

offences were committed in pursuance of political ends. A similar approach is also adopted in the case of some regional or sectoral conventions. But the effort to deal with international terrorism at the global or universal level in a more comprehensive way truly commenced with the establishment in 1996 of the UN *Ad Hoc* Committee with the mandate to elaborate legal instruments on the prevention and suppression of international terrorism. It may be recalled that India first mooted the establishment of the *Ad Hoc* Committee for considering the conclusion of a comprehensive International Convention on International Terrorism. India even prepared a draft convention on international terrorism for its consideration and submitted the same to the UN in 1996.[42]

However, the *Ad Hoc* Committee first took up the US proposals for a Convention on the Suppression of Terrorist Bombings. This was finalized in 1997. Later in 1998 it took up for consideration the Russian Federation proposal to suppress nuclear terrorism but failed to achieve a final conclusion. There was no consensus on some important issues including the proposal to exclude acts of armed forces from the scope of the Convention. Incidentally these acts of military forces were excluded from the scope of the 1997 Bombing Convention. However, in 1999 at the initiative of France, the Committee was able to adopt the Convention on the Suppression of Financing of Terrorism. This Convention makes notable advancement in the cause of fighting terrorism through legal means. First it struck at the source of terrorism by prohibiting contributions or collection of funds, "by any means, directly or indirectly, unlawfully and wilfully", "with the intention that they should be used or in the knowledge that they are to be used in full or in part in carrying out" an act of terrorism, as defined in Article 2(a) and (b). Article 2(a) referred to offences defined in the nine conventions on anti-terrorism and these are referred to in the annex to the Convention. Article 2(b) refers to "(A)ny other act intended to cause death or serious bodily injury to a civilian or to any other person not taking active part in hostilities in a situation of armed conflict, when the purpose of such act, by its nature or context, is to intimidate a population, or to compel a government or an international organization to do or to abstain from doing any act". In addition it provides for a wide-ranging obligations for the States to establish criminal offences, control legal entities, extradite, prosecute, assume extra-territorial jurisdiction, and monitor any unusual financial transactions and extend judicial and other assistance and cooperation to each other in pursuance of the objectives of the Convention. Bank secrecy cannot under the Convention pose a bar for the implementation of the obligations imposed by the Convention.

10. The Indian Proposal for a Comprehensive Convention on International Terrorism

In the year 2000, the UN *Ad Hoc* Committee finally took up the Indian proposal on the comprehensive Convention on the Prevention and Suppression of International

---

[42] Text of the Indian Proposal is available now at the www. meaindia.nic.in.

Terrorism.[43] The second round of consideration of the Indian Draft Convention took place within this Committee in 2001 in the aftermath of the September 11 attack on the World Trade Center at New York. A brisk progress was made and agreement was reached on most of the 27 draft articles, leaving only three articles still to be finally agreed upon. Even here, Article 2 on definition was agreed but its provisional adoption was withheld, pending consensus on Article 18, which deals with exclusions or exceptions to Article 2. An article on the relationship of the draft convention to other sectoral conventions is also pending but only raises some technical issues. Agreement on draft Article 18 is therefore crucial for the finalization of the Convention.

Under Article 18 two main issues have yet to be resolved: (a) status of struggles for self-determination involving tactics, which may otherwise be similar to terrorism, and (b) status of activities of military forces and the armed struggles of movements resisting foreign occupation. The question of the status of military activities in peacetime, as noted above, also remained unresolved in the context of conclusion of the Nuclear Terrorism Convention. The Financing Convention does not deal with the issue in any direct manner. The Indian proposal was to exclude such activities undertaken in their official capacity, in as much as those are governed by other rules of international law. It was so agreed when the Bombing Convention was concluded. An alternative proposal by the member States of the Organization of Islamic Conference suggested that the activities of military forces undertaken in the exercise of their official duties, in as much as they are *in conformity with international law* may be excluded from the scope of the draft convention. The problem appears to be that under the formula adopted in the Bombing Convention, the military activities cannot be regarded as terrorist as long as there is no clear prohibition in international law. Under the latter proposal, the presumption appears to be only that those activities, which are expressly authorized by international law, should be eligible for exclusion.

The difference in approach relates to a highly conceptual and controversial area of international law. In part it relates to the legality of use of nuclear weapons, which the ICJ left without full resolution in its advisory opinion. It also relates to a variety of military uses including the uses of the seas, which have never been directly dealt with in any convention relating to the law of the sea, including the 1982 UN Convention on the Law of the Sea. Partly it relates to the issues that arose in the Rainbow Warrior case, where the actions of the French military officials were in

[43] Pursuant to the General Assembly Resolution of 1999 on Measures to Eliminate International Terrorism, a Working Group of the Sixth Committee considered the draft comprehensive convention on international terrorism (Document A/C.6/55/1), proposed by India from 25th September - 6th October 2000.

question.[44] These issues therefore require a political solution, in respect of which India kept an open mind.

Another issue, which equally engaged the time of the negotiations without success, was about the status of the activities of armed forces on the one hand and the resistant movements opposed to foreign occupation on the other. This is in the overall context of armed conflict including in situations of foreign occupation, as those terms are understood within the terms of international humanitarian law. Claims concerning State terrorism on the one hand and the grant of the status of combatants, under international humanitarian law, to persons belonging to various national liberation movements, whether they strictly meet the criteria prescribed for such a status to be granted or not, on the other, are at issue. The classic and the most intractable conflict that unfortunately gripped the Middle East, locking Israel and Palestine, is at the root of disagreement during the negotiations at the UN. Israel and a few countries refused to countenance State terrorism. On the other hand, States members of the Organization of the Islamic Conference do not consider the activities of resistant movements opposing foreign occupation as terrorist acts.

The positions taken by the parties to the Middle East conflict have to be judged on their own merits in the specific context surrounding the conflict. But one point appears to be quite clear. That is, whatever be status of the participants in the conflict, the application of international humanitarian law either in the context of international armed struggles or internal armed struggle does not endorse terrorism as valid means to achieve the objectives involved.

11. International Humanitarian Law and the Prohibition of Terrorism

It may be recalled that international humanitarian law clearly prohibits any act of terrorism to be indulged by combatants. The prohibition against terrorism is equally applicable both in international and non-international armed conflicts. Article 33 of the fourth Geneva Convention common to the territories of the parties to the conflict and to the occupied territories prohibits any collective penalties and likewise all measures of intimidation or of terrorism against protected persons. In addition, it also prohibits pillage, and reprisals against such persons and their property. Article 34 of the same Convention also prohibits taking of hostages.

Article 1 (4) of Protocol I to the Geneva Conventions of 12 August 1949 and relating to the Protection of Victims of International Armed Conflicts makes it clear that international humanitarian law is applicable to peoples fighting "colonial domination and alien occupation and against racist regimes in the exercise of their right of self-determination". Article 51 (2) of Protocol I obliges the parties to such a conflict to not make the civilian population as such, as well as individual civilians the object of their attack. It further states that "acts or threats of violence, the primary

[44] Rainbow Warrior (New Zealand/France), R.I.A.A., vol. XX, p. 217 (1990).

purpose of which is to spread terror among the civilian population are prohibited". Similarly, Article 13 of Protocol II of the Geneva Convention of 12 August 1949 and relating to the Protection of Victims of Non-International Armed Conflicts that is applicable to non-international armed conflict is identical to Article 51(2) of Protocol I and prohibits acts or threats of violence, the primary purpose of which is to spread terror.

It must also be noted that international humanitarian law makes a fundamental distinction between permitted and prohibited types of violence. Any violence against non-combatants and protected persons including civilians and civilian targets is prohibited. Even violence permitted against adversary combatants has to conform to permitted methods and means of warfare and the requirements of proportionality, military necessity or advantage. Accordingly, all prohibited types of violence could be treated as acts of terrorism under international humanitarian law.

International humanitarian law considers certain prohibited acts of violence, given the seriousness of the breach involved as grave breaches. The four Geneva Conventions of 1949 defined grave breaches. Article 50 of the first Convention and Article 51 of the second Convention treat willful killing, torture or inhuman treatment including biological experiments, willfully causing grave suffering or serious injury to body or health and extensive destruction and appropriation of property not justified by military necessity and carried out unlawfully and wantonly as grave breaches. Article 130 of the third Convention in addition treats compelling a prisoner of war to serve in the forces of the hostile power, or willfully depriving a prisoner of war of the rights of fair and regular trial as a grave breach. Similarly, Article 147 of the fourth Convention includes unlawful deportation or transfer or unlawful confinement of a protected person, taking of hostages in the category of grave breaches. This is in addition to the prohibited categories of conduct referred to in Article 130 of the third Convention. Article 85 of Protocol I also deals with grave breaches. They may include: (a) willful targeting of civilian population or making individual civilians objects of attack; (b) launching an indiscriminate attacks on such civilian population and civilian objects in the knowledge that such attacks will cause excessive loss of life, injury to civilians or damage to civilian objects; and (c) launching an attack against works or installations containing dangerous forces in the knowledge that attack will cause excessive loss of life, injury to civilians or damage to civilian objects. Examples of works or installations containing dangerous forces are given in Article 56 of Protocol I which include dams, dykes, and nuclear plants. Attacks against cultural objects and places of worship are also prohibited (Article 53). The concept of grave breaches also found a place in the statues establishing the International Criminal Tribunal for the territories of the former Yugoslavia and Rwanda. Article 8(2)(a) of the Statute of the International Criminal Court also incorporated the concept including offences noted above as grave breaches to be tried as war crimes.

Article 35 of Protocol I prohibits employment of weapons, projectiles and the materials and methods of warfare of a nature to cause superfluous injury or unnecessary suffering. This is in accordance with the long-standing legal principle, which provides that the right of the parties to the conflict to choose methods and means of warfare is not unlimited. Perfidy (Articles 37) and refusal to give quarter (Article 40) are also prohibited under Protocol I.

In addition, international humanitarian law provides protection to the individual in the hands of an adverse party against arbitrary acts and violence. Articles 12 (2) of the first and second Geneva Conventions, and 13 (2) and 17 (4) of the third Geneva Convention govern these. These provisions are tantamount to a comprehensive ban on acts of terrorism against over-powered enemies.

Similar prohibitions against acts of terrorism are also available in the context of a non-international armed conflict. A non-international armed conflict is defined as an armed conflict between the armed forces of a State and the dissident armed forces or other organized armed groups which, under responsible command, exercise such control over a part of its territory as to enable them to carry out a sustained and concerted military operation. In addition, the dissident armed forces seeking the protection of the provisions of Additional Protocol II that deals with non-international conflicts should be willing and be able to implement the obligations of that Protocol. Thus it is clear that an individual or groups of individuals not conforming to the criteria of Additional Protocol II and engaged in violence within a State could be treated as terrorists. This is particularly so in situations involving only "internal disturbances and tensions, such as riots, isolated and sporadic acts of violence and other acts of a similar nature", which cannot be treated as situations of armed conflict (Article 1.2 of Protocol II).

In a situation of civil war or armed uprising against a State, Article 3 common to the four Geneva Conventions and provisions of Additional Protocol II, prohibits "violence to life and persons, in particular murder of all kinds, mutilation, cruel treatment and torture" and "the taking of hostages". Further Article 4 and Article 4(2)(b) of Additional Protocol II specifically prohibit all acts of terrorism.

International humanitarian law as described above is applicable to armed conflicts involving armed forces and military personnel of a State party on one side of the conflict and on the other, peoples or groups of individuals opposing such forces engaged in armed struggle against foreign occupation, aggression and colonization aimed at liberation and self-determination. Both sides are under an obligation to respect international humanitarian law and not engage in acts of terrorism.

As a separate matter, Indian sympathies for the Palestine cause are well-known. The position of India on the conflict in the Middle East region is recently restated and is worth noting in the words of the Ambassador and Permanent Representative of India to the UN offices in Geneva:

> We voted against the partition of Palestine, and recognized the PLO as the sole and legitimate representative of the Palestine people. We recognized the State Palestine in 1988, and opened our Representative Office to Palestine National Authority in 1996.

On the settlement of the conflict and the basic claims of Palestine, he added that:

> The negotiations should lead to the realization of the inalienable and legitimate right of the Palestine people to self-determination and a home land and to a just, comprehensive and lasting peace in the region based on UN Security Council Resolutions 242, 338 and principle of 'Land for Peace', with the State of Palestine existing alongside Israel within secure and internationally recognized borders ... India has extended its full support to vision contained in UN Security Council Resolution 1397. We fully endorse UN Security Council Resolution 1402 and 1403, which call on both parties to move immediately to a meaningful cease-fire, and for the withdrawal of Israeli troops from Palestine cities, including Ramallah. We support the recent peace initiatives of the international community, including the endorsement by the UN Security Council in its Resolution 1515 of the Quartet Roadmap and the call to restart negotiations ... We are not in favor of the unilateral disengagement plan...We are also not in favor of a separation fence which encroaches on Palestine territory and causes major humanitarian problems. [45]

On the question of the means used or to be used to settle the conflict, India is equally emphatic. It noted that "(B)oth sides must cease all acts of violence, including all acts of terror and fully cooperate with the efforts of the international community" [46] The above statement of India and its principled support for the cause of Palestine is worth reiteration if only for one reason. This is to emphasize that India holds terrorism in all its forms as criminal. In its view it cannot be a legitimate means whether in times of armed conflict or peace. Such a position is not at variance with its support for the legitimate causes of self-determination and upholding the sanctity of human rights and fundamental freedoms for all people. In spite of its clear stand, India was patient enough not to push the negotiations on its draft comprehensive convention on international terrorism and decided to wait for a

---

[45] Statement made by Ambassador and Permanent Representative of India at the 60th Session of the Commission on Human Rights, Geneva on agenda item 8, 24 March 2004, available at www.meaindia.nic.in. The same position is reiterated by A. Gopinathan, Acting Permanent Representative of India to the UN, New York, on 16 July 2004 at the Tenth Emergency Special Session of the UN General Assembly, following the delivery of the advisory opinion of the ICJ on "The Legal Consequences of the Construction of a Wall in the Occupied Palestinian Territory". India also called upon Israel 'to take into account the advisory opinion of the International Court of Justice in keeping with the overwhelming international opinion on the matter'. Available at www.un.int/India<Statements<Pleanary, 2004.

[46] *Ibid.*

better day and climate to revive and complete the negotiations to which it is committed.

12. Self-determination

On the issue of self-determination, which was also raised by Pakistan repeatedly in the negotiations on the conclusion of comprehensive convention on international terrorism and the choice of means available for its realization, the Indian position is equally clear. Terrorism as a means is not acceptable, and that in any case the right of self-determination in accordance with the principles of the United Nations is not applicable to situations beyond termination of colonialism. By way putting the Indian position in the current context of human rights, we may offer a few more comments.

The right of self-determination is clarified under the UN Charter (Articles 1(2), 55 and 73), the 1960 UN Declaration on Granting Independence to Colonial Countries and Peoples (General Assembly Resolution 1514 (XV) of 14 December 1960), the 1970 UN Declaration on Principles of International Law concerning Friendly Relations and Co-Operation Among States in accordance with the UN Charter and the two international Covenants concerning human rights. The Indian position has been very consistent and clear on struggles concerning self-determination against colonialism. India took the view that as far as possible such struggles should be non-violent like its own against the British occupation of India. But "if methods cannot be found for peaceful evolution from colonialism to freedom, then violence cannot be averted".[47] On the issue of the right of self-determination, India believed consistently and resolutely that it couldn't apply "to the integral part of any country or to sections of its population, or to enable such integrated parts or sections of populations to secede". Accordingly, it could be operative only "when one is dealing with a nation as a whole, and the context in which it can be applicable is the context of conquest or of foreign domination or of colonial exploitation".[48]

Further, it may be recalled that in addition to the 1970 UN Declaration, the subsequent 1993 Vienna Declaration and Program of Action adopted at the Conference on Human Rights dealt with the right of self-determination in the post colonial context. India reiterated its view of the essential limitation on the right of self-determination of all peoples in the post-colonial phase. In a statement on agenda item 5, before the 60th session of the Human Rights Commission, referring

---

[47] Statement of Vijayalaxmi Pandit, Leader of the Indian Delegation to the UN General Assembly, 11 October 1963, quoted in Nagendra Singh and P. Sreenivasa Rao, *supra* note 26 at 480

[48] Statements of Vijayalakshmi Pandit before the UN General Assembly on 30 September 1963 and M .C. Chagla in the Security Council on 5 December 1964, on the question of Kashmir, quoted in N. Singh and P. S. Rao, Id., at 461-462.

to these important instruments, Ambassador and the Permanent Representative of India to the UN Offices in Geneva, Hardeep Puri stated the position thus:

> They asserted that the right of self-determination shall not be construed as authorising or encouraging any action which would dismember or impair, totally or in part, the territorial integrity and political unity of sovereign and independent States conducting themselves in compliance with the principle of equal rights and self-determination of peoples and thus possessed of Government representing the whole people belonging to the territory without discrimination of any kind. It has also been recognized that any attempt aimed at partial or total disruption of the national unity and territorial integrity of a State or country or at its political independence is incompatible with the purposes and principles of the UN Charter. The principle of equal rights and self-determination of peoples enjoins that every State shall refrain from any action aimed at the partial or total disruption of the national unity and territorial integrity of any other State or country.[49]

It is also important to note that India made a reservation to Article 1 of the International Covenant on Civil and Political Rights, which provided for the right of self-determination for all peoples, stating that it applied only in the limited context of colonialism. Germany and other West European countries opposed the Indian reservation to the International Covenant on Civil and Political Rights. In their view the right of self-determination is universal and cannot be confined to only the colonial context. However, to make this point they rely on the UN Declaration on Friendly Relations adopted in 1970. Under that Declaration the possibility was envisaged for "people" to seek internal self-determination if a group of people are denied their fundamental human rights. India stands by the 1970 UN Declaration on Friendly Relations, in the preparation of which it took an active part. But as pointed out by the Indian Ambassador, the exercise of such a right has to be without undermining the territorial integrity and political independence of the State, if the Government of the State otherwise represents all sections of the people as a whole without any discrimination as to race, religion or creed or color. The concept of **internal** self-determination, which was developed under that Declaration, is different from the right of self-determination against colonialism. In view of the above we may state that the right of self-determination restricted only to the context of colonialism, may be rightly regarded as a peremptory norm of general international law.[50]

---

[49] Statement of 19 March 2004, available at www.meaindia.nic.in/speech/2004/03/15.

[50] The commentaries to the draft Article 48 cite the right of self-determination of people as an example of an obligation under peremptory norms of general international law. The draft articles of the ILC on State responsibility do not address directly the question of self-determination or for that matter define the obligations under such peremptory norms of general international law. It may also be noted that the Indian member stated his understanding that the right of self-determination was confined only to the colonial context. This was however opposed by the German and United States members. As the commentary also referred to the 1970 UN Declaration on Friendly Relations, which is considered by all

As for internal self-determination this is a separate matter and the same is governed by the law of human rights, the constitution of a country, peace, security and good order and is without any prejudice to the territorial integrity and political independence of a State. According to the law of human rights the struggle for self-determination cannot adversely impact upon the human rights enjoyed by the citizens of the country. These include the right to life, freedom from torture and arbitrary detention, rights of women and children, right to health, subsistence (food), democratic order, peace and security, the right to non-discrimination.[51]

In the context of the post-colonial phase, where claims of self-determination are made by minority groups, secession of a part of the territory belonging to State is not generally preferred. After surveying State practice since 1945, Professor James Crawford came to the conclusion that "outside the colonial context, the principle of self-determination is not recognized in practice as giving rise to unilateral rights of secession by parts of independent States". Further, according to him, self-determination "outside the colonial context is primarily a process by which the peoples of various States determine their future through constitutional processes without external interference".[52]

---

sides as providing the normative basis for dealing with the right of self-determination in the post -colonial stage of international relations, the members saw no need to further debate the matter. In any case that would have been outside the scope of the exercise of the ILC on State responsibility, which is not engaged in defining the content of any primary rule including the content of obligation under peremptory norms of general international law. Summary Records of the 2705th meeting of the 53rd Session (Second part) of the International Law Commission, Doc. No. 1/CN.4/SR.2705 (17 August 2001), p. 16. For the view of Professor Brownlie that the right of self-determination, involving secession of territory could exist outside the context of colonialism if there is international recognition and validation or certification, see Ian Brownlie, *supra* note 38 at 58-61. But such recognition and validation would come more as an exception rather than as a rule is borne out by the survey conducted by Professor James Crawford, See note 52 below.

[51] For an interesting discussion on the tension between the principles of self-determination and the territorial integrity, see Paul Szasz, "The Irresistible Force of Self-Determination Meets the Impregnable Fortress of Territorial Integrity: A Cautionary Fairy Tale About Clashes in Kosovo and Elsewhere", 28 *Georgia Journal of International and Comparative Law*, 1-8 (1999). The author proposed that "when terrorism becomes so strong that it can no longer be suppressed without an unacceptable level of State-terrorism, then the state concerned has, either as a victim of Violence or as a perpetrator, lost the legitimacy that enables it to insist on its Territorial integrity". But the solution in terms of accepting the right of self-determination need not be secession and hence the principle of territorial integrity could still be maintained while ensuring a suitable form of internal self-determination.

[52] James Crawford, "State Practice and International Law in Relation to Secession", *British Yearbook of International Law* 1998, 85-117 (1999). After surveying State practice, the author came to the conclusion that "outside the colonial context, the principle of self-determination is not recognized in practice as giving rise to unilateral rights of secession by parts of independent States. Self-determination outside the colonial context is primarily a process by which the peoples various States determine their future through constitutional processes

13. Principles of Non-Use of Force and Non-Intervention

Moreover, there is an obligation on the part of every State to respect the territorial integrity and political independence of another State by not undertaking or prohibiting acts which would amount to use of force or aggression against it. Such an obligation includes the duty for every State:

a to refrain from organizing or encouraging the organization of irregular forces or armed bands, including mercenaries, for incursion into the territory of another State; and

b to refrain from organizing, instigating, assisting or participating in acts of civil strife or terrorist acts in another State or acquiescing in organized activities within its territory directed towards the commission of such acts when such acts involve threats or use of force.[53]

The International Court of Justice in the case concerning the *Military and Paramilitary Activities in and against Nicaragua* examined the nature and the status of these obligations. The prohibited acts noted in point (a) if resorted to or tolerated by a State could be treated as acts of aggression by the affected State, giving rise to the inherent right of self-defence, against "armed attack" within the meaning of Article 51 of the UN Charter. The Court noted that it is agreed that an armed attack

> [m]ust be understood as including not merely action by regular armed forces across an international border, but also 'the sending by or on behalf of a State of armed bands, groups, irregulars, or mercenaries, which carry out acts of armed force against another State of such gravity as to amount to' (*inter alia*) an actual armed attack conducted by regular forces or 'its substantial involvement therein'. [54]

The description, which is based on the wording of paragraph 3 (g) of the Definition of Aggression annexed to (UN) Resolution 3314 (XXIX), according to the Court, reflected customary international law. Only frontier incidents are considered by the

---

without external interference". At 113. It may also be noted that plebiscite is not always regarded as essential for settling matters concerning the discharge of the obligations imposed by the right of self-determination.

[53] One of these duties is well-articulated in the paragraph 3(g) of definition of Aggression unanimously adopted by the UN General Assembly Resolution 3314 (XXIX) of 14 December 1974, 13 *International Legal Materials* 710 (1974). The other obligation is elaborated by the UN Declaration on Principles of International Law Concerning Friendly Relations and Cooperation among States in Accordance with the Charter of the United Nations, resolution 2625 (XXV) of 24 October 1970, 9 *International Legal Materials*, 1292 (1970).

[54] *Military and Paramilitary Activities in and against Nicaragua (Nicaragua v. Unites States of America),* Merits, Judgement, ICJ Reports 1986, p.14. Para. 195. Available at www.icj-cij.org/decisions

Court as not worthy of treatment as an armed attack, which is qualified as such because of its scale and effects.

With respect to point (b) noted above, the Court noted its importance in the context of the need to respect the principle of non-intervention that it is "part and parcel of customary international law".[55] In this connection it referred to its previous decisions, particularly the *Corfu Channel* case and the resolutions of the UN General Assembly 2131 (XX) on the Inadmissibility of Intervention in the Domestic Affairs of States and the Protection of their Independence and Sovereignty, and 2625 (XV) on Friendly Relations and Cooperation among States and pointed out that

> Intervention is wrongful when it uses methods of coercion in regard to such choices (that is, choices of a State in respect of political, economic, social, and cultural system and the formulation of foreign policy), which must remain free ones. The element of coercion, which defines, and indeed forms the very essence of, prohibited intervention, is particularly obvious in the case of an intervention which uses force, either in the direct form of military action, or in the indirect form of support for subversive or terrorist armed activities within another State. As note above (para. 191), General Assembly resolution 2625 (XXV) equates assistance of this kind with the use of force by the assisting State when the acts committed in another State 'involve a threat or use of force'. These forms of action are therefore wrongful in he light of both the principles of non-use of force, and that of non-intervention.[56]

Wrongful activities attributable thus to a State engage its international responsibility under international law.[57]

---

[55] *Id.*, para 203.

[56] *Id.*, para 205.

[57] Article 8 of the Indian draft on comprehensive convention on international terrorism submitted to the UN defines the primary obligation of States to prevent cross border terrorism, which if violated could attract State responsibility (available at www.meaindia.nic.in/warterror/draft/draft-convention). It reads as follows:

State Parties shall cooperate in the prevention of the offences set forth in article 2, particularly;

a. By taking all practicable measures, including, if necessary, adapting their domestic legislation, to prevent and counter preparation in their respective territories for the commission, by whom so ever and in whatever manner, of those offences within or outside their territories, including;
    i. Measures to prohibit in their territories the establishment and operation of installations and training for the commission, within or outside their territories, of offences referred to in article 2; and
    ii. Measures to prohibit the illegal activities of the persons, groups and organizations that encourage , instigate, organize, knowingly finance or engage in the commission, within or outside their territories, offences referred to in article 2;

14. State Responsibility

On the other elements of State responsibility, the International Law Commission completed a set of draft articles in 2001, which were under preparation for over forty years.[58] These articles exhibit high sensitivity to the needs of the people of the disadvantaged and disintegrating States. The draft articles no longer provide for the concept of State crimes, which was adopted by the ILC in its first reading in Article 19 in 1976. However, draft Article 40 provides for an alternative concept, which according to one view achieves the same objective.[59] It refers to international responsibility of a State for a serious breach of an obligation arising under a peremptory norm of international law. A breach is defined serious if it involves a "gross or systematic failure". Article 41 specified the particular consequences of such a serious breach. It involves the duty to cooperate to bring the serious breach to an end through lawful means. In addition, there is also the duty of non-recognition of the situation thus created and not to render aid or assistance in maintaining the situation.

The concept of differently injured States, which was not well formed in the earlier drafts, is abandoned. But in respect of breach of obligations owed to the international community as a whole, any State other than the injured State has been given the right to invoke the responsibility of another State. Article 48 (2) states the limits within which a State other than injured State could invoke the responsibility of a State. Such States could only seek cessation of the wrongful act and performance of the obligation, in the interest of the injured State or the beneficiaries of the obligation breached. The case of the plurality of the injured State is also separately covered (Article 46).

In respect of countermeasures,[60] Article 49 specifies that they could be taken only to induce the responsible State to comply with the obligation and not as a measure to punish or seek vengeance. They should also be reversible as far as possible after the cessation of the wrongful act and necessary reparation is made. Article 50 refers to obligations incumbent upon the State taking countermeasures to respect. These include respect for obligations under Article 2 (4) of the Charter of

---

iii. By exchanging accurate and verified information in accordance with their national law, and coordinating administrative and other measures taken as appropriate to prevent the commission of offences as referred to in article 2.

[58] For the text and commentaries of the 2001 draft articles, James Crawford, *The International Law Commission's Articles on State Responsibility: Introduction, Text and Commentaries* (Cambridge, 2002).

[59] Alain Pellet, "The New Draft Articles of the International Law Commission on the Responsibility of States for Internationally Wrongful Acts: A Requiem for State's Crime?", 32 *NYBIL*, 55-79 (2001).

[60] Pemmaraju Sreenivasa Rao, "Countermeasures in International Law: The Contribution of the International Law Commission", in Studi di diritto internazionale in onore di Gaetano Arangio-Ruiz, II Editoriale Scientifica, 853-880 (Napoli, 2004).

the United Nations, protection of the fundamental human rights, obligations of a humanitarian character prohibiting reprisals, and other obligations under peremptory norms of general international law. In addition, the State taking countermeasures is also required to honor any obligations it has under applicable dispute settlement procedure in force between it and the responsible State; and to respect the inviolability of the diplomatic or consular agents, premises, archives and documents. For lack of consensus among the members, the draft articles did not specify the need to seek resolution of the dispute by peaceful means as a precondition before countermeasures could be invoked. However, Article 52(3)(b) provides for not taking countermeasures, and if already taken, for suspension of the countermeasures if the dispute is pending before a court or a tribunal, which has the authority to make decisions binding on the parties. In addition under Article 52 countermeasures taken must be proportional to the injury suffered taking into account the gravity of the wrongful act and the rights in question.

15. *Jus Cogens* and *Erga Omnes* Obligations

The concepts of *jus cogens* and *erga omnes* obligations, which are now at the heart of the concern for "serious breaches of obligations arising from a peremptory norm under general international law", are important new elements in the structure of international law. They are an attempt to signify that international law is, going beyond the bilateral and State centric interaction, becoming more and more responsive to the needs of more globalized international relations and the demands of increasingly integrated international community interests. India along with other developing countries and the East European (Socialist) States supported the concept of *jus cogens* when it was first introduced in the Vienna Convention on the Law of Treaties in 1967.[61] Dr. S. P. Jagota, the Indian delegate to the Vienna conference on the Law of Treaties stated that "he was glad that the principle laid down in article 50 was generally recognized". "The text of the article", he said, "was a masterpiece of precision and simplicity and his delegation supported it unreservedly".[62]

As pointed out above (with respect to self-determination), India may have its reservations or views on the content of a principle of international law considered as *jus cogens*.[63] As a democratic country under a Constitution, which gives high priority

---

[61] West European countries and in particular U.K., France and Switzerland opposed the same on the ground that it was a vague concept. France even voted against the Convention because of Article 53 on *jus cogens*. See Ian Sinclair, *The Vienna Convention and the Law of Treaties* (2nd edition, 1984) at 66. According to Alain Pellet, France however seemed to have toned down its opposition in recent times. See Alain Pellet, *ibid. supra* note 59.

[62] It was Article 50 at the stage of consideration of the same in Committee of the Whole of the Conference. For the Statement of S. P. Jagota, see *The Official Records of the Vienna Conference, 1968 session*, Summary records of the Fifty-fourth meeting of the Committee of the Whole, 307.

[63] Commenting on the concept of *jus cogens*, Brownlie aptly explained that " more authority exists for category of *jus cogens* than exists for its content…". Ian Brownlie, *Principles of*

to the fundamental rights of human persons, it strongly supports any international principle or policy designed to suppress egregious breaches of human rights.

16. International Criminal Court and Jurisdiction

On the question of the suppression of genocide, "systematic" or "widespread" commission of egregious breaches of human rights or crimes against humanity or, commission of war crimes "as part of a plan or policy or as part of a large-scale commission of such crimes",[64] India was in favor of the idea of establishing an International Criminal Court to punish them. As Dilip Lahiri, the leader of the Indian Delegation to the Rome Conference stated in his opening remarks at that conference,

> India fully endorsed the view… which had stressed that the International Criminal Court should be based on the principles of complementarity, the sovereignty of States and non-intervention in the internal affairs of States, and that its Statute should be such as to attract the widest support and acceptance of States, State consent being the cornerstone of the Court's jurisdiction. [65]

But it could not join those States, which voted in favor of it at Rome in 1998 for other reasons it specified. Dilip Lahiri, noted that "he had always had in mind a court that would deal with truly exceptional situations, where the State machinery had collapsed". However, he continued, "the scope of the Statute had been so

---

International Law (6th edition, 2003) at 490. Professor Jennings, while agreeing with Brownlie, adds that there is also less authority for "its practical effects in given situations". Sir Robert Jennings, "The Pinochet Extradition Case in the English Courts", in Laurence Boisson de Chazournes and Vera Gowlland-Debbas (eds.), *The International Legal System in Quest of Equity and Universality: Liber Amicorum Georges Abi-Saab*, 677-698 (2001) at 697. The concept of *erga omnes* obligation enunciated by the ICJ in the *Barcelona Traction* case in comparison to the concept of *jus cogens* appears to give rise to less conceptual difficulties. It is an obligation a State owes to the international community as a whole. It is a procedural obligation, which gives *locus standi* for any State to invoke the responsibility of a State, even if it is not directly injured by the wrongful conduct. Again Article 48(2) (b) of the ILC draft article on State responsibility of 2001 is relevant, which specifies the limitation of this right. These States, which are not injured, could demand the performance of the obligation of reparation only "in the interest of the injured State or of the beneficiaries of the obligation breached". On the interrelationship of *jus cogens* and obligations *erga omnes*, See M. Ragazzi, *The Concept of International Obligations* Erga Omnes (1997).

[64] See Articles 7(1) and 8 (1) of the Rome Statute of the International Criminal Court, Official Records of the Rome Conference, Vol.1, Final documents, A/CONF.183/13 (Vol.1), 5 and 6.

[65] See Statement of Dilip Lahiri at the Fourth plenary meeting of the United Nations Diplomatic Conference of Plenipotentiaries on the Establishment of an International Criminal Court, Rome, 15 June-17 July 1998, Official records, Vol. III, Summary Records of the plenary meetings and of the meetings of the Committee of the Whole, A/CONF.183/13 (vol. II), para.47, at 86.

broadened that it could be misused for political purposes or to address situations for which the International Criminal Court was not intended". [66]

He also mentioned that it became difficult for India to accept the Statute for the special role given thereunder to the Security Council both to accord compulsory jurisdiction in certain cases and to require the Court to defer consideration of cases, if it so desired acting under Chapter VII of the Charter of the UN.[67] In addition India also regretted the fact that the conference did not even agree to consider its proposal to include use of nuclear weapons among those whose use was banned and treated as a crime.[68] The Statute also did not include international terrorism as a crime, the inclusion of which India and several other countries strongly supported.[69]

17. Emerging System of Multilateral Order and the UN

India recognizes the high political value of the United Nations and the normative character of its Charter. Speaking very early after the creation of the United Nations, Sir Benegal Rau, later judge of the ICJ, noted that the "Charter should be looked upon as a kind of fundamental law for every State".[70] Addressing the 59th Session of the UN General Assembly, Manmohan Singh, the Prime Minister of India, reiterated the consistent position of India that the United Nations and its Specialized Agencies "are the only instruments available for responding effectively to the challenges we face collectively", in the field of security, economic development and environment. However, noting that the UN was "often unable to exert an effective influence on global economic and political issues of critical importance", he pointed out that this was "due to its what may be called as 'democracy deficit'", which prevents effective multilateralism, a multilateralism that is based on a democratically-evolved global consensus". Stressing the need for reform and restructuring of the United Nations, the Prime Minister made it clear that the "expansion of the Security Council, in the category of both permanent and non-permanent members, and the inclusion of countries like India as permanent members, would be a first step in the process of making the United Nations a truly representative body".[71]

---

[66] *Id.*, P.122, para.11

[67] *Ibid.*, paras. 12-14.

[68] *Ibid.,* para. 16.

[69] See the Resolution E adopted at the end of the Conference as part of the Final Act, Annex 1, United Nations Diplomatic Conference of Plenipotentiaries on the Establishment of an International Criminal Court, Rome, 15 June -17 July 1998, Official records, Vol. I, Final documents, Rome Statute and the Final Act, A/CONF.183/13 (vol. I), p.71-72.

[70] Statement of 21 September 1949 in the 222 Plenary meeting of the UN General Assembly, available at www.un.int/india<Statements<Landmark speeches.

[71] For the full text of the Statement of the Prime Minister of India to 59th UN General Assembly, http://meaindia.nic.in/speech/2004/09/23. See also the statement of the Indian delegate P. S. Rao in the Sixth Committee of the United Nations General Assembly on the agenda item concerning the strengthening of the United Nations, GAOR, 39 Session,

Reacting to the recent events where the very foundations of the present world order as represented by the UN Charter were challenged by a series of unilateral acts of use of force, India took note of the challenges to multilateralism in the 21st Century. It noted that

> We must acknowledge that in the past few years, the very role and relevance of the UN system and the efficacy of the collective action has come under critical questioning. The unilateralist impulse, the tendency to ignore the principles and practice of Multilateralism and the disregard for established principles of international law are a matter for concern. [72]

It was also noted that

> The role played by the UN system on promotional aspects has come down but the regulatory dimension has been on the ascendant. This is so on a number of issues, be it human rights, or labour or technology. The UN system's role is not seen as the helping of the countries but of judging them. There is at the same time an imbalance between the security agenda and the development agenda, with latter losing its importance ... [E]ven in the application of norms or standards, often there is selectivity or double standards, based on political expediency. Countries are judged not on the objective criteria or through collective wisdom of the UNGA, but by a select few, based on expediency. [73]

Under the circumstances, India is skeptical about grafting the concepts of *jus cogens* and *erga omnes* on to the international system in the absence of truly and commonly acceptable international machinery to take decisions on behalf of the international community.[74] A more organized and non-discriminatory, hence institutionalized and uniform reaction and response to violations of international law, without regard to the status or power of the State involved, should be promoted.[75] In other words for

---

A/C.6/39/SR.30, 30 October 1984, para.36, p.9, where it was stated that "the system established by the United Nations was basically sound". It was added that the "Charter was not perfect and its provisions did not perhaps fully reflect the realities of the contemporary world, but it nevertheless remained the best instrument available to the international community".

[72] See the Statement of the Minister of State for External Affairs Rao Inderjit Singh of 19 August 2004, participating at the NAM Ministerial Meeting at Durban, South Africa, Available at http://meaindia.nic.in/speech/2004/08/19.

[73] *Ibid.*

[74] Bruno Simma noted the importance of developing truly representative international machinery to sustain and effectively operate the concepts representing the global community. Bruno Simma, "From Bilateralism to Community Interest in International Law", 250 *RdC* (1994-VI) at 249. For the concern of Prosper Weil that these concepts undermine the consent of State as the central element of international legal system, see P. Weil, "The Relative Normativity in International Law?", 77 *American Journal of International Law* 413-442 (1983).

[75] That such a system is possible has been established by the WTO dispute settlement procedures. It could be a model of sorts for other areas of international law including

India it may mean a better and more streamlined United Nations with a more effective and representative Security Council.[76] It also means that the permanent members of the Security Council should assume their role more as trustees of the System and shared values and act in defense of common interests and less as an instrument for narrow national policies or special interests.[77] It should act promptly and effectively by using more of its Chapter VI powers to prevent disputes and encourage settlement of the same through persuasion and less its mandatory and coercive Chapter VII powers, which should be used only sparingly. In this connection, India stressed the need to ensure the centrality of local actors in the political process and the imperative of having to avoid imposing models from outside.[78]

18. Peaceful Settlement of Disputes

This brings us to the question of settlement of disputes by peaceful means and the value of compulsory third party settlement. India strongly believes in peaceful settlement of disputes. Its non-violent struggle for freedom and the teachings of Mahatma Gandhi had an indelible impact on India and its leaders to pursue the theme of adopting the right means for achieving right ends. Jawaharlal Nehru, India's first Prime Minister, never lost an opportunity to emphasize this matter. Rejecting the use of force as well as cold war as a means of solving the world's problems, he stressed the need for nations of the world to set the right example by thinking always about the right means to be adopted to solve our problems. "That means", he said, "should always be peaceful, not merely in an external way in the

---

security See for an exposition in this regard, James Bacchus, "Groping Towards Grotius: The WTO and the International Rule of Law", 44 *Harvard International Law Journal* 533 (2003).

[76] On the need for the Security Council to be more representative, Pemmaraju Sreenivasa Rao, "The United Nations and International Peace and Security-An Indian Perspective", in Christian Tomuschat, *The United Nations at Age of Fifty* 143-184 (1995) at 182.

[77] For an Indian statement that questions the rationale of veto and the need to consider ways and means to overrule its use, see the Statement of A. Gopinathan, Deputy Permanent Representative of India to the United Nations, at the open-ended Working Group on Security Council Reform on April 19, 2004. Available at http://WWW.un.int/india<statements<Plenary, 2004. It is feared that any expansion of the Security Council and either enlarging the veto powers or removing them altogether may actually frustrate the working of the Security Council rather than make it more functional in the interest of international community, see David Bills, "International Human rights and Humanitarian Intervention: The Ramifications of Reform on the United Nations' Security Council", 31 *Texas International Law Journal* 107 (1996).

[78] See the Statement before the Security Council of V.K. Nambiar, Permanent Representative of India to the UN, on Post-Conflict National Reconciliation: Role of the United Nations, 26 January 2004. Available at www.un.int/india<statements<Security Council, 2004.

non-use of armaments, but in the approach of the mind".[79] Even when Kashmir was attacked or when the People's Republic of China made armed incursions across its Himalayan borders, India emphasized the need to settle the dispute in a peaceful manner, while reserving its right to defend its territory. India brought the question of aggression by Pakistan to the Security Council of the United Nations and urged China to negotiate the border issue.[80] India is now engaged in active bilateral negotiations with Pakistan on one hand and China on the other to settle all the outstanding disputes.

India thus is very committed to bilateral negotiations. India's preference for peaceful settlement of disputes through free choice of means,[81] and in particular, by direct negotiation among the parties to the dispute has several merits. B. S. Murty, an Indian authority on legal regulation of diplomatic relations explained:

> [F]rom different points of view negotiation is the most preferable method of settlement of disputes. First, since the resolution of the dispute is by mutual consent, reached after free bargaining, there is a high degree of probability of both the parties carrying out the agreement faithfully. Second, if the spirit of democracy is government by consent, bilateral diplomacy is nearest to the spirit. Third, arbitration and judicial settlement are, in game theoretic terms, zero sum games. One party's gain is the other party's loss, and the total pay-off is zero. By contrast, in bilateral diplomacy, it can be so worked out that each party gets something it desires, and the total pay-off of both is a variable sum, and there is scope for maximizing it. Fourth, any imposed

---

[79] Statement of 20 December 1956 before the UN General Assembly, New York. Available at www.un.int/india.

[80] For India's complaint dated 1 January 1948 against Pakistan to the Security Council of the United Nations, see S/628. India complained of the situation created by armed raiders and invaders, consisting of nationals from Pakistan and of tribesmen from the territory immediately adjoining Pakistan by their operations against Jammu and Kashmir, with the assistance from Pakistan, which is an act of aggression. See also Rahmatullah Khan, *Kashmir and the United Nations* (1969). On Chinese incursions, see the statement of V. K. Krishna Menon, before the UN General Assembly, New York, 6 October 1959, available www.un.int/india. Urging the Chinese to first remove their soldiers from the Indian territory, he noted that "... we subscribe to the principles of the Charter and to the set of ideas that were put forward at the African-Asian Conference held at Bandung in 1955 and by our own treaty relations with China based upon what are popularly called the 'Five Principles'. What is more, we shall strive as hard as we can to reach settlement on every problem by peaceful negotiation".

[81] While welcoming the adoption of the Manila Declaration on the Peaceful Settlement of Disputes in 1982, the Indian delegate to the Sixth Committee Mr. Sayeed said that the value of the Declaration lay in the fact that it stressed the "obligation to settle international disputes" on the basis of the sovereign equality of States and "in accordance with the free choice of means", thus incorporating one of the basic principles of the Declaration on Principles of International Law concerning Friendly Relations and co-operation among States in accordance with the Charter. UN Doc., GAOR, 37 Session, A/C.6/37/Sr.25, 25 October 1982, para. 10, p. 4.

> solution to a dispute is very likely to be reopened by the party who felt compelled to accept it at the time of settlement, and thus there may be no real settlement at all.[82]

India's position on peaceful settlement of disputes among States through means of their free choice should not however be misconstrued as a total opposition to recourse to the International Court of Justice or to recourse to arbitration[83]. India accepted the compulsory jurisdiction of the ICJ but with reservations. In a recent case before the ICJ, it pleaded that 'reservations do not by their terms derogate from a wider acceptance already given'. 'They operate', it is noted, 'to define the parameters of the State's acceptance of the compulsory jurisdiction of the Court'.[84]

19. Conclusions

The above survey of the Indian position on some general principles of international law illustrates the importance and consistency of the role India has been playing in the pre-colonial era and in the post-independent phase in promoting rule of law in international relations. Since independence it actively contributed to a world order based on equity and justice for all, rich or poor or big or small nations of the world. India's abiding faith in the UN system and its commitment to achieve universal world order is widely acknowledged. Its fight against colonialism, apartheid and racial discrimination, support for the right of self-determination with emphasis on the preservation and protection of territorial integrity and political independence of States has clearly influenced many of the law-making resolutions of the UN.

---

[82] B. S. Murty, *Diplomacy and Resolution of International Disputes*, paper presented to the UN Congress on Public International Law, New York, 14 March 1995, cited in Pemmaraju Sreenivasa Rao, *supra* note 76 at 172-173, note 74.

[83] In fact arbitration is noted as the method by which Article 51 of the Indian Constitution enjoined the State of India to 'encourage settlement of international disputes'. This however does not mean other means of settlement are excluded or the method of arbitration is to be preferred over any other method. If any method is preferred, as noted in the text above, it is direct negotiation. On the meaning and circumstance surrounding the adoption of Article 51 of the Indian constitution, see P. Chandrasekhara Rao, *supra* note 36 at 5-7. For reference to the Rann of Kutch Award of 19 February 1968, a case of arbitration between India and Pakistan, *ibid,*, 7. See also for a mention of the position under the Indian Constitution concerning the settlement of territorial boundary problems between India and Pakistan that no constitutional amendment was necessary for the implementation of the arbitral award, *ibid,*, 137. For a reference to the Berubari case, involving the Bagge Award, dividing the Berubari Union between India and Pakistan, and the Tin Bigha Agreement between India and Bangladesh, *ibid,*, 135-6. In the Berubari case it was held that for the transfer of an Indian territory to Pakistan would require a constitutional amendment. In the case of the perpetual lease agreement of Tin Bigha between India and Bangladesh, it was found that there was no need for a Constitutional amendment, as there is no surrender of sovereignty but only a grant in favor of Bangladesh of a set of limited rights.

[84] Statement of Soli Sorabjee, Attorney General of India, before the ICJ in the Case concerning the *Aerial Incident of 10 August 1999* (Pakistan v. India), (Jurisdiction), verbatim records, CR/200/2-4 April 2000, p. 2.

India strongly believes in international community interests and strives for representative global institutions. It is against unilateral acts and measures of self-help. It seeks to cope with violations not through enforcement mechanisms, but through diverse means of settlement of disputes. Its commitment to the peaceful resolution of disputes is evident in the manner it has been handling many of its problems with its neighbors. It prefers bilateral and direct negotiations for resolving inter-State disputes and agreeable to resort to third party settlement in appropriate cases only by mutual consent.

In recent year it is exercising its energies at the global level not only in securing economic justice to its people and poor countries allover the world but also in fighting international terrorism. This it seeks to achieve without minimizing basic and fundamental human rights.

TRADE IN SERVICES, WORLD TRADE ORGANISATION AND INDIA

Surinder Kaur Verma*

1. Introduction

In September 1986, the Uruguay Round of Multilateral Trade Negotiations (MTNs) on Goods and Services, started at Punta del E'ste, with an ambitious agenda of 15 sectors to negotiate including the trade in services. The decision to include trade in services in the MTNs was a natural culmination of a controversy centered on the issue of services started with the 1982 Ministerial meeting of the GATT, when the United States identified services as one of the future areas for trade negotiations among GATT signatories.

Inclusion of services along with intellectual property rights and investment measures, however, created an unprecedented controversy and confusion in the GATT negotiations. India, along with Brazil and Yugoslavia, opposed the inclusion of services as well as trade-related intellectual property rights in the MTNs as the GATT was primarily concerned with the trade in goods. The Uruguay Round ended in the adoption of an Agreement on World Trade Organization, 1994, which included a multilateral agreement on services – the General Agreement on Trade in Services (Annex 1B).[1] The GATS is an integral part of the World Trade Organization (WTO) and is *ipso facto* binding on all the members of the WTO.

The GATS is one of the most significant agreements of the WTO. It has put the service sector on the agenda of the policy planners of the member States because of its importance. Not only do services comprise a growing proportion of international trade overall, but the ways in which services are supplied provide potential to undermine the economic sufficiency, political sovereignty and cultural identity of the locality. Services, particularly those with intellectual content, carry far deeper messages than goods. They traverse fields clearly connected with social relations – professional, financial and communications fields that are likely to shape the structure of a global society. While services provide means to introduce fresh, foreign perspectives, and construct cross-border transactions and affiliations, they

---

* Professor of Law, University of Delhi.

[1] The other multilateral agreements adopted along with GATS are: the TRIPS Agreement (Annex IC); Agreement on Trade in Goods (Annex 1A); the Understanding on Rules and Procedures Governing the Settlement of Disputes (Annex 2); and the Trade-Policy Review Mechanism (Annex 3).

Bimal N. Patel (ed.), **India and International Law, 67-91.**

question the value of parochial knowledge and custom, and undermine the competence of local regulation.

Yet many services retain distinctive geographical, temporal and personal features. While international suppliers will use various strategies to try to overcome these particularities, the provision of services is likely to remain tied into their local contexts. In many sectors of services, effective supply still depends on being able to establish a presence in the locality, to be there at the right time, and to demonstrate familiarity with the local ways of doing things. But the suppliers who seek to obtain competitive conditions of access behind the border encounter a host of regulatory legalities that run counter to their own legalities of operation. As a consequence, both the suppliers and the locals become involved in attempts to reconcile these legalities.

The GATS is the first full-fledged multilateral legally binding set of rules, covering international trade in services. Services were to be a new field for the GATT, which was previously occupied with barriers to trade in goods. The essential approach taken by the GATT was to assimilate those trade barriers to a common measure of tariffs and then to seek reductions in these quantitative impositions on trade in goods. Services can be incorporated in goods, but often the real action on the supply of services is expressed through personal relationships between providers and users. It can be more difficult to keep track of the supply of services than it is to keep track of trade in goods. Certainly a wider range of domestic measures might be implicated by the application of trade norms to the supply of services. This lack of comparability between trade in goods and trade in services initially provided an argument for not making a trade agreement for services under the Uruguay Round and developing countries, led by India, Brazil and Yugoslavia, who were particularly opposed to it. It gave rise also to questions about the suitability of extending many of the GATT concepts to the GATS; one such example is the provision for anti-dumping procedures and remedies,[2] as is also the concept of subsidies (Art. XV).

The GATS produced a broad framework for negotiations over the liberalization of trade in services. It comprehends all possible modes of service supply. It then subjects the regulation of these supply activities and modes to the norms of national treatment (Art. XVII) and market access (Art. XVI). Regulatory arrangements operating deep behind the border and representing all sorts of economic, political and cultural concerns may become barriers to trade. But then all countries reveal strengths and weaknesses exposing their services sector to the competition of international trade.

---

[2] Christopher Arup, *The New World Trade Organization Agreements* (Cambridge University Press: 2000), pp. 97-98.

2. Nature and Role of Services in International Trade

For services no common definition exists. Generally, the term is related to all economic activities other than agriculture, mining, manufacturing, construction and utilities. It is a heterogeneous group of economic activities. Services in trade, for the most part, deal in intangibles, which include banking, insurance, transportation, communication and data processing, retail and wholesale trade, advertising, accounting, construction, design and engineering, management consultancy, real estate, professional services, entertainment, education, health care and tourism. Exceptions are the motion pictures and computer industry where service is embodied in tangible goods.

Most services operate on a contractual basis and, therefore, focus on fees, royalties, *premia* and margins. Some, such as tourism, provide output inside their respective nations to non-residents. Others offer parts of their services from their home country. Most depend heavily on the establishment of an overseas presence since, by their very nature, many services cannot easily be shipped or transported across national boundaries. Thus, while some services are related more to investment, requiring strong local presence, such as banking, communication, tourism, etc., others can be traded (applying the IMF definition that "trade" constitutes a transaction between residents and non-residents).

The GATS Agreement embraces all but a narrow category of services and does not give any elaborate definition of services except stating that term "services" includes "any service in any sector except services supplied in the exercise of governmental authority".[3]

A number of services have well defined international markets like shipping, air transportation, banking and motion pictures. Others, such as consulting services, do not. Government regulations also vary greatly among different services, being strongest in the areas of banking and insurance. But in most cases government regulation of trade in services is greater than that which exists in merchandise trade for reasons of sensitivity. Many services sectors touch on areas of national security (transportation, telecommunication), financial stability (banking) or cultural identity (motion pictures and television programming).

Although the service industry is generally regarded as being labour-intensive, there is substantial variation within the group. Accounting, management, consulting, architectural and engineering services are all labour-intensive and the labour involved is more skill-intensive, hence it is high-cost labour. On the other hand, reinsurance is capital-intensive industry.

---

[3] GATS, Article. I: 3(b).

Trade barriers for services are very different from trade barriers that affect goods. For most of the services, border controls are minimal (except where the movement of a natural person is involved in providing the service); there are generally no tariffs on services and quotas are very difficult to maintain. Rather, services are subject to a myriad of domestic regulations, often very sector-specific. Some service areas, such as telecommunications, are maintained as state monopolies. Some sectors are the subject of investment restrictions. For some professional services, such as doctors and attorneys, there are competency standards. In all areas, there are restrictions on immigration. Regulatory patterns differ greatly among countries. Consequently, trade liberalization in services is largely a negotiation based on divergent domestic regulations. In a sense, the GATS story resembles that of the GATT after border protection had been substantially dismantled: if the process of liberalization requires first dismantling border controls and then negotiating regulatory barriers, the GATS did not miss much by coming into force 45 years after the GATT.

Services, as a group, were never considered to be an issue before 1978, when the United States under the pressures of its aviation and insurance industry, brought it before the Trade Committee of the Organization of Economic Development and Cooperation (OECD).[4] Inclusion of services under the WTO is a reflection of growing share of services in national economies the world over. They accounted for around two-thirds of both GDP and employment, while manufacturing and agriculture played a minor role.[5] Currently they account for more than 50 per cent of world output whereas their share in world exports is around 25 per cent. The developed countries have the dominant share in traded services and the United States occupies the prime position.[6] It is further to be noted that though services do not account much in the world trade, they have dominated the GDP in most countries, particularly in developed countries with 67 per cent share in the GDP compared to 40per cent of the developing countries. Similarly, services share in employment has also increased tremendously in most of the countries in recent times. The services comprise an approximately 51per cent share of India's GDP.[7]

These developments in the services-sector had their resultant impact on the international economic and political arena. The developed countries became concerned and started insisting upon having a common policy and more free trade in services since the late 1970s. On the other hand, for developing countries, though services were less significant in GDP and employment, many of them were an integral part of import substitution policies. Various financial services such as

---

[4] Ronald K. Shelp, *Beyond Industrialization* (1981) 174.
[5] Shyoraj Singh Parmar, "Trade in Services and WTO," 30 *Journal of the Legal Studies* 137 (1999-2000).
[6] In the USA, services sector contribution to the GDP is 72 per cent. See *The Times of India,* 16 August 2004, p. 12.
[7] *Ibid.*

banking and insurance and others such as communications, utilities and advertising are areas in which most developing countries seek to build up their national industries and they are also part of nation building and development planning. In India, the banking and insurance sector were government-controlled and were in the public sector and they were obliged to follow the government directions in every aspect of their activity. National control of these industries is considered to be the symbol of economic development and independence from the industrial world. Foreign participation in them was restricted till recently because not only is it considered to be non-conducive to national objectives like earning foreign exchange, transferring technology, redistributing wealth but to ensure that socio-political, cultural and national security goals are achieved.

It should, however, be noted that such views are reinforced by developed countries that regulate and limit foreign participation in some of these sensitive industries. In the United States, for example, foreign investment in communications and advertising is restricted.[8] But the generally held view is that developing countries are more conscious of the need to limit service imports and this is understandable since they are the net importers of services except in the area of manpower, which is subject to immigration laws of developed countries and where most of the restrictions in the service sector are witnessed. Liberalizing international transactions in services is commonly considered to be a North-South issue with expected gains from trade for industrialized countries at the expense of the developing countries.[9] However, within industrial countries also, established producers have expressed concern on protecting domestic markets.[10]

Whatever definition of services one uses and whatever confidence one reposes in one set of statistics or another and whatever reservation one may have to the liberalization of services trade, it is now well entrenched in the world trade because of the GATS, which is binding on all Members, who are obliged to implement it. Hence, it is pertinent to examine the issues involved in services trade and their regulation under the GATS.

3. The Issues in Trade in Services

As already stated, it is difficult to define "services" and more so to define "trade in services". Trade in services cannot simply be equated with international transactions in services and still less so with international services "activities". It involves both trade and investment. Consequently, it is imperative to draw a

[8] Shelp, *supra* note 4, pp. 77-78.
[9] Andre Sapir "North-South Issues in Trade in Services", *The World Economy,* (March, 1985); Randhawa, "Punta del E'ste and After: Negotiations on Trade in Services and the Uruguay Round", 21 *JWTL* 163 (1987), p. 164.
[10] Henning Klodt, "International Trade, Direct Investment and Regulations in Services", 12 *World Competition* 47 (1988).

distinction between tradable and non-traded services, internal and international trade in services, trade-production and distribution, between market access conditions and the right to establishment, and between the purely trade issues and those relating essentially to foreign direct investment in services trade. This is a complex issue and a distinction is required to be made between trade and investment in this context.

An important characteristic of services that has far reaching implications for marketing of services is their inseparability, i.e., services cannot be separated from their providers, whether they are persons or machines. But all services do not require physical proximity of the provider and user. In this context, there are two broad categories of services:

3.1. Those that Necessarily Require the Physical Proximity of the Provider and the User

Those services that require the physical proximity of the provider and the user, and the services where physical proximity is essential fall into three categories:

a. The Mobile Provider and Immobile User: The mobile provider and immobile user characterize the first category. This involves cases where the mobility of the beneficiary to the place of the provider is not physically feasible. For example, an Indian firm which has a construction contract abroad will have to send the manpower required to the construction site for carrying out the work, or a technician may have to go to a plant abroad to rectify a problem with the plant.
b. The Mobile user and Immobile provider: This category consists of services, which involve some key elements, which are not normally transferable to the user's location. For example, certain experiments can be done only in those laboratories equipped for them or a patient who wants an open-heart surgery will have to go to a hospital where the required facilities are available.
c. Mobile user and Mobile provider: In this category, proximity may be achieved by either the provider going to the user or the user going to the provider such as professional services.

3.2. Services for which Physical Proximity Is Not Essential are Known as Long Distance Services

Services for which physical proximity is not essential are known as long distance services. Examples of this category include transmission "over the wire" and communication services. In advanced countries, traditional banking and insurance fall into this category since loans or insurance policies can be secured by mail or phone. The educational services in distance learning mode also fall in this category. Though they are closely linked to the advancement in technology, the scope for long distance transactions may increase without advancement in technology.

Even in respect of many long distance services, however, physical proximity between the provider and user may help to increase the efficiency of the service. A large number of service firms would, therefore, like to have places of business in countries with sufficient market. The "right to establish" is an important aspect of free trade in services, which also involves the right to employ people without restrictions on the nationality. International trade in many services involves international factor mobility, such as capital and labour. There are a number of international transactions involving temporary factor relocation services such as those requiring temporary residence by foreign labour to execute service transaction.

International trade in services, thus, involves intricate issues like the right to establish and factor mobility. These are special problems in liberalizing trade in services compared to trade in goods. Because of the special characteristic and the socio-economic and political implications of certain services, they are generally subject to various types of national restrictions. Protective measures include visa requirements, investment regulations, restrictions on repatriation of income, marketing regulations, restrictions on the employment of foreigners, compulsion to use local facilities etc. Heavily protected or restricted services in different countries include financial services, i.e., banking and insurance, transportation, motion pictures, transportation and communication etc.

There is a generally held misconception that developing countries are against negotiations in services. In fact, some developing countries are increasingly aware of the potential of services in the improvement of their overall economic development. Tourism is one of the service industries in which developing countries are particularly interested. As is evident that more than 50per cent of India's GDP comprises trade in services, it is very much concerned with the liberalizing of this sector according to its development goals.[11]

The reasons for lack of enthusiasm for negotiation on services among developing countries are: the way the services are generally understood to include principally financial services such as banking and insurance, and the belief, which is based on trade facts, that the comparative advantage in services lies with developed countries, which cannot be narrowed down easily. Their major pre-occupation has been the preponderant role of multi-national corporations (MNCs) in services, particularly by services conglomerates in banking and finance, telecommunications, insurance, advertising and other business services. These services from MNCs are also accompanied by monopolistic and restrictive business practices, which developing countries find difficult to curtail. Developing countries see this pressure particularly in so far as it is directed towards dismantling or modifying the national regulatory framework as a threat to their economies and sovereignty, particularly

[11] India has been in negotiation with the United States to conclude a Free trade Agreement in the services sector, which would provide the mutual market access in services to both the countries. See *The Times of India,* 7 August 2004, p. 16.

financial services are part of a national strategy of economic growth. These countries are concerned about their infant industries, balance of payment difficulties and the crucial role of services in infra-structure. This requires a differential and special treatment for them.

4. Services under the International Trade Organization (ITO) and the GATT

The origin of GATT can be found in the Charter of ITO (or the Havana Charter), which was envisioned as the principal international trade institution to be established after the Second World War. The echo of the trade in services could be heard in the ITO Charter, though the scope was limited. At the first session of the preparatory committee of the UN Conference on Trade and Employment, held under the auspices of the ITO, the view was expressed that the section on restrictive business practices would have no meaning if it failed to include services such as shipping, insurance and banking. Consequently, Article 50 in Chapter V (Restrictive Business Practices - RBPs) was incorporated, which stated that "the members recognize that certain services, such as transportation, telecommunications, insurance and banking are substantial elements of international trade, and that any restrictive business practices in relation to them may have harmful effects".

These practices were to be dealt with in accordance with the mode enumerated therein. The special provisions with respect to restrictive business practices (RBPs) in services remained in the final draft of the Havana Charter as well. The extension of the Charter to services was supported by developing countries and opposed by the major maritime powers. It is, however, to be noted that the Havana Charter, while included a provision on services, contained elaborate rules on restrictive business practices. In fact, services were discussed in the context of RBPs. On the contrary, the WTO does not contain any special provisions on restrictive business practices and leaves this aspect principally to Members. The Code on restrictive business practices, adopted by the United Nations General Assembly in 1980 covers the activities of MNCs and extended to trade in goods and services, is voluntary in nature.[12]

The Havana Charter also included general investment provisions, which, of course, extended to service investments also. Article 11 obligated members not to take unreasonable or unjustifiable action injurious to the international investments of other members. Article 12 obligated members to give reasonable opportunities for investments and adequate security for existing and future investments. Members were to negotiate commercial treaties on request, with the right to set up the terms with respect to the ownership of existing and future investments. The Charter did

---

[12] *The Set of Multilaterally Agreed Equitable Principles and Rules for the Control of Restrictive Business Practices*, UN Doc. TD/RBP/10, Annex (1980), cited in XIX ILM 813 (1980).

require, however, that these terms be "just and reasonable". It also allowed for the discussion of investment issues in the ITO and, at the insistence of any member, in the ICJ.[13]

These efforts to liberalize services went in vain because the efforts to establish the ITO failed. Only the section of the Charter dealing with commercial policy survived and became the basis for GATT, which lacked the broad scope and the organizational and procedural provisions of its progenitor, the ITO.

4.1. Services in the GATT

The GATT was principally designed for trade in goods and was not intended to cover services. Except for motion pictures, there was no provision specifically dealing with services. In the area of motion pictures, restrictions were allowed in the form of quotas. Article IV prescribed the form such quotas should take and seeks to prevent the screen time reserved for domestic films from being increased after 1947. It asserted that quotas are "subject to negotiations for their limitation, liberalization or elimination". Apart from this provision, the subject of motion pictures was never dealt with within the GATT. In fact, the Contracting Parties never discussed it except that there was a mention of motion picture restrictions in the list of non-tariff barriers, prepared for the Tokyo Round of Negotiations.

Notwithstanding this express provision for motion pictures, the real focus of the GATT in services was confined to transport insurance. Except for the freedom of transit (Art. V), the GATT did not expressly cover transportation matters also. Trade in services, for the first time, was comprehensively dealt with under the Uruguay Round of GATT negotiations.

5. The Framework of General Agreement on Trade in Services (GATS)

The immediate objective of negotiations, under MTN was the "expansion of trade in services" and not liberalization *per se*, though the expansion of trade was aimed at progressive liberalization. While vowing to free trade in services from existing restrictions, it recognized the regulatory concerns of Member countries. The Punta del E'ste Declaration stipulated that such a multilateral framework for trade in services "shall respect the policy objectives of national laws and regulations applying to services". Accordingly, the national laws and regulatory framework applying to services are clearly not being put up for negotiations. Generally speaking, these regulations govern for the most part the internal aspects of services sectors. Only where regulations impinge upon trade at the border, they would be looked at, but never with a view to questioning the objectives. The GATS "applies to measures by

---

13 UN Docs EPCT/C.II/25 at 4 (1946); EPCT/C.II/48 at 1 (1945); Ronald K.Shelp, *supra* note 4, at 151.

Members affecting trade in services".[14] It must be read with other documents contained in the Ministerial Declarations and Decisions of the Final Act, most importantly, the Understanding on Commitments in Financial Services.[15]

During the Uruguay Round negotiations, WTO Members negotiated, in principle, on everything (with the notable exception of the difficult issue of rights in air transport).[16] There was, in principle, no decision to conduct negotiations on specific sectors.[17] Sector-specific negotiations are, however, conducted on construction and related services, financial services, telecommunications services, and transport services, educational services, tourism, environmental, health and social services, tourism and energy services after the WTO Agreement entered into force. Currently negotiations are underway on educational services.

The Agreement in all has six parts. The opening section deals with the scope and definition. Part II (the longest), sets out the general obligations and disciplines, i.e., the rules that apply to all services and all members. Part III states rules governing the specific commitments in schedules. Part IV is concerned with future negotiations and the schedules of specific commitments. Parts V and VI cover institutional and final provisions. The Preamble to the Agreement provides insight into the intentions of negotiators and puts the reform process in perspective. It reflects the concerns of developing and least developed countries. It also sets out the long-term objectives of the agreement against the background of equitable and balanced economic development.

The GATS is primarily an enabling agreement, which creates a legal framework for trade in services and allows countries to specify the actual commitments to be undertaken in the schedule of commitment.

5.1. Scope and Coverage of the GATS

The GATS covers all manner of services except those supplied in the exercise of governmental authority,[18] i.e., any service which is supplied neither on a commercial basis, nor in competition with one or another service supplier. Four modes of trade in services are identified: cross border (Mode-1), consumption abroad (Mode-2),

---

[14] GATS, Article I:1.

[15] See Annex on the Financial Services.

[16] Michael J. Trebilcock and Robert Howse, *The Regulation of International Trade*, (2nd edition, 1999) (Chp. 11- trade in services); see also Annex on Air Transport Services to the GATS.

[17] For services sectoral classification, see WTO Doc.MTN/GNS/W/120, 10 July 1991. This classification is based on the International Classification of Occupation (ISCO-88).

[18] GATS, Article I: 3(b).

commercial presence in the consuming country (Mode-3), and temporary movement of natural persons (Mode-4).[19] The table below shows the operation of these modes.

Modes of Supply

Supplier Presence	**Other criteria**	**Mode**
Service supplier not present within the territory of the Member	Service delivered within the territory of the Member from the territory of another Member	Cross-Border Supply (Mode-1)
	Services delivered outside the territory of the Member in the territory of another Member to a service consumer of the Member	Consumption Abroad (Mode-2)
Service supplier present within the territory of the Member	Service delivered within the territory of a Member through the commercial presence of the supplier	Commercial Presence (Mode-3)
	Services delivered within the territory of the Member with supplier present as a natural person	Presence of Natural Person (Mode-4).

(1) "Cross border" services are where both provider and user remain in their home territory (e.g., services provided generally by facsimile, e-mail, phone, or other means of communication); (2) In "consumption abroad", services provided to the user who travels to the territory of the provider (e.g. tourist or student joining an education institution abroad); (3) In "commercial presence", services are provided where the provider establishes a commercial presence in the territory of the user (e.g., a UK bank, insurance, or financial services company establishes a branch or subsidiary in India). This is supposed to be the most important mode of supply of services, at least in terms of future development, and also raises the most difficult issues for host governments and for GATS negotiations. Under the investment

[19] GATS, Article I: 2.

laws, the supplier must belong to the country of consumption. WTO breaks new ground here compared to GATT which confined itself to trade in goods, originating in a foreign country; and (4) By "movement of natural persons", services are provided when a natural person – the provider of services temporarily travels to the territory of the user (e.g., an attorney, architect, interpreter, or teacher travels to another country to consult or lecture). The national governments have power to regulate this mode of service supply by regulating the entry through visas or entry permits to the prospective service providers.

The GATS disciplines, therefore, are relevant for not only services but also services suppliers (both natural and legal persons). Viewed from this angle, mode-3 essentially amounts to an international agreement to liberalize investment: for example, by allowing foreign banks to sell banking services under mode-3, a WTO Member is *de facto* opening up to foreign investment in the banking sector. However, it is mode 4, in which developing countries are particularly interested and about which developed countries are particularly apprehensive. As the services sector is mainly labour-intensive and most developing countries have labour in abundance, they are naturally interested in this mode. But entry of the natural persons has been made subject to the "Economic Needs Test" (ENT), Local Market Tests and Management Needs Tests by developed countries, that is, depending on their economic needs the entry of natural persons would be allowed under mode-4. The GATS applies to any "measure" taken by governmental bodies or non-governmental associations exercising delegated authority affecting any of these modes of trade in services.[20]

The broad scope of the GATS outlined above poses certain conceptual problems. First, the outer boundary of what is "services" for purposes of the GATS is not sharply defined. Services trade is defined more in terms of categories of transactions (the modes of supply) rather than substantive categories. Thus, although services can in most cases be distinguished from goods based upon the idea that services are simultaneously provided and consumed, but goods are storable for later use or enjoyment. There may nevertheless be overlap between the international rules for services and those for goods, especially given that GATS applies to all measures that "affect" services. Second, because trade in services is defined in terms of transactions, services trade under the GATS will inevitably involve more than just the bare services supplied. The transactional notion of services in the GATS means that services trade will also implicate in some instances certain international factor flows, notably (1) information; (2) technology; (3) capital or investment; and (4) labour or immigration.

The GATS obligations are divided into three major parts: (a) general obligations; (b) specific commitments; and (c) commitments relating to specific

---

[20] *Ibid.,* Article I: 1.

sectors, namely, financial services (banking and insurance), telecommunications, air transport and movement of labour (natural persons).

a. General Obligations

The explicit rules that are considered the foundation of the GATT are well known: the granting of non-discriminatory (most-favoured-nation MFN) treatment for goods of other contracting parties at the border (Art. I) and according national treatment to imported goods (Art. III). GATS incorporates these principles of MFN (Art. II) and National Treatment (Art. XVII) under specific commitments. The MFN clause makes it obligatory on GATT members to grant each other treatment as favourable as they give to any other country in the application and administration of import and export duties and charges. The aim of this rule is to make the extent of protection clear and to encourage as much competition as possible. In case of services, a Member must accord "immediately and unconditionally" to other Members treatment no less favourable than the treatment they accord to like services and service suppliers of any other country (Art. II: 1).

A Member can seek exemption from MFN treatment through the WTO waiver procedures over and above the Annex II exemptions (from Art. II: 1). Article II: 2 permits WTO Members to "maintain a measure inconsistent with paragraph 1 provided that such a measure is listed in, and meets the conditions of the Annex on Article II Exemptions". WTO Members can give advantages to its adjacent countries under regional trading arrangements (Art. II: 3). There is also an exception for national security (Art. XIV *bis*). These exemptions can be maintained for up to ten years, although they are subject to periodic review and negotiation. This means that MFN in the GATS is conditioned to prevent "free-riding" in the markets of more open WTO Members. No new exemptions can be added to the original ones unless recourse has been made to the waiver provisions of the WTO Agreement.[21]

GATS obligates Members to maintain transparency by publishing promptly all relevant measures of general application, which pertain to or affect the operation of this agreement. However, certain confidential information may be withheld, the disclosure of which may impede law enforcement, or would be against public policy or may affect legitimate commercial interests of particular enterprises (Art. III *bis*). Besides, international agreements relating to services must also be published. Members are also required to inform the Council for Trade in Services (CTS) promptly and at least annually of any new, or any changes to existing laws, regulations or administrative guidelines which significantly affect trade in services covered by its specific commitments (Art. III).

---

[21] Annex on Article II Exemptions enlists the exemptions granted on different grounds to various members.

GATS allows Members to enter into agreements resulting in integration of service markets as long as that agreement has substantial sector coverage and provides for elimination of substantially all discrimination between the parties in the covered sectors (Article V). It also allows Members to agree to full integration of the labour markets between them (Art. V *bis*). It requires Members to adopt domestic regulations to ensure that they are based on objective and transparent criteria such as competence to supply the services; they are not more burdensome than necessary to ensure the quality of the service; and in the case of licensing procedures, they are not a restriction on the supply of the service. The CTS can establish and develop "necessary disciplines" for domestic regulations (Article VI). Members may adopt criteria for recognition of the education or experience obtained in another country as long as such recognition does not operate as a means of discrimination between countries (Article VII). Such recognition may be based upon an agreement between the countries.

There are two provisions on anti-competitive practices that may undermine services liberalization. Article VIII does not prohibit national service monopolies, but prohibits "abuse" of a monopoly position and requires WTO Members to ensure that national monopolies do not operate in a manner inconsistent with GATS obligations. If "business practices" restrain or restrict trade in services, Article IX requires "consultations" at the request of any WTO Member and "full and sympathetic consideration" to complaints. This, however, is not a mandatory obligation and no follow-up action is provided, if the consultations fail to resolve the issue.[22]

GATS allows countries exemptions from their scheduled commitments for balance of payments reasons (Article XII). Additional exemptions are provided to enable a Member to protect its national security and for purposes of protecting public order, human, animal or plant life or health, prevention of fraudulent and deceptive practices, preventing or reducing double taxation and inequitable imposition of taxes and protection of privacy. Payments and transfers of capital must be open with respect to a Member's commitments.[23] Subsidies affecting services are subject to negotiation with a view to eliminating their trade distorting effects.[24]

Economic and market-to-market integration agreements are permitted to operate within the context of a Member's GATS commitments.[25] There is provision for emergency safeguard measures[26] and government procurement is exempt.[27] It

---

[22] Cf. Article XXII: 2.
[23] GATS Articles XI and XVI.
[24] *Ibid.,* Article XV.
[25] *Ibid.,* Articles V and VI.
[26] GATS Art. X.
[27] *Ibid.,* Article XIII.

also provides for negotiating on subsidies affecting services, and on the countervailing duties to compensate for the subsidy.[28]

The GATS also provides for progressive liberalization of services trade through future negotiations (Part IV). The increasing participation of developing countries is encouraged.[29] Their concerns are addressed through two requirements: (1) Members must negotiate specific commitments to benefit developing countries (Art. IV: 1); and (2) developed Members must establish "contact points" to facilitate access of developing countries to information (Art. IV: 2).

Article XIX mandates: "Members shall enter into successive rounds of negotiations ... with a view to achieving a progressively higher level of liberalization. Such negotiations shall be directed to the reduction or elimination of the adverse effects on trade in services of measures as a means of providing effective market access". The Council of Trade in Services (CTS) is entrusted to carry out an assessment of trade in services with a view of drawing guidelines and procedures for negotiations.

b. Specific Commitments

The general obligations assumed in the GATS do not, by themselves, guarantee market access. Any Member can, in principle, respect the MFN obligation and keep its market completely inaccessible to foreign services and service suppliers. Hence, specific commitments have to be made by Members related to market access and national treatment. The relevant provisions of the GATS in this regard are Article XVI, related to market access, Article XVII – the national treatment obligations, and Article XVIII – additional commitments. Members are required to accord market access through different modes of supply, identified in Article I, to a service and service provider of any other Member a treatment no less favourable than that provided under the terms, limitations and conditions agreed and specified in its Schedule. The "national treatment" rule is intended to ensure that a country must accord a foreign service provider the same treatment as domestic service suppliers.

National treatment is distinctly limited under the GATS and extends only to service sectors inscribed in an individual WTO Member's Schedule of Specific Commitments, and even commitments with respect to these service sectors can be conditioned and qualified.[30] A WTO Member may protect certain service sectors or modes of supply from national treatment by omitting it from its Schedule. However, with respect to market access in those sectors liberalized under a

---

[28] Article XV.
[29] *Ibid.,* Article IV.
[30] GATS Article II.

particular Member's Schedule, six measures are, in principle, prohibited, unless otherwise specified in its schedule measures:[31]

i. Limits on the number of service suppliers,
ii. Limits on the value of transactions or assets,
iii. Limits on the total quantity of service output,
iv. Limits on the number of natural persons that can be employed,
v. Limits on the type of legal entity or joint venture that can be used, and
vi. Limits on the participation of foreign capital or investment.[32]

In addition, WTO Members may negotiate commitments with respect to service sectors not covered by national treatment or market access Schedule commitments. It is important to note that, if India agrees to market access concessions, it cannot limit foreign equity participation in the sectors specified unless specified in its Schedule. Members may make additional commitments regarding qualifications, standards or licensing matters affecting trade in services. It may, however, be noted that a Member is free to deviate from its Article II (MFN Treatment) obligations, but not from its Article XVI and Article XVII commitments. Therefore, in such cases, a Member may accord treatment in that sector more favourable than the minimum standard to some Members, as long as all other Members receive at least that minimum standard of market access and national treatment appearing in its Schedule. In such cases, it is not possible for a Member to accord less favourable treatment to certain Members than that specified in its Schedule. The limitations on national treatment cover cases of both *de facto* and *de jure* discrimination. They are however not applicable to service supplier located in the territory of another Member. Similarly, subsidy to a service (Article XV deals with subsidies) located in the country of another Member will be excluded from the purview of the National Treatment provision.

Closely related to "national treatment", there is a serious conceptual problem with respect to the "country of origin" of services since they are produced and consumed simultaneously (in high technology goods, storing is possible). All that can be identified is the entity, whose nationality may not always be easy to establish and could quickly change with the corporate takeovers. Hence, considerable efforts and imagination would be required to fit such a trade within the WTO system of reciprocal concessions.

However, the developing countries' interests may be affected without proper safeguards (like a legally binding code on restricted trade practices at the international level). Furthermore, national treatment can only be a function of a degree of economic integration and homogeneity of economic structure and

---

[31] GATS Article XVI.
[32] In India, in insurance sector, the equity ratio for foreign participation has been fixed up to 26 per cent.

policies, which cannot be predicated when it comes to a multilateral framework, like GATS, to developed and developing countries alike.

Views have been expressed that these rules of GATS will lead to illogical ends when they are applied in the context of less apparent but even more fundamental basic expectations of major trading countries, signatories to the WTO, which although inherent in the Agreement, are less explicit. These are mutuality of benefits, reciprocity of obligations and increasingly, an expectation that other major contracting parties will seek to minimize barriers to trade, even if they are not obligated to do so.[33]

Observance of reciprocity is central to the functioning of the WTO/GATT and its breach by one party would lead to nullifying or impairing the benefits due to the other under the dispute-settlement procedure. Should reciprocity become a central theme in negotiations about services, there would almost certainly be some spill-over to goods and to negotiations when a Member which refuses to extend national treatment to a foreign bank risks retaliation in the form of withdrawal of tariff concessions on import of textiles or in the area of intellectual property rights. Such an approach would certainly open up a virtual Pandora's box of coercion and retaliation as the other side of the coin would be to penalise foreign-owned firms in retaliation for trade measures, for example, countervailing duties, imposed by the home-country under DSU.

A Member's Schedule of Specific Commitments[34] is intended to be progressively liberalized,[35] but commitments may also be modified and withdrawn.[36] Disputes are resolved according to the WTO Dispute Settlement Understanding.[37] Article XIX dealing with negotiations of specific commitments directs Members to hold successive rounds of negotiations not later than five years from the date of entry into force of the Agreement.[38] The negotiators will pay due respect to the national policy objectives and take note of the relative development of Member countries. The developing countries will be given more flexibility in undertaking market access and liberalization commitments. Once the member makes any commitment it becomes binding (just like under Art. XXVIII of the GATT in relation to goods) and can be modified at any time after three years from the entry into force of the Agreement in terms of Article XXI. Specific commitments refer to the degree of liberalization that each WTO Member deems optimal for its own

[33] See William Jr. Diebold and Helena Stalson, "Negotiating Issues in International Services Transaction" in W.R. Cline (ed.), *Trade Policy in the 1980's* (1983) 561.

[34] GATS Article XX.

[35] *Ibid.*, Article XIX.

[36] *Ibid.,* Article XXI.

[37] *Ibid.,* Articles XXII and XXIII.

[38] The negotiations have since been started from January 2000 and are to be concluded within the timeframe of up to 1 January 2005.

market. WTO Members are free (subject of course to the negotiating pressure from their trading partners) to open their services market in the sectors where they wish to do so and with the caveats they deem appropriate. Specific commitments are, consequently, sector specific. In such a case, a Member may restrict the area in a sector to be open for foreign-service providers. For example, currently negotiations are underway on educational services. The Government of India has kept the primary and secondary education outside its purview. In the higher education, the legal services have been kept out and the Government is ready to make commitments only in the areas where the country has a competitive edge. The commitments will be made on reciprocal basis.[39]

c. Specific sector-wise Commitments

Separate Annexes were attached to GATS on Financial services, Telecommunications, Air transport and Movement of natural persons, after negotiations were held and specific commitments made by Members thereto. Sectoral negotiations took place in the WTO on the movement of natural persons in 1995, on communications in 1997 and on financial services in 1998. Countries have made sector-specific commitments with limitations to market access and national treatment. Developed countries made commitments on two-thirds of all service activities – a coverage ratio that climbs to over 80 per cent - once audiovisual, postal, courier and basic telecommunication services, and transportation services are excluded.

Transition economies made commitments covering just over one-half of the 149 service activities. For them coverage ratio climbs to two-thirds for the sectors directly concerned with the Uruguay Round of Negotiations. Developing countries as a group have scheduled a much smaller share of activities than developed or transition economies – only 16 per cent of the 149 activities that are covered.

Activities where commitments have been made by most developing countries included the tourism-related services of "hotels and restaurants," reflecting the current importance of this sector in foreign exchange earnings of many developing countries. Insurance services have been the subject of commitments by one-half of the developing countries; one fifth have made commitments in banking, including India.[40] India has also allowed entry of foreign- service providers in this sector, limiting the equity to 26 per cent. In addition, several developing countries made commitments on basic telecommunications services and maritime transport, on an autonomous basis, since these sectors were generally considered as being excluded from the scope of final commitments.

---

[39] See WTO Doc. GATS/SC/42 on India's commitments.

[40] For India's commitments in Financial Services, see WTO Doc. GATS/SC/42/supp.1 and supp.4.

5.2. Movement of Natural Persons

This is an area of significant interest to developing countries and so to India, in which a minimum level of commitment has been made by the developed countries. For instance, horizontal commitments in mode-4 are subject to limitations in the case of more than 100 countries as opposed to only four countries for mode-2 (consumption abroad). As stated above, at the time of adoption of the GATS, a separate annex was attached to the GATS, which is applicable to measures affecting natural persons who are service suppliers of a Member. It establishes that the "Agreement shall not apply to measures affecting natural persons seeking access to the employment market of a Member, nor shall it apply to measures regarding citizenship, residence or employment on a permanent basis". The Annex further establishes that "the Agreement shall not prevent a Member from applying measures to regulate the entry of natural persons into, or their temporary stay in, its territory, including those measures necessary to protect the integrity of, and to ensure the orderly movement of natural persons across, its borders, provided that such measures are not applied in such a manner as to nullify or impair the benefits accruing to any Member under the terms of specific commitment".

Thus, the GATS allows Members to apply immigration laws to regulate the entry of persons into their territories and protect the integrity of national borders as long as these measures are not applied to nullify the benefits accruing to a Member under the terms of a specific commitment. Members are specifically allowed to apply visa requirements selectively to some countries and not to others.[41] However, the GATS allows Members to enter into agreements outside the GATS for integration of labour markets as long as these agreements result in exemption of citizens of parties to the agreement from residency and work permit requirements. Generally, such integration would provide citizens with a right of free entry to the employment markets of the parties (Article V). In addition, the GATS had established a negotiating group to discuss further liberalization of movement of labour after the conclusion of the Uruguay Round. This negotiating group was to submit a report to the Council on Trade in Services by January 1996. Commitments resulting from these negotiations shall be inscribed in a country's schedule of commitments.[42]

Movement of natural persons has remained a very contentious and thorny area to negotiate. Practically all the countries (including developing countries) have made it subject to the "economic needs test" or subject to quota.[43] Only a limited

---

[41] See Annex on Movement of Natural Persons. This kind of selective application of commitments is permitted under the GATS.

[42] *Ibid.*

[43] Only 12 members have made commitments in the category of independent professional, including those providing services within a service contract. As a matter of fact, the existing

number of developing countries have made specific commitments on movement of natural persons, with certain limitations.

What is important to remember is that the 'Annex on Movement of Natural Persons,' appearing at the end of the Agreement, lays down the basic limitations on the scope of possible negotiations in this area. It clearly states that "the agreement shall not apply to measures affecting natural persons seeking access to the employment market nor shall it apply to measures regarding citizenship, residence or employment on a permanent basis". It clarifies that the agreement shall not prevent a member from applying measures to regulate the entry of natural persons into, or their temporary stay in, its territory. Thus the scope for negotiations on export of labour and personnel is rather limited. Moreover, the regulation often tries, as part of the immigration regime will continue to operate as an effective limitation. This is not to speak of the specific conditionalities that will be attached to a particular sector or sub-sector of services by the country offering such an opening, a possibility explicitly recognized in the agreement itself.

Developed countries, on the other hand, attach foremost importance to supply of service through commercial presence. While being liberal on commercial presence they have evinced little interest in the movement of natural persons. In other words, the regime for movement of natural persons is more restrictive than that for the foreign enterprises. Further, self-employment by the foreign-service has been, by and large, effectively precluded.

It is also notable that in striking contrast to the rather narrow and hedged-in scope for negotiations on movement of labour, the provisions regarding movement of capital are generously liberal. The agreement lays down (Article XVI: 2) explicitly that in sectors where market access commitments are undertaken, the members shall not maintain measures which restrict or require specific types of legal entity of joint venture through which a foreign service supplier may supply a service. Also, no limitations will be prescribed on the participation of foreign capital in terms of maximum percentage limit on foreign shareholding or the total value of individual or aggregate foreign investment. Furthermore, if a member gives a market access commitment in relation to supply of a service across the border and if movement of capital is an essential part of a supply of such a service, the member shall be committed to allow such movement of capital. Similarly, if a service is being supplied through commercial presence in a member's territory, that member will have to permit the movement of capital necessary to establish such commercial presence. Note that by these clarifications, the agreement has established a 'right of establishment' for capital. But the 'right of residence', which is the corresponding equivalent in the case of labour or labour-intensive services, has been scrupulously excluded.

---

commitments are largely linked to commercial presence, which is of limited use to developing countries.

If access commitments are carried out, the developing countries may be affected by severally losing their right to control foreign firms, control of equity participation or expansion, restrictions on number of experts etc. In addition, there would be no state monopoly, de-nationalization in sectors like banking and insurance, as in the case of India.

6. The WTO model for Liberalization of Trade in Services

The GATS is based on the principle that trade in services will be progressively liberalized. In this respect, the GATS echoes the GATT tradition. In the GATT, no date for the launching of a multilateral round of negotiations is specified. The GATT provides that "[T]he Contracting Parties may therefore sponsor [tariff] negotiations *from time to time*".[44] In the GATS, however, the point in time when new negotiations must start is specified. The GATS provides that "[I]n pursuance of the objectives of this Agreement, Members shall enter into successive rounds of negotiations, beginning not later than five years from the date of entry into force of the WTO Agreement".[45] The GATS, therefore, required WTO Members to initiate negotiations on trade in services in January 2000.[46] It was not until March 2001, however, that guidelines and procedures for the negotiations were adopted.[47] The obligation to negotiate at a particular time is hard to enforce due to lack of incentives and the absence of a meaningful remedy. It is also important to note that distinction between goods and services becomes blurred in the context of information technology.

The GATS schedules, by and large, follow a classification, based on the United Nations Central Product Classification (CPC) system. This identifies 11 basic service sectors plus a twelfth category for miscellaneous services. These sub-sectors are further divided into some 160 sub-sectors or separate service activities. The 12 services recognized in the UNCPC system sectors are:

i. Business (including professional and computer) services,
ii. Communication services,
iii. Construction and related engineering services,
iv. Distribution services
v. Educational services,
vi. Environmental services,
vii. Financial (insurance and banking) services,
viii. Health-related and social services,
ix. Tourism and travel-related services,

[44] GATT Article XXVIII *bis*. 1 (emphasis added).
[45] GATS Article XIX: 1 (emphasis added).
[46] On the shaping of the agenda for the services negotiations, see Andre Sapir, "The General Agreement on Trade in Services: From 1994 to the year 2000", *33 Journal of World Trade Law* 1 (1999) at 51.
[47] GATS Article I: 1.

x. Recreational, cultural and sporting services,
xi. Transport services, and
xii. other services not included elsewhere.

The WTO Agreement provides for the establishment of a Council for Trade in Services (GATS Council), which operates under the general guidance of the General Council.[48] The mandate of the GATS Council is broadly described as,

> The Council for Trade in Services shall carry out functions as may be assigned to it to facilitate the operation of this Agreement and further its objectives. The Council may establish such subsidiary bodies, as it considers appropriate for the effective discharge of its functions.[49]

The GATS Council has established a series of subsidiary bodies to deal with sector-specific (e.g., financial services, telecommunications) or horizontal issues (e.g., the Working Party on GATS Rules established by the Council to pursue the mandate laid down in GATS Article X).

7. GATS and India

India's concern and interests in the service sector are common with other developing countries in the WTO. The Agreement on Services has shown some consideration for the concern and interests of the developing countries. It lays down (Article XIX.2) that

> The process of liberalization shall take place with due respect for national policy objectives and the level of development of individual members, both overall and in individual sectors. There shall be appropriate flexibility for individual developing countries for opening fewer sectors, liberalizing fewer types of transaction, progressively extending market access in line with their development situation and when making access to their markets available to foreign service suppliers, attaching to it conditions aimed at achieving the objectives referred to in Article IV.

Article IV is about the increasing participation for the developing countries. This objective is sought to be facilitated by "(a) strengthening domestic services capacity *inter alia* through access to technology on a commercial basis; (b) the improvement of their access to distribution channels and information network; and (c) the liberalization of market access in sectors and modes of supply of export interest to them". But this is only of operational significance, which will be relevant only upon

[48] WTO Agreement Article IV: 2.
[49] GATS Article XXIV: 2.

the improvement of their capacity in the service sector. For most of these countries, Mode 4 holds special interest due to their abundant labour force.

During the negotiations on the GATS, India sought deeper commitments by developed countries under Mode-4 of supply of services, particularly in horizontal commitments by developed countries. To this end, India submitted a detailed paper, identifying the key barriers to movement of professionals and the specific problems with the existing commitments undertaken by the Members. It has suggested bringing about transparency in concerned rules and procedure such as laws and regulations relevant to entry, stay, work authorization, etc.; doing away with additional tariffs and other such regulatory restrictions on the nationals of foreign countries which do not apply to one's own nationals; abolishing quantitative limits on the temporary movement of natural persons etc. It has also suggested a special GATS Visa for categories of personnel covered by horizontal and sectoral commitments undertaken by a Member under Mode-4. India also proposed non-application of the Economic Needs Test in sectors of interest to developing countries and fewer occupational categories to be made subject to such tests. It also desired a uniform definition and coverage of broader service personnel categories to bring greater certainty in these commitments. In this context, it has also insisted on the implementation of the existing Notification Requirements under Article VII on Mutual Recognition Agreements (MRAs), the text of which should be made available to all Members.[50]

Further, India sought provisions of special and differential treatment for developing countries as outlined in Articles IV (increasing participation of developing countries) and IX (business practices) of the GATS in modes other than Mode-4.[51] It raised the issues that Articles IV and XIX: 2 of the General Agreement on Trade in Services provide for special and differential treatment for developing countries.

But the actual history of the implementation since the conclusion of the Uruguay Round of Negotiations does not evidence the extension of such treatment to the developing countries. Also, the importance of Mode 4 for developing countries is obvious; and yet commitments made by the developed countries in this area are far from satisfactory. An assessment by the Council for Trade in Services under Article XIX is mandatory before embarking on negotiating guidelines for the new round of negotiations. Such an assessment must be carried out by the CTS in collaboration with the United Nations Conference on Trade and Development (UNCTAD), which has already commenced such work. Until such an assessment is complete, both, in overall terms and sector-wise, it is very difficult to conclude that developing countries have gained much from the GATS so far.

---

[50] India made a statement to this effect before the CTS in its meeting held on 6 October 2000 and insisted on compliance with Art. VII.4 (a), (b) & (c).
[51] WT/GC/W/224 of 2 July 1999.

Mode-4 commitments undertaken by developed countries being modest, there is a need to make substantially higher commitments in this area if the balance of benefits under GATS is to be preserved. Higher levels of commitments can be achieved on the basis of rules that are transparent; no additional tariff/tax or other regulatory restrictions on the nationals of foreign countries that do not apply to one's own nationals; no quantitative limits on temporary movement of natural persons; fees/charges applicable for providing social security nets should not apply to temporary movement of natural persons; no non-tariff barriers and no regulatory restrictions on the movement of natural persons. The Economic Needs Test should be applied exceptionally, which should be based on the transparent and objective criteria. In modes other than Mode-4, developing countries to be given special and differential treatment as outlined in Articles IV and IX of the GATS. India also submitted that any future negotiations in the GATS should be guided by the GATT approach, based on a "positive list", i.e., request and offer approach, with no prior exclusion of any mode and by the principles outlined in Article IX for developing countries.[52] For Mode-4, a new list of occupations using the ILO International Standard Classification of Occupations could be established.[53]

It is also incumbent on the CTS to establish modalities for the treatment of autonomous liberalization undertaken by Members since the Uruguay Round. And finally, Article IV is to be given real meaning in any new commitments by developed countries. Also, a monitoring mechanism is required to be set up for tracking implementation of Article IV of the GATS Agreement.

Despite these submissions, India is negotiating all service sectors which are open for the negotiations and has taken a cautious approach.[54] It is also pertinent to note that in legal services, due to the protests from the profession, the Government has kept it out of negotiation. But reading carefully, the Advocates Act, 1961 does not prohibit consultancy outside the courts (sec. 45). Thus the foreign professionals may render these services under Mode 3 or Mode 4 without violating the Advocates Act.

8. Conclusions

The GATS is best described as a forum of ongoing liberalization. Even though the argument could be made that the existing Schedules of Commitments do not

---

[52] In practice, however, India has just followed the developed countries, excluding certain specific areas and modes of services, as is evident from its negotiation on educational services.

[53] India's specific suggestion is to exclude applicability of Economic Needs Test to specified occupational categories of professional as contained in ISCO-88 under the relevant sectors/sub-sectors specified in WTO Doc. W/120.

[54] See WTO Documents GATS/SC/42/Supp.1. Supp.3 and Supp.4 on India's commitments in financial services, telecommunications and educational services.

represent meaningful liberalization in the services sector, one should always keep in mind that the GATS is the first attempt to liberalize trade multilaterally in this field and that existing examples at the regional level (such as the EU) have not been immediately successful. It may, however, be recalled that liberalization is a slow process, particularly when a country's sensitivities and national development issues are at stake. In the services sector, it is not only that the economic aspect, but social, cultural and political aspects are equally important, which a country needs to protect before embarking on the process of liberalization. One should not expect too much too soon. The current attitude of WTO Members toward services is one of caution.

GATS envisages objectives like establishing a sound multilateral framework or principle and rules for trade in services, which can expand under conditions of transparency and liberalization; it also aims at increased participation by developing countries. But the fact is that in the area of service trade, it is the industrial countries, which matter most because they control more than 80 per cent of the market. These countries have erected different kinds of non-tariff barriers to protect their nascent service industries. Developing countries on the other hand are minor players in the services trade and they may succeed only when the industrial countries take the initiative to liberalize services. While there is scope for the industrial countries to do away with some of their protectionist tendencies to respect GATT's obligations, some provisions have been legitimized by the GATT Uruguay Round in its escape clauses relating to Article XIV (security exceptions) in Part II of GATS. In GATS, there is an absence of a standard classification seeking the 'commercial presence', under which multinationals can produce and sell services in the territories of other countries. But the developing countries are not easily inclined to have foreign presence, affecting indigenous industries and interference in the autonomy of their service sectors.

In contrast to goods, services are subject to a number of non-tariff barriers, which mostly remain invisible. This, most of the time, makes it difficult to quantify the exchange of concessions. There is a need to have total transparency, along with a legally binding international code on restrictive business practices. It is pertinent that developing countries should have a proper legislative framework on restrictive practices. India has already adopted the Competition Act, 2002 (partly in force), which, though not service specific legislation, will address the anti-competitive practices of the enterprises.

INDIA AND THE INTERNATIONAL PATENT SYSTEM

V. G. Hegde*

1. Introduction

India's approach towards the evolution of the international patent system, as it exists today, is one of caution. There is an increasing realization in India in the last two decades, about the role of the international patent system in matters of industrial growth and economic development.[1] While this is so, it is to be noted that India was not a party to the Paris Convention on Industrial Property 1883 ('the Paris Convention' hereinafter), which embodied the main principles of the international patent system, till 1998.[2] India was, however, an active participant in the Diplomatic Conferences which took place during the latter part of the 1970s to comprehensively revise the Paris Convention.[3] The Paris Convention, containing

* Associate Professor of International Law, School of International Studies, Jawaharlal Nehru University, New Delhi.

[1] The debate concerning the role of the international patent system on economic development was first initiated within the United Nations, in the 1960s. There are a number of reasons for this. Firstly, the United Nations provided the perfect political setting to the emerging newly independent states to assert themselves. The decades of the 1960s and 1970s were the decades of 'developmental concerns' for developing countries. The United Nations General Assembly (UNGA) adopted on 14 December 1962 Resolution 1803 (XVII) on *Permanent Sovereignty over Natural Resources* which *inter alia,* referred to "the inalienable right of all states freely to dispose of their natural wealth and resources in accordance, with their national interests' and to 'respect for the economic independence of States". This was followed by the UNGA Resolution 3201 (S-VI) of 1 May 1974 containing a *Declaration on the Establishment of New International Economic Order.* On 12 December 1974 UNGA adopted the *Charter of Economic Rights and Duties*, see generally, R.P. Anand, *New States and International Law*, (Vikas Publications, Delhi, 1972); also see, R.P.Anand (edited) *Salient Documents in International Law*, (New Delhi, 1994). In this setting several studies emerged within the UN fora linking international patent system and economic development with particular reference to transfer of technology; see generally, *Report of the Group of Governmental Experts on the Role of the Patent System in the Transfer of Technology*, UNCTAD, TD/B/C-6/8,21 October 1975; *The Role of Patent System in Transfer of Technology to Developing Countries*, TD/B/AC 11/19 Rev. 2, 1975; *Study, Examination of the Economic Commercial and Developmental Aspects of Industrial Property in the Transfer of Technology to Developing Countries,* UNCTAD/TD/B/C.6/A.C.5/3,1981.

[2] India joined the Paris Convention on 7 December 1998. However, Article 2(1) of the TRIPS agreement extended the application of Articles 1 to 12 and 19 of the Paris Convention to all Members of the WTO with effect from 1 January 1995.

[3] The Paris Convention has been revised six times. Article 14 provides that periodic diplomatic conferences shall be held for revising the original text. Accordingly, it has been revised at Brussels on December 14, 1900, at Washington on 2 June 1911, at The Hague on 6 November 1925, at London on 2 June 1934, at Lisbon on 31 October 1958 and at Stockholm on 14 July 1967. India was not part of any of these negotiations.

***Bimal N. Patel (ed.),* India and International Law, 93-116.**

the substantive aspects of an international patent system, was considered to be inimical to the interests of developing countries, although they constituted its majority membership.[4] Accordingly, developing countries, including India, took a leading role during the mid-1970s to effectively revise the Paris Convention.[5] Despite several sessions of the Diplomatic Conferences and Consultative Meetings till 1985, developing countries failed to make any substantial gains in the negotiations crucial to their interests. From here, the focus of revising the international patent system shifted to the General Agreement on Tariffs and Trade (GATT) with the launching of its most ambitious Uruguay Round of Negotiations.[6] India played a crucial role in these negotiations *albeit* with little success particularly with regard to the evolution of the principles of IPR protection in the Agreement on Trade-related Aspects of Intellectual Property Rights (`TRIPs' hereinafter).

The present study proposes to focus on the role played by India, along with other developing countries, to revise the international patent system and its desire to be part of the system without compromising its basic economic and developmental objectives. The study also proposes to look at the negotiating positions taken by India with a view to reducing the rigours of the international patent system not only for itself, but for other similarly placed developing countries. The primary focus of the study will be to look at the international patent system with an evolutionary perspective, with special reference to India.

2. The Evolution of the International patent system

For nearly a century the international patent system was synonymous with the Paris Convention, which was concluded in 1883. The Paris Convention evolved in response to a need created during the last phase of the industrial revolution during the 19th century.[7] However, countries of the time, even within Europe where it evolved, were strongly divided over its utility, particularly in protecting their national

---

[4] As on 24 September 2004 the Paris Convention had a total membership of 168 countries. Among them, nearly 144 countries were developing countries. About 70 of them joined the Convention in the decade of 1991-2001.

[5] The objective of the Diplomatic Conference that commenced during February-March 1980 was to begin the Seventh Revision of the Paris Convention. The Revision Conference concluded without any tangible resulting 1991. Reasons for this failure have been dealt with elsewhere in this article.

[6] The GATT's Uruguay Round of Multilateral Trade Negotiations were launched on 20 September 1986 in Punta del Este, Uruguay. Among others, it included a negotiating agenda on Intellectual Property Rights (IPRs); see *Basic Instruments and Selected Documents*, (Geneva: General Agreement on Tariffs and Trade), 1987, Supplement 33, pp.19-28.

[7] The studies linking patent system and the industrial revolution basically deal with the issues of economic development. See Christine Macleod, *Inventing the Industrial Revolution: The English Patent System 1660-1880* (Cambridge, 1988); H.I. Dutton, *The Patent System and Inventive Activity During Industrial Revolution*, 1750-1852 (Manchester 1984); Eric Schiff, *Industrialization Without National Patents: The Netherlands 1869-1912, Switzerland, 1850-1902* (Princeton, 1971).

interests. The patent controversy of the early 19th century, for example, was fundamentally to protest against the international protection granted to patents. However, it is argued that the factors such as increasing inventive and innovative activity coupled with the industrial revolution necessitated the creation of an international patent system.[8] The Netherlands, for example, abolished its patent system in 1869, reintroducing it only in 1910. Germany introduced its patent system in 1871 and Switzerland in 1887, in both cases after initial opposition. European countries, in stark contrast to their position today, adopted patent laws which invariably protected national inventors and national industry. The majority of these patent laws acted like tariffs effectively barring foreign competition and was incompatible with the trends in commercial policy towards free trade. When viewed against the backdrop of the agreement on TRIPS, specifically on patent protection, it appears that the evolution of an international patent system in the last one hundred years has turned a full circle. It has shown that depending upon the level of technological development countries have sought to shift their emphasis on the level of patent protection.

India's response to the international patent system should be viewed in this context. The colonial English patent legislation was extended to India.[9] Patenting became a tool to import new inventions into the country which in turn was employed in such a manner as to produce goods in large scale. For this purpose, raw materials were shipped from the colonies of the Western countries. So, it is rightly

---

[8] For conflicting viewpoints existing during that period see E. Penrose, *The Economics of the International Patent System* (Baltimore, John Hopkins Press, 1951); Ulf Anderfelt, *International Patent Legislation and Developing Countries* (The Hague, Martinus Nijhoff, 1971).

[9] The Indian patent system had its origin in the "Act for Granting Exclusive Privileges to Inventors of 1856" which provided for the protection of inventions in India. A new enactment was introduced in 1859 modeled on the English Patent Act of 1852. Under this Act, an inventor of a new manufacture by filing a specification of his invention obtained the "exclusive privileges" of making, selling and using the invention in India and authorizing others to do so for a term of 14 years from the time of filing such specification. For the purpose of providing protection for designs, the "Patents and Designs Protection Act" was passed in 1872. An amendment Act affording protection to inventors desirous of exhibiting their inventions at exhibitions was passed in 1883. Subsequently, in 1888 the law contained in three Acts of 1859, 1872 and 1883 was consolidated into a single Act. The same was revised and replaced by the Indian Patents and Designs Act, 1911. This Act established for the first time in India a system of patent administration under the management of the controller of patents. In the period between 1911 to 1970 various amendments to this Act were introduced. See generally for the evolution of Indian Patent System, " Developments and Future Prospects on the National Level in India" in WIPO ed., *Current Trends in the Field of Intellectual Property* (Geneva: 1971); R Narayanan, *Patent Law* (Calcutta, 1985); *Indian Patent Laws vis-à-vis Paris Convention for the Protection of Industrial Property* (Bombay), Introductory papers by Forum for Preservation of Indian Patent Laws; *Protection of Intellectual Property-Indian Patents Act, 1970* (New Delhi, 1988) *Occasional Papers*, National Working Group on Patent Laws; Rajeev Dhavan, "A Monopoly by Any Other Name", *Occasional Papers*, National Working Group on Patent Laws.

asserted, "the history of the West in the East has largely been the history of repeated attempts to capture world markets as areas of exclusive domain. In its expansion, the West has used many techniques".[10] Patenting also served this purpose. For instance, it has been pointed out, in the 18th and 19th centuries numerous patent privileges were granted by several colonies, some for inventions and some for establishing new industries according to processes known elsewhere.[11] Accordingly, the national patent legislations were devised to meet the peculiar needs of each individual country.

While the national patent legislations in the European countries were undergoing change to suit their national interests and priorities, few other countries, mainly the Great Britain, the United States of America, France, Belgium and Austria-Hungary took an initiative to evolve an international patent system.

These countries had realized that this was one way of attracting foreign inventions on their soil. The deliberations conducted prior to the birth of the Paris Convention generally reflected the desires of these few countries to accumulate in their country as many fruits of the industrial revolution as possible.[12] This desire to attract new inventions by evolving an international patent system had other crucial dimensions as well. For example, one of the unsettled issues related to the "local working" requirement as contained in patent legislations of many countries. The dictates of domestic necessity were considered as a major reason for putting forward stringent principles relating to the effective utilization of the patent. Reasons for this were not far to seek. The industrial productivity of many European countries during the peak of the industrial revolution was not on an even keel. In order to realize the much needed competitive edge in foreign trade, countries of Europe at that time, initiated every possible move to bring into their country as many new inventions as possible. In order to realize this objective, understandably, the rights of the patentee acquired much significance in the existing national legislations. Compulsory licensing and revocation of patents for non-working in a host country did not evoke much interest.[13]

These conferences and exhibitions within Europe succeeded in laying down the broad principles for the evolution of an international patent system. The Paris

---

[10] Rajeev Dhavan, Lindsay Harris, and Gopal Jain, "Conquest by Patent: The Paris Convention Revisited", 32 *Journal of the Indian Law Institute* 131-78 (1990).

[11] Penrose, *supra* note 8 at 11.

[12] A leading American Science Journal *Scientific American* was fortnight in its criticism in this regard. See, S.P. Ladas, *Patents, Trademarks and Related Rights* (1975) at 59.

[13] It may be noted that some of the issues regarding the evolution of principles of an international patent system were raised at various industrial exhibitions in Europe, such as, the Vienna Exhibition, Paris Exhibition in 1878. Those inventors who exhibited their new inventions in the Exhibitions insisted on stronger protection of their exhibits, as the same was not forthcoming from some national legislations.

Convention for the International Protection of Industrial Property was finally concluded in 1883. The original members of the Paris Union were: Belgium, Brazil, Ecuador, France, Great Britain, Guatemala, Italy, the Netherlands, Portugal, El Salvador, Serbia, Spain, Switzerland and Tunisia.[14]

The substantive provisions of the Paris Convention were, mainly (a) the principle of national treatment; (b) the right of priority, and (c) working requirements. The principle of national treatment conferred the same protection to nationals of the other member countries as it granted to its own nationals (Article 2). The right of priority provided the prospective inventors to acquire exclusive rights on a first-come-first basis and thereby lessen the period of patent grant marginally. In other words, the provision allowed a patentee who had filed a patent application in one Member State, to acquire a priority right of 12 months during which he could file an application for a patent grant in any Member State without the risk of having third parties do it before him. The independence of patent grants was also recognized. Patents applied for in various countries of the Paris Union (i.e., members of the Paris Convention) by nationals of countries of the Union were regarded as independent of patents obtained for the same invention in other countries, whether members of the Union or not (Article 5 *bis*). The provision relating to the importation and the working of the patented invention constituted a major cornerstone of the Paris Convention. Importations of the patented products were allowed under Article 5 without attracting any sanction such as revocation and forfeiture of the patent grant. This single provision occupied a greater part of the deliberations of all the subsequent Revision Conferences of the Paris Convention. The working of a patented invention was defined in clear terms by providing for an obligation on the patentee to exploit his patent according to the laws of each particular State. This was termed as "local working". The Paris Convention of 1883 which began with strict "local working" requirements for the patent grants in its Article 5, after six Revision Conferences reached the other end by completely qualifying this requirement. Even the importation of the product was regarded as equivalent to "local working". The compulsory working requirement was scaled down to "compulsory licensing".

---

[14] Japan was the first Asian country to join Paris Convention along with the United States in 1900. It has been stated that the United States brought with it to Paris, abroad the same steamship, its Protectorates- Ecuador, El Salvador and Guatemala. Brazil too was brought in. France brought along Tunisia. But, Ecuador, El Salvador and Guatemala withdrew from the Convention in 1886, 1887 and 1895 respectively. The Netherlands, Serbia and Switzerland did not have any national patent laws at that time. Even then, they signed the Paris Convention. See, Surendra J. Patel, "Intellectual Property Rights in the Uruguay Round: A Disaster for the South?" 1 *Economic and Political Weekly*, XXIV 8 (1989) at 979; Also see Surendra J. Patel, "The Patent System and the Third World", 22 *World Development* .9, (1974) at 7; S.P. Ladas, *Patents, Trademarks and Related Rights* (1975).

The Revision Conferences of the Paris Convention, it may be noted, contributed to the evolution of an international patent system suited essentially to the interests of the industrialized countries of Europe. They were primarily confined to the prescription of limits to which national laws may require patentees to exploit their inventions and the types of sanctions allowed. Though the formulations relating to the exploitation of patens as embodied in Article 5, providing for compulsory local working originally were crucial for less industrialized countries, its evolution did not consider growing disparities in economic development. For less industrialized countries, it has been mentioned "economic cooperation or dependent status and affinity of legal traditions with the former mother country have been more important factors than for instance the country's state and evolution in the economic and technological field".[15]

The Revision Conferences for amending the Paris Convention were attended by many less industrialized and poor countries, the majority of them from the Latin American continent[16]. Most of these countries were represented at the conference by their colonial administrations. Accordingly, the evolution of the international patent system till the early part of the 1960s did not address the issues of economic development and transfer of technology crucial to less industrialized countries[17].

---

[15] Anderfelt, *supra* note 8 at 122; also see Penrose, *supra* note 8 at 91.

[16] One primary reason for this participation appears to be the proximity of Latin America with the continent of Europe. Accordingly, many Latin American countries initially joined the Paris Convention and left, in some cases, as hurriedly as they came in.

[17] The Revision Conference of Lisbon, 1958, held in the post-second world war era, for the first time, saw some developing countries making an effort to influence the outcome of the conference, *albeit* unsuccessfully. Ceylon and Indonesia joined the Paris Convention. Brazil, Yugoslavia argued that mere granting of compulsory licenses to a third party for non-working of the patent within a host country would not sufficiently be able to curtail the abusive practices arising out of patent grants. The Lisbon Revision Conference also introduced Article 5 *Quarter* which not only became a potential threat to the interests of developing countries, it also set in motion a new substantive agenda for the next three decades until the launching of GATT's Uruguay Round of Negotiations. The text of this article provided: "When a product is imported into a country of the union where there exists a patent protecting a process of manufacture of the said product, the patentee shall have all the rights, with regard to the imported product, that are accorded to him by the legislation of the country or importation, on the basis of the process patent, with respect to products manufactured in that country". The substance of this provision becomes clear only when the difference between process and product patent is recognized. A process patent in very simple terms means a patent that protects a process of manufacture and the product patent protects products only. The legislative measures provided in many countries identify two different kinds of process patents, namely, "pure process patents and product-by-process patents". As the name suggests, on pure process patents the scope of protection is limited strictly to the process of manufacture. In other words, under a pure process patent use by a third party of the patented process would constitute infringement but not use or sale of the

In 1961, Brazil, for the first time, brought into exclusive focus certain issues relating to the international patent system, which directly affected developing countries by way of a draft resolution in the Second Committee of the United Nations General Assembly, entitled "The Role of Patents in the Transfer of Technology to Underdeveloped Countries".[18] The resolution made critical references to the working of the international patent system which, *inter alia*, included broadly the following aspects: (a) accession to technical knowledge and the limitations placed by the system; (b) patents taken out by foreigners without the intention of local exploitation; (c) the harmful restrictive provisions in the license agreements; and (d) royalty payments constituting a heavy burden on the balance of payments, which may be further aggravated by imports of patented products carrying artificially high prices.[19] Some of these issues raised in the 1961 Brazilian Resolution set in motion a new thinking on the role of the international patent system.[20]

India played a significant role, along with other developing countries, when in 1975 preparatory work began for the revision of the Paris Convention by virtue of its membership of the 1967 Convention Establishing the World Intellectual Property Organization (WIPO).[21] By virtue of its membership with WIPO, India was also a member of the *Ad Hoc* Group of Government Experts which held three

---

product so produced. The effect of the product by process patent would be different. It not only restricts the use of process by a third party, but also the sale and use of its products would constitute infringement. This provision, accordingly, implicitly created an import monopoly for the patentee blocking thereby any kind of indigenous development of the product. Developing countries strongly argued for its deletion. See *The International Patent as an Instrument of Policy for National Development*, UNCTAD, TD/B/CC/AC.2/3.13 July 1975 p.28; Also see *World Intellectual Property Organization* PR/8/3/(1976); *Historical Trends in Protection of Technology in Developed Countries and Their Relevance for Developing Countries*, UNCTAD/IIP/TEC/18, 26 December 1990; Dhavan *supra* note 10 at 158.

18 UN Doc. A/C. 2/L.565, November 8,1961.

19 This Brazilian Resolution was totally modified. Its final version read: "*Affirming* that it is in the interest of all countries that the international patent system should be applied in such a way as to take wholly into account the special needs and requirements of the economic development of underdeveloped countries as well as the legitimate claims of patentees".

20 *The Role of Patents in the Transfer of Technology to Developing Countries*, UNDOC.E/3861/Rev. 1 March 1964. This report dealt with (a) major characteristics of the patent system; and (b) effects of patents on the economies of underdeveloped countries. The first part of the report discussed various aspects of national patent legislations (including India), including international and regional patent arrangements.

21 India had joined the World Intellectual Property Organization (WIPO) in 1975. WIPO provided the institutional framework to the Paris Convention. Initially, there were two offices, one for industrial property and another for copyright i.e., Paris Union for the Patents and Berne Union for the copyright. These two institutions were united in 1893. Later with a view to administering these institutions the United International Bureaux for the Protection of Intellectual Property (BIRPI) was established. WIPO succeeded BIRPI in 1967; see *Background Reading Material on Intellectual Property* (WIPO: Geneva: 1988) at 37.

sessions in February 1975(Geneva), December 1975 (Geneva) and in June 1976 (Lausanne).[22] India was also a member of the provisional steering committee of the Diplomatic Conference which established the provisional rules of procedure of the Diplomatic Conference and the provisional agenda of the Diplomatic Conference. The negotiations in the Diplomatic Conference were conducted in three main committees represented by three groups of countries. India was one of the members of the Group of Developing Countries. The objective of the Diplomatic Conference was to effect the Seventh Revision of the Paris Convention. These were to (a) examine the possibility of ensuring a proper balance between the needs of the developing countries and the rights granted by patents (b) promote the actual working of inventions; (c) establish the principal obligations and rights of owners of industrial property rights; (d) encourage creative inventions in the developing countries; (e) judge the real value of inventions for which protection is sought; (f) screen and control licensing contracts; (g) improve the means of information set up under national legislation; (h) create suitable institutional structures; (i) prevent or combat abusive practices in the field of industrial property; (j) consider the principle of equality of all forms of industrial property, of national treatment, of the independence of patents and of preferential treatment for developing countries; (k) assist the developing countries in strengthening their scientific and technological infrastructure and in the training of specialists, and (l) to give each country all latitude to adopt the legislative and administrative measures consistent with its needs and with its social and economic policy.[23]

The above objectives set for the revision of the Paris Convention were crucial for India. It had enacted a patent legislation in 1970, after a prolonged deliberation, taking into account its own economic and industrial development policies.[24] In other words, the above objectives were consistent with India's law and policy. Although India was part of the Group of Developing Countries, it did not make any substantive statements, on its own, on the various negotiating positions held by the developing countries. While the Brazilian delegate represented on behalf of the Group of Developing Countries, India was actively involved in the deliberations in various committees.[25]

---

[22] See WIPO, PR/SM/3, *Final Summary Minutes of the Diplomatic Conference on the Revision of the Paris Convention*, First Session, Geneva, 4 February to 4 March 1980.

[23] Declaration on the objectives of the Paris Convention, WIPO, WIPO, PR/DC/3, *Basic Proposals, Diplomatic Conference on the Revision of the Paris Convention*, Geneva, 25 June 1979, p.7.

[24] While "self-reliance" was fundamental to its primary policy objective, India laid emphasis on "the development of indigenous technology and efficient absorption and adaptation of imported technology appropriate to national priorities and policies"; see *Technology Policy Statement, 1983* of the Government of India.

[25] Upon the recommendation of the *Ad hoc* Group of Experts, the Assembly of the Paris Union established in September/October 1976 the preparatory Intergovernmental Committee on the Revision of the Paris Convention. This Intergovernmental Preparatory

The Revision of the Paris Convention and the proposals submitted by the developing countries were gradually diluted to meet the conditions steadfastly attached by developed countries. There was no consensus on issues, relating to the working of the patent grants in a host country.[26] The divide with regard to the perceptions of patent grants and its local working between developing and developed countries were getting wider. At the fifth consultative meeting for the revision of the Paris Convention which had met in September 1988 the Group of Developing Countries pointed out that the whole process of revision had already been "a rather long process, indeed too long process in certain respects".[27] The Group of Developing Countries which included India as well referred to three objectives of the revision, namely (a) to correct and prevent certain abusive practices that sometimes occurred in the industrial property field ; (b) to make the Paris Convention, in a new revised and improved version, capable of facilitating the technological development of the developing countries and improving the conditions of technology transfers to those countries on equitable terms; and (c) patents not to be merely used as a means of closing some markets and dividing others, speculating on prices or building up *de facto* monopolies that were always prejudicial to the weakest economies.[28] The developed countries, on the other hand, pointed out that they had no wish to revise the Paris Convention and that they considered the Stockholm Act of 1967 as satisfactory; and that it had wished to revise the Paris Convention keeping in view the problems of developing countries and at the same time without affecting the interests of developed country members. Reference was also made to the incidence of widespread infringement of industrial property rights, often referred to as counterfeiting and piracy and the consequent

---

Committee constituted four Working Groups. India was included in three of the Working Groups, namely (a) The Working Group on Article 5A of the Paris Convention (which dealt with local working of the patent grant, its forfeiture and revocation in case of non-working of the patent grant); (b) the working group entrusted with questions of special interest to developing countries, and (c) the working group on conflict between an appellation of origin and a trademark. India was also a member of the provisional steering committee of the Diplomatic Conference, which established the provisional rules of procedure of the Diplomatic conference and the provisional agenda of the diplomatic conference. See, WIPO, PR/SM/3, *Final Summary Minutes of the Diplomatic Conference on the Revision of the Paris Convention*, First Session, Geneva, 4 February to 4 March 1980, p.21.

26 The report of the chairman of the Main Committee I noted "in spite of all the efforts made both within main committee I and at the meetings of working Group-I unfortunately can only report that main committee I has failed to reach a consensus on Article 5 A and on the other questions relating to patents". See WIPO, PR/SM/12, *Final Summary Minutes of the Diplomatic Conference on the Revision of the Paris Convention, Fourth Session,* Geneva, 27 February to 24 March 1984, p.27. The revision of Article 5A dealt particularly with the importation of articles covered by patents, failure to work patents, abuse of patent rights, exploitation of patents in the public interest, and special provisions for developing countries.

27 See WIPO, PR/CM/V/4, Fifth Consultative Meeting on the Revision of the Paris Convention, Geneva, September 19 to 23, 1988, p.3.

28 *Ibid* at 4.

developments and discussion within GATT's Uruguay Round of Negotiations on Trade-related Aspects of Intellectual Property Rights (TRIPs).[29]

The developing countries, including India, had noted that the trend towards strengthening of the protection of industrial property rights in a number of areas was increasingly owing to the greater commercial and technological importance of those rights. The developing countries had also noted that this had the effect of promoting protectionism and technological secrecy, and in turn causing a reduction in technology transfers.[30]

The preparations for the creation of new norms and standards to protect IPRs were already set in motion in the GATT's Uruguay Round of Negotiations. By 1985, it should be noted, negotiations were in full swing not only in Geneva, but in the capitals of many developed countries. The dominant groups' multinational corporations had, by then, commenced lobbying for the inclusion of the issue of IPRs in the GATT's Uruguay Round Agenda. [31] Developed Countries, by 1987, were set to make detailed statement on the proposed negotiating objectives of the IPRs in the Uruguay Round of Negotiations. These statements, it should be noted, included a substantial section on the creation of new norms and standards of the protection of IPRs. These new norms and standards, however, totally discarded the work so far carried out within the Paris Revision Conferences.[32] Both India and Brazil had also circulated detailed statements on the proposed negotiating objective to be followed in the Uruguay Round Negotiations concerning IPRs.[33] In the next section we may look at the evolution of IPRs moving into an entirely new forum: the General Agreement on Tariffs and Trade.

3. Uruguay Round of Negotiations

The Punta del E'ste Declaration on IPRs was preceded by intense negotiations to present a compromise mandate. Differences were not easily bridgeable between

---

[29] *Ibid.*

[30] WIPO, *Sixth Consultative Meeting on the Revision of the Paris Convention*, [PR/CM/VI/I], Geneva, 18 to 22 September 1989, at 5.

[31] For an account on this see Chakravarti Raghvan, *Recolonization : GATT, the Uruguay Round and the Third World* (Penang: Third World Network, 1990).

[32] These new norms and standards within GATT were articulated by United States, European Communities and Japan. See MTN, GNG/NG 11W/2, 3 April 1987, *Statement by the United States,*; MTN , GNG/NG 11/W/7, 29 May 1987, *Submission by the European Communities*, MTN. GNG/NG 11/W/7, 29 May, 1987, Submission by Japan.

[33] MTN.GNG/NG 11/W/37, 10 July 1989, *Standards and Principles Concerning its Availability, Scope and Use, Communication from India. Brazil had made a statement earlier, See MTN. GNG/NG 11/W/ 30, 31 October 1988, Submission from Brazil.* It had become clear by 1985 that the Diplomatic conference to revise the Paris Convention and the subsequent consultative Meetings were leading nowhere.

developing countries mainly represented by India and Brazil and USA, the European Community and other developed countries on the other side. The GATT contracting parties had before them two drafts of a ministerial declaration on IPRs- one prepared by a group of Ten Third World Countries, namely, Argentina, Brazil, Cuba, Egypt, India, Nicaragua, Nigeria, Peru, Tanzania and Yugoslavia.[34] The second draft was termed "Colombian-Swiss Draft" supported by the United States, which was eventually adopted with certain modifications.[35] The GATT's Uruguay Round Mandate on IPRs was not only aimed at "clarifying" GATT provisions, it also sought to "elaborate… appropriate new rules and disciplines". The negotiating mandate for IPRs within the GATT framework had three strands, namely (a) effective and adequate protection of trade-related aspects of IPRs[36] (b) trade in counterfeit goods,[37] and (c) relationship between the negotiations in this area and initiatives in other forums, mainly WIPO.

---

[34] See Surendra J. Patel, *Trade Related Intellectual Property in Uruguay Round in GATT* (London: Commonwealth Secretariat: 1989) prepared at the request of the Commonwealth Secretariat; Also see Abdulqawi A. Yusaf, "Developing Countries and Trade-Related Aspects of Intellectual Property Rights" in *Uruguay Round: Papers on Selected Issues*, (New York: United Nations, 1989).

[35] The Punta del Este Ministerial Declaration provided: "In order to reduce the distortions and impediments to international trade and taking into account the need to promote effective and adequate protection of intellectual property rights and to ensure that measures and procedures to enforce intellectual property rights do not themselves become barriers to legitimate trade, the negotiations shall aim to clarify GATT provisions and elaborate as appropriate new rules and disciplines: negotiations shall aim to develop a multilateral framework of principles, rules and disciplines dealing with international trade in counterfeit goods, taking into account the work already undertaken in the GATT; these negotiations shall be without prejudice to other complementary initiatives that may be taken in the World Intellectual Property Organization and elsewhere to deal with these matters. See *Basic Instruments and Selected Documents* (Geneva: General Agreement on Tariffs and Trade, 1987, Supplement 33) , p.19.

[36] This is to "clarify and elaborate" existing GATT principles within the framework of " appropriate new rules and disciplines" to promote effective and adequate protection of IPRs. Subsequently the Uruguay Round Negotiations appear to have gone beyond this mandate when the Agreement on TRIPS set out new substantive uniform standards of IPR protection. Part II of the Agreement, it may be noted provided for the "Standard Concerning the Availability, Scope and Use of Intellectual Property Rights" See *Augment on Trade-Related Aspects of Intellectual Property Rights, including Trade in Counterfeit Goods,* in Final Act Embodying the Results of the Uruguay Round of Multilateral Trade Negotiations (Marrakesh: GATT, 1994), p.330.

[37] This matter was first raised in the GATT framework in July 1978 in the Tokyo Round Sub-group "Customs Matters". In the Tokyo Round Negotiations, the United States had proposed, with the general support of a number of other delegations, the negotiation of international rules on the prevention of commercial counterfeiting. However, agreement on a text for incorporation in the final results of the Tokyo Round was not reached. See MTN.GNG/NG11/W/4, 6 May 1987, *Work Undertaken in GATT Concerning Trade Related Aspects of IPRs, including Trade in Counterfeit Goods.*

The inclusion of IPRs on the GATT negotiating agenda, it is argued, was necessitated due to certain far-reaching changes which had taken place in the world economy. These changes have primarily taken place in the arena of technology. And the technology, in turn, played a crucial role in the global production and trade. Furthermore, the role of technology as a factor in the national development assumed new dimensions such as exercising control over the international market.[38] The reasons for this are quite complex. It has been pointed out that "the economic value of the intellectual assets of new technology is augmenting, but the technology is also becoming increasingly abstract and intangible".[39] The emerging new technological innovations were carriers of intensive scientific knowledge. This new knowledge facilitated the imitation and copying of intellectual property for it "makes it easy to separate the form that a product takes from the intellectual assets it embodies."[40] Considering these features of the new and emerging technologies, it has been argued that "a legal system suited to a conventional technological pattern of mechanical invention and printed forms of communication is not adequate for the new, scientifically-based, technological innovation that permits separation of the tangible from the intangible components, thereby facilitating diffusion of the latter."[41] Countries which owned and were worried about the international dimensions of the appropriation of technological innovation sought to create strong patent regimes for these reasons. The strong patent regimes, they argued would facilitate maximum return from the market in the shortest time. The life of the new and high technology was, it should be noted, shortened due to its faster diffusion rate and easy capability. Diffusion and comparability allowed fairly easy operation of the process of "reverse engineering" in reconstructing the whole technological innovation. This, on the other hand, favoured immensely the developing countries, including India. The nature of technological diffusion and its implications could be very crucial to a developing country. In a world of imposed North-South asymmetry, nowhere are the disparities between the industrialized countries and the Third World more marked than in the crucially important field of technological development.[42]

It is to be noted that at a time when some developing countries, and particularly India, had turned from import substitution to more aggressive export-oriented policies, the importance of creating comparative advantage and acquiring

---

[38] Paolo Bifani, "Intellectual Property Rights and International Trade", in *Uruguay Round: Papers on Selected Issues* (New York: United Nations, 1989) at 129.

[39] Paolo Bifani, "The New Mercantilism and the International Appropriation of Technology", in *Technology, Trade Policy and the Uruguay Round* (New York: United Nations, 1990) at 149.

[40] *Ibid.*

[41] *Ibid.*

[42] *The Technological Self-Reliance of Developing Countries: Towards Operational Strategies,* UNIDO/ICIS, 133, 15 November 1979,p.13.

technological competitiveness was paramount.[43] In such a scenario, the new technologies, with more easily available skills in developing countries, notably in the case of the biotechnological and informatics sectors, would provide a crucial technological leap with the possibilities of "reverse engineering". Realizing the potential of these possibilities, India had approached the GATT negotiations on IPRs with abundant caution. Its response to protection of IPRs along with other developing countries was shaped on certain factors, such as, realization of the potentialities for a strong science and technology base, the narrowing of the technological gap, the reduction of dependency, and a more active participation in the process of technological change.[44]

There were basically, two broad approaches in the TRIPs negotiations. A number of developed countries had made written submissions to the Negotiating Group of TRIPs, notably the United States, Japan, the European Community and Switzerland. In their submissions, these countries had an approach which was generally grounded on the premise that inadequate and discriminatory protection of IPRs constituted a major distortion of and impediment to trade and should as such be dealt with within the framework of GATT.[45] On the other hand, the developing countries' approach consisted mainly of questioning the conformity of the proposed substantive norms and standards with the mandate of the Negotiating Group. According to them, it was neither the role of GATT nor mandate of the Negotiating Group to consider the protection of IPRs through the elaboration of substantive norms and standards to be applied by all countries.[46]

The Indian submission to the Negotiating Group concerned itself with the structural aspects of a patent system and its trade-relatedness. It identified areas which were crucial in achieving the development objective set by the patent system, namely, (1) working of patents; (b) compulsory license; (c) license of right; (d) exclusions from patentability; (e) product versus process patents (f) duration of patents; (g) government's case of patent in public interest; (h) revocation of patents; and (i) restrictive and anti-competitive practices. The Indian submission also set out its views on "the provision of adequate standards and principles concerning the availability, scope and use of trade-related IPRs".[47] India considered only the restrictive and anti-competitive practices of the owners of the IPRs as trade-related, because, in its view, these alone distorted or impeded international trade. Any

---

[43] Bifani, n.36,p.164.

[44] *Ibid., at* 46; also see Technology Policy Statement of India, *supra* note 23.C.

[45] See MTN.GNG/NG11/W/2., 3 April 1987, *Statement by the United States* (GATT), MTN.GNG/NG11/W/7, 29 May 1987, *Submission by the European Communities* (GATT), MTN.GNG/NG 11/W/7, 29 May 1987, *Submission by Japan* (GATT).

[46] MTN.GNG/NG 11/W/30., 31 October 1988, *Submission from Brazil* (GATT); MTN.GNG/NG 11/W/37 10 July 1989, *Standards and Principles Concerning its availability, Scope and use, Communication from India.*

[47] *Ibid.*

principle or standard relating to IPRs, in India's view, should be carefully tested against the touchstone of the socio-economic, developmental, technological and public interest needs of developing countries.[48] According to India, the fundamental principle which should guide the discussions, was the freedom of the Member States to attune their intellectual properly protection system to their own needs and conditions.

The basic approach followed by India may be broadly described as:[49] (a) the evolution of the patent system, both in industrialized and developing countries would clearly establish the fact that there was a close, correlation between the level of the economic, industrial and technological development of a country on the one hand and the nature and extent of patent protection granted by it on the other,[50] (b) the patent system is an instrument of national economic policy for the industrialization and technological advancement of a country, (c) there should be no attempt at harmonization of the patent laws of the industrialized and developing countries nor should there be any imposition on developing countries of standards and principles that may be relevant to industrialized countries, but are inappropriate to developing countries, (d) Assuming that the patent system can play a part in promoting inventive activity and diffusion of technological knowledge, the protection of the exclusive rights of the patent owner could have serious adverse effects in sectors of critical importance to developing countries, such as food production, poverty alleviation, nutrition, healthcare and disease prevention, and (e) a patent law must focus equally on the duties and obligations of the patent owners as well as the remedial steps to be taken to prevent the possible abuse of monopoly rights by him. The essentials of the position taken by India, in general, reflected a view of patent protection that could be identified in its own patent legislation.[51]

---

[48] *Ibid.*

[49] *Ibid.*

[50] It may be noted that India's patent law and policy was primarily based on its own assessment. The Tek Chand Committee which was formulated in 1949, soon after India's independence, had noted that the existing colonial law on the subject i.e., Indian Patents and Designs Act, 1911 had failed to stimulate inventive activity. See S. Vedarman, "Patents; Recent Development and Future Prospects on the National Level in India" in WIPO, ed., *Current Trends in the Field of Intellectual Property* (Geneva, 1971) at 91; subsequently, the Rajagopala Ayyangar Committee in its Report on the Revision of Patent Laws in 1959 noted- "The Patent Law of an underdeveloped country like India should be so designed as to enable the country to achieve rapid industrialization and to attain, as quickly as possible, a fairly advanced level of technology giving inventors and investors sufficient inducement and protection by patent grants and at the same time safeguarding its national economic and social interest". See, N. Rajagopala Ayyangar, *Report on the Revision of the Patent Law*, (New Delhi, 1959), at 165.

[51] Section 83 of the Indian Patents Act, 1970 for example, provides- "Without prejudice to the other provisions contained in this Act, in exercising the powers conferred by the chapter, regard shall be had to the following general considerations, namely; (a) that patents are

The above negotiating stance, with regard to IPRs, proposed by India along with Brazil and other developing countries could not be sustained. By the time the Mid-Term Review of the Uruguay Round Negotiations took place in 1989, the United States and other industrialized countries were insisting on the negotiations of the substantive norms on IPRS.[52] India was actively involved in the back room negotiations and pursued its proposal to remit the issue of establishing substantive new norms, including dispute settlement to WIPO, UNCTAD and UNESCO where deliberations on some of the issues were in progress.[53] India also proposed that a report from these agencies could be sought.[54] It may be noted that the

---

granted to encourage inventions and secure that the inventions are worked in India on a commercial scale and to the fullest extent that is reasonably practicable without undue delay; (b) that they are not granted merely to enable patentees to enjoy a monopoly for the importation of the patented article; (c) that the protection and enforcement of patent rights contribute to the promotion of technological innovation and to the transfer and dissemination of technology, to the mutual advantage of producers and users of technological knowledge and in a manner conducive to social and economic welfare, and to a balance of rights and obligations; (d) that patents granted do not impede protection of public health and nutrition and should act as instrument to promote public interest specially in sectors of vital importance for socio-economic and technological development of India; (e) that patents granted do not in any way prohibit Central Government in taking measures to protect public health; (f) that the patent right is not abused by the patentee or person deriving title or interest on patent from the patentee, and the patentee or a person deriving title or interest on patent from the patentee does not resort to practices which unreasonably restrain trade or adversely affect the international transfer of technology; and (g) that patents are granted to make the benefit of the patented invention available at reasonably affordable prices to the public.

52 The US and other industrialized countries had systematically worked on this strategy. A well documented source points out that a powerful group of US chemical, pharmaceutical, computer, entertainment, publishing and electronics corporations lobbied the US government to introduce intellectual property issues into the multilateral trade negotiations under the GATT. The chairman of Pfizer, a large US pharmaceutical manufacturer, was considered to be the driving force behind this move. Mr. Ed Pratt who was the chairman of Pfizer at that time, was made the chairman of the Advisory Committee for trade negotiations by the US President Ronald Reagan in 1981 to shape the US Trade Policy. This Committee, it should be noted, played an active role in formulating the overall agenda of the Uruguay Round, particularly concerning issues in IPRs. Mr. Ed Pratt, in a systematic move, first formed alliances with the US motion picture and computer industries before approaching European and Japanese industrial groups. Thirteen major US corporations formed the "Intellectual Property Rights Committee" (IPC) which set down an agenda for what it wanted to achieve through international trade negotiations. See *Intellectual Property Rights in NAFTA: Implications for Health Care and Industrial Policy in Ontario* (Toronto: Ecumenical Coalition for Economic Justice:1993); for the US policy initiatives on these issues see R. Michael Gadbaw, "Intellectual Property and International Trade: Merger on Marriage of Convenience", 22 *Vanderbilt Journal of Transnational Law* 2 (1989) at .223.

53 See Raghavan, *supra* note 31 at 260.

54 *Ibid* at p.280; This reference that the TRIPs negotiations should be conducive to a mutually supportive relationship between GATT and WIPO as well as other relevant

outcome of the Mid-Term Review was not responsive to the concerns of the developing countries and also issues raised by India. India along with other developing countries agreed to negotiate issues of substantive norms and standards on IPRs, in the Uruguay Round of Negotiations. This sudden change in India's negotiating position and conceding to the proposals on TRIPs as embodied in the Mid-Term Review was on account of US Government's policy to approach the issue from a bilateral angle. It may be noted that while pronouncing GATT-based multilateral negotiations as preferred strategy for resolving trade problems, the United States government in particular had undertaken an intense programme of direct bilateral negotiations, coupled with the threat and use of unilateral economic sanctions, to protect its IPR owners.[55]

4. The Bilateral Approach of the United States and India

Although the United States had enough space to negotiate in the GATT, it resorted to bilateral handling of its foreign trade difficulties through the enactment of a new law entitled, "The Omnibus Trade and Competitiveness Act of 1988". Its central theme was to promote US exports to reduce the U.S. trade deficit.[56] The key technique was reciprocity of market opportunity, which could be obtained either through multilateral or bilateral negotiations, or, if necessary, through the use of Section 301 of the Trade Act of 1974.[57] These laws authorized the United States Trade Representative (USTR) to (a) identify countries that deny adequate and effective protection of IPRs, (b) identify "priority" countries that are the most egregious IPR transgressors and that do not undertake or make progress in accelerated section 301 investigations with regard to the practices of the identified priority countries.[58] On May 25, 1989, the Office of the USTR, in accordance with these newly termed "Special 301" provisions of the 1988 Trade Act placed Seventeen Countries on an intellectual property "Watch List" and eight countries on a "Priority Watch List".[59]

---

international organizations was retained in the mid-term Review; for a complete text of the mid-term Review see GATT, Decisions adopted at the mid-term Review of the Uruguay Round, 28 *International Legal Materials* 1023-1038 (1989).

[55] See Frederick M. Abbot, "Protecting First World Assets in the Third World: Intellectual Property Negotiations in the GATT Multilateral Framework", 22 *Vaderbilt Journal of Transnational Law* 4 (1989) at 707.

[56] Legality of section 301 was brought before a WTO Panel by EU in 1999 and its legality was upheld by the WTO panel in December 1999.

[57] John H. Barton and Bart S. Fisher, "Introductory Note: United States Omnibus Trade and Competitiveness Act of 1988" *International Legal Materials* (1989) at 15.

[58] *Ibid.*

[59] The timing of this notification by the USTR is crucial. This was the time when the Mid-Term Review of the Uruguay Rounds of Negotiations was in progress. Developing countries, including India, were consistently opposed to the setting of new substantive standards for the IPR protection. The seventeen countries on the Watch List included all the

The legal determination by the USTR concluded that no foreign country currently meets every standard for adequate and effective intellectual property protection as set forth in the US proposal on intellectual property tabled in the Uruguay Round. Thus the USTR has determined that all countries are eligible for potential priority designation based on the standards of the US Uruguay Round proposal, because all countries "deny adequate and effective protection of IPRs within the meaning of Statute".[60]

As regards India, the USTR sought the following: (a) Improved and adequate patent protection for all classes of inventions; (b) Elimination of discrimination against the use of Foreign Trade Marks; (c) Registration of Service Marks; (d) Effective protection of the well-known marks; (e) Improved access and distribution for US motion Pictures; (f) Improved enforcement against piracy; (g) Conclusion of an Intellectual Property Annex to the Bilateral Science and Technology Agreement; and (g) Constructive participation in the Multilateral Intellectual Properly Negotiations.[61]

5. Towards Uniform Standards of Patent Protection

India, along with other developing countries, was not in favour of evolving uniform standards for the protection of patents in the Uruguay Round of Negotiations. It had taken the view that the Negotiating Group should not deal with questions of what should be the proper level of protection of IPRs, but should confine itself to the negative effects on international trade of the implementation of existing laws and treaties for the protection of IPRs.[62] The major differences as regards the level of IPR protection pertained to: (a) the lack of subject-matter protection in certain fields (primarily pharmaceutical products) and the uncertainly about the extent of protection concerning applications of the new technologies (such as software, integrated circuits, data banks and biotechnology), (b) limitation on patentee's rights

---

eleven major developing countries, namely, Argentina, Malaysia, Pakistan, Chile, Philippines, Colombia, Egypt, Turkey, Indonesia, Venezuela and Yugoslavia. The other six countries were: Canada, Portugal, Spain, Greece, Italy and Japan. The other eight priority watch list countries including India were: Brazil, Republic of Korea, India, Saudi Arabia, Mexico, Taiwan, the People's Republic of China and Thailand. However, on November 1,1989, the USTR moved Saudi Arabia, Republic of Korea and Taiwan from Priority Watch List status to Watch List status. This move, it was argued, had some link with the ongoing Mid-Term Review of the Uruguay Round of Negotiations; see USTR Fact Sheets on Super 30 Trade Liberalization Priorities and Special 301 on Intellectual Property, reproduced in the XVI *Occasional Papers* (New Delhi, National Working Group on Patent Laws: 1989).

[60] *Ibid.*

[61] *Ibid.* India's negotiating stance changed thereafter, particularly during the Mid-Term Review in 1989.

[62] MTN. GNG/NG 11/W/12, Compilation of Written Submissions and Oral Statements (GATT).

(for example, as regards imports, forfeiture and compulsory licensing), (c) inadequate enforcement of conferred rights (lack of rapid administrative and judicial procedures, questions about the applicable burden of proof, and (d) inadequate duration of protection.[63] We may examine some of these areas, with particular reference to India's present law and policy.

5. 1. Patentable Subject Matter

The questions as regards what criteria actually constitute patentable subject matter are generally left to be decided by the national legislations. India, it may be noted, argued strongly for retaining this flexibility.[64] These criteria are formulated by the countries taking into account their industrial and economic development objectives. In addition to this, patentability criteria to allow a patenting of an invention or its subject matter should meet three conditions, namely, novelty, inventive step and industrial applicability.[65] It was, however, argued that rapid internationalization of technology and its use had necessitated uniform criteria to conclusively decide the scope of patentable subject-matter. Accordingly, the patent legislations of various countries provide more or less uniform standards while defining the patentable subject matter; a degree of variation may arise in the emphasis accorded to each criterion involving a considerable amount of subjectivity. This subjectivity, among countries, concerning patentable subject matter varies with the competence and effectiveness of patent agents who describe the invention in the complete specification, patent examiners and the patent office which examine them and the courts which look into its legality.[66]

Article 27 of the TRIPs Agreement provides for five uniform standards, namely (a) availability of patents for all kinds of inventions; (f) patent to be granted in all fields of technology, whether products or processes; (c) inventions to be

---

[63] *Trade and Development Report, 1991* (New York, UNCTAD, 1991) at 185.

[64] *See India's* Submissions, *supra* note 44.

[65] Section 2(j) of the Indian Patent Act, 1970 defined an "invention", before its amendment in 2002 as "any new and useful (i) and process method or manner of manufacture; (ii) machine, apparatus or other article; (iii) substances produced by manufacture and includes any new and useful improvement of any of them, and an alleged invention. The newly amended version of the definition, now provides- "a new produce or process involving an inventive step and capable of industrial application". The amended enactment (by Act 38 of 2002) provides the definition of an "inventive step" in Section 2(ja) as –"a feature that makes the invention not obvious to a person skilled in the art. The Indian Supreme Court in *Bishwanath Prasad Radhey Shyam v. Hindustan Metal Industries* stated that "the fundamental principle of patent law is that a patent is granted only for an invention which must be new and useful. That is to say, it must have novelty and utility. It is essential for the validity of a patent that it must be the inventor's own discovery as opposed to mere verification of what was already known before the date of the patent", See AIR 1982 Supreme Court 1444.

[66] R. S Crespi, *Patenting in the Biological Sciences* (New York, 1983) at 75.

patentable should fulfill the criteria of novelty, inventive step and industrial applicability; (d) patents should be available and patent rights enjoyable without discrimination as to the place of invention, the field of technology; and (e) patents granted irrespective of products' importation or local production.[67]

5. 2. Dilution of Concept of "Local Working"

One of the primary concerns for India is with regard to total dilution of the concept of "local working" in Article 27. The basic concept of the patent system emerges from the idea that the working of the patented invention is the price which society expects the patentee to pay for granting him monopoly rights. The history and evolution of the patent system reveals that the "working" of a patent grant has a unique role to play in the creation of knowledge and its sustenance.[68] The process of creating a patent itself creates a new asset and adds value to society in the form of knowledge. Article 27 of the TRIPs Agreement equates "working" of the patented invention with the importation of the patented product.[69] In other words, the importation of the patented product from another country could be regarded as fulfilling the criteria of meeting the "reasonable requirements of the public" and its "working" in the territory of a State. The Indian Patent act of 1970, amended in 2002, continues to emphasize on the requirements that "patented inventions are worked on a commercial scale in the territory of India without undue delay and to the fullest extent that is reasonably practicable".[70] This "working requirement" has, however, been qualified by another requirement in section 89 of the Indian enactment which, *inter alia*, provides, "... (f) that the interests of any person for the time being working or developing an invention in the territory of Indian under the protection of a patent are not unfairly prejudiced". If the patented inventions are not worked within India for more than three years, the Controller General of

67 The Agreement on TRIPs, *supra* note 36 at 330.

68 For the economic implications of "importation" of technology see: Sanjaya Lall, "The Patent System and the Transfer of Technology to Less-Developed Countries", 10 *Journal of World Trade Law* (1976); Also see A.K. Bagchi, P. Banerjee and P.K. Bhattacharya, "Indian Patents Act and its Relation to Technological Development in India- A Preliminary Investigation", 19 *Economic and Political Weekly* 7, 287-304 (1984); B.S. Chimni, "Political Economy of the Uruguay Round of Negotiations: A Perspective", 29 *International Studies* 2, 135-58 (1992); Constantine Vaitsos, "Patents Revisited: Their Function in Developing Countries", 19 *Journal of Development Studies* 71-97 (1972).

69 Article 27.1 of the TIRPS Agreement provides "... patents shall be available and patent rights enjoyable without discrimination as to the place of invention, the field of technology and whether products are *imported or locally produced*, (emphasis added).

70 Chapter XVI of the Indian Patents Act, 1970 was amended to give effect to the provisions of the TRIPs agreement relating to patents. Chapter XVI it may be noted deals with "Working of patents, compulsory Licenses and Revocation": see section 89 of the Indian Patents Act, 1970 which was inserted by way of an amendment –Act 38 of 2002 with effect from 20.5.2003.

Patents has the authority to grant a compulsory license on that patent to a third party.[71] Before he could do so, he has to satisfy himself of three conditions, namely – (a) that the reasonable requirements of the public with respect to the patented invention have not been satisfied, or (f) that the patented invention is not available to the public at a reasonably affordable price; or (c) that the patented invention is not worked in the territory of India.[72]

The above provisions in the Indian Patent Act of 1970, providing the working of the patented invention appear to be consistent with Article 27.2 of the TRIPs Agreement. Article 27.2 allows a member to "exclude from patentablity invention, the prevention within their territory of the commercial exploitation of which is necessary to protect *ordre public* or morality, including to protect human, animal or plant life or health or to avoid serious prejudice to the environment, provided that such exclusion is not made merely because the exploitation is prohibited by domestic law". While a member State may refuse to entertain patent application on any of the above grounds, Article 8.1 of the TRIPs Agreement is specific to create exceptions and the members could also use this "exclusion" while formulating their national legislation. These exclusions include: (a) public health and nutrition, and (b) promotion of public interest in sectors of vital importance to their socio-economic and technological development.[73]

5. 3. Patentability of Life Forms

Article 27.3 of the TRIPs Agreement provides the basis for patentability of life forms, although it begins with *chapeau* "members may exclude from patentability". On the contrary, it outlines what kind of life is patentable and what is not patentable. According to paragraph 3 of Article 27 "(a) diagnostic, therapeutic and surgical methods for the treatment of humans or animals; and (b) plants and animals other than micro-organisms, and essentially biological processes for the production

---

[71] Section 84 of the Indian Patents Act, 1970.

[72] *Ibid.* While India has done away with the provisions relating to 'Licenses of Right' in its Patents Act, 1970, it has retained the provisions relating to compulsory Licensing and Revocation of patents. These provisions, it may be noted, are qualified by requirements relating to working of the patented invention with a view to meet the reasonable requirement of the public. See also section 85 of the Indian Patents Act, 1970, as amended in 2002 which came into effect on 20 May 2003.

[73] See Article 8.1 of the TRIPs Agreement. This provision also provides that such exclusionary measures should be consistent with the provisions of the TRIPs Agreement. The issue of TRIPs consistency vis-à-vis amended Indian enactment is something on which we need to await the response of the US and other developed countries. Involving of WTO's dispute settlement by these countries on any interpretative questions and with regard to the WTO-consistency of the said provision could be one such response. It may be noted here that US took India to WTO Dispute Settlement Panel on the implementation of "exclusive marketing rights" under Article 70.8 of the TRIPs Agreement.

of plants or animals other than non-biological and micro-biological processes" were excluded from patenting. Further, paragraph 3 also provided that the plant varieties should be protected either by patents or by an effective *sui genesis* system or by any combination thereof.[74]

While Article 27 of the TRIPs agreement lays down the basic formulations for patenting of life forms for countries like India, patenting of genes and biotechnological products are posing unique challenges. Whether the formulation as contained in Article 27 allows patenting of genes and seeds or not is purely in the realm of interpretation. For instance, it has been pointed out that certain claims made in this arena do not easily subscribe to the criteria of patentability. It is, indeed, difficult to define these claims in such a manner so as to be understood by a "reasonably skilled person". There are also difficulties in establishing the criterion of novelty, apart from the problems of attaining stability and homogeneity in a biotechnologically evolved product.[75] It is also clear that a *sui genesis* system for plant varieties envisages a system, which does not allow propagation of seed varieties for commercial purposes. The International Convention for the Protection of New Varieties of Plants (the UPOV Convention) which is considered as a model for *sui genesis* protection for plant varieties allows national laws to decide the scope and limits of the farmer's rights.[76] As regards the gene sequences and micro-organisms developing countries generally did not favour patenting. There was a proposal to

---

[74] India did not make any reference to patenting of life forms in its submissions during the Uruguay Round of Negotiations. The Article 27.3 formulation reflected the position of European Union countries, in particular Article 53 of the European Patent Convention. The only one proposal submitted by Peru treated Biotechnology as a new science having application in various fields, such as agriculture, chemical and pharmaceutical products. See MTN.GNG/NG.11/W/26, 7 July 1988, *Guidelines and Objectives Progressed by the European Community for the Negotiations on Trade-Related Aspects of Substantive Standards of Intellectual Property Rights*; Also see MTN.GNG/NG11 W/45, 27 October 1989, *Guidelines for Negotiations that Strike a Balance between Intellectual Property Rights and Development Objectives: Communication from Peru.*

[75] See N.N. Mehrotra and Sheela Tandon "Biotechnological Patents and Developments in India: Some Policy Issues", 52 *Journal of Scientific and Industrial Research* (1993) at 315.

[76] India enacted in 2001 the Protection of Plant Varieties and Farmer's Rights Act. This enactment is regarded as a *sui genesis* (a class by itself) enactment. Its objective is to "provide for the establishment of an effective system for protection of plant varieties, the rights of farmers and plant breeders and to encourage the development of new varieties of plants". It also recognizes and protects the rights of the farmers in respect of their contribution made at any time in conserving, improving and making available plant genetic resources for the development of the new plant varieties. This enactment is also for giving effect to Article 27.3 (b) of the Agreement on TRIPs.

differentiate between "naturally-occurring" and "artificially bred" genes while considering patent grants to genetic material.[77]

The Indian Patents Act, 1970 was also modified to give effect to Article 27.3 (b). The phrase "diagnostic therapeutic" was inserted into Section 3(i) of the Indian enactment. The word "plants" was deleted. It may be noted that Section 3 outlines the criteria for "what are not inventions". Now, "any process for the medicinal, surgical, curative, prophylactic, diagnostic, therapeutic or other treatment of human beings or any process for a similar treatment of animals to render them free of disease or to increase their economic value or that of their products" is not regarded as inventions. A new clause (j) was added to Section 3 which excludes from inventions the following: "plants and animals in whole or any part thereof other than micro-organisms but including seeds, varieties and species and essentially biological processes for production on propagation of plants and animals". By juxtaposing these two exclusionary provisions along with Article 27.3 of the TRIPs Agreement, it would be deduced that under the Indian patent law the following life forms are patentable inventions, namely: (a) micro-organisms; (b) production of plants and animals by non-biological and microbiological processes; and (c) protection of plant varieties (not plants) by an effective *sui genesis* system.

5. 4. Term of Patent

In the past, the term of protection for patented invention was never specified. The Paris Convention, for example, did not specify any term. It was left to the countries concerned to decide on the term of protection taking into account their economic and technological priorities. The Indian Patents Act, 1970, before amending the term of protection in 2002, provided (a) in respect of invention claiming the method or process of manufacture of a substance, where the substance is intended for use, or capable of being used, as food or as a medicine or drug, the term be five years from the date of sealing of the patent, or seven years from the date of the patent whichever period is shorter; and (b) in respect of any other invention, the term be fourteen years from the date of the patent.[78] The Agreement on TRIPs in Article 33 accords twenty years as the term of protection counted from filing date of the patent specification. India and other developing countries did not agree with this long term of protection.[79] India, for example, sought the freedom to set the duration

[77] In India, this issue was considered in greater detail before a Parliamentary Standing Committee constituted by the Parliament of India. See *Department Related Parliamentary Standing Committee on Commerce (1993-94) in Draft Dunkel Proposals* (New Delhi: Rajya Sabha Secretariat, 1993).

[78] Section 53 of the Indian Patents Act, 1970, before its amendment in 2002.

[79] Developing countries viewed a 20 year uniform period as contrary to their need to master new technologies and to expand their own industrial capacity needs that become all the more acute when the foreign technology is neither worked locally nor effectively transferred by

at a level significantly lower than that of the industrialized countries in accordance with its own developmental, technological and public interest needs.[80] The Austrian proposal in this regard was significant according to which the harmonization of the various terms of protection should be achieved as the different length of protection in different states created different markets which was in itself an obstacle to trade.[81]

The intricacies of duration of patent should be viewed from the perspective of diffusion of high technology and its transferability. The fast rate of diffusion of high technology is essential as it reaches the optimum utilization point at a very short duration. According to one view uniform duration of twenty years is contrary to the needs of developing countries to master new technologies and to expand their own industrial capacity.[82] In the Indian context, the term of patent has now been fixed as twenty years from the date of filing. The amended Section 53 of the Indian Patents Act, 1970 provides that "... the term of every patent which has not expired and has not ceased to have effect, on the date of such commencement, under this Act, shall be twenty years from the date of filing of the application for the patent".

6. Conclusions

The international patent system and its evolution have a history of over hundred years. The Paris Convention which symbolized the emerging international patent system till the 1980s was the Euro-centric in its evolution. Although developing countries participated in its deliberations and Revision Conferences, they had no major role in shaping its various provisions. India was not part of the international patent system till the whole issue converged with the WTO Regime on IPRs. One of the crucial forums where developing countries, including India, had taken up the role of the international patent system vis-à-vis transfer of technology was the United Nations. The post Second World War era saw the emergence of new states. Their emergence from the colonial yoke had raised several key issues relating to economic and industrial development. The role of the international patent system as a factor in this process became an important subject matter for deliberations. Accordingly, the Euro-centric, rule-based approach attached to the evolution of an international patent system gave way to other factors, such as transfer of technology, local working of the patents to meet the reasonable requirements of the public and

---

other means. Developed countries, on the other hand, argued that the importance of the resources devoted to R and D require long periods of recovery if the continuity and expansion of the innovative process is to be ensured; see *Trade and Development Report, 1991,* n.61,p.186; Also see for the evolution of the India's legal position in Section 53 of the Indian Patents Act, 1970 *Ayyangar Report* ,*supra* note 48.

80 Indian Proposal, *supra* note 31.

81 MTN.GNG/NG11/W/55, 8 December 1989, Trade-Related Intellectual Property Rights-Submission by Austria.

82 See Trade and Development Report, *supra* note 61at 186.

the availability of medicines at affordable prices. It may be seen that some of these elements evolved in response to the concerns of developing countries found their way through the Indian Patent Act of 1970. The decades of the 1960s and 1970s were crucial for developing countries, including India, in evolving a meaningful national legislation on patents. India, while realizing this, constituted a one-man committee in 1957 known as Justice Rajagopala Ayyangar Committee, which went into various aspects of an international patent system with a view to evolve a suitable system for India. This committee submitted a substantive report on the issue of what kind of patent system India should have. The whole decade of the 1960s saw the Indian Parliament deliberating this and finally giving shape to the Patents Act of 1970. It may be noted that the Patents Act of 1970 incorporated all the then existing finer elements of an international patent system from the point of view of a developing country like India.

While India delved into the revision of the international patent system i.e., the Paris Convention by virtue of its membership of WIPO, the international technological and economic developments shifted the whole focus of the debate away from developing countries. The IPRs issue was taken up as a trade issue within the GATT forum. The Uruguay Round of Negotiations wherein India played a significant role was completely titled against the developing countries. GATT was a trade forum where developing countries had no bargaining power. The issues concerning IPRs, particularly the international context of IPR protection, were one among the several other important issues affecting developing countries. Textiles, for example, was a crucial sector for India and other developing countries as well. So, the focus on IPRs within the Uruguay Round of Negotiations got relegated to a low-priority area. Apart from these concerns, India also had to battle the bilateral approach taken by the United States through its "Special 301" mechanism. As could be seen in our discussions, some elements of this bilateral approach had a reference to "constrictive" negotiations on IPRs within WTO fora.

With the WTO regime on IPRs coming into force on 1 January 1995, India had a marginal space to accommodate its concerns. While for India, its concerns on IPRs, particularly on patent protection, were clear, its WTO obligations required it to modify its existing patents law. The last five years have seen India gradually amending its Patents Act of 1970 to meet its WTO obligations. Implications of these modifications are slowly sinking down into the Indian economic and industrial development process. While it appears that India has managed to withstand some of these changes, the precise legal and economic implications of these changes, particularly in the area of the pharmaceutical and chemical sector, needs long-term review. Currently, India is moving forward with the changes as envisaged under the WTO regime. Some of these changes, it may be noted, may become new battlegrounds for a new interpretative matrix within the WTO dispute settlement system.

SOVEREIGN ECONOMIC FREEDOM AND INTERESTS OF OTHER STATES

Ravindra Pratap*

> It clearly follows from the liberty and independence of Nations that each has the right to govern itself as it thinks proper, and that no one of them has the least right to interfere in the government of another.
>
> Emer de Vattel, *The Law of Nations* [1]

> There is no sensible alternative to the ongoing development of international law into a cosmopolitan order that offers an equal and reciprocal hearing for the voices of all those affected.[2]

1. Introduction

The lifting of economic sanctions on Iraq also brings to the fore a question different from the issue of their usefulness to achieve anything other than untold sufferings to the permanent population of a target State. If the territorial integrity and political independence of a sovereign State are contingent on its "good governance", and are therefore a legitimate concern of other States or a group of States, it is necessary that measures employed to that end must not harm the people of a target State when in force and legitimize the occupation of their territory once lifted.

This paper discusses States' freedom to take economic measures to the detriment of other States' interests under modern international law. The paper is in four parts. Part II gives a historical perspective; part III discusses treaty law, resolutions of international bodies and *jus cogens*; and part IV concludes the discussion.

2. Sovereign Economic Freedom in a Historical Perspective

Interstate relations gave birth to international law. The latter thus began to regulate States' freedom in relation to the conduct of international relations. The waning of isolationism and a renewed quest for peace gaining ground by the end of the nineteenth century laid the foundations of institutionalized cooperation among States. Reinforced by the devastating effects of the exercise of their economic freedom during the early 1930s and the events that followed it, this conviction of States grew and considerably institutionalized by the middle of the twentieth

---

* Assistant Professor, Indraprastha University School of Law, Delhi.

[1] (1758), Fenwick, trans. (Geneva, 1983), 131.

[2] Habermas, "The fall of the monument — II", *The Hindu* (Delhi), 6 June 2003, 10.

Bimal N. Patel (ed.), **India and International Law, 117-139.**

century. International law prohibition of the threat or use of force in international relations, indiscriminate human and serious environmental effects of modernized conventional and nuclear weapons, decolonization but the continuing economic dependence of newly independent States, growing economic transposition of technology and know-how, their crucial role in economic growth and "sustainable development" and their trade protection, sufficiently explain why economic measures began to be employed more frequently in the second half of the twentieth century and demonstrate why there has been an unprecedented increase in that frequency since the first quarter of the last decade of the twentieth century.[3]

---

[3] The US alone has applied sanctions for foreign policy purposes a total of 115 times since the First World War, 104 times since the Second World War, and according to the count of the President's Export Council, 61 times since 1993. Eizenstat, Under Secretary of State for Economic, Business, and Agricultural Affairs, Testimony Before the Senate Foreign Relations Committee Wash. DC, Jul. 1, 1999, <http://www.state.ov/www/policy_remarks/1999/990701_eizen_sanctions.html, 2>. See Kant, *Perpetual Peace* (1795) (New York, 1939); Carr, *The Twenty Years' Crisis, 1919–1939: An Introduction to International Relations* (London, 1939); Williams, "The Coming of Economic Sanctions into American Practice", 37 *AJIL* (1943), 386; Henderson, "International Economic History of the Inter-War Period", in Clay, ed., *The Inter-War Years and Other Papers, A Selection from the Writings of Hubert Douglas Henderson* (Oxford, 1955), 236; Allen, "State Trading and Economic Warfare", 24 *L. & Contemporary Problems* (1959), 256; Wilczynski, "Strategic Embargo in Perspective" 19 *Soviet Studies* (1967–68), 74; Tucker, *The Inequality of Nations* (New York, 1971); Kindleberger, *The World in Depression 1929–39* (Berkeley, 1973); Ruggie, "International Response to Technology: Concepts and Trends", 29 *Int. Org.* (1975), 557; Maw, "Historical Aspects and the U.S. Involvement in Boycotts", 71 *ASIL Proc.* (1977), 170; Barber, "Economic Sanctions as a Policy Instrument", 55 *Int. Aff.* (1979), 367; Polakas, "Economic Sanctions: An Effective Alternative to Military Coercion?" 6 *Brooklyn J of Int. L.* (1980), 289; Hufbauer and Schott, *Economic Sanctions in Support of Foreign Policy Goals* (Wash. DC, 1983); Axelrod, *The Evolution of Cooperation* (New York, 1984); Kopff, "The Influence of Technical Progress on Development of Creativity and the Law of Intellectual Property", 190 Hague *Recueil* (1985), 91; World Commission on Environment and Development, *Our Common Future* (Oxford, 1987); Lenway, "Between War and Commerce: Economic Sanctions as a Tool of Statecraft", 10 *Int. Org.* (1988), 397; Malloy, *Economic Sanctions and US Trade* (Boston, 1990); Ricupero, "Trade and Technology: Issues at Stake for Developing Countries", in *Technology, Trade Policy and Uruguay Round* (New York, 1990), 198; Sand, "International Economic Instruments for Sustainable Development: Sticks, Carrots and Games (1998), 599; Riedi, "US Economic Sanctions against India and Pakistan", 26 *Int. Bus. Lawyer* (1998), 354; Selden, *Economic Sanctions as Instruments of American Foreign Policy* (Westport, 1999); Eyffinger, *The 1899 Hague Peace Conference: 'The Parliament of Man, the Federation of the World'* (The Hague, 1999); Maier, "The Trade Embargo as an International Political Instrument", 34 *N. England L. Rev.* (1999), 51; McGlone and Trenkle, "Economic Sanctions and Export Controls", 33 *Int. Lawyer* (1999), 257; Munck, "Dependency and Imperialism in the New Times: A Latin American Perspective", 11 *EJIL* (1999), 56; Zeiler, *Free Trade, Free World: The Advent of GATT* (Chapel Hill, 1999).

3. Sovereign Economic Freedom under Modern International Law

3.1. Treaty Law

There is general agreement that the doctrine of sovereignty has undergone a considerable change, but few would agree that it is no longer of consequence. While it is true that every convention puts a certain degree of restriction upon the exercise of rights by parties, it has been held that "the right of entering into international engagements is an attribute of State sovereignty."[4] This neither suggests that there are no norms other than conventions creating obligations for States nor necessarily posits a normative hierarchy among them, it has been clarified that "a limitation of sovereignty must be construed restrictively."[5] Although the generality of this principle is unquestioned, the question whether a certain matter is within the jurisdiction of a State "depends upon the development of international relations".[6] Thus, a sudden discontinuance of these relations by one party or parties may amount to "an act of intervention",[7] if they create a situation of dependence and the other party necessarily suffers as a result thereof. Modern international economic law calls upon States to take into account the "valid interests"[8] of other States in exercising sovereignty. In certain cases, national boycott may "constitute an international delinquency for which liability may arise…under international law."[9]

---

[4] *S. S. Wimbledon*, Judgment, 1923, P.C.I.J., Series A, No. 1, p. 25.

[5] *Free Zones of Upper Savoy and the District of Gex*, Order of 6 December 1930, P.C.I.J., Series A, No. 24, p. 12.

[6] *Nationality Decrees issued in Tunis and Morocco*, Advisory Opinion, 1923, P.C.I.J., Series B, No. 4, p. 23–4. Further, on domestic jurisdiction, see Brierly, "Matters of Domestic Jurisdiction", 6 *British Yrbk. of Int. L.* (1925) at 8; Schapiro, "Domestic Jurisdiction in the Covenant and the Charter", 33 *The Grotius Society* (1948), 195; Preuss, "Article 2, paragraph 7, of the Charter of the United Nations and Matters of Domestic Jurisdiction", 74 Hague *Recueil* (1949), 550, Rajan, *United Nations and Domestic Jurisdiction* (Bombay, 1958); Verdross, "The Plea of Domestic Jurisdiction Before an International Tribunal and a Political Organ of the United Nations", 28 *Zeitschrift für ausländisches öffentliches Recht und Völkerrecht* (1968), 33; Cançado Trinidade, "The Domestic Jurisdiction of States in the Practice of the United Nations and Regional Organizations", 25 *ICLQ* (1975), 715.

[7] Abi-Saab, "Some Thoughts on the Principle of Non-Intervention", in Wellens, ed., *International Law Theory and Practice* (The Hague, 1998), 233–4.

[8] Simma, ed., *The Charter of the United Nations* (Oxford, 1994), 82.

[9] Bouvé, "The National Boycott as an International Delinquency", 28 *AJIL* (1934), 42. The author notes Politis of Greece characterizing systematic boycott organized and abetted by a government as a "kind of aggression and a flagrant violation of international law." Ibid. footnote 60. See also Hyde and Wehle, "Boycott in Foreign Affairs", 27 *AJIL* (1933), 1; Lauterpacht, "Boycott in International Relations", 14 *British Yrbk. of Int. L.* (1933), 125. Further see Mattern, *Concepts of State, Sovereignty and International Law* (Baltimore, 1928); Van Kleffens, "Sovereignty in International Law", 82 Hague *Recueil* (1953), 1; Korowicz, "Some Present Aspect of Sovereignty in International Law", 102 Hague *Recueil* (1961), 1; Henkin, "The Mythology of Sovereignty", in Macdonald, ed., *Essays in Honour of Wang Tieya* (London, 1993), 351; Lazhari, "The Role of Sovereignty in the Contemporary World Order", *Proc. of*

(a) The UN Charter

The Charter in Article 2, paragraph 4, enjoins States in their international relations from the threat or use of force not only against the territorial integrity and political independence of any State but also "in any other manner inconsistent with the Purposes of the United Nations." The latter strive for international cooperation in solving problems of economic or humanitarian character and respect for human rights.[10] For the settlement of disputes, the Charter prefers only pacific means, such as negotiation, enquiry, mediation, conciliation, arbitration, judicial settlement, or resort to regional agencies or arrangements.[11] While the UN shall promote "solutions of international economic problems", and "universal respect for, and observance of, human rights"[12] and "employ international machinery for the promotion of the economic and social advancement of all people"[13], [a]ll Members pledge themselves to take joint and separate action in co-operation with the Organization for the achievement of the purposes set forth in Article 55".[14]

The prohibition of the threat or use of force is a functional prerequisite for the maintenance of sovereign equality, territorial integrity and political independence of States. Debatable though it is whether "force" under Article 2, paragraph 4, includes economic force, a pressure can still be so surmountable as to constitute intervention, if it is "as great a threat to the political independence of States…as military force".[15] The ICJ has held:

---

the African Soc. of Int. and Comp. L., Fifth Ann. Conf., 20–4 Sept. 1993 (1994), 212; Chayes and Chayes, *The New Sovereignty: Compliance with International Regulatory Agreements* (Cambridge, Mass., 1995); Lyons and Mastanduno, eds., *Beyond Westphalia? State Sovereignty and International Intervention* (Baltimore, 1995); Linklater, "Citizenship and Sovereignty in the Post-Westphalian Age", 2 *EJIL* (1996), 77; Lauterpacht, "Sovereignty—myth or reality?", 73 *Int. Aff.* (1997), 137; Anghie, "Finding the Peripheries: Sovereignty and Colonialism in Nineteenth-Century International Law", 40 *Harv. Int. L. J* (1999), 1; Corell, "From Territorial Sovereignty to Human Security", http://www.un.org/law/counsel/ottawa.htm; Annan, "Two Concepts of Sovereignty", *The Economist*, Sept. 18, 1999, http://www.un.org/Overview/SG/Kaecon.htm.

[10] Article 1.3, UN Charter

[11] Article 33.1, UN Charter

[12] Article 55, UN Charter

[13] The preamble, UN Charter

[14] Article 56, UN Charter

[15] Goodrich et al., *Charter of the United Nations, Commentary and Documents* (New York, 1969), 48. See also Franck, "Who Killed Article 2 (4) or: The Changing Norms Governing the Use of Force by States", 64 *AJIL* (1970), 809; Delanis, "Force under Article 2 (4) of the United Nations Charter: The Question of Economic and Political Coercion", 12 *Vand. J of Int. L.* (1979), 101; Reisman, "The Emperor Has No Clothes: Article 2 (4) and the Use of Force in Contemporary International Law", in Saxena et al., *United Nations For a Better World* (N. Delhi, 1986), 3; Asrat, *Prohibition of Force under the UN Charter—A Study of Article 2 (4)* (Uppsala, 1991). Further see Blum, "Economic Boycott in International Law", 12 *Texas Int. L. J* (1977), 5; Lillich, "The Status of Economic Coercion Under International Law: United

> [It] was never intended that the Charter should embody written confirmation of every essential principle of international law in force. The existence in the *opinio juris* of States of the principle of non-intervention is backed by established and substantial practice. It has moreover been presented as a corollary of the sovereign equality of States.... A prohibited intervention must accordingly be one bearing on matters in which each State is permitted, by the principle of State sovereignty, to decide freely. One of these is the choice of a *political*, economic, social and cultural system, and the formulation of foreign policy. Intervention is wrongful when it uses methods of coercion in regard to such choices, which must remain free ones.[16]

Thus, it would be strange if, after more than a half century, the Charter were to stick to the same standards to adjudge upon "force". It is time that international law recognize the fact that consensus lies behind the acceptance of the principle of non-intervention. At a time when the principle of non-intervention is being eclipsed by the effects of internal acts upon the interests of third states,[17] it is necessary that non-intervention include all forms of indirect or effective non-intervention.[18] It is this principle of non-discrimination that forms the bedrock of what we now turn to.

Nations Norms", 12 *Texas Int. L. J* (1977), 17; Mani, "The Concept of Economic Coercion", *India Quarterly*, Jul.–Sept. (1977), 334; Parry, "Defining Economic Coercion in International Law", 12 *Texas Int. L. J* (1977), 1; Neff, "The Law of Economic Coercion: Lessons From the Past and Indications of the Future", 20 *Colum. J of Trans. L.* (1981), 427; Seidl-Hohenveldern, "The United Nations and Economic Coercion", 18 *Revue belge de droit international* (1984–85), 9.

[16] Case Concerning *Military and Paramilitary Activities in and against Nicaragua (Nicaragua v. United States of America), Merits, Judgment, ICJ Reports (1986)* ("the Nicaragua case"), 106 and 108, paras 202 and 205, respectively (emphasis added). Further see Benneh, "Economic Coercion, the Non-Intervention Principle and the Nicaragua Case", 6 *African Yrbk. of Int. L.* (1994), 235.

[17] See Simma, ed., n. 8, 81.

[18] Further see Stowell, *Intervention in International Law* (Wash. DC, 1921); Fawcett, "Intervention in International Law", 103 Hague *Recueil* (1961), 343; Zotiades, "Intervention by Treaty Rights, Its Legality in Present Day International Law", 6 *Jus Gentium, Series of Publication on International Law* (1965); Vincent, *Non-Intervention and International Order* (Princeton, 1976); Chimni, "Towards a Third World Approach to Non-Intervention through the Labyrinth of Western Doctrine", 20 *IJIL* (1980), 243; Schwenninger, "The 1980s: New Doctrine of Intervention or New Norms of Non-intervention", 13 *Rutgers L. Rev.* (1980–81), 423; Damrosch, "Politics Across Borders: Non-Intervention and Non-Forcible Influence over Domestic Affairs", 83 *AJIL* (1989), 1; Jackamo, "From the Cold War to the New Multilateral World Order: The Evolution of Covert Operations and the Customary International Law of Non–Intervention", 32 *Virg. J of Int. L.* (1992), 929; Zheng, "Neo-Interventionism—Modern Hegemonism", 53 *Foreign Aff. J* (1999), 56; Rajan, "The New Interventionism"?, 37 *Int. Studies* (2000), 31.

(b) General Agreement on Tariffs and Trade 1994 (GATT)

The general proposition in this regard has been stated by the ICJ:

> [A] State is not bound to continue a particular trade relations longer than it sees fit to do so, in the absence of a treaty commitment or other specific legal obligation; but where there exists such a commitment,…such an abrupt act of termination of the commercial intercourse as the general trade embargo…will normally constitute a violation of the obligation not to defeat the object and purpose of the treaty.[19]

The GATT 1947 rule that regulated contracting parties' freedom in accordance with not only its terms but also "reasonable expectations" has been retained in the WTO.[20] Further, it is generally established that exceptions to a rule should be interpreted narrowly. An exception to the GATT principle of non-discrimination is Article XXI, which admits of derogation on the ground of national security. The WTO has iterated on several occasions[21] what the Court has long clarified:

> [T]he measures taken must not merely be such as *tend* to protect the essential security interest of the party taking them, but must be "necessary" for that purpose.[22]

No doubt, "where a treaty excludes from its regulated reach certain areas, those areas do not fall within the jurisdictional scope of the treaty",[23] a determination as such is nevertheless required in accordance with the treaty that affords such an escape. In other words, a tribunal is not divested of jurisdiction otherwise vested in it simply because a party considers that its essential security interests render it "necessary". Unlike in the WTO, the question of jurisdiction is often before the ICJ. This was the issue which lay at the core of the Court's observations on GATT Article XXI.[24] Those remarks, coming as they do from no less a tribunal than the International Court of Justice are certainly persuasive, must however be seen in the light of both the issue before the Court and the relevant practice of the WTO.

Unilateral trade sanctions broadly violate WTO rules. Since retaliatory measures must be WTO-authorized, it excludes "*any residual right* to take countermeasures under general international law for breaches of the WTO and

---

[19] The *Nicaragua* case, *supra* note 16, 138, para 276.

[20] See subpara 1 (*b*) of GATT Article XXIII, and in particular *Korea – Government Procurement,* Panel Report, WT/DS163/R, adopted 19 Jun. 2000, para 7.95.

[21] See, in particular, Appellate Body Reports in *United States – Standards for Reformulated and Conventional Gasoline*, WT/DS2/AB/R, adopted 20 May 1996; *European Communities – Measures Concerning Meat and Meat Products (Hormones)*, WT/DS26/AB/R, adopted 13 Feb. 1998; *United States – Import Prohibition of Certain Shrimp and Shrimp Products*, WT/DS58/AB/R, adopted 6 Nov. 1998.

[22] The *Nicaragua* case, *supra* note 16, 141, para 282 (emphasis added).

[23] See the diss. op. of Judge Schwebel, ibid. 307, para 101.

[24] See the *Nicaragua* case, *supra* note 16, 116, para 222.

related agreements".[25] The US refusal to submit the so-called "political disputes" to the WTO is inconsistent with its GATT 1994 obligations.[26] Even otherwise, a State lawfully taking counter-measures is required to fulfil its obligations under "*any other binding dispute settlement procedure in force* between the injured State and the State which has committed the internationally wrongful act".[27] It has been suggested that resort to countermeasures should be made conditional upon the "refusal by the wrong-doing State of an offer to settle the matter through a binding third-party procedure".[28]

Thus, the national security argument of the US is not sufficient to justify the extraterritorial applications of sanctions to third countries that have nothing to do with the terrorist activity that such sanctions are aimed to punish.[29] There was no state of warfare or an emergency situation between the US on the one hand and Iran and Libya on the other.[30] Moreover, "a security escape clause would be invalid when the invoking state has full discretion to interprete [sic] its terms and determine its scope."[31] A tribunal confronted with the interpretation of a treaty exception advanced by a party may not accept it if it renders nugatory other treaty provisions on the rights of other parties.

(c) Human Rights Treaties

Together with treaties on international humanitarian law, human rights treaties represent the conscience of States. But they also testify to the nature and extent of both States' willingness to be bound by, and States' reliance on, them. What else if

---

[25] Crawford, *Third Report on State Responsibility*, UN Doc. A/CN.4/507/Add.3 (18 Jul. 2000); para 342 (emphasis added). Further see my *India at the WTO Dispute Settlement System* (N. Delhi, 2004), ch. V, s. 8.

[26] Argued by the US Ambassador to the WTO in a preliminary hearing of the Helms-Burton case. See Swardson, "U.S. Comes Out Ahead in Trade Skirmishes", *Seattle Times*, Oct. 16, 1996, A3.

[27] Draft Article 48 (2) on State Responsibility, *ILC Yrbk (1996-I)*, i, 135 (emphasis added).

[28] Crawford, *supra* note 25, para 304.

[29] Giardina, "The Economic Sanctions of the United States Against Iran and Libya and GATT Security Exception", in Hafner et al., eds., *Liber Amicorum Professor Ignaz Seidl-Hohenveldern* (The Hague, 1998), 230.

[30] Hahn, "Vital Interests and the Law of the GATT: An Analysis of GATT's Security Exceptions", 12 *Mich. J of Int. L.* (1991), 558.

[31] Van Houtte, "Treaty Protection Against Economic Sanctions", 18 *Revue belge de droit international* (1984–85), 46. Further see Dattu and Boscariol, "GATT Article XXI, Helms-Burton and the Continuing Abuse of the National Security Exception", 28 *Canadian Bus. L. J* (1997), 198; Kuilwijk, "Castro's Cuba and the US Helms-Burton Act, An Interpretation of the GATT Security Exemptions", 31 *J of World Trade* (1997), 68; Bhala, "National Security and International Trade Law: What the GATT Says, and What the United States Does", 19 *Univ. of Pennsyl. J of Int. Econ. L.* (1998), 275; Perez, "WTO and UN Law: Institutional Comity in National Security", 23 *Yale J of Int. L.* (1998), 301.

not state sovereignty which underlies here.[32] The sovereignty is not a shield to justify human rights violations either in times of peace or war; it is the people who suffer "when robust and comprehensive economic sanctions are directed against authoritarian regimes".[33] In its General Comment, the UN Committee on Economic, Social and Cultural Rights has observed:

> Just as the international community insists that any targeted State must respect the civil and political rights of its citizens, so too must that State and the international community itself do everything possible to protect at least the core content of the economic, social and cultural rights of the affected people of that State.[34]

While, it has been held, States are free to form their "own appraisal of the situation as to the respect for human rights"[35] in another State, "the use of force could not be the appropriate method to monitor or ensure such respect".[36] The fact that a State or group of States has not ratified the Covenant, does not exonerate it from the obligation not to defeat its object and purpose,[37] and precludes it from doing

[32] Further see Doehring, "The Relationship between State Sovereignty and Human Rights", *Acta Juridica* (1994), 83; Tyagi, "The Conflict of Law and Policy on Reservations to Human Rights Treaties", 71 *British Yrbk. of Int. L.* (2001), 181.

[33] Annan, *We the Peoples, the Role of the United Nations in the 21st Century* (New York, 2000), 50. Calling for the immediate lifting of economic sanctions imposed on his country by its neighbours, the representative of Burundi told the Second Committee (Economic and Financial) that sanctions had resulted in reduction of food production by 30 per cent and decline in industrial growth by 10 per cent. UN Doc. GA/EF/2724, 17 Oct. 1996, 1. The representative of Columbia decried the allocation of increased resources to resolve financial crises caused by speculative ventures at a time when restrictions were placed on official assistance flows to combat poverty. Ibid. 1. Further see Damrosch, "The Civilian Impact of Economic Sanctions", in Damrosch, ed., *Enforcing Restraint: Collective Intervention in Internal Conflict* (New York, 1993), 274; Weiss, ed., *Political Gain and Civilian Pain: Humanitarian Impact of Economic Sanctions* (Lanham, 1997); Haas, "Sanctioning Madness", 76 *Foreign Aff.* (1997), 80; Wall, "Human Rights and Economic Sanctions: The New Imperialism", 22 *Fordham Int. L. J* (1998), 577; Davidson, "The Economic Sanctions against the People of Iraq", <http://www/lancs.ac.uk/ug/greenrd/project/elias.htm>.

[34] No. 8, *Seventeenth Sess., UN Econ. and Soc. Council*, UN Doc. E/C.12/1997/8, 12 Dec. 1997, 2. It concludes by suggesting that three steps be taken, which follow from the recognition of economic social and cultural rights. First, these rights must be fully taken into account when a sanction regime is being designed; second, effective monitoring should be undertaken throughout the period that sanctions are in force; and finally, the party or parties responsible for the imposition, maintenance or implementation of the sanctions have the obligation "to take steps, individually and through international assistance and co-operation, especially economic and technical", in accordance with Article 2, para 1, of the Covenant, in order to respond to any disproportionate suffering experienced by vulnerable groups within the targeted country. Ibid. 4.

[35] The *Nicaragua* case, n. 16, 134, para 268.

[36] Ibid. para 268.

[37] Article 18 of the 1969 Vienna Convention on the Law of Treaties. Further see *Reservations to Genocide Convention, ICJ Reports (1951)*, 23.

anything which militates against "full realization of the rights recognized in the present Covenant...."[38] Sovereign economic freedom does not therefore extend to "conduct which derogates from basic human rights".[39] While it is not intended "unduly to restrict a State's ability to take effective countermeasures in respect of certain wrongful acts involving obligations *erga omnes*, for example, violation of human rights".[40] A conduct by the injured State is not exempted, "which is legally required of it under human rights norms: *however consistent with humanitarian considerations such exemptions may be*, a State is not in general obliged by human rights law to allow humanitarian activities be carried out by its nationals or officials on the territory of other States".[41] There is enough evidence that States "do not, in fact intervene to safeguard human rights, though they may use that pretext."[42] Considering its inevitable adverse effects on the intervened State, it has been stated that "human rights obligations (whether or not qualified as "basic" or "fundamental") may not themselves be the subject of countermeasures."[43] A UN report has emphasized:

> Sanctions should be judged against the standards of universal human rights, particularly the Convention on the Rights of the Child. The primary consideration when developing a sanctions regime should always be the potential human impact, which should influence the choice of sanctions, their duration, the legal provisions and the operation of the sanctions regime. Sanctions should not be imposed without advance assessment of the economic and social structure of the target country.[44]

Clearly, the failure to take a timely preventive action is as much, if not more, a failure of the international community as an act of intervention.

---

[38] Article 2.1 of the International Covenant on Economic, Social and Cultural Rights.
[39] See Draft Article 50 (*d*) on State Responsibility, n. 27, para 135. The ILC debates reflect that there was no consensus as to the phrase "basic human rights". Ireland suggested that the enumeration of Article 4 of the International Covenant on Civil and Political Rights be included in draft Article 50 and recommended that "countermeasures involving a derogation from any of the rights specified in paragraph 2 of Article 4" of the Covenant as well as "countermeasures which are discriminatory on any of the grounds mentioned in para 1 of Article 4 should be expressly prohibited." Crawford, n. 25, para 317.
[40] Ibid. para 307.
[41] Ibid. para 312 (d) (emphasis added). See also Brownlie, "International Law at the 50th Anniversary of the United Nations", 255 Hague *Recueil* (1995), 206.
[42] Henkin, n. 9, 358. Further see Mani, "Humanitarian Intervention and International Law", 33 *IJIL* (1993), 1; Tyagi, "Concept of Humanitarian Intervention Revisited", 16 *Mich. J. of Int. L.* (1995), 883; Reisman, "Unilateral Action and the Transformation of the World Constitutive Process: The Special Problem of Humanitarian Intervention", 11 *EJIL* (2000), 3; Woollacott, "Humanitarian action—how legitimate is it?", *The Hindu*, Apr. 3, 2004, 15.
[43] Crawford, n. 25, para 349.
[44] The Machel Report on the Impact of Armed Conflict on Children; Note by the Secretary General, UN Doc. A/51/306, 26 Aug. 1996. See also Arts. 3, 6, 24, 27–8 and 38 of the Convention of the Rights of the Child.

(d) Charter of the Organization of American States (OAS)

Unlike the UN Charter, the OAS Charter prohibits "not only armed force but also any other form of interference or attempted threat against the personality of a State or against its political, *economic* and cultural elements".[45] Thus:

> No State may use or encourage the use of *coercive measures of an economic or political character* in order to force the sovereign will of another State and obtain from it advantage of any kind.[46]

The phrase "advantage of any kind" would encompass any kind of advantage that the intervener is not entitled to "as a matter of right under international law."[47] In addition, the proportionality principle would apply to a lawful advantage. Otherwise, "a measure of economic and/or political coercion which was either out of proportion to the lawful purpose pursued or of such a nature and weight as to amount to an act of military aggression."[48] Thus, speaking in the Security Council on 10 May 1985, the representative of Argentina said that the US measures against Nicaragua:

> Contravene the provisions of Article 19 of the Charter of the OAS. In the context of our organization, furthermore, they have been clearly rejected in the Charter of Economic Rights and Duties of States and in many General Assembly Resolutions, particularly in Resolution 38/197 and 39/210.[49]

Earlier, the 1960 US import embargo of Cuban sugar was generally regarded as a violation of the OAS ban on economic measures. The OAS provision on economic coercion has been adopted in the UN Resolutions and seems to have become a generally accepted UN standard. However, it is not always clear "where does the zone of free bargaining end, and where does it slide into that of coercion which annihilates free will."[50] It is said that Articles 23 and 24 of the OAS Charter, which urge parties to settle their disputes by negotiation, enquiry, mediation, conciliation, arbitration or judicial settlement, are "too vague to forbid economic countermeasures",[51] but "any alleged violation of the Treaty by either party could not have the effect of precluding that party from invoking the provisions of the

---

[45] Article 18.
[46] Article 19 (emphasis added).
[47] Arangio-Ruiz, "Human Rights and Non-Intervention in the Helsinki Final Act", 157 Hague *Recueil* (1977), 262.
[48] Ibid. 262.
[49] SCOR, Doc. S/PV. 2580, 10 May 1985, 66.
[50] Abi-Saab, n. 7, 234. Further see Ferguson, "Reflections on the Inter-American Principle of Non-Intervention: A Search for Meaning in Ambiguity", 32 *J of Politics* (1970), 628.
[51] Malenczuk, "Countermeasures and Self-defence as Circumstances Precluding Wrongfulness in the International Law Commission's Draft articles on State Responsibility", *Zeitschrift für ausländisches öffentliches Recht und Völkerrecht*, (1983), 737. Further see van Wijnen and Thomas, *Non-Intervention: The Law and Its Import in the Americas* (Dallas, 1956).

Treaty concerning pacific settlement of disputes".[52] And such means of dispute settlement do not exhaust earlier than provided for in the treaty.[53]

(e) Vienna Convention on the Law of Treaties[54]

Article 26 underlines the principle of good faith. The ICJ has held, "[j]ust as the very rule of *pacta sunt servanda* in the law of Treaties is based on good faith, so also is the binding character of an international obligation…."[55] The principle has been characterized as the basic principle of the "creation and performance of legal obligations".[56] And, pursuant to rules of interpretation contained in Article 31 (2) of the Convention, the preambular paragraph of the 1970 UN declaration on Principles of International Law concerning Friendly Relations and Co-Operation Among States in accordance with the UN Charter would include not just armed force but also other forms of coercion. Further, Article 60 states that the termination or suspension of the operation of a treaty as a consequence of its breach does not apply to "provisions relating to the protection of the human person contained in treaties of a humanitarian character".[57] It has been argued that if a treaty provides for the allocation of payment exclusively for strictly medical or humanitarian purposes and, in humanitarian circumstances, foodstuffs, the obligations arising under it cannot be ignored on the ground of being part of coercive economic measures.[58]

---

[52] *United States Diplomatic and Consular Staff in Teheran, ICJ Reports (1980)*, 28, para 53.

[53] See the WTO Dispute Settlement Understanding. "[A]n obligation relating to dispute settlement may not be suspended as a countermeasure." Crawford, n. 25, para 339. Further see Schachter, "Dispute Settlement and Countermeasures in the International Law Commission", 88 *AJIL* (1994), 471; Arangio-Ruiz, "Counter-measures and Amicable Dispute Settlement Means in the Implementation of State Responsibility: A Crucial Issue before the International Law Commission", 5 *EJIL* (1994), 20.

[54] See generally Rosenne, *The Law of Treaties—A Guide to the Legislative History of the Vienna Convention* (Leiden, 1970); Sinclair, *The Vienna Convention on the Law of Treaties* (Manchester, 1973).

[55] *Nuclear Tests (Australia* v. *France), ICJ Reports (1974)*, 268, para 46.

[56] *Border and Transborder Armed Actions (Nicaragua* v. *Honduras), ICJ Reports (1988)*, 105, para 94. Further see Lachs, "Some Thoughts on the Role of Good Faith in International Law", in Akkerman et al., eds., *Declaration on Principles: A Quest for Universal Peace* (Leyden, 1977), 47; O'Connor, *Good Faith in International Law* (Aldershot, 1991).

[57] Article 60, *Ibid.,* 112.

[58] Elagab, "Coercive Economic Measures Against Developing Countries", 41 *ICLQ* (1992), 691.

3.2. Resolutions of International Bodies

(a) General Assembly Resolutions[59]

In a series of resolutions adopted since the first decade of its coming into existence, the UN General Assembly has addressed a number of issues concerning international peace and security. As early as 1949, it stated that every State has a duty to refrain from intervention in the internal or external affairs of any other State.[60] Later, this principle of non-intervention was understood to mean that:

> No State may use or encourage the use of *economic*, political or any other type of *measures to coerce* another State in order to obtain from it the subordination of the exercise of its sovereign rights and *to secure from it advantages of any kind*.[61]

The principle of sovereign equality of States was explained to mean that "[e]ach State has the right freely to choose and develop its political, social, *economic* and

[59] 375 (IV) of 6 Dec. 1949, Rights and Duties of States; 1236 of 14 Dec. 1957, Peaceful and Neighbourly Relations among States; 2131 of 21 Dec. 1965, Inadmissibility of Intervention in the Domestic Affairs of States and the Protection of their Independence and Sovereignty; 2160 of 30 Nov. 1966, Strict Observance of the Prohibition of the Threat or Use of Force in International Relations, and of the Right of Peoples to self-determination; 2625 (XXV) of 24 Oct. 1970, Principles of International Law Concerning Friendly Relations and Cooperation among States in Accordance with the Charter of the United Nations (the Friendly Relations Declaration); 3201 of 1 May 1974, the Establishment of a New International Economic Order; 3281 of 12 Dec. 1974, Charter of Economic Rights and Duties of States; 3314 of 14 Dec. 1974, Definition of Aggression; 34/103 of 14 Dec. 1979, Inadmissibility of the Policy of Hegemonism in International Relations; 36/103 of 9 Dec. 1981, Inadmissibility of Intervention and Interference in the Internal Affairs of States; 37/10 of 15 Nov. 1982, Manila Declaration on the Peaceful Settlement of International Disputes; 42/22 of 18 Nov. 1987, Enhancement of the Effectiveness of the Principle of Refraining from the Threat or Use of Force in International Relations; 46/62 of 9 Dec. 1991, Development and Strengthening of good-Neighbourliness Between States; 46/210 of 20 Dec. 1991 and 50/96 of 20 Dec. 1995, Economic Measures as a Means of Political and Economic Coercion against Developing Countries; 47/19 of 24 Nov. 1992, Necessity of Ending the Economic, Commercial and Financial Embargo Imposed by the United States of America Against Cuba; 51/22 of 27 Nov. 1996, 53/10 of 26 Oct. 1998 and 55/6 of 26 Oct. 2000, Elimination of Coercive Economic Measures as a Means of Political and Economic Compulsion; 52/181 of 18 Dec. 1997, 54/200 of 22 Dec. 1999, 56/179 of 21 Dec. 2001 and 58/198 of 23 Dec. 2003, Unilateral Economic Measures as a Means of Political and Economic Coercion against Developing Countries; 52/120 of 12 Dec. 1997, 53/141 of 9 Dec. 1998 and 54/172 of 17 Dec. 1999, Human Rights and Unilateral Coercive Measures; 54/107 of 9 Dec. 1999, Implementation of the Provisions of the Charter of the United Nations Related to Assistance to Third States Affected by the Application of Sanctions; 57/5 of 16 Sept. 2002, Elimination of Unilateral Extraterritorial Coercive Economic Measures as a Means of Political and Economic Compulsion.

[60] Res. 375 (IV).

[61] Res. 2131 (XX) (emphasis added).

cultural *systems*."[62] The texts of Resolution 2131 and the Friendly Relations Declaration confirm the definition of actions prohibited as unlawful intervention, as codified in the Inter-American system, and as covered implicitly by the general provisions of Article 2(4) of the UN Charter.[63] In 1991, the General Assembly expressed its concern that the use of coercive economic measures adversely affects the economy and development efforts of the developing countries.[64] And, in 1995, it urged the international community:

> [T]o adopt urgent and Charter of the United Nations and the relevant rules of the World Trade effective measures to eliminate the use by some developed countries of unilateral coercive measures against developing countries which are not authorized by relevant organs of the United Nations.[65] In a near unanimous resolution adopted in 1997, while reiterating its earlier concern about unilateral economic measures, the Assembly characterized these measures as contravention of "the basic principles of the multilateral trading system",[66] and "instruments of intervention in matters that are essentially within the domestic jurisdiction of any State.[67]

Later, "[d]eeply concerned that Member States are continuing to apply extraterritorial coercive laws in violation of the norms of international law....", the Assembly in 1998 believed that:

---

[62] Decl. 2625 (emphasis added). This principle is reiterated in Article 1 of Res. 3281.

[63] Arangio-Ruiz, n. 47, 274. Further see Nawaz, *The Legal Principle Governing Friendly Relations and Cooperation Among States in the Spirit of the United Nations Charter* (Leyden, 1966).

[64] Res. 46/210.

[65] Res. 50/96.

[66] Res. 52/97.

[67] *Report of an ad hoc Group set up by the Secretariat as a follow-up to the Assembly's 1995 Resolution on Unilateral Measures*. UN Doc. A/52/459/97, para 73. The Report admits the following exceptions to this prohibition: multilateral economic sanctions mandated by the Security Council; other situations where the Security Council has determined the existence of a threat to peace, breach of the peace, or act of aggression; where the Security Council has merely recommended economic sanctions, provided that any limits specified by the Security Council are observed; where the General Assembly recommends sanctions by consensus or by large majorities over a period of time; certain instances where regional organizations impose economic sanctions for cause against their own members; where one or more States adopt unilateral measures in response to a clear violation of universally accepted norms (*jus cogens*) standards, or obligations (*erga omnes*), provided these States are not seeking advantages for themselves but are pursuing an international community interest; and where the economic measures constitute proportional countermeasures by a State for a prior injury, provided *inter alia* that the measures are not designed to endanger the territorial integrity or political independence of the target State. Ibid. para 76.

> [P]rompt elimination of such measures would be consistent with the purposes and principles embodied in the Organization.[68]

In the same year, the Assembly rejected these measures because of their negative effects on the realization of all the human rights of vast sectors of their populations, in particular children, women and the elderly.[69] Later, on the report of the Sixth Committee, the Assembly stressed that in the formulation of sanctions regimes, due account should be taken of the potential effects of sanctions on third States.[70]

While it is held that the functions and powers conferred by the Charter on the General Assembly are "not merely hortatory",[71] of what normativity are resolutions adopted by it in the exercise of that power has been the subject of much debate. It has been suggested that the resolutions must be distinguished according to various factors, such as the intention of the General Assembly, the content of the principles proclaimed and the extent of support for their adoption. And in the case of unanimously adopted resolutions, it has been argued, "a contributory effect towards the creation of a new rule of customary international law cannot be ruled out".[72] To the extent that they were interpretation agreed by all the member States, according to one author, they fitted comfortably into an "established source of law".[73] Thus, "[i]nternational law derives whatever substance and validity it has from the democratic deliberation of sovereign nations."[74] But there has been "a tendency to project the choices of a State or a group of States as community decisions without basing those choices on the common interest which could be developed only through the democratic participation of all States...."[75] The argument that the

---

[68] GA/RES/53/10, 3 Nov. 1998, 2. Later, the Assembly expressed its grave concern that the use of unilateral economic measures adversely affects the economy and developments efforts of developing countries in particular and has a general negative impact on international economic cooperation and on worldwide efforts to move towards a non-discriminatory and open multilateral trading system. See GA/RES/54/200, 20 Jan. 2000, 2.

[69] Res. 53/141, 2. Reiterated in Res. 54/172, 3.

[70] Res. 54/107, 3. The resolution reaffirms the important role of the General Assembly, the Economic and Social Council and the Committee for Programme and Coordination in mobilizing and monitoring, as appropriate, the economic assistance efforts by the international community and the United Nations System to States confronted with special economic problems arising from the carrying out of preventive or enforcement measures imposed by the Security Council and, as appropriate, in identifying solutions to the special economic problems of those States, ibid. 5.

[71] *Certain Expenses of the United Nations, Advisory Opinion, ICJ Reports (1962)*, 163.

[72] Castañeda, *Legal Effects of the General Assembly Resolutions* (New York, 1969), 35.

[73] Schachter, "International Law in Theory and Practice, General Course in Public International Law", 178 Hague *Recueil* (1982), 113. See also Arangio-Ruiz, "The Normative Role of the General Assembly of the United Nations and the Declaration of Principles of Friendly Relations", 137 Hague *Recueil* (1972), 607.

[74] Sellers, "Republican Principles in International Law", 11 *Connecticut J of Int. L.* (1996), 426.

[75] Rao, Draft Article 48 (2) on State Responsibility, *supra* note 27 at 158.

outcome of democratic deliberation is largely devoid of a normative content is not new;[76] noticeable is "democratization"— a norm of international law at the "threshold" of the twenty-first century.[77]

(b) Security Council Resolutions

States' freedom to act to the detriment of other States is not without limits when exercised by a body primarily responsible to maintain international peace and security.[78] All States have undertaken to carry out the decision of the Council and the latter is mandated to act in accordance with the Purposes and Principles of the Charter.[79] Authorized to take economic measures under Chapter VII, the Council has in one of its resolutions:

> Reaffirmed its readiness, whenever measures are adopted under Article 41 of the Charter of the United Nations, to give consideration to their impact on the civilian population, bearing in mind the needs of children, in order to consider appropriate humanitarian exemptions.[80]

---

[76] That these are "only a statement of political intention and not a formulation of law", *GAOR, First Committee,* UN Doc. A/C.1/SR.1423, 436.

[77] Pastor Ridruejo, "Le Droit International à la Veille du Vingt et Unième Siècle: Normes, Faits et Valeurs", 274 Hague *Recueil* (1998), 21. Further, on General Assembly resolutions, see Kelsen, "The Draft Declaration on Rights and Duties of States", 42 *AJIL* (1948), 259; Higgins, *The Development of International Law through the Political Organs of the United Nations* (Oxford, 1963); Asamoah, *The Legal Significance of the Declarations of the General Assembly of the United Nations* (The Hague, 1966); Falk, "On the Quasi-Legislative Competence of the General Assembly", 60 *AJIL* (1966), 782; Bleicher, "The Legal Significance of Re-Citation of General Assembly Resolutions", 63 *AJIL* (1969), 444; Brower and Tepe, "The Charter of Economic Rights and Duties of States: A Reflection or Rejection of International Law?", 9 *Int. Lawyer* (1975), 295; Tiewul, "The United Nations Charter of Economic Rights and Duties of States", 10 *J of Int. L. and Economics* (1975), 645; Khan, "The Legal Status of the Resolutions of the United Nations General Assembly", 19 *IJIL* (1979), 554; Schwebel, "The Effects of Resolutions of the United Nations General Assembly", *ASIL Proc.* (1979), 302; Mendelson, "The Legal Character of General Assembly Resolutions: Some Considerations of Principle", in Hossain, ed., *Legal Aspects of New International Economic Order* (London, 1980), 95; Joyner, "United Nations General Assembly Resolution and International Law: Rethinking the Contemporary Dynamics of Norm-Creation", 11 *Calif. Wes. Int. L. J* (1981), 445; Skubiszewski, 61 *Annuaire de l'Institut de droit international, Session d' Helsinki* (1985), 93; Chodosh, "Neither Treaty nor Custom: the Emergence of Declarative International Law", 26 *Texas Int. L. J* (1991), 87; Sloan, *United Nations General Assembly Resolutions in Our Changing World* (New York, 1991); Sohn, "Enhancing the Role of the General Assembly of the UN in Crystallizing International Law", in Makarczyk, ed., *Theory of International Law at the Threshold of the 21st Century* (The Hague, 1996), 549.

[78] Article 24.1 of the UN Charter.

[79] Article 24.2. Further see Schwarzenberger, "The Purposes of the United Nations: International Judicial Practice", 4 *Israel Yrbk. of Int. L.* (1974), 11.

[80] See Article 17 (c), Res. 1261 of 25 Aug. 1999, 3. The same provision has been repeated in Article 16 of Res. 1265 of 17 Sept. 1999, 2–3. "Even when based on collective efforts, this

Earlier, it was stated that any adverse humanitarian consequence on civilian population should be avoided. And any sanctions regime is required to take "fully into account international human rights instruments and humanitarian standards established by the Geneva Conventions".[81] Later, the Council was asked to look at ways to make itself more accessible to consultation by third States experiencing economic problems due to sanctions imposed on their neighbours or fading partners.[82]

These safeguards do address widespread concerns, but they do not set out the means of ensuring compliance to satisfy the criteria of justice and international law.[83] "The pre-eminence of Charter obligations…never meant a blank check given by UN members to the Security Council to override or dispose of sovereign rights through decisions reached on the basis of a political process by a largely unaccountable organ, without the requirements of legal process and under the influence of a few powerful states."[84] This is not to suggest that the determination of a threat to peace is always and necessarily legal in nature, a determination of such a threat by consensus would be as good as by a judicial body.[85] The repute of the

---

potentially devastating economic weapon must satisfy the general rule of proportionality, notwithstanding the fact that economic countermeasures and Chapter VII measures are two distinct domains having distinct legal bases." See the *Case Concerning Gabčikovo-Nagymaros Project (Hungary/Slovakia)*, *ICJ Reports (1997)*, 56, para 85. Further see Christiane, "The Security Council of the United Nations and the Implementation of International Humanitarian Law", 20 *Denver J of Int. L. and Policy* (1992), 335; Fruedenschuß, "Between Unilateralism and Collective Security: Authorization of the Use of Force by the UN Security Council", 5 *EJIL* (1994), 465; Reisman, "Assessing the Lawfulness of Non-Military Enforcement: The Case of Economic Sanctions", 89 *ASIL Proc.* (1995), 250; Wall, "Human Rights and Economic Sanctions: The New Imperialism", 22 *Fordham Int. L. J* (1998), 577.

81 See Statement by the Inter-Agency Standing Committee to the Security Council on the Humanitarian Impact of Sanctions, UN Doc. S/1998/147, 29 Dec. 1997, 2. Reisman and Stevick have proposed five legal principles for mandatory economic sanctions: that highly coercive sanctions follow prescribed contingencies; that they be necessary and proportionate; that the sanctioners reasonably maximize discrimination between combatants and non-combatants; that sanctions programmes be periodically assessed; and that relief be provided to injured third parties. "The Applicability of International Law Standards to United Nations Economic Sanctions Programmes", <http://www.ejil.org/journal/Vol9/No1/art4.html>. See also Higgins, "Policy and Impartiality: The Uneasy Relationship in International Law", 23 *Int. Org.* (1969), 914.

82 See the text introduced by the representative of Ghana, Sixth Committee, Press Release GA/L/3133, 30th Mtg., 12 Nov. 1999, 1. See also Delbrück, "International Economic Sanctions and Third States", 30 *Archiv des Völkerrechts* (1992), 95; Hailbronner, "Sanctions and Third Parties and the Concept of International Public Order", ibid. 2.

83 See Purposes of the UN.

84 Burci, "Legal Aspects of UN Economic Sanctions", Lecture at Lauterpacht Research Centre for International Law, Friday Lecture Series 2000, Cambridge, U.K. <http://www.law.cam.ac.uk/rcil/Burci.doc>.

85 See Mani, "The U.N. & human rights", *The Hindu*, Sept. 6, 2000, 10. Further see Blum, *Eroding the United Nations Charter* (Dordrecht, 1993), 239; Freudenschuss, "Article 39 of the

UN can suffer if it tries "to "heal" what cannot be healed."[86] Yet this is what Resolution 1483 essentially does by lifting the economic sanctions on Iraq sans putting in place verifiable safeguards against abuse of the situation.[87] That it does not seek to solve every issue, as the representative of the United Kingdom puts it, such as the function of the IAEA,[88] is what speaks for how it legitimizes the invasion and the occupation of the country. Needless to say, only the UN weapons inspectors were competent to determine whether or not there were weapons of mass destruction, a task well begun and was being reported to the Security Council. But a determination of their non-existence if made before the invasion would only have made it more difficult for the occupying powers, if now made would hardly help them—already in a quagmire while the mission is far from complete.

(c) Resolutions Adopted by the International Law Commission

Perhaps the most important contribution of the Commission relevant to the subject is on state responsibility.[89] It is remarkable that the international community has moved away from reprisals to countermeasures as temporary steps taken in response to prior internationally wrongful conduct.[90] Now, even a State injured by an internationally wrongful act "shall not resort, by way of countermeasures, to:

> (*b*) Extreme *economic* and political *coercion* designed to endanger the territorial integrity or *political independence* of the State which has committed the internationally wrongful act.[91]

One view held this formulation as "extremely vague and unhelpful",[92] the other viewed it "very important because it reflected an aspiration and a reality and was

---

UN Charter Revisited: Threats to the Peace and the Recent Practice of the UN Security Council", 46 *Austrian J of Public Int. L.* (1993), 1; Bedjaoui, *The New World Order and the Security Council, Testing the Legality of Its Acts* (Dordrecht, 1994).

[86] Habermas, *supra*, n. 2, 10. See also Alvarez, "Hegemonic International Law Revisited", 97 *AJIL* (2003), 888; Falk, "What Future for the UN Charter System of War Prevention", ibid. 590; Franck, "What Happens Now? The United Nations After Iraq", ibid. 607; Mani, "The U.N. and post-war Iraq", *The Hindu*, Apr. 30, 2003, 10; Rajagopal, "U.N. credibility at stake", ibid. Sept. 5, 2003, 10; Steele, "The U.N. and the Iraqis", ibid. Apr. 23, 2004, 10. Further see Doxey, *Economic Sanctions and International Enforcement* (London, 1980); Segall, "Economic Sanctions: Legal and Policy Constraints", 81 *Int. Rev. of the Red Cross* (1999), 763; Simons, *Imposing Economic Sanctions: Legal Remedy or Genocidal Tool?* (London, 1999).

[87] S/Res/1483, 22 May 2003.

[88] Press Release 7765, 22 May 2003.

[90] See Draft Articles on State Responsibility, *ILC Yrbk. (1980-II)*, ii, 30 *et seq.*

[91] Crawford, "The Relationship between Sanctions and Countermeasures", a contribution to the colloquium of the Graduate Institute of International Studies, Geneva, on *United Nations Sanctions and International Law*, Jun. 1999, <http://www.law.camb.uk/RCIC/ILCSR/State.htm>, 7.

[91] See Article 50 of Draft Articles on State Responsibility, n. 27, 135 (emphasis added).

[92] Rosenstock, ibid. 177.

grounded in the Charter of the United Nations".[93] Indeed, the provision "would help prevent the situation in which a small country which had committed an internationally wrongful act was brought to its knees through economic or political coercion".[94] Another member wanted the Commission to make it very clear that it was "fully aware of the fact that the prohibitions contained in subparagraph (*a*) and (*b*), threat or use of force, and extreme economic or political coercion, were circumvented by qualifying the countermeasures concerned as self-defence".[95]

The commentary on Article 50 justifies the exclusion of the measures described above on the ground that consequences arising therefrom "may have consequences as serious as those arising from the use of armed force".[96] As was to be expected, States were divided on their attitudes to the formulation of paragraph (*b*) of the Draft Article 50. Support to the formulation lay in the conviction of those States who believed that countermeasures favour more powerful States. Some of the States who opposed paragraph (*b*) argued that it had "no basis in customary law".[97] However, it was clarified that the provision did not prohibit "conduct capable of remotely and unintentionally endangering the territorial integrity or political independence of the State".[98] While noting the paragraph (*b*) formulation as "deficient",[99] the report notes that "countermeasures must not be taken as an excuse to intervene in other issues internal to the responsible State, *distinct from the question of its compliance with its international obligations*; such issues *continue* to be protected by the principle of domestic jurisdiction".[100] Thus, the issue of compliance with international obligations is an *international* question, not a matter of a State's or group of States' "choosing".

(d) Resolutions of Other International Bodies

Mention must be made to the OAS resolution of 28 April 1982, which:

> [D]eplores the adoption by the European Economic Community and other States of coercive measures of an economic and political nature, which are prejudicial to the Argentine nation and to urge them to lift those measures indicating that they constitute a serious precedent, inasmuch as they are not covered by Resolution 502 (1982) of the United Nations Security Council and are incompatible with the Charters of the United Nations and the

---

[93] Villagrán Kramer, ibid. 177.
[94] Fomba, ibid. 177.
[95] Arangio-Ruiz, ibid. 177.
[96] Crawford, n. 25, para 311 (b).
[97] Ibid. para 315.
[98] Ibid. para 315.
[99] Ibid. 31.
[100] Ibid. (emphasis added). In addition, countermeasures otherwise necessary must be proportional, i.e. "commensurate with the injury suffered, taking into account the gravity of the internationally wrongful act and its effects" on the injured party". Ibid. para 346. For other procedural limitations, see ibid. para 360.

> Organization of American States and the General Agreement on Tariffs and Trade(GATT).[101]

Later, the imposition of a total embargo on trade by the United States against Nicaragua was characterized as coercive economic measure and "a violation of international law, in particular the Charter of the Organization of American States".[102] In its Declaration of 2 June 1997, Affirming Respect for the Personality, Sovereignty, and Independence of States, the OAS General Assembly has called upon member states to respect the personality, sovereignty, and independence of states, refrain from taking any unilateral action which is inconsistent with the purposes and principles of the Charter and settle disputes by peaceful, non-coercive procedures and means consistent with the spirit and the letter of the Charter.[103]

Earlier, on 22 November 1996, the EC Council adopted a Regulation protecting against the effects of the extra-territorial application of legislation adopted by a third country, and actions based thereon or resulting therefrom. The Regulation enumerates a number of possible damage to EU interests,[104] and suggests various measures to protect its economic or financial interests, such as the imposition of sanctions by a Member State in the event of breach of any relevant provisions of the Regulation.[105] A number of non-governmental organizations have concurred in the view that "individual states; subnational entities or *ad hoc* coalitions should be forbidden from imposing sanctions..., [the latter] might themselves be considered a breach of law that might provoke sanctions by the international community"[106] But what if those States were to do that in the name of international community?

---

101 21 *ILM* (1982), 670–1

102 OAS General Assembly, Second Committee, Economic and Social Matters, Doc. AG/Com.11, 12/85, 6 Dec. 1985. The United States Representative stated that the measures in question were intended to promote "peace and security of the region.... There is no general principle of customary law which obliges one State to trade with another. The OAS Charter did not, and was not intended to, create such a rule." The draft resolution was not put to vote for want of a quorum. Further see Domb, "Defining Economic Coercion in International Law: The Possibility of Regional Action by the Organization of American States", 11 *Cornell Int. L. J* (1978), 85.

103 <http://www.oas.org/En/prog/juridico/english/ga-res97/dec14.htm>.

104 See Regulation 2271/96 of 22 Nov. 1996, 36 *ILM* (1997), 131.

105 Article 9, ibid. 129. Further see Chudzicki, "The European Union's Response to the Libertad Act and the Iran-Libya Act: Extraterritoriality without Boundaries?" 28 *Loyola Univ. Chicago L. J* (1996–97), 505; van den Berg, "Cuban Liberty and Democratic Solidarity Act: Violation of International Law and the Response of Key American Trade Partners", 21 *Maryland J of Int. L. and Trade* (1997), 279.

106 "Perspectives on Sanctions, Abolition of Comprehensive Economic Sanctions", Peace Action Congress, July 1998, <http://www.webcom.com/peaceact/sanctions_perspectives.html>. Further see Pinto, "Democratization of International Relations and its implications for Development and

3.3. *Jus Cogens*

Rules of *jus cogens* can be derived from customary international law, treaties, such as the UN Charter and from treaties against torture.[107] As early as 1966, the International Law Commission stated, "the law of the Charter concerning the prohibition of the use of force in itself constitutes a conspicuous example of a rule in international law having the character of *jus cogens*".[108] The other examples include the law of genocide and crimes against humanity.

(a) Vienna Convention on the Law of Treaties

The Convention characterizes *jus cogens* as a peremptory norm of general international law, which "is a norm accepted and recognized by the international community as a whole as a norm from which no derogation is permitted and which can be modified only by a subsequent norm of general international law having the same character".[109] The Convention closely connects international *jus cogens* with the consensual character of general international law, excluding any possibility of identifying it with "natural law standing above the will of States".[110]

The International Law Commission, which earlier adopted the Convention, in its Draft Articles on State Responsibility states in Article 50 that even "an injured State shall not resort, by way of countermeasures to:

> (*e*) "any other conduct in contravention of a peremptory norm of general international law".[111]

The Commission was however aware of the real difficulty, which lay "in identifying existing peremptory norms whose application is not already excluded either by the conception of countermeasures itself, or by other specific exclusions".[112] Since the possibility of new peremptory norms is manifest in the use of "emerges" in the formulation of Article 64 of the Convention, the Commission thought it necessary

---

Application of International Law", 5 *Asian Yrbk. of Int. L.* (1995), 111; Detter, "The Effect of Resolutions of International Organizations", in Makarczyk, ed., n. 77, 381.

[107] Simma, ed., n. 8, 1118. See also ibid. 122 and 779. Further see Verdross, "*Jus Dispositivum* and *Jus Cogens* in International Law", 60 *AJIL* (1966), 59; Suy, *The Concept of Jus Cogens in International Law*, Papers and Proceedings II, Conference on International Law, Lgonissi, Greece, 3–8 Apr. 1966 (Geneva, 1967).

[108] See *ILC Yrbk.* (1966), ii, 247. See also Schwelb, "Some Aspects of International *Jus Cogens* as Formulated by the International Law Commission", 61 *AJIL* (1967), 946.

[109] Article 53.

[110] Alexidze, "Legal Nature of *Jus Cogens* in Contemporary International Law", 172 Hague *Recueil* (1981), 253–4.

[111] Article 50 (*e*), n. 27, 135.

[112] Crawford, n. 25, para 342.

to retain Draft Article 50 (*e*), for, once a new peremptory norm emerges, "countermeasures derogating from that rule are prohibited".[113]

(b) Judicial Pronouncements

In the *Corfu Channel* case, the ICJ referred to the "elementary considerations of humanity", which are "more exacting in peace than in war"[114]. Later, in the *Barcelona Traction* case, the Court distinguished between:

> [T]he obligations of a State towards the international Community as a whole, and those arising vis-à-vis another State…. By their very nature the former are the concern of all States. In view of the importance of the rights involved, all states can be held to have a legal interest in their protection; they are obligations *erga omnes*.[115]

And it is worth recalling what the Court said in the *Nicaragua* case:

> It was never intended that the Charter should embody written confirmation of every essential principle of international law in force. The existence in the *opinio juris* of States of the principle of non-intervention is backed by established and substantial practice. It has moreover been presented as a corollary of the sovereign equality of States.[116]

Thus, in the absence of a customary rule of contrary effect, the principle of non-intervention must be treated as part of *jus cogens*. Whether or not it is justified to take a "judicial perspective on peremptory norms",[117] the absence of cases involving reference to *jus cogens* is not the evidence of the absence of the existence of either a normative category of *jus cogens* or a norm that otherwise satisfies the criteria of *jus cogens*.[118] Violation of international law, like domestic law, proves its existence; it does not make legal what is otherwise illegal.

---

113 Ibid. para 342. France and Ireland suggested deletion of para (*e*). The US noted that "the content of the peremptory norms is difficult to determine outside the areas of genocide, slavery and torture". Ibid. para 318. Further see Murty, "*Jus Cogens* in the Law of Treaties", *ISIL Proc., 5th Ann. Conf.* (1968), 10; Dhokalia, "Problems Relating to *Jus Cogens* in the Law of Treaties", in Agarwala, ed., *Essays on the Law of Treaties* (N. Delhi, 1972), 149; Nageshwar Rao, "*Jus Cogens* and the Vienna Convention on the Law of Treaties", 14 *IJIL* (1974), 362; Sztucki, *Jus Cogens and the Vienna Convention on the Law of Treaties: A Critical Appraisal* (Wien, 1974); Magallona, "The Concept of *Jus Cogens* in the Vienna Convention on the Law of Treaties", 5 *Philippine L. J* (1976), 521; Rozakis, *The Concept of Jus Cogens in the Law of Treaties* (Oxford, 1976).

114 *ICJ Reports (1949)*, 22.

115 *ICJ Reports (1970)*, 32 (italics in the original).

116 *ICJ Reports (1986)*, 106, para 202. See also the sep. op. of Judge Sette-Camara in the *Nicaragua* case (1986), 199.

117 Gaja, "*Jus Cogens* Beyond the Vienna Convention", 172 Hague *Recueil* (1981), 286. Further see Ford, "Adjudicating Jus Cogens", 13 *Wisconsin Int. L. J* (1994), 145.

118 Further see Alexidze, n. 111, 232.

(c) The Writings of Publicists

It is widely believed that *jus cogens* rules constitute "a lowest common denominator below which states cannot sink",[119] but differences in attitudes of States work against their identification. The fact that there were so divergent views must be seen as a "proof that the legal conscience of the international community distinguishes between different types of international duties and responsibilities".[120] And it is generally agreed that the "lack of acceptance or even opposition on the part of one or a few States is no obstacle to a norm becoming peremptory"[121] Further, since the norms of *jus cogens* are "in constant development, the system was thus open-ended, ensuring that countermeasures would always be subject to certain restrictions".[122] Even those States, which interpret *jus cogens* restrictively have admitted that they will not "apply trade sanctions, particularly if such sanctions are prohibited…."[123] Thus, if rules relating to the prohibition of use of force by States "have the status of peremptory norms",[124] together with the principle of non-intervention,[125] economic measures that bring the population of a target State to the brink of starvation or trigger its exodus can hardly be treated other than either intervention or the use of force.

4. Conclusions

Economic interests have become a routine cause of international politics. While States remain sovereign, and to that extent also remain independent, the expanding domain of international law is nothing but a measure of diminishing sovereignty and deepening dependence.

---

[119] Davidson, "United States' Use of Economic Sanctions, Treaty Bending and Treaty Breaking in International Aviation", 59 *J of Air L. and Commerce* (1993), 291.
[120] Ago, *ILC Yrbk.* (1976), ii, 32.
[121] Gaja, *supra* note 117 at 283.
[122] Elaraby, *supra* note 27 at 178.
[123] de Vries, in *Contemporary International Law Issues: New Forms, New Applications* (1998), 275.
[124] Crawford, n. 25, para 335. Further see generally Glaser, "International Peremptory Norms", 7 *Revue Roumaine d'etudes internationales* (1973), 57; Onuf and Birney, "Peremptory Norms of International Law: Their Source, Function and Future", 4 *Denver J of Int. L.* (1974), 194; Whiteman, "*Jus Cogens* in International Law with a Projected List", 7 *Georgia J of Int. L.* (1977), 609; Kreća, "Some General Reflections on Main Features of *Ius Cogens* as Notion of International Public Law", in Girardot et al., eds., *New Directions in International Law: Essays in Honour of Wolfgang Abendroth* (Frankfurt am Main, 1982), 27; Minagawa, "Essentiality and Reality of International *Jus Cogens*", 12 *Hitotsubashi J of Int. L. and Politics* (1984), 1; Hannikainen, *Peremptory Norms (Jus Cogens) in International Law: Historical Development, Criteria, Present Status* (Helsinki, 1988); Danilenko, "International *Jus Cogens*: Issues of Law-Making", 2 *EJIL* (1991), 42; Paust, "The Reality of *Jus Cogens*", 7 *Connecticut J of Int. L.* (1991–92), 81; Czaplinski, "Concept of *Jus Cogens* and Obligations *Erga Omnes* in International Law in the Light of Recent Developments", 23 *Polish Yrbk. of Int. L.* (1997–98), 87.
[125] Pratap, R. "International Humanitaian Law and Contemporary Realities—A Report on New Delhi Symposium", 40 *IJIL* (2000), 58.

Treaties are the most normative evidence of the growth of relations between States. And yet the sovereign equality of States and non-intervention, which lie at the core of the treaty *primus inter pares*, remain as illusory today as they were more than half a century ago. This explains why some States can act in disregard to the sovereignty of other States. Implicit in the sovereign equality of States and non-intervention are a good faith exercise of rights by States and the obligation to cooperate. They must be verified to have been discharged before treaty-conforming sanctions may be allowed to be imposed on a target State.

Resolutions of international bodies are the result of democratic deliberation at the international level. And if democratization has become a norm of international law, and is good enough to justify even acts derogating from the essentials of modern international law, repeatedly adopted consensual resolutions of at least the most representative body, the UN General Assembly, may not be brushed aside solely on the basis of the absence of resolutions of international bodies in the formulation of international law sources devised more than half a century ago.

In a system of law drawn from sources of various kinds, it is necessary that there should exist norms permitting no derogation. It is natural for a developing system of law not to have an immutable inventory of those norms. It is enough for an advancing society that the criteria for peremptoriness are defined, for the identification of those norms is a function of the progressive development of international law to give vent to the needs of its time. One wish the norms against denying the permanent population of a target State means of sustenance had not been identified in international law or the time had not come for it to treat them as peremptory.

LAWS OF HUMAN RIGHTS AND THE INDIAN CONSTITUTION

Manoj Kumar Sinha*

1. Introduction

The Indian experience on the promotion and protection of human rights at the national level, despite India's numerous social and economic problems, most importantly its stark poverty, may be of some interest at the international level, particularly to countries in Europe, Asia and Africa. India's experience may reveal with clarity that democracy, freedom and rule of law are not luxuries which only the western societies can afford.

Considering India's extensive territorial domain, the vastness of its population and the complexity of its social structure, cases of violation of rights, whether attributable to the agencies of the State or to private individuals or groups, may occur despite its best efforts.[1]

It is pertinent here to highlight the problems in implementation of human rights highlighted by commentators like V.S. Mani.[2] They are as follows:

a. Human rights are evolving ideals which the human society cherishes, no nation in the world can verily claimed to have lived up to these ideals,
b. Nations differ in the level of rights performance achieved, and often the level of rights performance is relatable to the level of economic development achieved,
c. The politics of human rights, both domestic and international often casts a veil of exaggeration, if not mendacity, on issues of human rights violations,
d. Wild allegations of rights violations must be distinguished from those supported by verifiable proof,

---

* Currently Visiting Professor at Raoul Wallenberg Institute of Human Rights and Humanitarian Law, Lund, Sweden, Assistant Professor (Research) Indian Society of International Law, New Delhi. My Special thanks to my wife Preet Kumar Sinha for her encouragement and support.

1 The magnitude of India's diversity is indicated by the 1991 census, which recorded a population of 879 million with growth rate of less than two per cent per annum (since the mid 1980s), while its linguistic diversity is reflected in the eighteen major languages which are recognised in Schedule VIII of the Constitution and the 844 dialects spoken by its people. Cf. Third Country Report submitted by India, CCPR/C/76/Add.6, 17 June 1996, at 3-4.

2 V.S. Mani, "Human Rights in India: An Overview" (unpublished paper, Germany: Konrad Adenauer Foundation, 1997) 1-63.

Bimal N. Patel (ed.), **India and International Law, 141-174.**

e. The problems of criminal law overlap those of human rights, and
f. Situations related to terrorism and threats to territorial integrity of a nation actively aided from across the border, it is at times difficult to sit in judgement as to the proportionately of use of force by the state against groups and individuals.

This paper examines the implementation mechanism available under the Indian Constitution, keeping in mind these considerations. For a proper understanding of the implementation mechanism under the Indian Constitution, it is essential here to cover the crucial role played by the judiciary, executive and legislature in implementation of human rights in general.

2. The Constitutional Regime

The Indian Constitution[3] envisages a noble democracy which ensures freedom under the law and the dignity of the individual. Part III of the Indian Constitution enumerates the fundamental rights[4] and Part IV sets out the Directive Principle of State Policy.[5]

The Indian Constitution provides certain rights for individuals in Part III of the Constitution which are known as the `fundamental rights'. The word `fundamental' means that these rights are inherent in all human beings and basic and essential for the individual. These rights represent the basic value of a civilized society and the Constitution makers declared that they should be given pride of place in the Constitution. These rights are aimed at protecting the dignity of the individual and create conditions in which every human being can develop his personality to the fullest extent.[6] No law, ordinance, custom, usage or administrative order can abridge or take away one's fundamental rights.[7]

---

[3] Durga Das Basu, *Commentary on the Constitution of India* (Calcutta, 1994); M.P. Jain, *Indian Constitutional Law* (Bombay, 1986), H. Seervai, *Constitutional Law of India: A Critical Commentary* (4th edition, Bombay, 1991).

[4] Articles 12 to 35 of the Indian Constitution deal with Fundamental Rights. The Indian Constitution groups the Fundamental Rights under several sub-heads. A) Right to Equality (Arts.14-18). B) Right to Freedom (Arts.19-22); C) Right against Exploitation (Arts.23-24); D) Right to Freedom of Religion (Arts.25-26); E) Cultural and Educational Rights (Arts.29-30); F) Right to Constitutional remedies (Art.32).

[5] Articles 38 to 51-A contain the Directive Principles of State Policy. The idea to have such principles in the Constitution has been borrowed from the Irish Constitution. The Directive Principles are not enforceable by the Court of Law.

[6] H.O. Agarwal, *Implementation of Human Rights Covenants with Special Reference to India,* 112-52 (Allahabad, 1983).

[7] Article 13(2) of Indian Constitution says, "The State shall not make any law which takes away or abridges the rights conferred by this Part and any law made in contravention of this clause shall, to the extent of the Contravention, be void.

There are two fundamental human rights under the Indian Constitution which have acquired the status of non-derogable human rights. They are contained in Articles 20 and 21, respectively.

Article 20 stipulates:

1. No person shall be convicted of any offence except for violation of a law in force at the time of the commission of the act charged as an offence, nor be subjected to a penalty greater than that which might have been inflicted under the law in force at the time of the commission of the offence.

2. No person shall be prosecuted and punished for the same offence more than once.

3. No person accused of any offence shall be compelled to be witness against himself.

Article 21 provides:

> No person shall be deprived of his life or personal liberty except according to procedure established by law.

The Constitutional rights under Article 20 prohibit *ex-post facto* operation of criminal law and confer immunity against double jeopardy and protection against self-incrimination. Article 21, which has sprung into life with the decision of the Supreme Court in *Maneka Gandhi vs. Union of India*[8], provides that no person shall be deprived of his life and personal liberty except according to procedure established by law. This judgement marks a watershed in the history of the constitutional law of the country. In fact, the Supreme Court of India, for the first time, took the view that Article 21 affords protection not only against executive action but also against legislation, that no law can deprive a person of his life or personal liberty unless it prescribes a procedure which is reasonable, fair and just and that if it is not, the Court will strike down the law as invalid. After the *Maneka Gandhi* case, Article 21 assumed a new dimension and the Supreme Court

---

(3) In this Article, unless the context otherwise requires:
(a) "law" includes any Ordinance, order, bye-laws, rule, regulation, notification, custom or usages having in the territory of India the force of law;
(b) "laws in force" includes laws passed or made by a Legislature or other competent authority in the territory of India before the commencement of this Constitution and not previously repealed, notwithstanding that any such law or any Part thereof may not be then in operation either at all or in particular areas.

8 *Maneka Gandhi vs. Union of India*, AIR 1978 SC 597.

introduced substantive and procedural due process in the constitutional law of India through creative interpretation inspired by judicial activism.[9]

3. Directive Principles of State Policy and International Obligations

The Indian Constitution has laid down the implementation procedure in Parts III and IV. While the former guarantees certain rights to the individual, the latter gives direction to the State to provide economic and social rights to its people in specified matters. They together constitute the conscience of the Constitution. However, the rights guaranteed and provided in the Constitution are required to be in conformity with the International Covenant on Civil and Political Rights and the International Covenant on Economic, Social and Cultural Rights in view of the fact that India has become a party to these Covenants by ratifying them.[10] The Constitution of India lays down clearly the bases on which foreign policy should be framed and respected, [11] Article 51 of Indian Constitution highlights this principle. Article 51 stipulates:

> The State shall endeavour to:
>
> (a) promote international peace and security;
> (b) maintain just and honourable relations between nations;
> (c) foster respect for international law and treaty obligations in the dealings of organised peoples with one another; and
> (d) encourage settlement of international disputes by arbitration.

The key provision to the Directive Principles of State Policy is found in Article 37 which says:

> The provisions contained in this part shall not be enforceable by any Court, but the principles therein laid down are nevertheless fundamental in the governance of the country it shall be the duty of the State to apply these principles in making law.

The reason to make these principles judicially non-enforceable appears to be that the Directive Principles impose positive obligations on the State to secure a new

---

[9] P.N. Bhagwati, "Human Rights in the Criminal Justice System", 27 *Journal of the Indian Law Institute* (1985) 1-22. The major setback to fundamental rights was noticed when emergency was declared on 26 June 1975 on the pretext that the security of India was threatened by "internal disturbances". Once there was a Presidential order under Article 359 suspending the enforcement of fundamental rights to life and liberty guaranteed by Article 21 to a person who is deprived of his liberty by a detention could not approach the Court for redress.

[10] United Nations, Human *Rights International Instruments: Signatures, Ratification, etc.,* 1 July 1982 (New York, 1982) at 52.

[11] P.C. Rao, *The Indian Constitution and International Law* (New Delhi, 1993) at 3.

socio-economic order for the promotion of the welfare of the people of India and that this cannot be achieved here and now. It is clear from Article 12 that the term "the State" for the purpose of Parts III and IV of the Constitution, includes the constituent states of the Union of India. The basic thrust of Article 51 is international peace and security, international relations and international obligations, matters which, under the Indian Constitution, fall exclusively within the domain of the Union.[12]

In reality, Article 51(c) does not deal with the enforcement of implementation of treaties, it only obligates the State to foster respect for "international law and treaty obligations" in inter-state relations. This Article embodies the object of India in the international sphere. It does not lay down that international treaties or agreements entered into by India shall have the force of municipal law without appropriate legislation undertaken under Article 253.

Article 253 provides,

> Notwithstanding anything in the foregoing provisions of this Chapter, Parliament has power to make any law for the whole or any part of the territory of India for implementing any treaty agreement or convention with any other country or countries or any decision made at any international conference, association or other body.

This Article is in conformity with the objectives as declared by Article 51(c), i.e., treaty-making, implementation of treaties. Article 51(c) does not deviate from the well-established principle that every State is bound by the principles of international law.

Technically speaking, obligations arising from treaties are not judicially enforceable in India unless backed by legislation.[13] In other judgments it was highlighted that there was, however, no need to incorporate a treaty into law if its implementation was possible at the administrative level and without legislative endorsement.[14]

The State is directed to promote the welfare of the people by securing social order in which justice, social, economic and political, shall form the institution of

---

[12]Articles 73, 254(2) and 253 and entries 1 and 10 to 21 of the Union list in the Seventh schedule to the Constitution. For details see, Rao, *Ibid.*, 126-78.

[13] *See State of West Bengal vs. Jugal Kishore*, AIR 1969 SC 1171; *State of Gujarat vs. Vora Fiddali*, AIR 1964 SC 1043; *Jolly George Varghese vs. Bank of Cochin*, AIR 1980 SC 470; *Birma vs. State of Rajasthan*, AIR 1951 Raj.129; *C.R.V. Committee, S.L.S.R.C.C.L. vs. Union of India*, AIR 1983, Knt. 85.

[14] *State of Gujarat vs. Voru Fiddali*, AIR 1969 SC 1051; *Maganbhai vs. Union of India*, AIR 1969 SC 783.

national life. The Directive Principles are intended to ensure dignity of human life and the Parliament and State Legislatures are to secure these objectives.

4. Emergency Provisions[15]

A remarkable feature of the Indian Constitution is the way in which the normal, peacetime federation can be adapted to an emergency situation. The Constitution envisages mainly three types of emergencies: (i) emergency arising from a threat to the security of India, (ii) breakdown of constitutional machinery in a State, and (iii) financial emergency.[16]

Article 352(1) of the Indian Constitution[17] empowers the President to make a declaration of emergency by issuing a Proclamation of Emergency.

---

[15] *See* for further reading, H.M. Seervai, *The Emergency, Future Safeguards and the Habeas Corpus Case, a Criticism* (Bombay, 1978); G.O. Koppel, "The Emergency, the Courts and Indian Democracy", 8 *Journal of Indian Law Institute* (1966) 287-337; Charles Henry Alexandrowich, "Personal Liberty and Preventive Detention", 3 *Journal of Indian Law Institute* (1961) 445-53.

[16] Jain, *supra* note 3 at 358-78. [Article 15(1) of the European Convention on Human Rights permits the member States to take measures derogating from their obligations under the Convention in respect of the guaranteed fundamental freedoms; Article 4(1) of the International Covenant on Civil and Political Rights provides ground for suspension during public emergency; Article 27(1) of American Convention on Human Rights, provides suspension of Human Rights in Certain situations.

[17] Part XVIII of Indian Constitution contains emergency provisions from Articles 352 to 360. Articles 352 to 360 deals with emergency provisions:

- i. Art.352 - Proclamation of Emergency arising from threat to the security of India.
- ii. Art.353 - Effect of Proclamation of Emergency
- iii. Art.354 - Application of Provisions relating to distribution of revenues while a Proclamation of Emergency is in operation.
- iv. Art.355 - Duty of the Union to protect States against external aggression and internal disturbance.
- v. Art.356 - Provisions in case of failure of Constitutional machinery in States.
- vi. Art.357 - Exercise of legislative powers under Proclamation issued under Article 356.
- vii. Art.358 - Suspension of provisions of Article 19 during emergency.
- viii. Art.359 - Suspension of the enforcement of the rights conferred by Part III during emergencies.

Article 359A - Application of this Part in State of Punjab was repealed by the Sixty third Amendment Act, 1989, s.3 (w.e.f. 6 January 1990).

- ix. Art.360 - Provisions as to financial emergency.

> If the President is satisfied that a grave emergency exists whereby the security of India or of any part of the territory thereof is threatened, whether by war or external aggression or internal disturbance, he may, by proclamation, make a declaration to that effect.

Before 1978, emergency could be declared because of war, external aggression or internal disturbance. The expression 'internal disturbance' was too vague and broad. The 44th amendment substituted the words 'armed rebellion' for 'internal disturbance'[18] with a view to excluding the possibility of an emergency being proclaimed on the ground of internal disturbance only not involving armed rebellion. This change, effected to prevent recurrence of a 1975-77 type of emergency, has somewhat restricted the scope of what may be called an internal emergency.

A Proclamation issued under Article 352(1) may be varied or revoked by a subsequent proclamation.[19] The 44th Amendment has introduced a clause[20] to the effect that the President shall not issue a proclamation of emergency or a proclamation varying the same, unless the Union Cabinet has taken the decision[21] and that such a proclamation may be issued has been communicated to him in writing. This implies that the decision to issue such a proclamation has to be arrived at collectively by the Cabinet and not by the Prime Minister alone without consulting the Cabinet as happened in 1975 when the President proclaimed emergency on the advice of the Prime Minister and the Cabinet was later presented with a *fait accompli*.

It has so far been the practice to treat the question whether or not the security of India is threatened to be within the subjective satisfaction of the President acting on the advice of the Cabinet. The question was raised several times whether this satisfaction of the President was justiciable. In *Bhut Nath vs. West Bengal*,[22] the Supreme Court, refusing to hold the continuance of the emergency under Article 352 'void', stated that the question is "a political, not justiciable issue and the appeal should be to the polls and not to the Courts". However, to put the matter beyond doubt, the Constitution (38th Amendment) Act, 1975 amended the Constitution by inserting Clause 5 in Article 352 which declared that the "satisfaction" of the President mentioned in Article 352 (1) and (3) "shall be final and conclusive" and "shall not be questioned in any Court on any ground".

---

[18] Substituted by the Constitution (Forty-Fourth Amendment) Act, 1978, S.37, for "internal disturbance" (with effect from 20 June 1979).
[19] Article 352(2). Subs. by the Constitution (Forty-Fourth Amendment) Act, 1978, Sec.37, for Clauses (2), (2A) and (3) (with effect from 20 June 1979).
[20] Article 352(3).
[21] The Council consisting of the Prime Minister and Ministers of Cabinet rank, appointed under Article 75.
[22] AIR 1974 SC 806.

But by the 44th amendment the situation was once again brought back to what had existed before the 38th amendment. Thus, it will be for the Supreme Court or even a High Court to decide whether it will treat the 'satisfaction' of the President to issue a proclamation of emergency, or to vary it or to continue as 'final' and 'non-justiciable' or as subject to judicial review on some grounds.[23]

As a result of the declaration of emergency, the President becomes more powerful and assumes a number of additional powers and functions to those already provided under the Constitution during normal times.[24] The power of the Union Government extends to the giving of direction to the States as to the manner in which the executive power of the State is to be exercised. The financial arrangements between the State and the Union as provided in Articles 268 to 279 may be altered.

During the operation of an emergency, Article 358 suspends the fundamental rights guaranteed by Article 19[25], authorising the State during the period of proclamation of emergency to make laws in derogation of the rights conferred in Article 19 to take executive action under those laws.

Article 358:

(1) While a Proclamation of Emergency declaring that the security of India or any part of the territory thereof is threatened by war or by external aggression is in operation, nothing in Article 19 shall restrict the power of the State as defined in Part III to make any law or to take any executive action which the State would but for the provisions contained in that Part be competent to make or to take,

---

[23] *P.N. Awasti vs. State*, AIR 1976 All.414; *P. Venkataseshamma vs. State* (FB), AIR 1976 A.P. 2; *Shersingh vs. State*, AIR 1976 M.P.87.
[24] K. Rao, *Parliamentary Democracy of India: A Critical Commentary* (Calcutta: 1961).
[25] Article 19(1) guarantees that all citizens have the right:

(a) to freedom of speech and expression;
(b) to assemble peaceably and without arms;
(c) to form associations or unions;
(d) to move freely throughout the territory of India;
(e) to reside and settle in any part of the territory of India;
(f) to practise any profession, or to carry on any occupation, trade or business.

*Ins. by the Constitution (Forty-Second Amendment) Act, 1976, S.52 (with effect from 3 January 1977).
**Subs. by the Constitution (Forty-Fourth Amendment) Act, 1978, S.39 (with effect from 20 June 1979).
+Ins. by the Constitution (Forty-Fourth Amendment) Act, 1978, S.30, S.39 (with effect from 30 June 1979).

but any law so made shall, to the extent of the incompetency, cease to have effect as soon as the Proclamation ceases to operate, except as respects things done or omitted to be done before the law so ceases to have effect:

Provided that [where such proclamation of emergency] is in operation only in part of the territory of India, any such law may be made, or any such executive action may be taken, under this Article in relation to or in any State or Union territory in which or in any part of which the Proclamation of Emergency is not in operation, if and in so far as the security of India or any part of the territory thereof is threatened by activities in or in relation to the part of the territory of India in which the Proclamation of Emergency is in operation.

(2) Nothing in clause (1) shall apply:

(a) to any law which does not contain a recital to the effect that such law is in relation to the Proclamation of emergency in operation when it is made; or

(b) to any executive action taken otherwise than under a law containing such a recital.

Article 359 does not[26] suspend any fundamental rights of its own force, but authorises the President to deprive an individual of his right to approach any Court for the enforcement of any or all of the rights conferred by Part III of the Constitution, except Articles 20 and 21.

Both Articles 358 and 359 (1-A) provides that as soon as the proclamation of emergency ceases to operate, the effect of the suspension vanishes except in respect of things done or omitted to be done during the emergency. It would be wrong to hold that the protection for otherwise invalid laws during an emergency is converted into their validation which derogated the rights conferred under the Constitution. A law inconsistent with the fundamental rights made during the emergency would not be validated, but only its invalidity is suspended.[27] Quite possibly, the chastened, post-emergency Supreme Court of today would not hesitate to be the arbiter of permissibility of such laws, even during an emergency.

---

[26] Article 359(1) where a Proclamation of Emergency is in operation, the President may by order declare that the right to move any Court for the enforcement of such of [the rights conferred by Part III (except Articles 20 and 21)] as may be mentioned in the order and all proceedings pending in any Court for the enforcement of the rights so mentioned shall remain suspended for the period during which the Proclamation is in force or for such shorter period as may be specified in the order.

[27] *Madan Mohan Pathak vs. Union of India*, AIR 1978 SC 803.

5. Emergency and the Writ of Habeas Corpus

The issue relating to the suspension of the writ of *habeas corpus* during the period of emergency declared under Article 352 came up before the Supreme Court in the controversial case *A.D.M. Jabalpur vs. Shivakant Shukla.*[28] In 1975, the President on the advice of the Prime Minister proclaimed emergency under Article 352 on the ground that the security of India was threatened by internal disturbance and also issued an order under Article 359 suspending the right of access to the Courts for the enforcement of fundamental rights enshrined in Articles 14, 21 and 22.[29] The Parliament, thereafter, amended the Maintenance of Internal Security Act, 1971 and conferred extraordinary powers on the government to detain a person without trial. A question arose whether the writ of *habeas corpus* under Article 226 could be issued to release a detenu on the ground that his detention was inconsistent with the provision of the MISA or was *malafide.*

It was contended that the object of the Presidential order under Article 359(a) was to remove fetters on the legislature so that during emergency it was free to make laws even in derogation of the fundamental rights mentioned in the order and that suspension of the right to enforce fundamental rights could not confer any right on the government to flout the law, be it emergency or times of peace. It was further contended that the obligation on the government to act in accordance with law stemmed from the inherent compulsion of the rule of law, and the suspension of Article 21 did not automatically entail the suspension of the rule of law. The inquiry in a *habeas corpus* petition raised the question whether the detention is justified by law, and it was not shut out by the suspension of the right to enforce fundamental rights, otherwise it would necessarily mean that during the emergency no person had any right to life or personal liberty. The Supreme Court, with the dissent of Justice Khanna, legitimised the suspension of the writ of *habeas corpus* during the period of emergency on the basis of higher claims on national security. In other words, the detenu had no *locus standi* to file the writ petition and question the reasons or grounds of detention.

The majority view in the *Shivakant Shukla* case was completely negated by the 44th amendment of the Constitution as well as subsequent judicial interpretation thereof and therefore it is no longer good law.

The ultimate justification for an emergency in a democratic State is to enable it to preserve vital values of a democratic society temporarily endangered on account of unexpected situations of exceptional gravity. Emergency cannot be declared for undermining the basis of democracy. The rule of law is an

---

[28] AIR 1976 SC 1207.

[29] Ved P. Nanda, "From Gandhi to Gandhi: International Legal Response to the Destruction of Human Rights and Fundamental Freedoms in India", 6 *Denver Journal of International Law* (1976) 19-42.

indispensable feature of democracy. In the absence of the rule of law, lawlessness predominates, especially government lawlessness, when there is no authority to question the government's action, no mechanism to control it and no institution to make it accountable and to check its excesses.

6. The Indian Constitution and Due Process of Law

The genesis of due process of law can be traced back to the Indian Constituent Assembly Debates, 1947-49.[30] The first time it reflected was in K.M. Munshi's draft in its chapter on Rights to Freedom which provided:

> No person shall be deprived of his life, liberty or property without due process of law.

The other provision, which in effect elucidated the "due process" clause guaranteed to every person the right to be informed within 24 hours of his deprivation of liberty by what authority and on what grounds the action was taken. It had laid down further that no person would be subjected to prolonged detention preceding trial, to excessive bail or unreasonable refusal of bail, to inhuman or cruel punishment or to denial of adequate safeguards and proper procedure.[31] B.R. Ambedkar not only strongly supported this view in his draft Article, but also included a provision that the State should not deprive any person of life, liberty or property without "due process of law".[32]

The Sub-Committee on Fundamental Rights discussed the subject on 25, 26 and 29 March 1947 and included in its draft two clauses 11 and 29.[33]

> 11. No person shall be deprived of his life, liberty or property without due process of law.
>
> 29. No person shall be subjected to prolonged detention preceding trial, to excessive bail, or unreasonable refusal thereof, or to inhuman or cruel punishment.

[30] K.M. Munshi's draft Article in B. Shiva Rao, *The Framing of Indian Constitution: Select Documents* (vol. II, Bombay: 1969) at 75.
[31] Munshi's draft Articles V(i) and V(4) and Articles XII(3), Rao, *supra* note 30, 4(ii)(b), at 75-79.
[32] Ambedkar's draft Article (11)(2), Rao, *op. cit.,* note 30, 4(ii)(a), at 86.
[33] Minutes and Draft Report of the Sub-Committee, Annexure, Clauses 11 and 29. Select Documents II, 4(iii) and (iv), pp.119-20, 122, 132, 139, 141. The provision regarding the right to be informed of the authority and grounds of deprivation of one's liberty within twenty four-hours was omitted in view of "the due process of law" provision clause 11.

Commenting on the draft report, B.N. Rau, the Constitutional Adviser, pointed out that Clause 11 had been adopted from the Fifth and the 14th amendments of the Constitution of the United States, while Clause 29 was based on the Sixth and the Eighth Amendments of that Constitution.

B.N. Rau reproducing Clause 16 of his Draft Constitution of October 1947, restricted the scope of the expression "liberty" by adding the word "personal" before it. He justified the change on the ground that the word "liberty" by itself might be construed widely unless it was qualified by the word "personal". The change had the approval of the Drafting Committee which accepted it at its meeting on 31 October 1947 despite Munshi's opposition.[34]

Meanwhile, during his visit to the United States of America, B.N. Rau had discussion with Justice Frankfurter of the United States' Supreme Court who was of the opinion that the power of review implied in the "due process" clause was not only undemocratic because it gave a few judges the power of vetoing legislation enacted by the representatives of the nation, but also threw an unfair burden on the judiciary. In fact, this view was communicated by B.N. Rau to the Drafting Committee which introduced a far-reaching change in the clause by replacing the expression "without due process of law" by the expression "except according to procedure established by law". The text of the provision, thus redrafted by the Committee, was incorporated in Article 15 of the Draft Constitution.

> No person shall be deprived of his life or personal liberty except according to procedure established by law nor shall any person be denied equality before the law or the equal protection of the law within the territory of India.[35]

Draft Article 15 evoked a keen controversy regarding the respective merits of the expressions "due process of law" and "procedure established by law" when the issue came up for consideration in the Assembly on 6 December 1948. Almost the entire debate centred on the controversy, with all the speakers including Munshi, favouring the restoration of the expression "due process of law". Syed Karimuddin and Mehboob Ali Beg pointed out that the use of the phrase "procedure established by law" stripped a court of the power to go into the merits and demerits of the grounds on which a person was deprived of his life or liberty; a Court could not look into the injustice of any law since its function would cease the moment it was satisfied that the "procedure established by law" had been complied with.[36]

---

[34] Minutes, also see Draft Constitution, Rao, n.30, Select Documents III, 5 & 6, pp.328, 406, 523.
[35] Rao, *supra* note 30.
[36] C. A. Deb, *Indian Constituent Assembly Debates*, (vol.II, 1949) 843-45.

Thakurdas Bhargava explaining the import of the use of the words "without due process of law" highlighted that if this phrase was used the Courts could go into the question of substantive as well as procedural law; in other words, the Courts would have the right to go into the question whether a particular law enacted by the Parliament was just or not, whether it was good or not, as a matter of fact, it protected the liberties of people; and if the Supreme Court came to the conclusion that any law was constitutional, unreasonable or unjust, such a law would cease to have effect. Z.H. Lari expressed the opinion that the essence of the "due process of law" provision was two-fold. There would first be an enquiry before a man was condemned, and then there would be a judgement after trial. If the words "procedure established by law" were adopted, it would mean that the legislature was all powerful. He said:

> Men as well as assemblies or any mass of people are subject to passing emotions...and if the present state on things, particularly keeping in view the Constitution that we are going to have, namely a parliamentary government, the legislature is controlled by a Cabinet, which means by the executive.[37]

The lone voice in support of "procedure established by law" as against the "due process" provision, Alladi Krishnaswami Ayyar, argued that the verdict of three or five gentlemen sitting as a Court of law on what exactly was "due process" according to them in a particular case could not be regarded as more democratic than the expressed wishes of the legislature or the action of an executive responsible to the legislature. He expressed his fear that the clause "due process of law" might prove to be a great handicap for all social legislation, for the ultimate relationship between the employer and the labourer, for the protection of children and for the protection of women.

The feeling in favour of incorporating in the Constitution "due process of law" even outside the Assembly was so deep that the vote of the Assembly against it evoked a great deal of criticism. It was felt that draft Article 15 gave to Parliament a *carte blanche* to provide for the arrest of any person under any circumstances it deemed fit.[38]

Introducing this Article in the Assembly on 15 September 1949, B.R. Ambedkar observed that they were "making, if I may say so, compensation for what was done in passing Article 15", while it might not satisfy those who believed in the absolute personal freedom of the individual, he claimed, it contained the substance of the law of "due process". The first two clauses of the Article embodied two of the most fundamental principles of justice recognised by every civilised country and which were already contained in the Criminal Procedure

[37] C. A. Deb, *Indian Constituent Assemble Debates*, (vol.VII, 1949) 855-6.
[38] C. A. Deb, *Indian Constituent Assembly Debates*, (vol.IX, 1949) 1496-7.

Code.[39] Ambedkar was satisfied that the draft Article provided adequate protection against arbitrary or illegal arrests, and that the inclusion of further safeguards against inroads by the executive and the legislature upon the personal liberty of the individual, urged by some members, was unnecessary.[40]

The new draft Article 15-A, as amended by the suggestions made or accepted by Ambedkar, was adopted by the Assembly:

Draft Article 15-A

1. No person who is arrested shall be detained in custody without being informed, as soon as may be, of the grounds for such arrest nor shall be denied the grounds for such arrest nor shall be denied the right to consult and be defended by a legal practitioner of his choice.

2. Every person who is arrested and detained in custody shall be produced before the nearest magistrate within a period of twenty-four hours of such arrest excluding the time necessary for the journey from the place of arrest to the Court of the magistrate and no such person shall be detained in country beyond the said period without the authority of a magistrate.

3. Nothing in Clauses (1) and (2) of this Article shall apply:

   a) to any person who for the time being is an enemy alien; or

   b) to any person who is arrested under any law providing for preventive detention;

   Provided that nothing in sub-clause (b) of clause 3) of this Article shall permit the detention of a person for a longer period than three months unless -- a Advisory Board consisting of persons who are or have been or are qualified to be appointed as judges of a high court has reported before the expiration of the said period of such detention; or (3-a) where an order is made in respect of any person under sub-clause (b) of clause (3) of this Article, the authority making an order shall, as soon as may be, made and afford him the earliest

[39] *See* Sections 60, 61, 81 and 167 of the Criminal Procedure Code, 1898. Sections 53, 54 and 167 of Criminal Procedure Code, 1973, which are aimed at affording procedural safeguards to a person arrested by the police.
[40] Deb, *supra* note 38 at 1497-8.

opportunity of making a representation against the order.

(3-b) Nothing in clause (3-a) of this Article shall require the authority making any order sub-clause (b) of clause (3) of this Article to disclose the facts which such authority considers to be against the public interest to disclose.

4. Parliament may by law prescribe the circumstances under which, and the class or classes of cases in which, a person who is arrested under any law providing for preventive detention may be detained for a period longer than three months and also the maximum period for which any such person may be so detained, and Parliament may also prescribed by law the procedure to be followed by an Advisory Board in an enquiry under clause (a) of the proviso to clause (3) of this Article.

In the course of the revision, the Drafting Committee renumbered draft Articles 15 and 15-A as Articles 21 and 22, respectively. The other changes were: (1) the "legal equality" provision which had been coupled with the "Protection of life and liberty" provision in draft Article 15 was separated and transferred under the heading "Right to Equality" as Article 14, the renumbered Article 21 being confined to guaranteeing that no person would be deprived of life and personal liberty (2) the provision to clause (3) of draft Article 15-A was converted into an independent clause (4) in the renumbered Article 22; and (iii) clauses (3-a)(3-b), and (4) were redrafted and renumbered as clauses (5),(6) and (7), respectively. Interestingly, when the text of Article 21 thereafter remained unaltered, that of Article 22 underwent further modifications when the revised Draft Constitution was considered by the Assembly on 14, 15 and 16 November 1949. The provisions of Article 22 was severely criticised and several amendments were moved to it on behalf of the Drafting Committee itself. T.T. Krishnamachari moved two amendments which sought to redraft clauses (4) and (7) so as to indicate clearly that there would be a maximum period laid down by the Parliament for which any person or any class or classes of persons could be detained by any law providing for such detention. Even in cases where the Advisory Board approved of detention beyond three months, no authority in India could in any circumstances order the detention of a person beyond the maximum limit so laid down by the Parliament.[41]

Drafting Committee's amendment as moved by Krishnamachari were adopted and Article 22 of the Constitution assumed its present form.[42] The two Articles as adopted read:

[41] Indian Constituent Assembly Debates, (vol.XI, 1949) 466-67 and 531-32.
[42] *Ibid* at 575-6, and 600.

Article 21

No one shall be deprived of his life or personal liberty except according to procedure established by law.

Article 22

1. No person who is arrested shall be detained in custody without being informed, as soon as may be, of the grounds for such arrest nor shall be denied the right to consult, and to be defended by, a legal practitioner of his choice.

2. Every person who is arrested and detained in custody shall be produced before the nearest magistrate, within a period of twenty-four hours of such arrest excluding the time, necessary for the journey from the place of arrest to the Court of the magistrate and no such person shall be detained in custody beyond the said period without the authority of a magistrate.

3. Nothing in clauses (1) and (2) shall apply

   (a) to any person who for the time being is an enemy alien; or

   (b) to any person who is arrested or detained under any law providing for preventive detention.

4. No law providing for preventive detention shall authorise the detention of a person for a longer period than three months unless:

   (a) An Advisory Board consisting of persons who are, or have been, or one qualified to be appointed as, judges of a High Court has reported before the expiration of the said period of three months that there is in its opinion sufficient cause for such detention: provided that nothing in this sub-clause shall authorise the detention of any person beyond the maximum period prescribed by any law made by Parliament under sub-clauses (a) and (b) of clause (7).

5. When any person is detained in pursuance of an order made under any law providing for preventive detention, the authority making the order shall, as soon as may be, communicate to such person the

grounds on which the order has been made and shall afford him the earliest opportunity of making a representation against the order.

6. Nothing in clause 5 shall require the authority making any such order as is referred to in that clause to disclose facts such authority considers to be against the public interest to disclose.

7. Parliament may by law describe

a. The circumstances under which, and the class or classes of cases in which, a person may be detained for a period longer than three months under any law providing for preventive detention without obtaining the opinion of an Advisory Board in accordance with the provisions of sub-clause (a) clause (4);

b. the maximum period for which any person may in class or classes of cases be detained under any law providing for preventive detention; and

c. to procedure to be followed by an Advisory Board in an inquiry under sub-clause (a) of clause (4)

A substantial number of the framers of the Indian Constitution were in favour of keeping a "due process of law" provision under the Indian Constitution, although this phrase was replaced by "procedure established by law".[43]

It was not until 1978 that the Supreme Court infused life into Article 21 by subjecting state action interfering with life or liberty to a test of reasonableness; requiring not only that procedures be authorised by law that they are "right, just and fair"[44] and not arbitrary, fanciful or oppressive. The Court has also expanded horizons of procedure established by law which bears its testimony in the *Hussainara Khatoon*[45] case. The post-emergency Supreme Court was indeed a different incarnation. Having learnt the bitter lessons of emergency, it had its lost prestige to retrieve, it had to redefine its Constitutional role. From now on there would be no difference between "due process of law" and "procedure established by law".

[43] This provision is similar to Article 31 of Japanese Constitution.

[44] *Maneka Gandhi vs. Union of India*, *supra* note 8.

[45] *Hussainara Khatoon vs. State of Bihar*, AIR 1979 SC 1360. [In this case a writ of *habeas corpus* was filed before the Supreme Court of India for the release of undertrials subjected to prolonged detention in prison. These undertrials included men, women and children and some of them were behind bars for periods ranging from three to ten years without trial having been commenced so far].

7. Implementation Mechanism at National Level

The fundamental rights enumerated in Part III of the Constitution would remain ineffective if there were no strict implementation mechanism. The framers of the Indian Constitution were fully aware that the supreme importance of judicial remedies to enforce fundamental rights was evident from the fact that not only did they expressly lay down that any law which contravened any of the fundamental rights should be "void", but they also incorporated in the Constitution itself certain extraordinary remedies for enforcing these rights against any deviant State action, legislative or executive. Further, the right to make use of these constitutional remedies is itself made a fundamental right guaranteed by the Constitution, so that nothing short of an amendment of the Constitution can take away the power of the superior courts, that is, the Supreme Court and the State High Courts, to apply these constitutional remedies for the protection of individual rights guaranteed by the Constitution. The Courts have made it clear that they cannot refuse to entertain an application for an appropriate constitutional remedy where a fundamental right has been infringed. Indeed, it is doubtful if powers of the High Courts and the Supreme Court can be abridged even by a Constitutional amendment.[46]

8. Justiciability of Fundamental Rights

The justiciability of fundamental rights is itself guaranteed under Article 32 which provides:

> 1. The right to move the Supreme Court by appropriate proceedings for the enforcement of the rights conferred by this part is guaranteed.
>
> 2. The Supreme Court shall have power to issue directions or orders or writs, including writs in the nature of *habeas corpus*, *mandamus*, *prohibition*, *quo warranto* and c*ertiorari*, whichever may be appropriate for the enforcement of any of the rights conferred by this part.
>
> 3. Without prejudice to the powers conferred on the Supreme Court by clauses (1) and (2), Parliament may by law empower any other Court to exercise within the local limits of its jurisdiction all or any of the powers exercisable by the Supreme Court under Clause (2).
>
> 4. The right guaranteed by this Article shall not be suspended except as otherwise provided for by this Constitution.

---

[46] Bhagwati, *supra* note 9, at 1-22.

Article 32 has been described as "the Cornerstone of the democratic edifice",[47] as "the protector and guarantor of fundamental rights",[48] or as the "*qui vive*".[49] In one of the judgments, the Supreme Court held that it is the duty of the Courts to guard the remedial fundamental rights and to protect it "zealously and vigilantly".[50] The High Courts have the power under Article 226 that the fundamental rights can be enforced by moving the High Courts. Indeed, the High Courts' powers are broader than those of the Supreme Court. The responsibility for the enforcement of the fundamental rights lies on the Supreme Court by virtue of Article 32. It is often alleged that this would involve the Court in making decisions on policy,[51] which in reality is a matter to be left to the legislature, and that this would contravene the constitutional framework for the separation of powers. The general principle is that any person whose fundamental right is violated can seek remedy under Article 32 of the Constitution. The violation of a fundamental right of the petitioner is the condition precedent for moving the Court under Article 32.[52] To be actionable, it is not necessary for actual infringement of the fundamental right, a petition can be moved even if there is an imminent danger of infraction of a fundamental right.[53] It appears from the above discussion that the primary duty of the Supreme Court is to set right the violation of the fundamental right of concerned individual. Secondly, it would have to ensure that the State is compelled to observe the law, in view of interpreting its duty under Article 32 and that it has always attempted to redress substantive violations of the rights rather than refuse relief on the basis of technicalities.

[47] *Prem Chand vs. Excise Commissioner*, AIR 1963 SC 996; "the fundamental rights guaranteed by Part III which have been made justiciable, form the most outstanding and distinguishing feature of the Indian Constitution" (Para 2), at 998.

[48] *Romesh Thapar vs. State of Madras*, AIR 1950 SC 124 at 126.

[49] *State of Madras vs. V.G. Row*, AIR 1952 SC 96.

[50] *Daryao vs. State of U.P.*, AIR 1961 SC 1457 at 1461.

[51] AIR 1984 SC 802 at p.812; see also W.E. Dellinger, "Of Rights and Remedies: The Constitution as a Sword", 85 *Harvard Law Review* (1971) at 1532.

[52] *Romeshwar Prasad vs. Commrs., LRsJ*, AIR 1959 SC 498. "It is well settled that no petition under Article 32 is maintainable, unless it is shown that the petitioner has some fundamental rights. The fundamental right claimed in these case is that the property which the State of Madhya Pradesh Bharat (now Madhya Pradesh) is not permitting the petitioners to remove from the forests is property which they have right to hold and dispose off. This could only be so if the property in the trees or the charcoal or katha which have been manufactured passed to the petitioners. No such property, however, passed to the petitioners. In the circumstances they have no right to hold and dispose petitioners. In the circumstances they have no right to hold and dispose of their property, in the absence of any law authorising the state to deprive them of it" (K.M. Wanchoo) para 15; *Haji Ismail vs. Competent officers*, AIR 1967 SC 1244; *Kuriakose vs. State of Kerala*, AIR 1977-SC 1509.

[53] *Hans Muller vs. Supdt. Presidency Jail*, AIR 1955 SC 367.

8.1. The Writs

An important aspect of the Indian Constitution is the jurisdiction it confers on the Supreme Court and the High Courts to issue writs. Under Article 32 the Supreme Court and under Article 226, the High Courts have power to issue orders, directions or writs including writs in the nature of *habeas corpus*, *mandamus*, prohibition, *certiorari* and *quo warranto* for the enforcement of the fundamental rights. For the High Courts this power is available for "any purpose", including the enforcement of any other legal rights as well. These writs are indeed a contribution of British Constitutional jurisprudence.[54]

8.1.1. *Habeas Corpus*

The fundamental right to personal liberty is meaningless if there does not exist the writ of *habeas corpus*.[55] The writ of *habeas corpus* is used to secure the release of a person who has been detained unlawfully or without legal justification.[56] The writ of *habeas sub jiciendum* as it was originally named, has proved to be a very effective legal remedy to secure personal liberty, it enables an immediate determination of a person's right to freedom.[57] In India, detention may be unlawful if, *inter alia*, it is not in accordance with law,[58] or the procedure established by law has not been

---

[54] Seervai, *op. cit.,* note 3; V.G. Ramacharan, *Fundamental Rights and Constitutional Remedies: Law of Writs* (Lucknow: 1963).

[55] See also, Luis Kutner, "World Habeas Corpus, Human Rights and World Community", 17 *De Paul law Review*, 3-37 (1967).

[56] The writs have been among the great safeguards provided by the British judicial system for upholding the rights and liberties of the people and it was an act of great wisdom and foresight on the part of the Constitution-makers to introduce the writ system in India. In the Pre-Constitution era, only the High Courts of Calcutta, Madras and Bombay enjoyed the jurisdiction to issue writs.

[57] *Ranjit vs. Pepsu*, AIR 1959, SC 893.

[58] *Bihar vs. Kameshwar Prasad*, AIR 1965 SC 575. In this case a convict Bipat Gope sentenced to imprisonment was released from custody on grounds of ill-health but was subsequently rearrested and detained in jail. On an application under Article 226 for a writ of *habeas corpus*, the state did not file any return showing the provisions under which the convict was released or rearrested.

In this connection the observations of Lord Atkin in *Eshugbal Eleko vs. Administering Govt. of Nigeria*, 1931 AC 661 at p.670: (AIR 1931 PC 298) are appropriate as observed by Subba Rao, J.:

> In accordance with British jurisprudence no member of the executive can interfere with the liberty or property of a British subject except on the condition that he can support the legality of his action before a court of justice. And it is the tradition of British justice that judges should not shrink from deciding such issues in the face of the executive.

It is the same jurisprudence which was adopted in this country on the basis of which the Courts of this country exercise jurisdiction. It has not been shown in this case

followed in detaining a person,[59] or there is no valid law to authorise detention or the law is invalid because it infringes a fundamental right, or the legislature enacting it exceeds its limits.

The purpose of the *habeas corpus* is to secure the release of a detenu from unlawful detention and not to punish the detainee.[60] The detention should not contravene the provisions of Article 22, which says, if a person is not produced before a magistrate within 24 hours of his detention he is entitled to be released.[61] The power of detention vested in an authority if exceeded, abused or exercised malafide makes the detention unlawful.[62] The efficacy of the *habeas corpus* depends, to a large extent, on the operative part of the law under which the curtailment of an individual's liberty is authorised, as for example, the Preventive Detention Act, which has given rise to numerous cases on this writ, authorises detention in the subjective satisfaction of administrative officers and the scope left for judicial review is thus very limited.[63]

---

that there was any lawful authority under which Bipat Gope was rearrested and in the absence of such lawful authority Bipat Gope's detention cannot be supported and is illegal. In the circumstances the remedy under Article 226 is rightly applicable to the facts of this case.

[59]*Makhan Singh vs. Punjab*, AIR 1964 SC 387, *Biren Dutta vs. Chief Com of Tripura*, AIR 1965 SC 596.

[60]*Kedarnath vs. State of Punjab*, AIR 1960 Punjab 122. The Court observed that writ of *habeas corpus* was meant to determine the legality or illegality of the detention and not for punishing the detainee.

[61]In *Gunapati vs. Nafisul Hassan* (AIR 1954 SC 636). In this case a person was arrested in Bombay and taken to Lucknow in custody to be produced before the speaker of the U.P. Legislative Assembly to answer a charge of breach of privilege. The arrest was made on a warrant issued by the Speaker. He remained in the speaker's custody at Lucknow and was not produced before a magistrate within twenty-four hours of his arrest. The court held that this was a clear breach of the peremptory provisions of Article 22(2) and hence the petitioner was released.

[62]*Jagannath Misra vs. State of Orissa*, AIR 1966 SC 1140; *Ram Manohar Lohia vs. State of Bihar*, AIR 1966 SC 746; *Inder Singh vs. State of Punjab*, AIR 1995 SC 312; *Sanju vs. Shobanath* AIR 1995 SC 922.

[63]*Ram Bali vs. State of West Bengal* AIR 1975 SC 623, "on a *habeas corpus* petition, what has to be considered by the Court is whether the detention is *prima facie* legal or not, whether the detaining authorities have wrongly or rightly reached on every satisfaction of the Court. Courts have no doubt to zealously guard the personal liberty of the citizen and to ensure that the case of detenu is justly and impartially considered".

8.1.2. Mandamus

Mandamus is a command issued by a court asking a public authority to perform a public duty belonging to its office[64]. For example, when a tribunal omits to decide a matter which it is bound to decide, it can be commanded to determine the question which it has left undecided.[65] Mandamus can be granted only when a legal duty is imposed on the authority in question and the petitioner has a legal right to compel the performance of his duty.[66]

A mandamus also lies where the discretion is exercised on irrelevant or extraneous considerations or where the exercise of discretion is delegated to someone else or where its exercise is improperly declined.[67] But where the discretion has not been exercised in good faith the Court would not intervene; it is not the function of the Court to substitute their wisdom and discretion for that of the persons to whose judgement the matter is entrusted by the law.[68]

8.1.3. *Certiorari*

The writ of *certiorari* is issued to a body acting in a judicial or quasi-judicial manner and not to one which acts in a purely administrative manner.[69] In the modern law c*ertiorari* goes to a quasi-judicial body when it violates the principles of natural justice[70] when it assumes jurisdiction which it does not possess or where the order passed by it contains an error of law apparent on the face of record. *Certiorari* would be available against administrative bodies, not having any quasi-judicial obligation, if they affect rights of individuals without conforming to the principles of "fair play".[71]

In *T.C. Bassapa vs. T. Nagappa*, the Court observed:

---

[64] *Mysore vs. Chandrasekhara*, AIR 1965 SC 532; *NHRC vs. State of Arunachal Pradesh* AIR 1996 SC 2351; *N.S. Ziyauddin Ahmed vs. Union of India*, AIR 1995 Mad 129; *K. Vaithianathan vs. Union Territory of Pondicherry*, AIR 1995 Mad.197.

[65] *Parry & Co., vs. Commercial Employees Ass.,* AIR 1952 SC 179; *Bhopal Sugar Industries vs. Income Tax Officer*, AIR 1961 SC 182.

[66] *Madhya Pradesh vs. Mandavar*, AIR 1954 SC 493; *Sohan Lal vs. India*, AIR 1957 SC 529; *K.V. Rajyalakshmi Setty vs. Mysore*, AIR 1967 SC 993.

[67] *T.G. Goakar vs. R.N. Shukla*, AIR 1968 SC 1050; *Bombay Union of Journalists vs. State of Bombay*, AIR 1964 SC 1617.

[68] *Vice-Chancellor Utkal University vs. S.K. Ghosh*, 1954 SCR 883; *Prabodh vs. State of U.P.,* AIR 1985 SC 167; *NHRC vs. State of Arunachal Pradesh*, AIR 1996 SC 1235.

[69] Yadley, "The Grounds for Certiorari and Prohibition", 37 *Canadian Bar Review*, 294-307 (1959).

[70] *T.C. Basappa vs. T. Mayappa*, AIR 1954 SC 440.

[71] *Union of India vs. Nambudri* (1991), 2 UJSC, 302.

> One of the fundamental principles in regard to the issuing of a writ of certiorari, is that writ can be availed of only to remove or adjudicate on the validity of judicial acts. The expression "judicial acts" includes the exercise of quasi-judicial functions by administrative bodies or other authorities or persons obliged to exercise such functions and used in contrast with what are purely ministerial acts. The second essential feature of a writ of certiorari is that the control which is exercised through it over judicial or quasi-judicial tribunals or bodies is not in appellate but supervisory capacity. In granting a writ of certiorari the superior court does review or reweigh the evidence upon which the determination of the inferior tribunal purports to be based. It demolishes the order which it considers to be without jurisdiction or palpably erroneous but does not substitute its own views for those of inferior tribunal.[72]

It is already established that these writs recline to control the administrative act also if there is a duty on the person or authority acting administratively to act fairly. The landmark English decisions propounded this view, are *Ridge vs. Baldwin*[73] and in re H.K.,[74] and the leading Indian decisions are *A.K. Kraipak vs. Union of India*[75] and *Maneka Gandhi vs. Union of India.*[76]

8.1.4. Prohibition

The writ of prohibition is issued to prevent a court or quasi-judicial tribunal from exceeding its jurisdiction,[77] or acting contrary to natural justice. The object of prohibition is prevention rather than cure. It differs from *certiorari* not so much in its nature as in the fact that it is issuable at a stage when the matter is being proceeded with and has not yet been disposed of. After disposal of the matter, the proper writ is *certiorari* for it is the decision to be quashed. Prohibition is issued only if there are proceedings pending in a Court or a quasi-judicial body. Prohibition restrains the adjudicatory body concerned from proceeding further in excess of jurisdiction or against natural justice.

8.1.5. *Quo Warranto*

Quo warranto is a discretionary remedy which the Court may grant or refuse according to the facts and circumstances of each case. The Court may refuse it

---

[72] Yadle, *supra* note 69 at 440.
[73] (1963) 2WLR 935.
[74] (1967) 2KB 617.
[75] AIR 1970 SC 150.
[76] AIR 1978 SC 12.
[77] *East India Comm. vs. Collector of Customs*, AIR 1962 SC 1893.

where the application was actuated by ill-will or malice, or ulterior motive.[78] The Constitution of India retains the writ of *quo warranto* under Articles 32 and 226.

These are five writs available under Article 226; the most effective writ among all these available writs is *habeas corpus*, which is directly related with personal liberty.

8.2. Access of Public Interest Litigation

Access to justice is one of the most basic human rights and without its realisation many of the human rights may stay merely on paper. The Indian judiciary has tried to bring law into the service of the poor and oppressed. The Courts have widened their jurisdiction for enforcement of fundamental human rights under Public Interest Litigation (PIL).[79] Unlike the case of PIL, in the United States, the PIL movement in India has been almost entirely initiated and led by the judiciary.

In India, PIL is channelled through basically two ways. First, if the complaint is of a 'legal wrong' the appropriate forum is the High Court of the State under Article 226 of the Constitution. Second, if a fundamental right is alleged to have been violated the remedy may be sought from the High Court or directly from the Supreme Court.[80]

The Supreme Court has thrown its doors open by broadening the doctrine of *locus standi* and making it possible for the problems of the poor to be brought

[78] *Mukhtiar Singh vs. State of Punjab*, AIR 1991, P&H 20; *Satish Chandra vs. Rajasthan University,* AIR 1970 Raj 186 (para 12).
[79] Moin Qazi, "Social Action Litigation: Reality or Mirage of Justice", 4 *Lex et Juris* 26-27 (1989); Beena Choudhary, "Public Interest litigation and *locus standi*", 28 *Civil and Military Law Journal*, 236-43 (1992); P.N. Bhagwati, "Judicial Activism and Public Interest Litigation", 23 *Columbia Journal of Transnational Law*, 561-77 (1985); S.K. Agarwal, *Public Interest Litigation in India* (Indian Law Institute Publications, New Delhi: 1986); N.R. Madhav Menon, "Public Interest Litigation: A Major Breakthrough in the Delivery of Social Justice", 5 *Journal of Bar Council of India*, 15-58 (1982); Clark D. Cunningham, "Public Interest Litigation in Indian Supreme Court: A Study in the Light of American Experience", 30 *Journal of the Indian Law Institute*, 19-44 (1988); Jamie Cassels, "Judicial Activism and Public Interest Litigation in India: Attempting the Impossible?", 37 *American Journal of Comparative Law*, 495-519 (1989); Rajeev Dhavan, (ed.), *Judges and Judicial Power: Essays in Honour of Justice V.R. Krishna Iyer* (London: Sweet & Maxwell Ltd., 1995). S.K. Aggarwal, *Public Interest Litigation in India: A Critique* (Bombay, 1985); Rajeev Dhavan, "Law as Struggle: Public Interest Law in India", 36 *Journal of Indian Law Institute*, 302-38 (1994); Mani, *op. cit.,* note 2, at 51-54.
[80] Article 32(1), "The right to move the Supreme Court by appropriate proceedings for the enforcement of the rights guaranteed by this part is guaranteed".

before the Courts. The Indian Supreme Court in *Maharaj Singh vs. Uttar Pradesh*[81] has discussed *locus standi*. Following this case the Indian approach to PIL has extended the rules of standing to the point that they may be said to have ceased to present any real obstacle to the PIL so long as it does not amount to the abuse of process of the Court. PIL has been initiated by individuals on behalf of other individuals and groups, by academicians, journalists and by many social action organisations.[82]

The Supreme Court has in the *Judges Appointment and Transfer case*[83] said that though the ordinary rule of Anglo-Saxon jurisprudence is that an action can be brought only by a person to whom legal injury has been caused. This rule can and must be departed from having regard to the massive poverty and ignorance of the people and where legal injury is caused to a person or class of persons, who by reason of poverty or disability or socially or economically disadvantaged position cannot approach the Courts for judicial redress. In such a situation, any member of the public or social action group, acting bonafide, can maintain an application in the High Court under Article 226 and in the Supreme Court under Article 32 seeking judicial redress for the legal injury caused to such person or class of persons. And in such a case, the Courts will not insist on a regular writ petition to be filed by the public spirited individual or social action group espousing their cause and readily respond on a letter addressed by an individual or social action group.[84]

The public interest litigation has already covered wide areas combating inhuman prison conditions,[85] and the horrors of bonded labour.[86] Public interest has also now established the right to a speedy trial,[87] the right to free legal aid,[88] the

[81] AIR 1976 SC 2609. Justice Krishna Iyer observed, "Where a wrong against community interest is done, "no *locus standi*" will always be a plea to non-suit an interested body chasing the wrong doer in Court ... *locus standi* has a larger ambit in current legal semantics than the accepted individualistic jurisprudence of the old' (para 21).

[82] Cassels, *op. cit.,* note 79, at 495.

[83] *S.P. Gupta vs. Union of India*, AIR 1982 SC 149.

[84] For an examination of the areas see, Dhavan, *op. cit.,* note 79, at 307; Mani, *op. cit.,* note 2, at 53.

[85] *Sunil Batra vs. Delhi Administration*, AIR 1978 SC 1675; *Upendra Baxi vs. State of Uttar Pradesh* (1983) SCC 2, p.308.

[86] *People's Union for Democratic Rights vs. Union of India*, AIR 1982 SC 1473; Bandhua Mukti *Morcha vs. Union of India*, AIR 1984 SC 802.

[87] *M.H. Hoskot vs. State of Maharashtra*, AIR 1978 SC 1548; *Hussainara Khatoon vs. Home Secretary, State of Bihar*, AIR 1979 SC 1360.

[88] *Suk Das vs. Union Territory of Arunachal Pradesh*, 1986 SCE, 401; *Sheela Barse vs. Union of India*, AIR 1983 SC 378.

right to livelihood,[89] rights against pollution,[90] a right to be protected from individual hazards,[91] right to human dignity,[92] reforming hospital or jails.[93]

There are numerous cases which deal with procedural aspects and basic approach,[94] *locus standi*[95] and mode of entertaining.[96] The widening of the rule of *locus standi* and creation of epistolary jurisdiction[97] have opened a new vista of a totally different kind of litigation for enforcing basic human rights of the poor and deprived sections of the community and basic human dignity.

The development of PIL has strengthened the human rights cases implementation. The Supreme Court has made the following significant observation in the *Peoples Union for Democratic Rights vs. Union of India:*[98]

> Public Interest Litigation which is a strategic arm of the legal aid movement and which is intended to bring justice within the reach of the poor masses, who constitute the low visibility area of humanity, is a totally different kind of litigation from the ordinary traditional litigation which is essentially of an adversary character where there is a dispute between two, one making claim

---

[89] *Olga Tellies vs. Bombay Municipal Corporation*, AIR 1986 SC 180.

[90] Rural Litigation and Entitlement, *Kendera Dehradun vs. State of Uttar Pradesh*, AIR 1985 SC 652.

[91] *M.C. Mehta vs. Union of India*, AIR 1987 SC 982; *Ratlam Municipality vs. Vardichand*, AIR 1980 SC 1622.

[92] *Francis Coralie Mullin vs. Administrator, Union Territory of Delhi*, AIR 1981 SC 746; *Upendra Baxi vs. State of Uttar Pradesh* (1986), 4 SCC 106.

[93] *Rakesh vs. State of Bihar* (1991), Supp (2), SCC 626; *Mathur vs. State of U.P.* (1993), Supp (1) SCC 722.

[94] Gupta *op. cit.,* note 82, at 149.

[95] *D.C. Wadhwa vs. State of Bihar*, AIR 1987 SC 579; *Fertiliser Corporation of India vs. Union of India*, AIR 1981 SC 344; *V. Satyam Reddy vs. Union of India*, AIR 1996 A.P.175.

[96] *State of H.P. vs. Parent*, AIR 1985 SC 910; *Shivajirao vs. Mahesh*, AIR 1985 SC 194.

[97] The Supreme Court of India also felt that when any member of a public or social organisation espoused the cause of the poor, he should be able to move the Court by just writing a letter, because it would not be fair to expect a person acting *pro bono publico* to incur expenses from his own pocket in order to go to a lawyer and prepare a regular petition to be filed in Court for endorsement of the fundamental rights of the poor. In such a case, a letter addressed by him to the Court can legitimately be regarded as an appropriate proceeding within the meaning of Article 32 of the Constitution. The Supreme Court thus evolved what has come to be known as "epistolary jurisdiction", where the Court can be moved by just addressing a letter on behalf of the disadvantaged class of persons. Epistolary jurisdiction was a major breakthrough achieved by the Supreme Court in bringing justice closer to the large masses of people.

[98] AIR 1982 SC 1473.

or seeking relief against the other and that other opposing such claim or resisting such relief.[99]

Public Interest Litigation is brought before the Court not for the purpose of exercising the right of one individual as against another as happens in the case of ordinary litigation, but it is intended to promote and vindicate public interest which demands that violations of the constitutional or legal rights of a large number of people who are poor, ignorant or in a socially or economically disadvantaged position should not go unnoticed and unredressed.

9. Preventive Detention[100]

The Supreme Court has occasion to deal with the (a) the nature of preventive detention under the Indian Constitution, (b) no-justiciability of nature of executive satisfaction, (c) the requirement of application of mind by the detaining authority, (d) relevance of the grounds for detention, and (e) safeguards of detenu.

There is no authoritative definition of the term "Preventive Detention" in Indian law. According to Lord Finlay, "it is not a punitive but a precautionary measure."[101] Lord Macmillan observed in *Liversridge vs. Anderson* that the object is not to punish a man for having done something but to intercept him before he does it and to prevent him from doing it. No offence is proved, nor any charge formulated; and the justification of such detention is suspicion or reasonable probability and not criminal conviction which can only be warranted by legal evidence.[102]

---

[99] *Ibid.*

[100] C.M. Jariwala, "Public order under prevention detention: The judicial and legislative responses", 6 *Indian Bar Review*, 168-69 (1989); K. Narayana Rao, *Right to Compensation for unlawful detention in India* (vol. 26, 1986) at 516-8; C.M. Jariwala, "Justice Bhagwati and Personal liberty", 16 *The Banaras Law Journal*, 51-81 (1980); K.D. Gaur, "Personal Liberty and National Emergency: A Critical Appraisal", 4 *Kurukshetra University Law Journal* 116, 18-34 (1978); S.V. Pulla Reddy, "Preventive Detention and National Security: The Scope for Judicial Scrutiny", 9 *Cochin University Law Review*, 473-81(1985); Satvinder Mohan Mehta, "Preventive Detention Laws, Their Enforcement and the Judiciary *vis-à-vis* Personal liberty", 4 *Kurukshetra University Law Journal* 116, 116-30 (1978); Chandra Pal, "Personal Liberty and Preventive Detention", 4 *Kurukshetra University Law Journal* 116, 143-52 (1978).

[101] *Rex vs. Halliday*, 1917, A.C. 260.

[102] C.M. Jariwala, "Justice Bhagwati and Personal Liberty", 16 *Banaras Law Journal*, 55-75 (1980).

Preventive detention[103] has received constitutional recognition under Article 22,[104] Clauses 4 to 7 under Part III of the Indian Constitution. The first enactment

---

[103] The term finds mention in entry 9 of List I which empowers the central legislature to pass law with regard to preventive detention. It also appears in entry 3 of list III under schedule VII which empowers both the central and the state legislatures to make laws on preventive detention.

[104] Article 22(4) to (7) stipulates:

> (4) No law providing for preventive detention shall authorise the detention of a person for a longer period than three months unless:
>
> (a) An Advisory Board consisting of persons who are, or have been, or are have qualified to be appointed as Judges of a High Court has reported before the expiration of the said period of three months that there is in its opinion sufficient cause for such detention:
>
> Provided that nothing in this sub-clause shall authorise the detention beyond the maximum period prescribed by any law made by Parliament under sub-clause (b) of clause (7); or
>
> (b) such person is detained in accordance with the provisions of any law made by Parliament under sub-clauses (a) and (b) of clause (7).
>
> (5) When any person is detained in pursuance of an order made under any law providing for preventive detention, the authority making the order shall, as soon as may be, communicate to such person the grounds on which the order has been made and shall afford him the earliest opportunity of making a representation against the order.
>
> (6) Nothing in clause (5) shall require the authority making any such order as is referred to in that clause to disclose facts which such authority considers to be against the public interest to disclose.
>
> (7) Parliament may by law prescribe:
>
> (a) the circumstances under which, and the class of case in which, a person may be detained for a period longer than three months under any law providing for preventive detention without obtaining the opinion of an Advisory Board in accordance with the provisions of sub-clause (1) of clause (4);
>
> (b) the maximum period for which any person may in class or classes of cases be detained under any law providing detention; and

on the subject was the Preventive Detention Act, passed by the Indian Parliament in 1950. The Act was not meant to punish a man for having done something but to prevent him before he does it. The peculiarity of the provisions of the preventive detention law under the Indian Constitution is that it is not limited to times of emergency, but it is recognised even during normal times.

The first case under the Preventive Detention Act 1950 was *A.K. Gopalan vs. State of Madras.*[105] The petitioner prayed for the issue of a writ of *habeas corpus* on the ground that the detention order was illegal and void. The Preventive Detention Act takes away or abridges the rights of an individual guaranteed under Part III of the Constitution in general, and under Articles 21, 22 and 19(1)(a) in particular.

A Special Constitution Bench of the Supreme Court dismissed the petition by a majority of four to two. The Court declared that the Preventive Detention Act, 1950, was valid, and upheld the detention. In spite of this, the Court criticised the inclusion of preventive detention in the Chapter on fundamental rights as a peacetime legislation which did not exist in any free and democratic Constitution. In *Ram Singh vs. State of Delhi*[106] again this rationale was applied by the Supreme Court.

In *State of Bombay vs. Atma Ram,*[107] it was held by a majority of judges that the subjective satisfaction of the government was not subject to an objective test in a Court of Law. Hence, it was made a non-justiciable issue. The Court observed that it was true that the interpretation was moulded by laying down a distinction between vague grounds and irrelevant grounds. The Court rejected the contention of the petitioner based on the vagueness of the grounds.

(c) the procedure to be followed by an Advisory Board in an inquiry under sub-clause(a) of clause (4).

105 AIR 1950 SC 27. [The case arose from a petition filed by Gopalan under Article 32(1) of the Constitution of India for a writ of *habeas corpus* against his detention in a Madras Jail. While he was under detention under one of the orders of the Madras State Government, on 1st March 1950 he was served with an order made under S.3(1), L, Preventive Detention Act (IV) 4 of 1950. He challenged the legality of the order as he contended that Act (IV) 4 of 1950 contravenes the provisions of Articles 13, 19 and 21 and the provisions of the Act were not in accordance with Article 22 of the Constitution.

106 AIR 1951 SC 270 [In this case a man was detained under the Preventive Detention Act for making allegedly prejudicial speeches, detenu was unable to challenge his detention on the grounds of a violation of his rights under Article 19(1) (g) because the legislation did not attempt directly to control citizen's freedom of speech.

107 AIR 1951 SC 187.

In *Rameshwar Shah vs. District Magistrate, Burdwan*[108], the Court stipulated that as an abstract proposition of law, it may be said that a detaining authority had power to pass a detention order against a person who is already in detention or in jail; but in every case, the detaining authority had to apply its mind to the question whether a detention order was necessary. In *Bitu Mahato vs. District Magistrate, Dhanbad*[109], the detaining authority had passed a detention order against a person already in jail, but the detaining authority was not aware of the fact. In this case, Justice Desai, observed:

> [T]he detention order must show on the face of it that the detaining authority was aware of the situation. Otherwise detention order will suffer from the vice of non-application of mind. The awareness must be of the fact that person against whom the detention order is made is already under detention or in jail in respect of some offence.

It is necessary that the authority who is detaining a person must apply its mind. The satisfaction may be subjective or objective.[110]

10. Relevancy of grounds of Preventive Detention

The ground of detention must be relevant to the order of detention. In *Gora vs. State of West Bengal*[111] the ground of detention referred to only one incident which narrated that the petitioner along with other associates armed with lethal weapons, including fire arms, raided the house of one 'A' and looted cash, ornaments etc. It was further contended that the action of the petitioner created such a panic in the locality that the local people felt a sense of insecurity and thus he acted in a manner prejudicial to the maintenance of public order. Justice Bhagwati observed that there was clearly a disturbance of public order by the appellant, and thus upheld the detention.

11. Other Safeguards

One of the important safeguards under Article 22(5) is that the authority passing the order of detention must afford the detenu the earliest opportunity of making a representation against the order of detention. Justice Bhagwati insisted that opportunity should be "comprehensive and effective".[112] In another case *John*

---

108 AIR 1964 SC 334.

109 AIR 1984 SC 104.

110 *Binod Bihari vs. State of Bihar*, AIR 1974 SC 2125; *State of Orissa vs. Manilal Singhania*, AIR 1976 SC 456; *Kishori Mohan vs. State of West Bengal*, AIR 1972 SC 1949; *Akshoy Konai vs. State of West Bengal*, AIR 1973 SC 300.

111 AIR 1975 SC 473; *Gandhi Sardar vs. Union of India*, AIR 1975 SC 755.

112 *Ibid.*

Martin vs. State of West Bengal[113] one of the contentions on behalf of the petitioner was that the order of the government, made after considering the representation of the detenu, did not disclose any reasons for rejecting the representation of the detenu that the order was invalid. Justice Bhagwati, following *Hardhan* case[114] held that "there need not be a speaking order ... all that is necessary is that there should be a real and proper consideration by the government".

The power of preventive detention is a draconian power and justified only in the interest of public security and order and it is tolerated in a free society only as a necessary evil. The power to detain without trial is an extraordinary power constituting encroachment on personal liberty and it is the solemn duty of the Courts to ensure that this power is exercised strictly in accordance with the requirements of the Constitution and the Law. The Courts should always lean in favour of upholding personal liberty, for it is one of the most cherished values of mankind, without it life would not be worth living.[115]

11.1. The Right to Compensation

The rationale for awarding compensation under Article 32 for the violation of a fundamental right, is that the right in question has been violated by the executive whose sworn duty it is to uphold the right of an individual. Under the CP Covenant there is clear provision for compensation in Article 9(5) which says,

> Anyone who has been victim of unlawful arrest or detention shall have an enforceable right to compensation.[116]

India has already ratified[117] this Convention but with reservations, specifically with Article 9(5) of the CP Covenant. It says

> With reference to Article 9 of International Covenant on Civil and Political Rights, the Government of the Republic of India takes the position that the provisions of the Article shall be so applied as to be in consonance with the provisions of Clauses (3) to (7) of Article 22 of the Constitution of India. Further under the Indian legal system, there is no enforceable right to

---

113 *Khudiram Das vs. State of West Bengal*, AIR 1975 SC 550.
114 *Hardhana Saha vs. State of West Bengal*, AIR 1975 SC 775.
115 Jariwala, *op. cit.,* note 102, at 50-82.
116 *Human Rights: A Compilation of International Instruments* (New York, 1988), at 23.
117 For the text of India's instrument of accession, see 20 *Indian Journal of International Law*, 118-19 (1980).

> compensation for persons claiming to be victims of unlawful arrest or detention against the state.[118]

However the Supreme Court overlooked this reservation in various cases and established the rule of compensation. In *Nilabati Behera vs. State of Orissa*,[119] a sum of Rs.1.5 lakhs was awarded to a mother whose son had died in police custody. In this case the Court also referred to the CP Covenant:

> We may also refer to Article 9(5) of the International Covenant on Civil and Political Rights, which indicated that an enforceable right to compensation is not alien to the concept of enforcement of a guaranteed right. Anyone who has been the victims of unlawful arrest or detention shall have an enforceable right to compensation.

The Court also rejected the principle of sovereign immunity in this case, it stipulates:

> A claim in public law for compensation for contravention of human rights and fundamental freedoms is available under Article 32 by Supreme Court or by the High Court under Article 226 of the Constitution is a remedy available in public law, based on strict liability for contravention of fundamental rights to which the principle of sovereign immunity does not applly, even though it may be available as a defence in private law in an action based on tort.

The fixing of monetary liability on the state through the award of compensation under Article 32 is no longer a question of debate after the landmark judgement delivered in *Rudul Shah vs. State of Bihar*.[120] In this case, which involved the petitioner's claim for compensation for his incarceration for fourteen years after his acquittal in a full dressed trial.[121] Chief Justice Chandrachud opined that the Indian Constitution had no provision similar to Article 9(5) of the CP Covenant which entitles a victim of unconstitutional arrest or detention to claim compensation from the State. The absence of this provision from the Indian Constitution is certainly not accidental. Aware of this fact, the Chief Justice nevertheless said that if in a case of gross violation of liberty the Court refuses to pass an order of compensation, it would only be paying lip-service to liberty. He said:

---

[118] United Nations, New York, *Human Rights International Instruments: Signatures, Ratifications, Accessions, etc., 1 July 1982* (1982), at 52.

[119] AIR 1993, SC 1960.

[120] AIR 1983 SC 1086.

[121] In this case the petitioner (Rudul Shah) was acquitted by the Session Court of Muzaffarpur on 3 June 1968, unfortunately he languished in jail for another fourteen years, finally released on 16 October 1982.

> Article 21 which guarantees the right to life and liberty, will be denuded of its significant content if the power of the Court were limited to passing orders of release from illegal detention. One of the telling ways in which the violation of that right can reasonably be prevented and due compliance with the mandate of Article 21 secured is to mulct its violators in the payment of compensation.[122]

Keeping this in view the Court awarded a sum of Rs.30,000 as compensation. Through this judgment the Court has incorporated the provision of Article 9(5) of the CP Covenant *via* Article 21 and enlarged the jurisdiction of the Court under Article 32 and of the High Courts under Article 226 to enforce fundamental rights through compensatory remedies. In another important case, *Sebastian M. Hongray vs. Union of India*,[123] the Supreme Court by a writ of *habeas corpus* required the Government of India to produce two persons, but the Government failed to produce them. The Supreme Court in the circumstances, keeping in view the torture, agony and the mental oppression through which the wives of C. Daniel and C. Paul, the persons directed to be produced had to pass, instead of imposing a fine, directed payment as a measure of exemplary costs, of Rs.1 lakh to the two women. There have been numerous other cases[124] where the Court has granted compensation against the sovereign immunity concept. It is clear that the Supreme Court is not helpless; the Court under Articles 32 and 21 has assumed wide power. The Court is free to forge new tools necessary to impart complete justice and enforce the fundamental rights guaranteed in the Constitution.

12. Conclusions

The provisions of the Constitution, embodying fundamental rights basic to political democracy are not static. It is true that in the context of the non-inclusion of certain human rights in the Indian Constitution and the non-incorporation of the International Covenant on Civil and Political Rights into India's municipal law the Indianization of the needed human rights by the judges looks like Constitution-making. However, a closer analysis of all these significant judgments reveals that the judges have not usurped the role of law-maker or of Constitution-maker.

The judges are not duty-bound to adopt those conceptions and meanings, as they have to only interpret the Constitution in terms of what Constitution-makers wanted. In fact, they may clothe the concepts with new conceptions and the

---

122 AIR 1983 SC 1080.

123 AIR 1984 SC 1026.

124 *Bhim Singh vs. State of J&K*, AIR 1986 SC 494; *People's Union for Democratic Rights vs. state of Bihar*, AIR 1987 SC 355; *Saheli, a Women's Resource Centre vs. Commissioner of Delhi Police*; AIR 1990 SC 513; *State of Maharashtra vs. Ravikant S. Patil*, 1991 AIR SCW 871; *Kumari vs. State of Tamil Nadu*, AIR 1992 SC 2069.

words with new meanings to make them serve life. Thus the power to interpret includes the power to make law. Through its various judgments the Supreme Court has rationalized the needed human rights into justiciable fundamental rights. The Court has enriched and enlarged the right of access to justice through public interest litigation, transformed the distant Supreme Court into a poor man's court. The Supreme Court has made remarkable advances in the field of human rights. The main emphasis has been on making basic civil and political rights meaningful for the large masses of people who are living a life of poverty and destitution and to whom these basic human rights have so far no meaning or significance because of constant and continuous deprivation and exploitation.

THE LEGAL STATUS OF REFUGEES IN INDIA

B.C. Nirmal*

1. Introduction

India has an age-old unbroken history of welcoming and providing warm hospitality to an endless inundation of men and women of diverse creeds, cultures and races who came to this ancient land from distant regions and climes in the noble tradition of 'live and let live' and Guests are Gods.[1] At the heart of this tradition was the country's resolve that 'none shall be turned away from the shores of this vast sea of humanity that is India'. This Karuna (compassion) model of refugee protection greatly enriched India in all possible dimensions and made this country a symphony of diverse creeds, faiths and cultures all combining to make India a nation of unity in diversity.[2] And these who reached here earlier became the proud citizens of this country.

In keeping with its old noble tradition of according humanitarian protection to refugees and asylum seekers, India has been following a very liberal refugee policy since its independence although till today it has neither become a party to the 1951 Refugee Convention or its 1967 Protocol nor has it enacted any refugee specific legislation. The successful handling of the refugee problems in the past and the presence of thousands of refugees either recognized by the Government or by the UNHCR[3] are an eloquent testimony of India's commitment to the cause of refugee protection. This is in accord with its commitments under the human rights treaties as well as the constitutional provisions requiring the Indian Government to accord protection to refugees. Yet in the absence of a refugee specific legislation issues relating to determination of the refugee status, rights and duties of refugees,

* Professor of Law, Law School, Banaras Hindu University, Varanasi

1. See *Re Kerala Education Bill* (1959) SCR 995 at 1017-8.

2. Sir Radhakrishnan was more eloquent in this regard : "India is a symphony where there are, as in an orchestra, different instruments, each with its particular sonority, each with its special sound, all combining to interpret one particular score. It is this kind of combination that this country has stood for. It never adopted inquisitorial methods. It never asked the Parsis or the Jews or the Christians or the Muslims who came and took shelter there to change their creed or become absorbed in what might be called a uniform Hindu humanity. It never did this. 'Live and let live' that has been the spirit of this country." *Constituent Assembly Debates*, vol. I, p. 38 quoted in P.P.Rao in *Report on Judicial Symposium on Refugee Protection* (1999) 110.

3. For further details see Mahendra Kumar, *Refugee Law and Policy in India* (a LLM (HRDE) dissertation, Law School BHU, submitted under the supervision of Dr. B.C. Nirmal, 2002).

Bimal N. Patel (ed.), **India and International Law, 175-188.**

cessation and exclusion of the refugee status, local integration, re-settlement and voluntary repatriation remain unresolved.

2. Constitutional Framework for Refugee Protection

The Constitution of India establishes the supremacy of law[4] and accords a pride of place to customary and conventional law in the governance of the country and the formulation of the governments' policy.[5] In consequence, both the Union Government and the courts are under a constitutional duty to have due regard to customary rules and treaty obligations regarding refugee protection. The Constitution also confers certain fundamental rights on refugees. Thus, the right to equality (Article 14), right to life and personal liberty (Article 21) right to protection against arbitrary arrest (Article 22), right to protect in respect of conviction of offences (Article 20), freedom of religion (Article 25) right to approach the Supreme Court for the enforcement of fundamental rights (Article 32) are as much available to non-citizens including refugees as to citizens. Time and again, the Supreme Court has made it clear that refugees are entitled to the protection of their lives and personal liberty and the State is duty bound to safeguard the life, health and well-being of refugees.[6] But as the Supreme Court held in *Khudiram Chakma case*, Article 21 does not include the right to reside and settle in the country since these rights are only available under Article 19 which is limited to the citizens of this country and moreover the machinery of Article 14 cannot be invoked to obtain the right to reside and settle in this country. The forceful way in which the Supreme Court came to the rescue of Chakma refugees exhibits a liberal and humanitarian approach to the refugee problem. In *NHRC v. State of Arunachal Pradesh*[7] the Supreme Court reminded the Government of Arunachal Pradesh (an Indian state) of its constitutional duty to safeguard the life, health and well-being of Chakmas residing in the state without being inhibited by local polities. The Court also held that by refusing to forward their applications, the State Government was denying the Chakmas rights, constitutional as well as statutory, to be registered as citizens of India.

---

4. Rule of Law is a basic feature of the Indian Constitution. See *Smt Indira Gandhi Nehru vs. Raj Narain* AIR 1975 SC 2299. In *S. G. Jaisinghani vs. UOI,* AIR 1967 SC 1427. The Court declared, "it is important to emphasize that the absence of arbitrary power is the first essential element of the rule of law upon which our whole constitutional system is based. In a system governed by rule of law, discretion, when conferred upon executive authorities must be confined within clearly defined limits. *In State of Orissa vs. Dr. (Ms) Bina Pani Dei,* AIR 1967 SC 1269. The Court declared, "an order by the State to the prejudice of a person in derogation of his vested rights may be mode only in accordance with the basic rules of justice and fair play if the essentials of justice are ignored and an order to the prejudice of a person is made, the order is a nullity. This is a basic concept of the rule of law and importance thereof transcends, the significance of a decision in any particular case."

5. See Article 51 C of the Indian Constitution, which is a Directive Principle of State Policy.

6. *Louis De Raedt vs. Union of India*, (1991) 3 SCC 544, *State of Arunachal Pradesh vs. Khudiram Chakma* 1994 Supp (1) SCC, 615.

7. *NHCR vs. State of Arunachal Pradesh*, AIR 1996 S.C. 1235.

Thus, refugees are entitled to the protection of their lives and personal liberty in accordance with the constitutional provisions. They also have the right to live so long as they are in India with human dignity. It is important to note here that for the purpose of Article 21, the term life is wide enough to include dignified life[8] and the expression 'personal liberty' is much more than the liberty of the physical body and covers a variety of rights which go to constitute the personal liberty of man. A dynamic Supreme Court has widened the scope of Article 21 to include the right to privacy,[9] the right to go abroad,[10] the right to legal aid,[11] the right to speedy trial,[12] the right against the bar fetters,[13] the right against solitary confinement,[14] the right against custodial violence[15], the right to medical assistance,[16] the right to shelter,[17] the right to free education up to the age of fourteen years[18], the right to livelihood,[19] the right to live with dignity free from exploitation,[20] the right to protection against torture,[21] the right to a safe and decent environment[22] and the right to protection from sexual harassment.[23] It is true that the right to life and personal liberty can be curbed by procedure established by law, but the procedure has to be just, fair and reasonable, not fanciful, oppressive or arbitrary. Considering that refugees are frequently at risks of various acts of violence in the country of asylum, the constitutional guarantee of the life and personal liberty of refugees in India are bound to help them immensely.

As noted above the right to equality before the law and equal protection of the laws is available to every person in India whether he is a citizen or refugee. The equality before the law is an integral part of what Dicey has called the 'rule of law' in England and means that no body is above law and that every person, whatever be his rank or condition, is subject to the jurisdiction of the court. In fact, the very purpose of Article 14 is to strike arbitrariness in state actions and ensure fairness and equality of treatment.[24] The expression 'equal protection of the laws' means that

8. *Francis C. Mullin vs. Administrator*, AIR 1981 SC 746.
9. *Govind vs. State of MP.* AIR 1975 SC 1378.
10. *Satwant Singh vs. Assistant Passport Officer*, New Delhi, AIR 1967 SC 1834.
11. *M.H. Hoskat vs. State of Maharashtra*, AIR 1978 SC 1548.
12. *A.R. Antulay vs. R. S. Nayak*, AIR 1992 SC 1701.
13. *Charles Sobraj vs. Superintendent, Central Jail*, AIR 1978 SC 1574.
14. *Sunil Batra vs. Delhi Administration*, AIR 1978 SC 1675.
15. *Sheela Barse vs. State of Maharashtra*, AIR 1983 SC 378.
16. *Parmanand Katara vs. UOI*, AIR 1989 SC 2039.
17. *Shantistar Builders vs. N. K. Totame* AIR 1996 SC 786.
18. *Unnikaishnan vs. State or A.P.*, AIR 1993 SC 2178.
19. *Olga Tellis vs. Bombay Municipal Corporation* AIR 1986 SC 180.
20. *Francis C. Mullin vs. Administrator*, AIR 1987 SC 746.
21. *D.K. Basu vs. State of West Bengal*, AIR 1997 SC 610.
22. *M.C. Mehta vs. UOI*, AIR 1987 SC 945.
23. *Visaka vs. State of Rajasthan* (1997) 6 SCC 241.
24. In *E.P. Royappa vs. State of Tamil Nadu*, AIR 1974 SC 555. The Supreme Court held, "in fact equality and arbitrariness are sworn enemies; one belongs to the rule of law in a republic,

equal law should be applied to all the same situations and there should be no discrimination between one person and another. The rule is that the like should be treated alike and not that unlike should be treated like. In the context of refugee protection Article 14 means the protection of refugees from the discriminatory and arbitrary actions of the official authorities and a positive and affirmative action to their favour wherever it is needed.

Refugees living in India are bound to be benefited by the power of judicial review[25] and the independence of the judiciary recognized by the Indian Constitution. Like citizens they too have unfettered access to courts in India for judicial protection against arbitrary and illegal action of the state in violation of their fundamental rights. Any violation of their fundamental rights can be remedied through a recourse to the judiciary. A refugee can approach the Supreme Court or High Court for vindication of his fundamental rights. Indian courts have even allowed NGOs and the National Human Rights Commission to intervene on behalf of refugees and the system of public interest litigation has widened the access of asylum seekers and other aliens to the justice delivery system in this country.

3. Human Rights Treaties and Refugees Protection

As already noted, India is not a party to the 1951 Convention on the Status of Refugees and its Protocol of 1967. But those provisions of these treaties which have now acquired the status of customary international law may be regarded as incorporated into the domestic law to the extent of their consistency with the existing municipal laws and also when there is a void in the domestic law.[26] In any case there is an obligation on the courts to remain alive to these treaties and construct a statute in the light of their provisions when there is no inconsistency between them and domestic laws.[27] It is to the credit of the Indian judiciary that it has not only recognized the importance of human rights,[28] but has also relied on the

---

while the other, to the whim and caprice of an absolute monarch. Where an act is arbitrary, it is implicit in that it is unequal, both according to political logic and constitutional law and is therefore, violative of Article 14." The Court reiterated in *Maneka Gandhi vs. UOI* that Article 14 strikes at arbitrariness of state action and ensures fairness and equality of treatment. AIR 1978 SC 597.

25. *L. Chandrakumar vs. Union of India*, AIR 1997 SC 1125 (Power of Judicial review is a basic feature of the Indian Constitution).

26. See *Indian Gramophone Co vs. Birendra Bahadur Pandey and another,* AIR 1954 SC 667, *Vellore citizens Welfare Forum* case (1996) 5 SCC 746. By virtue of this reasoning the principle of *non-refoulement* may be deemed incorporated into the Indian municipal law.

27. *Visaka and others vs. State of Rajasthan* and others 1997 (6) SCC 241. In *Apparel Export Promotion Council vs. A. K. Chopra*, 1999 (1) SCC 759. Chief Justice Anand held, "in cases involving violation of human rights, the courts must remain alive to the international instruments and conventions and apply the same to a given case when there is no inconsistency between the international norms and the domestic law occupying the field."

28. See Maneka Gandhi vs. UOI AIR 1978 SC 597; M.S. Hoskot vs. State of Maharashtra, AIR 1978 SC 1548, Hussainara Khatoon & Ors vs. Home Secretary, State of Bihar, AIR 1979 SC 1360 Randhir Singh vs. UOI, AIR 1982 SC 879. M.C. Mehta vs. UOI, AIR 1987 SC

provisions of the human rights treaties, conventions, declarations and agreements for widening the ambit of fundamental rights and for filling the gaps and voids in the domestic human rights law.[29] It now seems to be more willing to incorporate the provisions of human rights treaties into the domestic law without insisting on the requirement of their transformation into the law of the land through a formal legislation.[30]

The fact that India is a member of the Executive Committee of the Office of the United Nations High Commissioner for Refugees (UNHCR), an honour bestowed upon it in recognition of its demonstrated interest in and devotion to the solution of the refugee problem puts a moral if not legal obligation on it to set an example for others to emulate by developing a constructive partnership with the UNHCR and by following the provisions of the 1951 Refugee Convention.

India is a party to various human rights treaties and conventions that contains provisions relating to the protection of refugees, such as, the Genocide Convention, International Covenant on Civil and Political Rights, International Covenant on Economic, Social and Cultural Rights, International Convention on the Elimination of All Forms of Discrimination against Women, Convention against Torture and Other Cruel, Inhuman or Degrading Treatment or Punishment (signed but not ratified) and Convention on the Rights of Child. As a party to human rights treaties India is under a legal obligation to protect the human rights of all persons be they citizens or non-citizens including refugees by taking appropriate legislative, administrative and other measures. India is also a member of various human rights treaty bodies which seek to ensure the observance and implementation of the basic rights of all human beings irrespective of their nationality. India sends periodic

---

965, D.K. Basu vs. State of W.B., AIR 1997 SC 410 Nilabati Behra vs. State of Orissa, (1993) 2 SCC 746, Apparel Export Promotion Councils vs. A. K. Chopra, 1999 (1) SCC 759; Visaka vs. State of Rajasthan, 1997 (6) SCC 241, J.P. Unnikrishnan vs State of A.P., AIR 1993 SC 2178. M.C. Mehta vs. State of Tamil Nadu, AIR 1997 SC. 699.

29. See *Visaka's case* 1997 (6) SCC 241; *Apparel Export promotion Council's Case.* 1999 (1) SCC 759; *PUCL vs. Union of India* AIR 1997. SC 568. Applying the *Visaka* Principles to refugee protection the then Chief Justice Mr. J.S. Verma observed, "in the absence of national laws satisfying the needs (to protect refugees), the provisions of the (1951 refugee) convention and its protocol can be relied on when there is no conflict with any provisions in the municipal laws. This is a cannon of construction recognized by the courts in enforcing the obligations of the state for the protection of the basic human rights of individuals." Inaugural speech at a seminar on *Refugees in the SAARC Region*, held in New Delhi, May 1997.

30. Until recently the Indian courts insisted on the requirement of transformation of human rights treaties into the domestic law for their implementation and enforcement. *Jolly George Verghese vs. Bank of Cochin*, AIR 1980 SC 970; *Xavier vs. Canara Bank* Ltd 1969 Kerl. Times 927, *Vigilance Rights Committee case*, AIR 1983, Karn. 85. *Bishambhar Singh vs. State of Orissa*, AIR 1957 Orissa 1957, 247 at 256. The application of the doctrine of incorporation in the case of human rights treaties, though laudable, ignores Articles 253 of the Indian Constitution and the prerogative of the Union Government to become or not to become a party to any international convention and even overlooks the issues of state responsibility in international law for the violation of any treaty.

reports to human rights treaty bodies on the state of implementation of the provisions of the relevant human rights treaty in the country.

Besides the mechanisms at the international level for the promotion and protection of human rights and courts, National Human Rights Commission and State Human Rights Commissions[31], NGOs and members of civil society keep a constant vigil on the implementation of human rights obligations of the Government under international and domestic laws. Refugees living in India are bound to be benefited by these mechanisms.

4. Statutory Laws and Refugees

Among the principal Indian laws that are relevant to refugee protection the Passport (Entry into India) Act, 1920 and the Passport Act, 1967 occupy an important place. Since these two enactments make no distinction between genuine refugees and other categories of aliens, refugees run the risk of arrest by the immigration authorities and of their prosecution if they enter India without a valid passport/travel documents[32] or illegally depart or attempt to depart from India without a valid passport or travel documents[33]. When a refugee is detained by the

---

31. National Human Rights Commission (NHRC) and State Human Rights Commissions have been established under the Protection of Human Rights Act, 1993. The National Human Rights Commission performs a wide range of functions for refugees. NHRC has received complaints from and on behalf of refugees, intervened in court proceedings, visited special camps and detention centres and opened a dialogue with the Central Government in regard to human rights treaties. The Commission's interventions in respect of the protection of Chakma refugees in Arunachal Pradesh and Tripura, and in regard to Sri Lankan Tamil refugees in special camps in Tamil Nadu are noteworthy *Report on Judicial Symposium on Refugee Protection*, 69-70 (13-14 Nov, 1999).

32. Section 30 of the Passport Act 1920 read with Rule 6A of the Indian Passport Rules, 1950 makes entry into India from outside without a passport an offence punishable with imprisonment for a term which may extend to three months or with a fine or with both. The police and customs authorities may arrest without warrant any person who has contravened or against whom there is reasonable suspicion that he had contravened any rule or order made under Section 3 of the Act.

33. If a person, whether he is an Indian citizen or an alien, departs or attempts to depart from India without a valid passport or travel document, he is liable to be punished with imprisonment for a term not exceeding two years or with a fine which may extend to a five thousand rupees or with both (Section 3 the Passport Act, 1967). Making of an application by a foreigner for obtaining a passport or obtaining a passport by suppressing his nationality or holding a forged document is punishable with imprisonment which shall not be less than one year but which may extend to five years and with a fine which should not be less than ten thousand rupees but which may extend to fifty thousand rupees. See the *Mehmud Ghazaleh* is case in which an First Information Report was lodged against an Iranian refugee u/s 419/420/468/471 read with Section 31 of the Passport Act for traveling on forged and fabricated travel documents. Two Afghan refugees Shah Ghazal and his minor son were apprehended at the Atari border, Amritsar while attempting to illegally exit India for Afghanistan via- Pakistan. See also *State vs. Asghar Nilooker Rahimi*, the decision of the District Munsif cum Judicial Magistrate, Alandur Chennai, dated 17th July 1998

customs, immigration or police authorities for commission of any of the offences under these enactments[34], he is generally handed over to the police and a first information report is lodged against him.[35]

Although the courts have come to the rescue of refugees in many cases by taking a lenient view in the matter of punishment for their illegal entry[36] or illegal activities in India[37] and also by releasing detainees pending determination of refuges status[38] staying deportation[39] and giving them opportunity to approach the

---

(unreported). It is important to note that under Section 20 of the Passport Act 967 the Central Government can issue passport and travel documents to non-citizens in the public interest. The Government has also power to exempt any person or class of persons from the operation of the provisions of the Act and rules made there under (Section 22). These provisions may be suitably adapted to provide better refugee protection. For the discussion of the unreported cases see, T. Ananthachari, "Refugees in India: Legal Framework, Law Enforcement and Security", 1 *Indian Society of International Law Year Book of International Humanitarian and Refugee Law*, 118-143 (2001); K. C. Saha, "Legal Status of Asylum Seekers in India: A study of Selected Cases", 2 *Indian Society of International Law Year Book of International Humanitarian and Refugee Law,* 190-206(2002).

34. Section 13, Indian Passport Act, 1967, Section 4 Indian Passport Act, 1920. Under Section 14 of the 1967 Act, customs immigration and police authorities have power to search any place and seize any passport or travel documents.

35. Section 4 (2) Indian Passport Act, 1920 and Section 13 Passport Act 1967.

36. *State vs. Teresi* Case no. 406 of 1996, the decision of the Chief Judicial Magistrate, Kozhikode Kerala, dated 2nd January, 1997 (unreported); *State vs. Akhtar Mohd*, AF/6433, the decision of the CJM, Amritsar, dated 9 January, 1997 (unreported), *State vs. Kishan Chand and Habib Iranpur* criminal case No. 66/96, the decision of the Chief Judicial Magistrate, Ajmer, dated 31 May, 1996 (unreported). In *State vs. Md. Hashim* (1997) an Afghan national was charged under Sections 420/471 Indian Penal Code (IPC) and Section 14 of the Foreigners Act but the Court took a lenient view in the matter of punishment. In *State vs. Benajamin Tang Neng* (1994) although, the refugee served out the sentence for illegal entry his prayer for his release and handing him over to the UNHCR was not accepted by the court.

37. *State vs. Winston Vanojan Rajyasingham*, FIR No. 438/93, the decision of the Additional Chief Metropolitan Magistrate, New Delhi, dated 9 September 1994 (unreported). (A Sri Lankan refugee was charged 4/5 419/471 IPC for cheating by impersonation using a foreged passport at the Indira Gandhi International Airport), *State vs. Mohd, Riza Ali*, FIR No. 414/93. The decision of the Chief Metropolitan Magistrate, New Delhi, dated 6 July 1995 (unreported). This case related to the prosecution of an Iranian refugee under Sections 420/421 IPC and the relevant provisions of the 1946 Act. In *State VS. Eva Massur Ahmad* (1995) a Sudanese lady was detained and charged under the relevant provisions of the Foreigners Act as she could not produce any document regarding her stay in India. The court, however, took a lenient view in the matter. In *State vs. Farid Ali Khan* (1995) the Court discharged the accused because no offence was made out against the accused. See also, *State vs. Hudson Vilvraj*, decision of the Metropolitan Magistrate Delhi, dated 6 May 1998 (unreported). In this case a Sri Lankan national who had been granted asylum and who was living in Chennai, was detained from a hotel in Delhi and charged under the relevant provisions of the Foreigners Act. But the Court took a lenient view.

38. See *Zothatnsangpuii vs. the State of Manipur* Civil Rule No. 1847/89, the High Court of Guahati dated 28 Sept 1989 (unreported); *Biyogi vs. Union of India*, Civil Rule No. 1847/87,

UNHCR, refugees continue to run the risk of apprehension, detention and prosecution for the violation of the Foreigners Act 1946[40] and the Foreigners Order 1948.[41] The power of the Central Government to expel or deport a foreigner (even a refugee) is absolute. A refuge can be deported on the ground of national security if he is found indulging in activities undesirable and prejudicial to the security of India and international law and conventions can not be applied in such a case.[42] Leave

---

Guahati High Court dated 28 Sept 1989 (unreported); *Shar Aung A.K. Aung Thant Mint vs. Union of India*, Crl. WP No. 110 of 1989. Delhi High Court, dated 4th March 1989 (unreported); *Khy-Htoon* & 7 others *vs. Union of India*. Civil Rule No. 515 of 1990. Guahati High Court, dated 11 Sept 1990 (unreported); *Umyat Kyaw & Mr. Nyazin vs. State of Manipur*, Guahati High Court dated 26 Nov 1991 (unreported); *State vs. K. Htoon and 4 others*, decision of the Chief Judicial Magistrate, Churchandpur Manipur, dated 23 December, 1994 (unreported). In all these cases refugees were released in order to enable them to approach the UNHCR in Delhi for the Refugee Status. In earlier cases the Guahati High Court released the detained asylum seekers on bail on furnishing sureties, but in subsequent cases they realized the difficulties of the asylum seekers and allowed bail on personal bond.

39. *Maiwand 's Trust of Afghan Human Freedom vs. State of Punjab*, Crl WP No. 125 & 126 of 1986; *N.D. Pancholi vs. State of Punjab and others* (WP civil) No. 1294 N 1987, (unreported); *Malavika Karlekar vs. Union of India*, Crl WP No. 243 of 1988. In *Syed Ata Mohammadi vs. Union of India*, Crl W.P. No. 7504/ 1994, the Bombay High Court was pleased to direct that "there is no question of deporting the Iranian refugee to Iran since he has been recognized as a refugee by the UNHCR.." In some cases the prosecution pending against the asylum seekers for illegal entry into India was withdrawn and exit permit was issued when on the initiative of the UNHCR third countries agreed to resettle them. See *Shar Aung A.K. Aung Thant Mint vs. Union of India* (1989), *Maung Maung Kyo Myunt vs. Union of India* (1994) Delhi High Court (unreported). In *State vs. Kishan Chand and Habib Iranpur,* the Chief Judicial Magistrate, Ajmer directed that on completion of the sentence he be handed over to the custody of UNHCR.

40. Entry of foreigners to India, their presence therein and their departure therefrom in violation of any provision made by the Central government under Section 3 is an offence punishable with imprisonment for a term not exceeding 5 years and also with fine (Section 14).

41. The Foreigners Order, 1948 requires a foreigner to enter India only through ports or places prescribed by the Registration Officer for the purpose of entry. A foreigner may be refused leave to enter the country on the grounds of public safety and non-possession of a valid passport or visa. Where leave to enter is refused the foreigner in question may be detained at some place approved by the authority. If he has come by sea route, then he may be placed temporarily on shore for that purpose. The civil authority may by order in writing impose on any foreigner conditions in respect of his place of residence, his movement etc. A foreigner is required to obtain the permission in writing of the civil authority for getting an entry in premises relating to or employed in or in connection with any undertaking for the supply to government, or to the public of light, petroleum, power or water, or any other undertaking, which may be specified in the central government. A foreigner may also be directed by the military officer for the time being in command of the forces in a cantonment to remove himself from the said cantonment.

42. *Mst Khadija a.k. a. Khudija and others vs. Union of India*, Crl W.P. No. 658 of 1997 and Crl, Ms. No 4855/97 & 6657/97, the High Court of Delhi, dated 19 December 1997

India notices may be issued to an alien either on the order of the court or when he fails to obtain extension of his travel permits. When leave India notices are issued by the Foreigner's Regional Registration Officer (FRRO), the only available remedy is to obtain stay from the appropriate court.

In view of the provision of the relevant statutes a refugee may face the prospects of forced deportation at the established sea ports, airports or the entry points on the international border, if he is detected without valid travel documents. Alternatively, he may be detained and interrogated pending decision by the administrative authorities regarding his plea for refugee/asylum. In all such cases refugees are ultimately handed over to the local police and first information reports are lodged against them, and whilst he is detained, he shall be deemed to be in legal custody and not to have entered India.

It is mandatory for a foreigner to depart or exit from India only from the prescribed departure points after obtaining leave of the civil authority having jurisdiction of such places of departure.[43] The civil authority may examine any person who seeks leave to enter India or to depart therefrom or during his stay in India for the purpose of the Foreigners Act, 1946 or order made thereunder. A foreigner entering India on the authority of a visa is required to obtain from the registration officers a travel permit. An alien entering India otherwise than on the authority of a transit or tourist visa is also required to obtain a residential permit. Unless the period of stay is extended by the Central Government every foreigner should leave India before the expiry of the period indicated in the residential permit. At the time of his departure the foreigner leaving India must surrender the permit to the registration officer having jurisdiction of the place from which he departs.

The movement of a foreigner, whether he is a refugee or any other alien, in India is subject to reasonable restrictions to be imposed by the Government as per the provisions of the law of the land. Thus, it is not possible for any foreigner to visit or reside in any prohibited place as defined in the Official Secrets Act. Any foreigner or any class of foreigners may also be prohibited by the civil authority from entering or remaining in the prohibited areas. Their entry into or presence in the protected areas is subject to such restrictions and conditions as the civil

(unreported). In this case the Delhi High Court dismissed the writ petition but stayed the deportation of petitioners for a period of four weeks so that the Afghan refugees could seek re-settlement in a third country through the good offices of UNHCR. In *Mohammad Sedique vs. Union of India*, the Delhi High Court held that the Union of India could deport even that refugee who had valid authority to stay in India if his activities were found to be prejudicial to the interests of the state.

43. Leave shall be refused if the civil authority is satisfied that (a) the foreigner has failed to comply with the, formalities of departure prescribed under the Registration of Foreigners Rules; (b) the foreigners presence is required in India to answer a criminal charge; (c) the foreigner's departure will prejudice the relations of the Central Government with a Foreign power; (d) the departure of the foreigner has been prohibited under an order issued by a competent authority.

authority may impose under the Foreigners Order, 1948. Where a refugee enters India on the basis of a visa and passport, which subsequently is detected to be forged, it constitutes a very serious and grave offence and may serve as a ground for non- acceptance of his prayer that he be not deported from India. The plight of refugees may be compounded further if they are required to bear the expenses of deportation[44] basis for which is already provided under paragraph 14 of the Foreigners Order, 1948. A very important point that merits attention here is the designation of transit areas at airports and other points of entry into Indian territory as 'International Zones' which are considered as being outside Indian territory and the normal jurisdiction of Indian courts. In the case of detention of a refugee/foreigner in such zones administrative remedies and not legal remedies are available.

A refugee also faces the prospects of prosecution for violation of the Registration of Foreigners in India, 1939 and rules[45] made thereunder and if he is found guilty of any offence under this Act he may be punished with imprisonment which may extend to one year or with a fine up to one thousand rupees or with both. [46] Besides, a fugitive refugee runs the risk of extradition to his country of origin or nationality if his case falls under the Indian Extradition Act, 1962 and bilateral extradition treaties. This in turn raises the question of relationship between extradition and the principle of *non-refoulement*.[47]

It is evident from the forgoing that existing laws create serious legal abstracts to the refugee protection in this country despite several progressive, liberal and humanitarian pronouncements of the Supreme Court and the High Courts on the one hand and a very sympathetic and helping attitude of the subordinate judiciary. The courts have given due weight to the UNHCR's refugee status certificate not only in the determination of the quantum of punishment but also in the release and deportation of the detained asylum seekers. In few cases prosecution against the detained asylum seeker was withdrawn subsequent to the grant of refugee certificate to him by the UNHCR or UNHCR's arrangement for his re-settlement in a third country. Notwithstanding these laudable developments in the field of refugee

---

44. For example, the *Mazid Ahmad 's case*, a Palestinian refugee had to bear the expenses of his air flights from Kathmandu to Delhi and then from Delhi to Kathmandu and finally from Kathmandu to Delhi and the expenses for his 25 days detention at the Indira Ghandhi Air Port and for his final deportation to Bangladesh.

45. Registration of Foreigners Rules 1939, amended in 1963 and 1965, Registration of Foreigners (Exemption) order, 1957.

46. Section 5 of 1957 Order, Under Section 3 the Central Government can frame rules with respect to foreigners for the purpose of reporting etc.

47. It is clear from Article 33 (2) of the 1951 Refugee Convention that in the case of those persons who represent a danger to the security of the country or who have been convicted by a final judgment of particularly serious crimes, the principle of *non-refoulement* may not apply. Article 32 of the European Convention on Extradition provides that a person charged with a lesser crime shall not be extradited, if it is believed that *refoulement* would lead to the threat to the life and freedom of the person concerned.

protection, the status of a refugee with UNHCR's certificate is uncertain and the judicial approach towards such refugees is not coherent and uniform. For these reasons foreigners related statutes require a re-look to make them refugee friendly.

5. Emerging Refugee Jurisprudence

India does not define 'refugee' in terms of a victim of 'persecution' but rather adopts the broad definition of 'refugee' as given under the Convention Governing the Specific Aspects of Refugee Problems in Africa (OAU Refugee Convention of 1969). While admission of group refugees in this country is governed and regulated by the broad policy guidelines issued by the Central Government from time to time, in the absence of a refugees[48] specific legislation there is no legal process for identification of individual refugee[48] in this country and matters relating to admission and treatment of asylum are handled by the bureaucratic minds who may not have adequate knowledge of the humanitarian principles of international refugee law and the attending consequences of the decision-making process. While India's preference to deal with refugees bilaterally or even unilaterally may perhaps be useful in cases of mass influx of refugees, the lack of a just, fair, impartial, transparent and expeditious individualized procedure for the determination of refugee states are nor conducive to the rule of law in this country. There is therefore an urgent need to put a refugee specific legislation in place. Such legislation would provide great relief to genuine refugees and asylum seekers and necessary guidelines to the authorities concerned and to all those whose work is to apply the humanitarian principles of refugee law. It would also introduce transparency, accountability and fairness in India's refugee policy.

Turning to the observance of the cardinal principle of international refugee law in this country, it is heartening to note that the principle of *non-refoulement* is well entrenched in the refugee law and policy of India[49] and Article 14 of the Universal Declaration of Human Rights,[50] the Bangkok Principles Concerning Treatment of

---

48. UNCHR, *Handbook on Procedure and Criteria for Determining Refugee Status* along with the conclusions of EXCOM may be used for evolving suitable criteria for determination of refugee status in this country. A fair and expeditious procedure with an emphasis on full access by the asylum seekers to the appropriate body and the opportunity for independent review of negative decisions may be put in place. If UNHCR is requested, it can help in the effective identification of refugees in the following ways: (i) assessment of the applicant's credibility in the light of the claim and of conditions known to exist in his or her country of origin; (ii) providing information on the treatment of similar cases or similar legal points in other jurisdiction; and (iii) representation of the international community interests by providing authoritative interpretation etc.

49. The principle of non-refoulement can be traced to Article 21 of the Indian Constitution, which guarantees the right to life and personal liberty. See *Kfaer Abbas Al Qutaifi vs. Union of India*, *Gujrat Law Herald*, (vol. XVIII (3)), 1005. In this case the Gujrat High Court held that the principle of *non-refoulement* is encompassed in Article 21 of the Constitution, so long as the presence of refugee is not prejudicial to the law and order and security of India.

50. Though not legally binding Article 14 of the Universal Declaration on Human Rights provides a basis for grant of asylum to refugees. This Article, according to the Supreme

Refugees (1966) and India's age-old noble tradition of not turning away any person from its seashore continue to guide and shape the asylum policy of the Central Government. As already noted the Indian Constitution extends the protection of a few fundamental rights to refugees. But beyond that there is a state of uncertainty with regard to the basic human entitlements of refugees[50a] which has been responsible for a lack of consistency and uniformity in the treatment of different refugee communities.[51] This is the additional reason why a refugee specific legislation should be enacted. As far as the treatment of women and child refugees is concerned, India initiated a gendered refugee policy and adopted pro-refugee child programmes way back in 1947 itself.[1] This however does not mean that all is well on this front. According preferential treatment to women and children belonging to certain refugee groups but denying the same to Chakma (women and children) refugees speaks about the arbitrary and discriminatory nature of the government's policy in this regard. Human rights treaties and the programme of Action adopted at Beijing along with the arbitrary and discriminatory nature of the government's refugee policy require that a gender conscious and pro-child refugee policy is put in place and a well-structured, predictable and rights based framework is created for the protection of the basic human rights of women and children refugees.[52]

While India has received worldwide acclamation for the successful local integration of lakhs (one lakh equals to an hundred thousand) of partition refugees and a great number of refugees have been assimilated in this country, India considers voluntary repatriation of refugees as the most preferred solution to the refugee problem and has successfully repatriated Bangladeshi, Sri Lankan and

---

Court, carries considerable moral authority and implies that a state which has granted him asylum must not later return the asylum obtaining person to the country whence he came. *State of Arunachal Pradesh vs. Khudiram Chakma* NOS 1994 Supp 1 SCC 615.

50a. The 1951 Refugee Convention recognizes a wide range of rights of refugees. For the discussion of the basic human rights of refugees see. B.C. Nirmal, "Refugees and Human Rights", 1 *ISIL Yearbook of International Humanitarian and Refugee Law*, 94-117 (2001).

51. It has been claimed that India follows the following provisions of the 1951 Refugee Convention in its treatment of refugees. Article 3 (policy of non-discrimination), Article 31 (no penalty for illegal entry), Article 4 (religious freedom), Article 16 (free access to courts), Articles 17 and 18 (wage earning rights), Article 2 (freedom of housing) and article 27 and 28 (issues of identity and travel cards). See J. N. Saxena "Legal Status of Refugees-Indian Position, 26 *Indian Journal of International Law*, (1986) at 50. This claim is vigorously contested by human rights activists who cite the cases of Jammu, Chin and Chakma refugees to show that while certain refugee groups have been given preferential treatment, others received neglect and suffering. Jammu and Chakma refugees were forced to live inside camps and severe restrictions were imposed on their freedom of movement. During 1995-96, approximately 5000 Chin refugees were pushed back over the border. As the Government does not issue residence permits to all refugees, they are unable to open bank accounts, rent houses and set up a business. Moreover, educational institutions did not admit sons and daughters of the less fortunate refugees.

52. See Vikas Singh, *Refugee Women and their Protection* (LLM Dissertation, Law School, B.H.U. 2002, submitted under the supervision of Dr. B.C. Nirmal).

Chakma refugees. It took all steps to ensure the voluntary nature of repatriation of refugees and allowed those Sri Lankan refugees to remain in India who were not willing to return to their country. The Courts also came to the rescue of those refugees who were unwilling to return to their country.[53] In *P. Nedumaran v. Union of India*[54] the Madras High Court emphasized the need for the voluntary nature of repatriation and held that since the UNHCR was involved in ascertaining the voluntariners of the refugees return to Sri Lanka, hence being a World Agency it was not for the court to consider whether the consent was voluntary. In *NHRC v. State of Arunachal Pradesh*, the Supreme Court also directed the State Government to protect the Chakma refugees from threatened eviction from the state.

6. Conclusions

It is to the credit of India that it not only hosted a number of refugees from different countries in the past but even accorded them humanitarian treatment and protection in the spirit of the UN Charter, human rights treaties and the cardinal principles of international refugee law and successfully repatriated the Bangladeshi, Chakma and Sri Lankan refugees in the most commendable way without being bound by the 1951 Refugee Convention or its 1967 Protocol. In keeping with its age-old humanitarian and secular tradition it continues to host more than 251,400 refugees. India can rightfully boast that it has been able to deal with the numerous refugees problems in a satisfactory manner even in the absence of a refugee specific legislation and that its human rights commissions and courts are better placed to provide the necessary protection to individuals as well as group refugees. But as is evident from the review of the existing statutory laws as well as the refugee policies adopted by the Central Government from time to time, there are many gaps and ambiguities in the relevant law and the refugee policy is beset with a lack of uniformity, predictability, accountability and transparency. There may be obvious advantages in dealing with the case of mass influx of refugees at the political and administrative levels, according to broad guidelines issued by the Central Government, but this approach is of doubtful utility in the case of individual asylum seekers, particularly in view of the absence of any refugee specific legislation and the applicability of the Foreigners Act and other alien specific legislations to foreigners in general and genuine refugees. In the absence of any legal process for identification of individual refugees, matters relating to admission and treatment of asylum seekers are handled by the administrative authorities according to certain vague and general guidelines. This is not in accord with the rule of law and the right to equality and non- discrimination, which the Indian Constitution pledges to secure for all citizens and non-citizens (including refugees). It is true that in recent cases the Supreme Court and the High Courts have come to the rescue of certain refugees and provided them with appropriate reliefs. But judicial intervention is a measure of last resort for refugees who because of being in an alien land are hardly in a position

53. See *Gurunathan and others vs. Government of India* WP No. S 6708 and 7916 of 1992; *A.C. Mohd Siddique vs. Government of India and others* 1998 (47) DRJ (DB) 74.
54. *P. Nedumaran vs. Union of India*, Aug 27, 1992.

to approach the court and whose first and foremost concern is protection against *refoulement* and the grant of asylum. There is, therefore, a long-felt need to enact a domestic legislation to provide for the protection, rehabilitation and repatriation of refugees. Enactment of a refugee specific legislation would not only serve to codify India's international legal obligations for refugees and establish transparency, fairness, predictability and certainty in its refugee policy but it would also enhance its credibility and standing in the international community, and enable the courts and human rights institutions to protect the rights of refugees in a better way. The proposed legislation should cover broadly the following areas; the refugee definition, exclusion from refugee status, *non-refoulement,* procedure for refugee status determination, cessation of refugee status, rights and duties of refugees, the situation of mass influx, the situation of refugees unlawfully in the country of refugee and voluntary repatriation of refugees. The proposed legislation should adopt a balanced and practical approach to the refugee issues by ensuring a harmonious balance between humanitarian concerns involved in the refugee situation on the one hand and security concerns and the national interest of the country on the other.

INTERNATIONAL CRIMINAL LAW: CRIME PREVENTION AND PUNISHMENT

Vishnu Dutt Sharma*

1. Introduction

Peace, security and physical integrity are a must for a human being to think in the right direction, to discharge duties in a perfect manner, to enjoy basic freedoms, and to contribute to the evolution of a healthy environment in the world.

Since the beginning of human society, and throughout the history of its development, no era has been absolutely free of evil/crime. Good and evil walked always together. The best example that can be given from Indian society is that during Lord Rama's age also evil was present in the shape of Ravana and other Rakshashas, who used to commit crimes against the innocent people. According to the traditional Indian faith, when crime reaches its peak, Lord Vishnu takes birth on the earth in human shape to rid the earth of inhuman/criminals or in other words to clear the earth of all kinds of evils.

This has always been the dream of every good human being to establish peace and security in the world, which could not see the reality because of anti-peace elements. Without going into the debate on what sows the seeds of the element of criminality in the human mind, which is a separate and highly debatable subject, there is no denying that greed, selfishness, jealousy, illiteracy, inefficiency, incompetency and the race for victory, are among other factors responsible for instigating the human to commit wrongs and violations.

Human society on the planet earth is seriously threatened by variety of crimes of international character. These crimes endangered international peace and security, maintenance of which is one of the purposes of the Charter of the United Nations. The world community has always been engaged in exploring and adopt measures at national, regional and international levels for the prevention of crimes and dealing with them firmly, by prosecuting and punishing, in the case of their occurrence.

* Legal Officer, Ministry of External Affairs, Government of India, New Delhi. The views expressed are the personal views of the author and do not reflect the views of the Government of India.

Bimal N. Patel (ed.), **India and International Law, 189-222.**

Prevention can essentially be ensured by correcting the demeanour or by creating deterrence through the adoption of international legal instruments such as, treaties, conventions, agreements, protocols and declarations. They characterize the criminal acts as offences/crimes, which has the effect of defining criminalities, and provides punishment for the commission thereof. These instruments also contain measures of cooperation between states aimed to prevent crimes ranging from information sharing to the adequate legal action leading to punishment.

Prosecution and punishment of crimes is carried through the national or international judicial organ, depending upon the factor of jurisdiction. The treaties or legislations establishing such organs also provide legal procedure including the rules and principles of evidence and proof for the purpose of investigation and trial.

The present paper is an attempt to focus on the discussion of international crimes and analysis of international law for the prevention and punishment thereof.

2. International Crimes

International criminal law is an era of definitional ambiguity.[1] Some eminent scholars have said even to the extent that, "international criminal law in any true sense does not exist,"[2] rather, the so-called international crimes like piracy are classified solely as municipal law crimes and the only question of international law being the extent of a state's jurisdiction to apply its criminal law to an accused foreigner acting outside the territorial jurisdiction of the prescribing state.[3] On the other hand, under the "naturalist" model, certain crimes including piracy are considered crimes against international law "seeking only a tribunal with jurisdiction to apply that law and punish the criminal".[4] Accordingly, "a crime against international law is an act committed with an intent to violate a fundamental interest protected by international law or with knowledge that the act would probably violate such an interest, and which may not be adequately punished by the exercise of the normal jurisdiction of any state."[5]

It is evident from the conflicting views that over the time, there has been a controversy as to the international character of laws related to criminal activities, the deciding factors of the internationality element of a crime being its nature, content and jurisdictional aspects. International criminal law can be thus divided into

---

[1] John F. Murphy, "Civil Liability for the Commission of International Crimes as an Alternative to Criminal Prosecution" In 12 *Harvard Human Rights Journal* (Spring 1999), at 2.
[2] Georg Schwarzenberger, "The Problem of an International Criminal Law" In Gerry Simpson, *War Crimes Law* (vol. 1, 2004) 5-38, See Murphy, *Ibid.*, at 3.
[3] Alfred P. Rubin, *The Law of Piracy* (Naval War College Press, 1988) 328. See, Murphy, *Ibid.*
[4] *Ibid.*
[5] Professor Quincy Wright, as quoted in an article entitled "The Law of Nuremberg Trial" in 41 *American Journal of International Law* (1947), at 56.

international criminal law *stricto sensu* – the so-called core crimes - and crimes of international concerns – the so-called treaty crimes.[6] According to Mueller, "transnational crime" is a criminological rather than a juridical term, coined by the UN Crime Prevention and Criminal Justice Branch "in order to identify certain criminal phenomena transcending international borders, transgressing the laws of several states or having an impact on another country".[7] The term "transnational crime" is a general concept that contains different types of crime, including organized, corporate, professional and political crime.[8] Further, the "transnational law" has been described as the law, which regulates actions or events that transcend national frontiers.[9] It means cross-border relations of a legal kind involve international and national elements that do not fit within the traditional divisions. Thus, focusing on the trans-boundary dimension, transnational criminal law is used for the indirect suppression by international law through domestic penal law of criminal activities that have actual or potential trans-boundary effects.[10]

Transnational criminal law is considered by some to be part of international criminal law in the general sense of international laws concerned with penal measures.[11] However, several distinctions can be drawn between the two on the basis of direct and indirect criminal liability in international law, extra-territorial jurisdiction, values and interests, and the suppression of different types of threats that impact on international society.[12]

Since the most important goal of international treaties is to ensure prosecution of the accused, many of them strongly state the obligation either to extradite or to submit the accused for prosecution.[13] Under normal circumstances, it

---

[6] Neil Boister, "Transnational Criminal Law"?, 14 *European Journal of International Law* 953-976 (2003), at 953.

[7] S. Mueller, "Transnational crime: Definitions and Concepts", in P. Williams and D. Vlassis (eds.), *Combating Transnational Crime* (2001) at 13. Bassiouni cites Mueller as the author of the term. See Bassiouni and Vetere, "Towards Understanding Organized Crime and its Transnational Manifestations", in M. C. Bassiouni and E. Vetere (eds.), *Organized Crime: A Compilation of UN Documents, 1975-1998* (1998) 31. See Neil Boister, *ibid*, at 954.

[8] Cyrille Fijnaut, "Transnational Crime and the Role of the United Nations", 8 *European Journal of Criminal Law and Criminal Justice* (2000) at 120. See Neil Boister, *ibid.*

[9] P. Jessup, *Transnational Law* (1956), at 2. Neil Boister, *ibid.*

[10] Neil Boister, *ibid*, at 955.

[11] *Ibid*, at 961.

[12] *Ibid*, at 961-974.

[13] See, *e.g.*, Convention on Prevention and Punishment of Crimes Against Internationally Protected Persons, Including Diplomatic Agents, which entered into force on 20 February 1977. Art. 7 of the Convention states that "The State Party in whose territory the alleged offender is present shall, if it does not extradite him, submit, without exception whatsoever and without undue delay, the case to its competent authorities for the purpose of prosecution, through proceedings in accordance with the laws of that State." See Murphy, *supra* note 1, at 3.

is solely up to the state where an accused is apprehended to decide whether to extradite him or to prosecute.[14] To ensure that the prosecution option is realizable, each state party is required to take such measures as may be necessary to establish its jurisdiction over the offence in cases where the alleged offender is present in its territory and it decides not to extradite him.[15]

So, as discussed above, an "international crime" is an act that is defined as criminal under international law. In most instances, this will be done through international agreements, but customary international law also plays a role. Normally, an act will initially be defined as a crime by an international agreement and then, after the agreement has been ratified by a large number of states and generally accepted in practice even by those states which do not become parties, the act may be regarded as a crime under customary international law.[16] If an act is defined as an international crime under customary international law, this creates an international legal obligation to refrain from the commission of the act. The classic example of this process is the 1907 Hague Convention No. IV Respecting the Laws and Customs of War on Land,[17] which the International Tribunal at Nuremberg explicitly recognized as having become customary international law, at least by 1939.[18]

There is no definitive list of what acts qualify as international crimes. However, a survey of conventions that criminalize certain acts, provided the following list of criminal acts[19] under the interests the conventions are designed to protect: (A) Protection of Peace – aggression; (B) Humanitarian Protection During Armed Conflicts, the Regulation of Armed Conflicts, and the Control of Weapons – war crimes, unlawful use of weapons, unlawful emplacement of weapons, and mercenarism; (C) Protection of Fundamental Human Rights – genocide, crimes

---

[14] As examples of abnormal circumstances can be cited the efforts undertaken before the UN Security Council against Libya for its support of international terrorism by refusing the surrender of two Libyan members of the Libyan secret service who were indicted by a Grand Jury of the District of Columbia, United States in November, 1991 and the counteraction taken by Libya before the International Court of Justice. In response, the Security Council adopted several resolutions that, *inter alia*, demanded that Libya surrender the two accused, as well as cease its support for all terrorist activities, and imposed economic sanctions against Libya. See S.C. Res. 731 (1982), reprinted in 31 I.L.M. 731 (1992); S.C. Res. 748 (1992) reprinted in 31 I.L.M. 750 (1992). See Murphy, *ibid*, at 4.

[15] See, e.g., Article 5 of the Montreal Convention for the Suppression of Unlawful Acts against the Safety of Civil Aviation, 1971.

[16] Richard R Baxster, "Multilateral Treaties, as evidence of customary international law", 41 *British Yearbook of International Law* 275 (1965-66). See Murphy, *supra* note 1, at 4.

[17] Murphy, *ibid*, at 5.

[18] Judgement of the International Military Tribunal, 6 F.D.R. 69 (1946), at 130. See Murphy, *ibid.*

[19] The table may be found in Jordan Paust et. al., *International Criminal Law (Carolina Academic Press, 1996),* 11 . See Murphy, *ibid.*

against humanity, apartheid, slavery and related crimes, torture, and unlawful human experimentation; (D) Protection Against Terror-Violence – piracy, aircraft hijacking and sabotage of aircrafts, threat and use of force against internationally protected persons, taking of civilian hostages, and attacks upon commercial vessels and hostage-taking on board such vessels; (E) Protection of Social Interests – drug offences, and international traffic in obscene publications; (F) Protection of Cultural Interests – destruction and/or theft of national treasures; (G) Protection of Environment – environmental protection, and theft of nuclear materials; (H) Protection of Communication Means - interference with submarine cables; (I) Protection of Economic Interests – falsification and counterfeiting, and bribery of foreign public officials.

Some of these crimes are generally regarded as covered by *jus cogens* norms, i.e., peremptory norms of international law that preempt any other inconsistent law.[20] Examples commonly cited include aggression, genocide, crimes against humanity, war crimes, piracy, slavery, and torture.[21] In such cases, an agreement by a state or an individual to commit the crime would be unlawful and void *ab initio* as a matter of law.[22] Also, some of these crimes are distinguished from the other crimes by referring to them as "core crimes". For example, the statute of the International Criminal Court (ICC) only covers genocide, crimes against humanity, war crimes, and aggression.[23]

Unfortunately, some of the conventions that cover these crimes do not create an obligation or authorization to prosecute or extradite.[24] In sharp contrast, with respect to war crimes, the Geneva Conventions of 1949,[25] in particular designate

[20] Article 53 of the Vienna Convention on the Law of Treaties, 1969 provides: "A treaty is void if, at the time of its conclusion, it conflicts with a peremptory norm of general international law. For the purpose of the present Convention, a peremptory norm of general international law is a norm accepted and recognized by the international community of states as a whole as a norm from which no derogation is permitted and which can be modified only by a subsequent norm of general international law having the same character." Although by its terms Article 53 limits its definition of a peremptory norm to the purposes of Vienna Convention, the definition is regarded as a general standard for other purposes as well. See R.Y. Jennings & A. Watts (eds.) Oppenheim's International Law 7-8 (9th edition, 1992). See also Murphy, *ibid*, at 6.

[21] Murphy, *ibid.*

[22] See Vienna Convention on the Law of Treaties, *supra* note 20, Article 53. Article 64 of the Vienna Convention complements Article 53 by providing: "If a new peremptory norm of general international law emerges, any existing treaty which is in conflict with that norm becomes void and terminates."

[23] Rome Statute of the International Criminal Court (ICC), Article 5.

[24] Paust, *supra* note 19, at 10. See Murphy, *supra* note 1, at 6.

[25] Geneva Conventions: for the Amelioration of the Conditions of Wounded and Sick in Armed Forces in the Field, 12 August 1949, Article 49; for the Amelioration of the Conditions of Wounded, Sick and Shipwrecked Members of Armed Forces at Sea, 12

certain "grave breaches" as universal and extraditable offences within the criminal jurisdiction of each state party. Each of the four 1949 Geneva Conventions obligates states parties: (1) to enact any legislation necessary to impose effective criminal sanctions on persons committing, or ordering to be committed, any grave breaches of the conventions; (2) to search for alleged offenders and to submit them for prosecution before their own courts, whatever their nationality, or, alternatively, and in accordance with their legislation, to extradite them to another state party, provided that the requesting party has made out a *prima facie* case; and (3) to ensure to accused persons a fair trial with judicial safeguard specified in the Third Convention on Prisoners of War.

Primary focus of many of the conventions on international crimes remains on the prosecution and punishment of individuals who perpetrate the crimes. Moreover, it has long been established that the official position of the perpetrator, as head of state or as a government official, does not relieve him or her of criminal responsibility.[26] It has long been equally well established that states that sponsor international crimes may be held civilly liable, at least at the international level, for such sponsorship.[27] Much more controversial, however, has been work of the International Law Commission on state responsibility. Specifically, in 1996, the Commission adopted a complete set of draft articles on state responsibility at first reading.[28] Draft Article 19 drew a distinction between international "crimes" and international "delicts". Under the Commission's approach, states would be subject to additional consequences for the commission of state crimes.[29] Several states have

---

August 1949, Article 50; Relative to the Treatment of Prisoners of War, 12 August 1949, Article 129; Relative to the Protection of Civilian Persons in Time of War, 12 August 1949, Article 146; and their two Protocols.

[26] The decision of the International Military Tribunal at Nuremberg stated this principle most emphatically: "It was submitted that international law is concerned with the actions of sovereign States, and provides no punishment for individuals; and further, that where the act in question is an act of State, those who carry it out are not personally responsible, but are protected by the doctrine of the sovereignty of the State. In the opinion of the Tribunal, both these submissions must be rejected. That international law imposes duties and liabilities upon individuals as well as upon States has long been recognized." It stated "Crimes against international law are committed by men, not by abstract entities, and only by punishing individuals who commit such crimes can the provisions of international law be enforced. Further, it stated "The principle of international law, which under certain circumstances protects the representatives of a State, can not be applied to acts which are considered as criminal by international law. The authors of these acts cannot shelter themselves behind their official position in order to be freed from punishment in appropriate proceeding. Judgement of the International Military Tribunal, *supra* note 18, at 110.

[27] Murphy, *supra* note 1, at 8.

[28] Report of the International Law Commission on the work of its Forty-eighth session: Draft Articles on State Responsibility, U.N. GAOR, 51st Session, Supp. No. 10, U.N. Doc. A/51/10 (1996).

[29] See Articles 51-53 of the Draft Articles on state responsibility.

sharply criticized this concept.[30] The Commission's approach raises the complex issue relating to states that sponsor international crimes, regardless of the fate of Article 19 and related articles.

It is pertinent to note that by adopting the Statute of the ICC with jurisdiction over core crimes, the international community has focused attention on these crimes, and has accepted the challenge of dealing with international criminal law in a more coherent manner. But identifying all forms of international cooperation in criminal laws with the core crimes gives a distorted view of the extent and nature of this cooperation because it ignores the role of the suppression conventions.[31]

This is a fact that the issue related to the controversy over the existence of international criminal law has lost its poignancy because of the establishment of several international criminal tribunals (like the Yugoslavia and Rwanda tribunals). These tribunals exercise jurisdiction over crimes that are clearly international crimes because they appear in and are defined by the statutes of the tribunals, which were established by the binding UN Security Council resolutions. As the Rome Statute has come into force, the ICC will be exercising jurisdiction over crimes defined under the Statute.[32]

It is thus evident from the above discussion that crimes of international character have evolved over the course of time and have been embodied in a number of multilateral conventions. This process is, however, characterized by unevenness and lack of systematization. It has long been debated what constitutes

---

[30] See Draft Articles on State Responsibility: Comments of the Government of the United States of America, 37 ILM 468, 474-78 (1998).

[31] Nail Boister, *supra* note 6, at 111.

[32] Since the coming into force of the Rome (ICC) Statute on 1 July 2002, no case has so far been instituted before it. However, the Prosecutor of the ICC, Luis Moreno Ocampo, has received a referral from the President of the Democratic Republic of Congo on the situation in that country concerning the Lord's Resistance Army (LRA). The LRA has been accused of regularly attacking in December 2003 civilians of northern Uganda. Attacks by this rebel group have resulted in a pattern of serious human rights abuses against civilians in the region, including summary execution, torture and mutilation, recruitment of child soldiers, child sexual abuse, rape, forcible displacement, and looting and destruction of civilian property. The reference has requested the Prosecutor to investigate in order to determine if persons involved should be charged with such crimes, and the authorities committed to cooperate with the ICC. The ICC has jurisdiction over the most serious crimes of concern to the international community as a whole committed after the 1st July 2002: genocide, crimes against humanity and war crimes, all of which are defined in the Rome Statute. States Parties as well as the UN Security Council can refer situations to the Prosecutor for investigation. The Prosecutor has also power to initiate investigation on his or her own on the basis of information received from reliable sources with the authorization of the Pre-Trial Chamber.

an international crime, and why.[33] The fabric of international penal law in terms of defining offences as well as in determining sanctions remained relatively primitive.[34]

"Terrorism" and the crime of "aggression" are still away to be brought within the bounds of authentic international definitions having universal application. The devastating effects of the acts of terrorism are every moment attracting the attention of the international community toward this objective. It often disrupts international relations, strikes at internationally protected persons and plays States and societies against each other. Its object and form are of a trans-national character. In legal doctrine, it is often classified as a crime against humanity. Since the terrorist offence strikes not only at the established regime, but all too often at innocent bystanders as well; since terrorism is indiscriminate, consisting of mass intimidation which terrorizes, disregards and negates recognized and established norms of human rights, it is a crime against humanity. Ideologically, terrorism is directed against a particular political system, against society and against the State system as such. It is, thus, the enemy of a specific socio-political ideological system common to a considerable number of States. It threatens not only one specific State, but also the system of all or many of them.[35]

Although acts of terrorism have got definitions in various countries' national laws, so far no definition has been accepted as universally applicable by the international community. Currently the attempt for defining the term terrorism is pending consideration before the UN General Assembly as a provision in the proposed "comprehensive convention on terrorism". Given the nature and effects of a terrorist offence, the terrorist offender is an international criminal, carrying international responsibility. But the existing laws are not adequate to suppress terrorism, since a State is prevented from asserting extra territorial jurisdiction over the terrorist in the absence of a universally applicable definition of "terrorism" and universal jurisdiction. Because normally a State applies international law only to the extent it is transformed into its domestic law, subject to limitations upon the type of jurisdiction it may exert. Therefore, addition of the acts of terrorism to the list of defined international crimes is extremely necessary from the point of view of international peace and security.[36]

---

[33] M. Cherif Bassiouni, *Crimes Against Humanity in International Criminal Law,* (2nd revised edition, 1999), at 253. See, Vishnu Dutt Sharma, "International Crimes and Universal Jurisdiction", 42 *Indian Journal of International Law* 2 (2002), at 139.

[34] For more discussion see Lombois Claude, *Droit penal international,* (Paris, Dalloz: 1971), at 171. See Noemi Gal-Or, *International Cooperation to Suppress Terrorism* (1985), at 124. See also, Sharma, *supra* note 33, at 140.

[35] Noemi, *ibid*, at 153.

[36] Sharma, *supra* note 33, at 141.

Regarding the crime of aggression, it has been in principle included in the list of crimes in the ICC Statute, but has not yet been defined.[37] The ICC would be able to have jurisdiction over the crime of aggression once a provision is adopted in accordance with its Statute,[38] defining the crime of aggression and setting out the conditions under which the court would exercise jurisdiction with respect to this crime.[39] However, the Statute of the ICC has defined the international crimes of genocide, crimes against humanity and war crimes.[40] It is noteworthy that there was a move during the negotiations on the Statute for defining terroristic crimes and bringing them also within the jurisdiction of ICC. But due to the divergence of opinions, it could not come through.

A clear distinction is necessary between prohibited conduct that falls within the legally defined criminal category and that which does not.[41] Because, it is a well-established truism in international law that if a given conduct is permitted by general or particular international law, such permissibility deprives that conduct of its criminal character under international criminal law.[42] But if a given conduct is prohibited by general or particular international law, it does not mean that it is criminal *ipso jure*.[43] Therefore, international criminal law requires the existence of a legal prohibition which is deemed to have primacy over national law, and which defines a certain conduct as criminal, punishable or prosecutable, or violative of international law.[44]

3. Prevention and Punishment of Crimes

International law has walked through centuries to reach the present day reality. It creates the rights and obligations for the international community and provides for sanctions against violations. The greater part of international peace and security depends upon the extent of the prevention of crimes and effective dealing thereof by the implementation of international conventions/treaties, through international cooperation.

---

[37]ICC, *supra* note 23.
[38] Ibid, Articles 121 & 123.
[39] Ibid, Article 5 (2).
[40] Ibid, Articles 5-8.
[41] Bassiouni, note 33, at 145.
[42] A distinction exists between different violations of international law. As Kelsen puts it "not every act which constitutes a violation of law is a punishable crime." Hans Kelsen, *Peace Through Law* (1944), at 116; and Georg Dahm, Zur Problematik des Volkerstrafrechts (1956), at 49. The punishability of international crimes rests on the fact that such acts injure the international community in whole or in part and its prevention, control and repression are not based on the individual victim but on the international community as a whole. See Lassa Oppenheim, 1 International Law 192 (Hersch Lauterpacht 7th ed. 1955). See also Bassiouni, *ibid.*
[43] Bassiouni, *ibid.*
[44] Sharma, *supra* note 33, at 142.

The international community remained seized of adopting international legal measures such as the treaties and conventions, with a view to combat international crimes and to achieve the objective of world peace and security. The treaties have not only defined the crimes in their respective areas, but have also created obligations for states either to prosecute the criminals if found in their territory or to extradite them to the state by whom they are wanted for prosecution in respect of the crime committed

International legal measures dealing with international crimes may be dated back to the Paris Declaration of 16 April 1856 Respecting Maritime Law. Since then a number of conferences have been held and instruments adopted establishing principles to prevent and fight international crimes.[45]

---

[45]See, Timeline of International Humanitarian Law, at http://www.globalpolicy.org/intljustice/general/2001/timeline.htm, which lists out the following humanitarian legal measures contributing in the preventing and fighting crimes: April 16, 1856: Declaration Respecting Maritime Law, Paris; April 24, 1863; The Lieber Code, a field manual instructing the US Army how to behave in war; October 26-29, 1863; International conference was held in Geneva to discuss the laws of war; August 22, 1864; Convention for the Amelioration of the Condition of the Wounded in Armies in the Field was adopted at Geneva, the First Geneva Convention; December 11, 1868; A declaration renouncing the use of certain explosives projectiles was adopted at St. Petersburg; July 29, 1899; An International Peace Conference was held at The Hague which gave birth to: - Regulation concerning the Laws and Customs of War on Land - The Adaptation to Maritime Warfare of the Principles of the Geneva Convention of 1864, The Prohibition for five years of launching projectiles and explosives from balloons - Limits on the use of asphyxiating gases - Limits on the use of expanding bullets; October 18, 1907; A Second International Peace Conference at The Hague was convened, which established several other conventions: - Convention III relative to the Opening of Hostilities - Convention IV respecting the Laws and Customs of War on Land - Convention V respecting the Rights and Duties of Neutral Powers and Persons in Case of war on Land - Convention VI relating to the Status of enemy Merchant ships at the Outbreak of Hostilities - Convention VII relating to the Conversion of Merchant Ships into War-Ships - Convention VIII relative to the Laying of Automatic Submarine Contact Mines - Convention IX concerning Bombardment by Naval Forces in Time of War - Convention X for the Adaptation to Maritime warfare of the Principles of the Geneva Convention - Convention XI relative to certain Restriction with regard to the exercise of the Right of Capture of Naval war - Convention XII relative to the Creation of an International Prize Court - Convention XIII concerning the Rights and Duties of Neutral Powers in Naval War - Convention XIV Prohibiting the Discharge of Projectiles and Explosives from Balloons; February 26, 1909: A Conference was convened in London, which establishes the Laws of Naval War; June 17, 1925: Another conference in Geneva established the Protocol for the prohibition of the use of Asphyxiating, Poisonous or Other Gases, and of Bacteriological Methods of Warfare; July 27, 1929. A major diplomatic conference was held in Geneva, which established the Convention relative to the treatment of Prisoners of War; 1934. An International Convention on the Condition and Protection of Civilians of enemy nationality who are on territory belonging to or occupied by a belligerent was adopted in Tokyo; April 15, 1935; A Treaty on the Protection of Artistic and Scientific

Institutions and Historic Monuments called the Roerich Pact was adopted in Washington; 1938; A Draft Convention for the Protection of Civilian Populations Against New Engines of War was introduced in Amsterdam; August 8, 1945; The Allied powers of World War II created an International Military Tribunal to prosecute Nazi war criminals in Nuremberg, London; November 21, 1945 — October 1, 1946; Some 21 Nazi leaders were prosecuted for crimes of aggression, war crimes and crimes against humanity in Nuremberg. Eleven are sentenced to death, 3 are acquitted and the rest are imprisoned; October 1946: In the wake of the precedent set by Nuremberg, an international congress was convened in Paris calling for the adoption of an international criminal code prohibiting crimes against humanity and the prompt establishment of an International Criminal Court (ICC); January 19, 1946; The Allied Powers of World War II announced the establishment of a second war crimes court, the Military Tribunal for the Far East, to prosecute Japanese war criminals; December 11, 1946; UN General assembly affirmed the Principles of International Law recognized by the Charter of the Nuremberg Tribunal; April 29, 1946 — November 12, 1948; The International Military Tribunal for the Far East prosecuted Japanese soldiers for war crimes, crimes against peace and crimes against humanity. Seven were sentenced to death; December 9, 1948; - UN General Assembly adopts the Convention on the Prevention and Punishment of the Crime of Genocide. - An International Law Commission is asked to study the possibility of establishing an International Criminal Court; December 10, 1948; The UN General Assembly adopted the Universal declaration of Human Rights detailing human rights and fundamental freedoms; 1949-1954; The International Law Commission drafted statutes for an International Criminal Court but opposition stymied the effort and the General Assembly effectively abandoned the effort pending agreement on a definition of the crime of aggression and an international Code of Crimes; August 12, 1949; Another diplomatic conference was held in Geneva, establishing: - Convention I for the Amelioration of the Condition of the Wounded and Sick in armed forces in the field. - Convention II for the Amelioration of the Condition of wounded, Sick and shipwrecked Members of armed Forces at Sea. - Convention III relative to the Treatment of Prisoners of War. - Convention IV relative to the Protection of Civilian Persons in time of War; May 14, 1954; Meeting at The Hague established. - Protocol for the Protection of Cultural Property in the Event of Armed Conflict. - Resolutions of the Intergovernmental Conference on the Protection of Cultural Property in the Event of Armed Conflict; 1956; The International Committee of the Red Cross drafted rules for the Limitation of the Dangers incurred by the Civilian Population in Time of War; May 12, 1968: An International Conference adopted a Resolution on the Human Rights in armed Conflicts in Teheran; November 26, 1968; The UN General Assembly decided that there is no statute of limitations to war Crimes and Crimes Against Humanity; June 8, 1977: Additional Protocols of the Geneva Conventions were adopted: - I relating to the Protection of Victims of International armed Conflicts. - II, relating to the Protection of Victims of Non-International Armed Conflicts; October 10, 1980: A UN Conference in Geneva established: - Prohibitions on the Use of Certain Conventional Weapons Which May be Deemed to be Excessively Injurious or to Have Indiscriminate Effects. - Protocol on Non-Detectable Fragments. - Protocol on Prohibitions or restrictions on the Use of Mines, Booby-Traps and Other Devices - Protocol on Prohibitions or Restrictions on the Use of Incendiary Weapons; December 10, 1984; UN General Assembly adopted the Convention against Torture and Other Cruel, Inhuman or Degrading Treatment or Punishment; June 1989: Trinidad and Tobago resurrect the proposal for an International Criminal Court and the UN General Assembly asked the International Law Commission to prepare a draft statute; December 4, 1989; UN General

4. The Centre for International Crime Prevention and the Commission on Crime Prevention and Criminal Justice[46]

The United Nations has acknowledged the importance of crime prevention and criminal justice in the maintenance of international peace and security, since its early days. In 1948, it set up the Centre for International Crime Prevention, with a view to fight international crimes. The Centre is mandated to work out plans for crime prevention, criminal justice and criminal law reforms, with special attention toward transnational organized crime, corruption and illegal trafficking in human beings. The Centre is part of the United Nations Office for Drug Control and Crime Prevention. It cooperates with national, regional and international institutions for exchange of expertise while dealing with issues relating to organized crimes, money laundering and drug control. Further, towards the goal of preventing crime, the Economic and Social Council of the United Nations established in 1992 the Commission on Crime Prevention and Criminal Justice. The Commission, which arose from a ministerial meeting held in Versailles in 1991, is a subsidiary body of

---

Assembly adopted an International Convention against the Recruitment, Use Financing and Training of Mercenaries; May 25, 1993; the UN Security Council established an International Criminal Tribunal to prosecute war crimes in the former Yugoslavia; 1993; The International Law Commission submitted a draft Statute for an International Criminal Court to the General Assembly; November 8, 1994; The UN General Assembly established a second International Criminal Tribunal to prosecute war crimes in Rwanda; December 9, 1994; The International Law Commission presented a final draft Statute on the International Criminal court to the UN General assembly and an ad hoc committee was appointed to work on establishing the court; December 11, 1995; UN General Assembly established Preparatory Committee for the Establishment of a permanent International Criminal Court; May 7, 1997; The UN Tribunal for Yugoslavia handed down its first conviction, sentencing a Bosnian Serb concentration camp guard to 20 years in prison for crimes against humanity and violations of the laws and customs of war; September 18, 1997; Convention on the prohibition of the Use, Stockpiling, Production and Transfer of Anti-Personnel Mines and on their Destruction; March 26, 1998; US Senator Jesse Helms, chairman of the Foreign Relations Committee, declared any International Criminal Court "dead on arrival" in the United States Senate unless the United States was given control over the court; June 17, 1998; Rome Statute establishing the International Criminal Court was finalized and adopted; September 2, 1998; The UN Tribunal for Rwanda handed down its first conviction finding a Rwandan Hutu leader guilty of genocide; October 16, 1998; British authorities arrested former Chilean dictator, Augusto Pinochet on an extradition request from a Spanish judge who brought charges of genocide, torture, and other crimes during his rule in the 1970s-80s: January 31, 2000; A UN Commission recommended that the Security Council should establish a tribunal to prosecute war crimes in East Timor, but member nations ignored the recommendation and instead asked the Indonesian government to mete out justice; August 14, 2000: UN Security Council called for the establishment of a "Special Court" to prosecute war crimes in Sierra Leone; January 3, 2001; Cambodian National assembly passed legislation to establish a tribunal in conjunction with the United Nations to prosecute "senior leaders" of the Khmer Rouge for atrocities from 1975-1979.

[46] See, http://www.uncjin.org/CICP/cicp.html, p.1.

the Council. It was preceded by a more technically focused Committee on Crime Prevention and Control, formed in 1971 to replace an earlier expert advisory committee and to tackle a broadened scope of UN interest in criminal justice policy. The Commission has been mandated by the Council to focus on several priority areas, which include: international action to combat national and international crime; promoting the role of criminal law in protecting the environment; crime prevention in urban areas, including juvenile crime and violence; and improving the efficiency and fairness of criminal justice administration systems. The Vienna based Commission selects aspects of these principal themes for discussion at its annual sessions. It provides policy guidance to the UN in the field of crime prevention and criminal justice, and to facilitate coordination of activities of the UN institutes for the prevention of crime and the treatment of offenders.

The Commission offers the nations a forum for exchanging information and to establish ways to fight crime on a global level. The Commission also provides substantive direction for the periodic UN Congress on the Prevention of Crime and the Treatment of Offenders.[47] The principal objective of the Commission thus relates to the prevention and combating of crimes. Achieving this objective requires effective cooperation between States by assisting in the collection of evidence, and by making the criminals available for prosecution. The Centre for International Crime Prevention is responsible for carrying out the decisions of the Commission.

5. Tribunals

Achieving the goal of the establishment of international peace and security requires efficient apprehension and successful prosecution of criminals including terrorists. The international community needs to employ powerful and effective tools for that purpose in the form of courts or tribunals.

The International Court of Justice (ICJ) is the principal organ among the international judicial fora with competence to deal with international crimes. According to the Statute of the ICJ, its jurisdiction comprises all cases which the parties may refer to it and all matters specially provided for in the Charter of the United Nations or in treaties or conventions in force.[48] While deciding cases, the Court applies: international conventions, whether general or particular, establishing rules expressly recognized by the contracting States; international custom, as evidence of a general practice accepted as law; the general principles of law recognized by civilized nations; and judicial decisions.[49] The Court also takes into account teachings of the most highly qualified publicists of the various nations, as subsidiary means for the determination of rules of law.[50] The Court, however, has

[47] *Ibid*, at 4.
[48] Statute of the ICJ, Article 36 (1).
[49] *Ibid*, Article 59.
[50] *Ibid*, Article 38.

jurisdiction only with respect to disputes between States. Criminal acts of individuals are thus beyond its purview. Unless sponsored by a government, such acts would not fall within the competence of the ICJ.

The court has dealt with several cases involving issues relating to international criminal law. Presently, the court is seized of many cases pertaining to the conventions on international crimes and the legality of the use of force.[51]

5.1. *Ad-hoc* Tribunals

Another type of international tribunal is the *ad-hoc* variety created by the Security Council of the United Nations. Under Chapter VII of the United Nations Charter, the Security Council has the power to take measures for the maintenance of international peace and security.[52] It was under this power that the Security Council established the International Criminal Tribunal for the former Yugoslavia (ICTY);[53] and the International Criminal Tribunal for Rwanda (ICTR).[54]

It is worth mentioning that in Security Council Resolution 1373, adopted on September 28, 2001, the Security Council stated that the acts committed on September 11, 2001, "like any act of international terrorism, constitute a threat to the peace and security" of the international community.[55] Resolution 1373 raised the possibility that the Security Council could establish an ad-hoc tribunal to prosecute acts of terrorism. Such a tribunal could exercise peremptory jurisdiction over individuals suspected of having committed these acts. However, instead of establishing an *ad hoc* tribunal a special Iraqi court has been designated to investigate and prosecute Mr. Saddam Hussein and his accomplishes in accordance with the procedure under the Iraqi laws. As they would be facing the charges of violation of international laws, it might give rise to a controversy as to the identification of the

---

[51] The cases pending before the ICJ concerning conventions on international criminal law, and on criminal law issues include: Applicability of the Convention on the Prevention and Punishment of the Crime of Genocide (Bosnia and Herzegovina v. Serbia and Montenegro), (Croatia v. Serbia and Montenegro); Armed activities on the territory of Congo (Democratic Republic of Congo v. Uganda), (Democratic Republic of Congo v. Rwanda); Certain criminal proceedings in France (Republic of Congo v. France); Legality of use of force (Serbia and Montenegro have instituted these proceedings separately against Belgium, Canada, France, Germany, Italy, Netherlands, Portugal, and United Kingdom. See for more details, "*List of pending cases before the Court*", *at* http://www.icj-cij.org/icjwww/idocket.htm.

[52] UN Charter, Article 39.

[53] Established by Resolution 827 of the United Nations Security Council on 25 May 1993, acting under Chapter VII of the UN Charter.

[54] Created by Resolution 955 of 8 November 1994 of the UN Security Council, under Chapter VII of the UN Charter.

[55] U.N. SCOR, 56th Sess., 4385th mtg., U.N. Doc. S/RES/1373 (2001). See, Richard J. Goldstone and Janine Simpson, "Evaluating the Role of the International Criminal Court as a Legal Response to Terrorism", 16 *Harvard Human Rights Journal*, (Spring 2003), at 20.

relevant international laws and procedure to be adopted for their application, and jurisdiction of the Iraqi courts.

5.2. Perplexities with the *Ad-hoc* Tribunals

The creation of tribunals by the Security Council pursuant to its power under the UN Charter presupposes Chapter VII discrete threats to international peace and security. Accordingly, the tribunals have a defined and limited temporal and geographic competence, and once they have completed their task, are dissolved. Whether such a tribunal could be dedicated to prosecuting acts of terrorism has been a perennial phenomenon with motivations as varied as its targets have been widespread. Another difficulty with such a tribunal remains that if the tribunal is to rely on the support of the Security Council for the establishment and enforcement of its jurisdiction, it will face the danger of political sabotage by the use of the veto by one or more of the permanent members of the Security Council. The delay in establishing an ad-hoc tribunal might also result in the loss of valuable evidence and witnesses.[56]

It would thus always be preferable to prosecute international crimes in a permanent tribunal like the ICC rather than to establish an ad-hoc tribunal, whose temporal and geographic competence would almost necessarily be limited. The ICC for instance, can yield all kinds of efficiencies: its "start-up" cost is one-time expenditure; it can in a single forum manage the prosecution of crimes other than terrorism and so avoid the necessity of creating other ad-hoc tribunals as they become necessary; its permanency does away with delays associated with initiating ad-hoc tribunals; and its funding comes from States Parties to its Statute rather than the United Nations, whose strapped budget may prelude the creation of new tribunals.[57]

5.3. Tribunal by a Treaty

A tribunal can also be created under a treaty by coalition of different international players as an alternative to municipal courts for the purpose of the prosecution of criminals, accused of the commission of international crimes.[58] The parties to such a treaty may be a country and the United Nations as happened in the case of the Independent Special Court for Sierra Leone. Such a treaty could be between several states, as was the case with the Nuremberg and Tokyo tribunals. The Nuremberg trials, for instance, were held in accordance with the London Agreement pursuant to which the four victorious allies of World War II agreed to prosecute major Nazi

---

[56] Goldstone and Simpson, *Ibid,* at 20-21.
[57] ICC, *supra* note 23, Article 115(a).
[58] Goldstone and Simpson, *supra* note 55, at 18.

leaders.[59] However, the tribunals' jurisdiction was not so much universal as it was the concentration of the national jurisdiction that each of the allied powers possessed to prosecute war crimes.[60]

The partners to such a tribunal may more likely reach a timely consensus regarding an acceptable definition of a crime not defined under international law, for example, terrorism. Moreover, by working together, the coalition members would have the benefit of international or transnational financial, legal, and policing services. A multilateral tribunal formed by such a coalition might be more reflective of different nations' legal systems and political ideals, and so benefit from an aura of greater legitimacy and impartiality in the eyes of the international community.

The coalition would, however, be powerless to compel other nations to cooperate in the production of evidence and suspects. Coalition members would consequently have to rely on existing extradition and cooperation treaties as well as principles of customary law like *male captus, bene detentus*.[61] Further impediments to tribunals of this nature include their cost, the delays associated with their inception, and the possibility that they may be perceived as applying "victor's justice" in spite of their multinational origins.

6. International Criminal Court (ICC)

There has been tremendous progress over the past century in fashioning global laws against the most serious of international crimes. As a result, the world now has the first effective international instrument to enforce those laws. Since the establishment of the ICC pursuant to the entry into force of its Statute on 1st July 2002, the international community is hoping that the ICC will provide a key forum for the prosecution and punishment of criminals and would thus prove helpful in the prevention of crimes. The basic role that the ICC would have is the provision of an effective tribunal in which perpetrators of certain crimes can be prosecuted under international criminal law. In the light of this primary mission, it is interesting to note that the Rome Statute does not envisage the ICC as the primary tribunal for such prosecutions. Instead, the responsibility for investigating and prosecuting perpetrators of crimes within the ICC's jurisdiction remains first with the domestic courts. This responsibility arises from the "principle of Complementarity", which grants jurisdiction to the ICC only when a country with primary competency is unwilling or unable to investigate or prosecute the crime at issue.[62] Complementarity has various consequences. First, it allays fears that the ICC may encroach upon the

---

[59] London Agreement, Aug. 8, 1945, Nuremberg Trial Proceedings, vol. 1, at http://www.yale.edu/lawweb/avalon/imt/proc/imtchart.htm. See, Goldstone and Simpson, *Ibid*, at 18-19.

[60] Goldstone and Simpson, *Ibid*, at 19.

[61] *Ibid.*

[62] ICC, note 23, Article 17.

sovereignty of nations. Second, the mere existence of the potential jurisdiction of the ICC over certain crimes can act as an incentive for nations to incorporate those crimes into their domestic laws and to become vigilant in investigating alleged violations. Third, in the event that the domestic courts do not adjudicate a matter within the jurisdiction of the ICC, the ICC itself will be able to do so, thereby both ensuring that serious crimes do not go unpunished and that a measure of retribution sanctioned by the international community is meted out against the perpetrators of heinous acts. A problem with Complementarity is that it does not prevent a country from initiating sham investigations to preclude the ICC jurisdiction. If this happened, however, the ICC could still assume jurisdiction, but precious time and evidence may have been lost during the interval.[63]

6.1. ICC Rules of Evidence

The rules of evidence, witness protection, testimony, and trial in the ICC Statute have been specially tailored to fit the crimes within the Court's jurisdiction.[64] Additionally, the ICC's punitive guidelines make provisions for both restorative and compensatory measures[65] and institutional support will be further provided through the Victims and Witnesses Unit.[66] These schemes are expected to yield positive results for law enforcement, victims, and the communities in which the crimes are perpetrated. A single set of procedural and substantive laws will apply to all parties and proceedings before the ICC. It will lead to consistency and greater legal certainty. The laws, moreover, are contained in the detailed definitions of elements of crimes incorporated into the ICC Statute. As they are the products of extensive negotiations by States Parties, they indicate that the Statute not only reflects the legal norms of various regions of the world but also represents the new frontier of global developments in international law.[67]

6.2. Referral by the Security Council

A State Party to the ICC or the Security Council may refer a case to the ICC. Alternatively, the ICC Prosecutor may initiate an investigation.[68] On the issue of referral by the Security Council, where some held it as an extraordinary political interference, others by linking it to the operation of the ICC have interpreted that the ICC is not solely dependent on Security Council referral and is therefore less vulnerable to the political will of the Security Council's Permanent Members. In their view, the most that the Security Council can do to obstruct the Court's operation is to instruct the ICC to defer an investigation for a renewable period of

---

[63] Goldstone and Simpson, *supra* note 55, at 21.
[64] ICC, note 23, Articles 68-70, and Part-6.
[65] *Ibid*, Article 75.
[66] *Ibid*, Article 43 (6).
[67] Goldstone and Simpson, *supra* note 55, at 22.
[68] ICC, *supra* note 23, Article 15.

twelve months.[69] A single permanent member will not therefore be able to use its veto right to suspend an investigation. Further, the believers in this approach are of the view that in this war prospective cases are less likely to be stymied, although, having a case referred to the ICC by the Security Council will always be advantageous, insofar as the ICC's jurisdiction over individuals and evidence will not then depend upon the ratification of the Rome Statute by any given state.[70] Security Council referral will make it possible to prosecute genocide, crimes against humanity or war crimes committed within a single state, when the territorial state and the state of nationality of the accused are one and the same. It is, however hard to be convinced that a political body should exercise control over a judicial forum, may it be by referral of a case or even more seriously by deferral of proceedings.

6.3. Jurisdiction

The ICC will be able to prosecute those who fall within its jurisdiction, provided that either the state on whose territory the crime was committed, or the state the accused is a national of, is a party to the ICC.[71] This means, according to one interpretation, that a perpetrator cannot escape the ICC's jurisdiction by fleeing to a state that is not a party to the ICC, so long as his own country, or the country where he committed the crime, is a party.[72] Even if neither of these states in such a scenario is a party to the ICC, either of them can specially submit to the ICC jurisdiction for the prosecution of the alleged perpetrator.

With this assumption, the whole world is asserting that the ICC is based on universal jurisdiction, binds not only the States Parties, but non-states parties also through the potential exercise of jurisdiction over their nationals.

These claims, however, seem to be a misrepresentation both of the jurisdictional provisions of the ICC Statute and of the existing state practice under general international law and international treaties.[73] The Statute therefore, by making the ICC jurisdiction subject to the consent of the state of nationality or that of the territory, establishes a very conservative regime, which perhaps is more restrictive than the regimes embodied in other international treaties, and does not represent the universal jurisdiction as such.

---

[69] *Ibid*, Article 16. See, Goldstone and Simpson, *supra* note 55, at 22.
[70] The Security Council can use its Chapter VII powers to compel any UN member to cooperate with the ICC. See, Goldstone and Simpson, *Ibid.*
[71] ICC, *supra* note 23, Article 12.2.a,b.
[72] Goldstone and Simpson, *supra* note 55, at 22-23.
[73] Human Rights Watch, *The ICC Jurisdictional Regime; Addressing U.S. Arguments, at* hrw.org/campaigns/icc/docs/icc-regime.htm, at1.

The consent requirement clearly creates a room for nationality veto, which may in practice reduce the ICC to an extremely limited system of *ad hoc* justice, based on political expediency.

Many treaties, such as hijacking or anti-terrorism conventions, confer jurisdiction over states other than the state of nationality of the accused to prosecute the serious crimes dealt therein.[74] Those treaties provide for the state of territory or for the state of the offender's nationality to exercise jurisdiction as an obligation. In most cases they go beyond, providing that the state of the nationality of the victim[75] should also do so. And all contain provisions for all states parties who find an offender on their territory to either prosecute or extradite. These treaties like the ICC Statute do not require that the state of nationality be a party to the treaty or consent to prosecution. Such a requirement imposes preconditions on the exercise of ICC jurisdiction that would not be imposed on the exercise of universal jurisdiction by any state. It is hard to conceive of an anti-terrorism treaty, that required ratification or consent by the state of the nationality of the accused being acceptable in world public opinion. So the assertions that the ICC is empowered to exercise universal jurisdiction seem spurious,[76] and casts doubts as to its expected efficiency in proving a great breakthrough in the prevention and punishment of crimes. However, the Court could most likely have jurisdiction in cases with an "international" element, where the state of nationality and territory are distinct states.

Further, the fact that the ICC Statute should stimulate the incorporation of universal jurisdiction into national law is widely unforeseen, since the Statute imposes no obligation on states parties to prosecute the crimes it defines, whether on a universal or any other basis. Rather it provides a limited incentive to prosecute

---

[74] See the Convention on Offences and Certain Other Acts Committed on Board Aircraft, 12 December 1969 U.N.T.S. 220-241; Convention for the Suppression of Unlawful Seizure of Aircraft, 21 September 1971, 860U.N.T.S. 105; Convention for the Suppression of Unlawful Acts Against the Safety of Civil Aviation, 23 September 1971, 24 UNT 564; International Convention Against the Taking of Hostages, G.A.Res.34/146, 34 U.N.GAOR Supp. (No.39), UN Doc A/39/819(1979); Convention on the Prevention and Punishment of Crimes Against the Internationally Protected Persons, Including Diplomatic Agents, Doc 14, 1973, 1035 U.N.T.S. 167; Convention Against Torture and Other Cruel, Inhuman and Degrading Treatment or Punishment, Dec. 10, 1984, 1465 U.N.T.S. 113; International Convention on the Suppression and Punishment of the Crime of Apartheid, Nov. 30, 1973, 1015 U.N.T.S. 243; the Convention on the Physical Protection of Nuclear Material, 1456 U.N.T.S. 2463; See Human Rights Watch, *Ibid*, at .3.

[75] The International Convention against the Taking of Hostages, the Montreal Convention, the Protected Persons Convention, the Convention against Torture and the Apartheid Convention.

[76] Human Rights Watch, *supra* note 73, at 2-3.

crimes committed by nationals or on the territory of other states parties.[77] Also, the Statute does not bind non-states parties or impose upon them any obligations toward the Court.[78] It scarcely needs saying that in these cases the ICC will not have the power to compel a non-party state to surrender a suspect, which is true of any tribunal in the absence of a prior agreement with the surrendering state or the conferral of powers under Chapter VII of the UN Charter. In any case, some states may prefer to surrender a suspect to the ICC rather than to extradite him to a country whose legal system is a matter of concern (such as one that imposes the death penalty). However, with respect to States Parties, the ICC does not have to rely on complicated extradition treaties and other cooperation treaties in order to obtain suspects and evidence as all States Parties are obliged to cooperate with the Court.[79]

The greater international cooperation, which is possible through the ICC, should give rise to greater international stability and efficacy in the fight against crimes. The very nature of crimes creates the need for international cooperation if they are to be suppressed efficiently. The flip side of this coin, however, is that the ICC's success will largely depend on international cooperation, especially insofar as the Court commands no police force of its own. The Rome Statute and Rules of Evidence and Procedure contain detailed provisions relating to such cooperation. Should a State Party fail to comply with a request, the matter may be referred to the Assembly of States Parties or, when the reference has come from it, to the Security Council.[80]

The effectiveness of the ICC as a forum for the prosecution of serious crimes is hampered by the fact that the crimes of terrorism may only be included within the ICC's jurisdiction by way of amendment, which can happen no earlier than seven years from the entry into force of the Statute i.e., 2009.[81] Moreover, if such an amendment is made to the Statute, it will only be binding on those States Parties that accept it.[82] In the interim, other kinds of fora must be used to prosecute any acts of terrorism that occur, unless of course the acts also fall under the definition of one of the crimes already within the ICC's competence. Naturally, it is possible that

---

[77] Bruce Broomhall, "Towards the Development of an Effective System of Universal Jurisdiction for Crimes Under International Law", 35 *New England Law Review* 2 (2001), at 408; See also, Sharma, *supra* note 33, at 154.

[78] Part 9 of the Rome (ICC) Statute, dealing with the state cooperation with the court, specifically obliges only "states parties" to cooperate fully and without undue delay; a clear distinction is drawn in a number of provisions between state parties and non-state parties. Those who have put forward these concerns would not dispute this. Rather their concerns relate to the prosecution of non-state parties nationals without its consent. See, Human Rights Watch, *supra* note 73, at 3. See also, Sharma, *Ibid*

[79] ICC, *supra* note 23, Article 86.

[80] *Ibid*, Article 87.7.

[81] *Ibid*, Article 121.1.

[82] *Ibid*, Article 121.5.

the States Parties will continue to disagree on the definition of terrorism, or that they will adopt only a narrow definition of the crime. The latter scenario may not be ideal, but it is preferable to the ICC having no jurisdiction whatsoever.[83]

6.4. Position of Non-party States

The critical extrinsic factor that may affect the ICC is the fear of some nations including the United States of jurisdiction of the ICC over the nationals of non-party States and politicized prosecutions including that of high dignitaries of a state. This prompted the United States to embark on a series of measures aimed at ensuring impunity for its nationals brought before the ICC.[84]

In the light of US opposition to the Court on this issue, the Security Council adopted a resolution on 12 July, 2002, in which it instructed the ICC to defer any investigation or prosecution involving current or former officials or personnel from non-States Parties for acts or omissions related to United Nations peace-keeping operations.[85] This resolution followed pressure and threats from the United States that it would veto a Security Council decision to extend the peacekeeping mandate in Bosnia. This order was made consistent with the provisions of Article 16 of the ICC Statute with one-year validity from 1 July 2002, unless the Security Council decided otherwise. At the initiative of the US, this Resolution was renewed in 2003 for another year. On its expiry, the US brought the proposal for its renewal for another year in 2004 also. However, because of international protest and strong opposition from most other nations, the US announced on 23 June 20044 that it would not proceed with the Security Council Resolution that would have extended for a third consecutive year the immunity of UN peacekeepers from prosecution by the ICC. The Deputy US representative to the UN, Ambassador James B. Cunningham said that while Washington still had the same concerns about the ICC that led to the resolution in 2002, it "has decided not to proceed with further consideration and action on the draft at this time to avoid a prolonged and divisive debate". Further, Ambassador Cunningham said, "The US would consider the risk of review by the ICC in deciding its future contributions to the UN peacekeeping

---

[83] Goldstone and Simpson, *supra* note 55, at 24.

[84] In this regard reference may be made to the American Service Members Protection Act (ASPA) passed by the US House and Senate on July 24, 2002 and signed into law by the US President on 2 August 2002. the SPA includes the following provisions: The prohibition of cooperation with the ICC; the restriction on American participation in United Nations peace-keeping operations; the prohibition of direct or indirect transfer of classified national security information (including law enforcement intelligence) to the ICC; the prohibition of United States military assistance to States Parties to the ICC; Pre-authorized executive authority to free member of the armed forces of the United States and certain other persons detained or imprisoned by or on behalf of the ICC (the so-called "Hague Invasions Clause"). See, Goldstone and Simpson, *Ibid*, at 24-25.

[85] Security Council Resolution 1422, UN SCOR, 4572d Meeting, UN Doc. S/RES/1422 (2002).

operations". He added that the US would continue to seek bilateral agreements with individual member states to protect US nationals from the reach of the ICC."[86] In reaction to the US announcement, UN Secretary General Kofi Annan said through his spokesperson that this move would help maintain the Security Council's unity at a time when it faces difficult challenges. Mr. Annan further said that if the exemption from prosecution was extended, it would hurt the credibility of the Security Council and the UN. He said, "The blanket exemption is wrong. It is of dubious judicial value, and I don't think it should be encouraged by the Council". Further, he said that, "it would be unfortunate for one to press for such an exemption, given the prisoner abuse in Iraq."[87]

Still not satisfied by the Security Council Resolution, the United States further made use of Article 98 of the ICC Statute, which provides that the Court may not proceed with a request for surrender or assistance if doing so would require the requested State to act inconsistently with its international law obligations. The United States approached many nations of the world and requested the signing of an agreement, thereby creating an international obligation guaranteeing that US nationals will not be surrendered to the ICC without the permission of the Unites States.[88]

The extent of support for the Statute in Rome, and the diverse range of states that have accepted the Statute, provide indication of the faith of the world community in the ICC with a hope of the positive deterrent value of the Statute. With sufficient support, the ICC could be a powerful mechanism, and it could be an especially credible one by virtue of its transparency and commitment to the legal ideals respected by most domestic legal systems. It would be a serious setback if the Court were allowed to emerge stillborn.[89]

6.5. Impediments to the Prosecution of Crimes

It would be relevant in this discussion to throw a light on the possible obstacles in the prosecution of serious international crimes including aggression, genocide, war crimes, crimes against humanity, and torture.

Aggression: Among the crimes covered by the ICC Statute, the crime of aggression has been the most troublesome and controversial. The precedent for the crime of aggression was the crime against peace charge filed against the defendants at the Nuremberg Trials. Article 6(a) of the London Charter that established the

---

[86] UN News Service, 23 June 2004, "US drops measures on immunity for troops in UN peace operations", at http://www.un.org/apps/news/printnews.asp?nid=11129.
[87] UN News Service, *ibid.*
[88] Such agreements, for example, were signed by the US with Tajikistan, Romania, Israel and India.
[89] Goldstone and Simpson, *supra* note 55, at 26.

Nuremberg Tribunal defined crimes against peace as "planning, preparation, initiation or waging of a war of aggression, or a war in violation of international treaties, agreements or assurances, or participation in a common plan or conspiracy for the accomplishment of any of the foregoing." The term, "aggression," however, is nowhere defined in the London Charter; nor was the term defined in the Tribunal's opinion. Rather, the aggressive nature of the Nazi attacks was assumed, and the primary focus of the Tribunal was on the defendants' allegation that the charge constituted *ex post facto* law.

The United Nations Charter uses the term "aggression" only in Chapter VII, where it authorizes the Security Council to determine the existence of an act of aggression and to make recommendations or decisions on measures to be taken by member states in order to maintain international peace and security.[90] Nowhere in the UN Charter is the concept of aggression defined either. This absence is deliberate, for many states, including the United States, opposed defining aggression. U.S. President Harry Truman described such an effort as "a trap for the innocent and an invitation to the guilty" and noted that under the Charter system as adopted, "the appropriate U.N. organ, in the first instance the Security Council, would determine on the basis of the facts of a particular case whether aggression has taken place."[91]

Despite this and later U.S. reservations, in 1974 the U.N. General Assembly adopted by consensus a resolution defining aggression.[92] The Assembly's definition, however, was not adopted for the purpose of imposing criminal liability, and was intended only as a political guide for the Security Council.[93]

As a consequence, the definition of aggression was not included in any multilateral convention, nor was it generally included as a crime in national criminal legislations. Most significantly, it does not appear in the statute of either the Yugoslavia or Rwanda tribunals, and there have been no prosecutions for crimes against peace or aggression since the Nuremberg and Tokyo Trials and the trials of German and Japanese defendants that followed in their wake.[94]

---

[90] The UN Charter, *supra* note 52.

[91] Marjorie Whiteman, *Digest of International Law* (Washington D.C.: Department of State Publications, 1965) 740. See Murphy, *supra* note 1, at 10.

[92] Res.3314 (XXIX) *on the Definition of Aggression*, G.A. Res.3314, 29 U.N. GAOR, 26th Session, Supp. No. 31, at 142, U.N. Doc. A/9631 (1974). See Murphy, *Ibid.*

[93] Julius Stone, "Hopes and Loopholes in the 1974 Definition of Aggression", 71 *American Journal of International Law* 224 (1977). See Murphy, *Ibid.*

[94] In addition to the trials of Nazi leaders held before the International Military Tribunal, numerous prosecutions of Nazis below the level of those tried before the International Military Tribunal were held at Nuremberg under *Punishment of Persons guilty of War Crimes, Crimes against Humanity,* Allied Control Council Law No.10, 20 December 1945, Official

One reason for this inactivity may be that prosecution for the crime of aggression would arguably raise serious due process questions. Past efforts to define aggression have been replete with vagueness and ambiguity.[95] It is thus perhaps surprising that aggression would appear in the ICC Statute.[96] The court's jurisdiction would be deferred, however, until such time as the states parties have defined the crime and set out the conditions under which the Court shall exercise jurisdiction with respect to this crime.[97] It remains to be seen whether the states parties will be able to accomplish this task.

Genocide: Scholars and practitioners of international law often regard genocide as the most heinous international crime."[98] A primary reason for this view is the extraordinary barbarism that characterized the Holocaust, history's most traumatic instance of genocide. The Charter of the Nuremberg Tribunal did not expressly use the term "genocide,"[99] but the definition of the crimes against peace charge covered many acts today regarded as constituting genocide,[100] the indictment of the defendants expressly charged them with genocide,[101] and the prosecution used the term during the proceedings.[102] Moreover, unlike the other crimes against humanity, the crime of genocide has been defined in a widely ratified multilateral

---

Gazette of the Control Council for Germany, No.3 Berlin, January 31, 1946, *reprinted in* Benjamin B. Ferencz. An International Criminal Court: A Step Toward World Peace: A Documentary History and Analysis (1980) 488. In these trials the judicial machinery was part of the occupation administration for the American zone. The Tokyo Tribunal, which consisted of eleven judges, was appointed by General MacArthur. Charter of the International Military Tribunal for the Far East, Jan.19, 1946, *amended* April 26, 1946. The Tribunal tried 28 Japanese leaders and convicted 25. Other allied tribunals tried over 5000 other Japanese for war crimes. *See* M. Cherif Bassiouni, *Editor's Note*, in 3 International Criminal Law 97-98 (M. Cherif Bassiouni, ed. 1986). See Murphy, *Ibid.*

[95] For an examination of ambiguities in the General Assembly's definition of aggression, see Julius Stone, *supra* note 93 at 226-37, see also Murphy note 1, at 11.

[96] ICC, *supra* note 23, Article 5.1.d.

[97] *Ibid*, Article 5.2.

[98] Steven Ratner and Jason Abrams, *Accountability for Human Rights Atrocities in International Law: beyond the Nuremberg Legacy* (1997), at 24. See Murphy *supra* note 1, at 11.

[99] Rather, Article 6 (a) of the London Charter charged the defendants with crimes against humanity, defined as: murder, extermination, enslavement, deportation, and other inhumane acts committed against any civilian population, before or during the war, or persecutions on political, racial or religious grounds in execution or in connection with any crime within the jurisdiction of the Tribunal, whether or not in violation of the domestic law of the country where perpetrated. See Agreement for the Prosecution and Punishment of the Major War Criminals of the European Axis (London Charter), Art.6, August 8, 1945, 59 Stat. 1544, 82, U.N.T.S. 279.

[100] For example, "Persecutions on Political, Racial or Religious Grounds" in the definition of Crime Against Humanity under Article 6 of the Nuremberg Tribunal Charter.

[101] Ratner and Abrams, *supra* note 98, at 25.

[102] *Ibid.*

convention—the Genocide Convention of 1948,[103] and the prohibition against genocide is generally regarded as a *jus cogens* norm. However, the Genocide Convention's definition of "genocide" remains controversial and, most importantly, the Convention has been a singular failure, both as a deterrent to acts of genocide[104] and as a legal instrument facilitating prosecution and punishment of the crime.[105] This failure is not surprising, since the Genocide Convention is a seriously flawed instrument, besides being limited in scope, does not cover so-called political genocide.[106] By its very nature most often genocide is committed by government officials as a matter of national policy and because the Convention calls for prosecution in the court of the state in which the crime was committed, it casts doubts as to impartial prosecution or even any prosecution at all.[107] The Convention also provides that states parties may "call upon the competent organs of the United Nations to take such action as they consider appropriate for the prevention and suppression of acts of genocide"[108] and that disputes between states parties regarding the "interpretation, application, or fulfillment of the present Convention, including those relating to the responsibility of a State for genocide shall be submitted to the International Court of Justice at the request of any of the parties to

---

[103] Convention on the Prevention and Punishment of the Crime of Genocide, G.A. Res.260A (III), U.N. GAOR, 3d Sess. 179th Plen. Mtg. at 174, U.N. Doc. A/810 (1948).

[104] Since adoption of the Genocide Convention in 1948, the world has witnessed, among others, the genocidal acts of the Khmer Rouge in Cambodia, the slaughter of the Kurds in Iraq, the massacres in Bosnia of Muslim, Croats and Serbs, and the ethnic slaughters in Rwanda of Tutsis and Hutus. See Murphy, *supra* note 1, at 11-12.

[105] Murphy, *Ibid*, at 12.

[106] Genocide Convention, *supra* note 103, Article II. It defines genocide as "any of the following acts committed with intent to destroy, in whole or in part, a national, ethnic, racial or religious group, as such: (a) Killing members of the group; (b) Causing serious bodily or mental harm to members of the group; (c) Deliberately inflicting on the group conditions of life calculated to bring about its physical destruction in whole or in part; (d) Imposing measures intended to prevent births within the group; and (e) Forcibly transferring children of the group to another region". Earlier drafts of the convention had included political and certain other groups. In large part because of the strong opposition of the then Soviet Union to its inclusion, political groups were omitted from the convention's coverage. See Ratner and Abrams, *supra* note 98, pp. 32-33. See also, Murphy, *Ibid.*

[107] Georg Schwarzenberger states, after reviewing arguably genocidal actions by a number of governments, "Hardly any of these alleged crimes have been committed spontaneously by irresponsible individuals. Yet the whole Convention is based on the assumption of virtuous governments and criminal individuals, a reversion of the truth in proportion to the degree of totalitarianism and nationalism practiced in any country. In any event, even if this assumption were correct, the criminal law of every civilized State provides sufficiently against any individual act of the kind, which are enumerated in the Convention." As it was once put by Sir Hartley Shawcross, murder remains murder whether committed against one or a million. In either case a criminal can be hanged only once. See Georg Schwarzenberger, The Problem of an International Criminal Law, *in* 3 *Current Legal Problems (1950)*, at 292. See also, Murphy, *Ibid.*

[108] Genocide Convention, *supra* note 103, Article VIII.

the dispute."[109] These provisions have been invoked only once i.e., by Bosnia and Herzegovina.[110] Moreover, some states, including India have made reservations to the jurisdiction of the ICJ that preclude their calling by another state party to account for the commission of genocidal acts.[111] The Yugoslavia and the Rwanda Tribunals have jurisdiction over the crime of genocide.[112] The definition of genocide in their statutes as well as the statute of the ICC tracks the definition in the Genocide Convention. Accordingly, ambiguities in this definition, as well as its exclusion of protection for political, economic, and social groups, may pose problems in successful prosecution for genocide.

On 6 July 1998, the Yugoslavia Tribunal began the trial of a Bosnian Serb charged with the crime of genocide, the first time an international trial for genocide has taken place in Europe,[113] which unfortunately came to an abrupt halt when, on August 1, 1998, the defendant died in his cell of an apparent heart attack.[114] The Rwanda Tribunal is also trying dozens of defendants on charges of genocide committed during the ethnic massacres in Rwanda in 1994. A former prime minister of Rwanda has "pleaded guilty to charges of genocide after long negotiations with the prosecutors"[115] for the Rwanda Tribunal, and the tribunal has found a former mayor in Rwanda guilty of genocide—the first time an international criminal tribunal has convicted someone of that crime.[116] Rwanda's national courts also have convicted some members of the Hutu ethnic group of genocide under the local law.

---

[109] *Ibid*, Article IX.

[110] Cases before the ICJ concerning the applicability of the Convention on the Prevention and Punishment of the Crime of Genocide brought by Bosnia and Herzegovina, note 51. See Murphy, *supra* note 1, at 12-13.

[111] The Indian reservation to the dispute settlement clause in Article IX of the Genocide Convention provides: "With reference to article IX of the Convention, the Government of India declares that, for the submission of any dispute in terms of this article to the jurisdiction of International Court of Justice, the consent of all the parties to the dispute is required in each case." Many other countries have made similar reservation including Algeria, Argentina, Bahrain, Bangladesh, Malaysia, Morocco, Singapore, Spain, United States, Venezuela, Viet Nam, and Yemen. See the *Status of Genocide Convention in the Multilateral Treaties.*

[112] ICTY Statute, *supra* note 53, Article 4; and Statute of the ICTR, *supra* note 54, Article 2.

[113] Murphy, *supra* note 1, at 13.

[114] Murphy, *Ibid.*

[115] Barbara Crossette, "U.N. Chief Pays a visit to Tribunal for Rwanda", *New York Times*, 6 May 1998, at A27. See Murhpy, *Ibid.*

[116] James C. MicKinley, Jr., "U.N. Tribunal, in First Such Trial Verdict, Convicts Rwandan Ex-Mayor of Genocide", *New York Times*, 3 September 1998, at A14. See Sara Darehshori, "Inching Toward Justice in Rwanda", *New York Times*, 8 September 1998, at A25. See, Murphy, *Ibid.*

War Crimes: The United Nations General Assembly adopted a resolution[117] in 1973 that, *inter alia*, provides that war crimes and crimes against humanity are subject to universal jurisdiction, calls upon states to assist each other in detecting, arresting and bringing to trial persons suspected of having committed such crimes and, if they are found guilty, in punishing them. It also provides that persons accused of war crimes and crimes against humanity should be tried in the countries where they committed crimes, that states shall cooperate on questions of extraditing such persons and that states shall not grant asylum to any person who is suspected of having committed a "crime against peace, a war crime or a crime against humanity."

It is worth mentioning that the laws of war crimes were arguably well established even by the time of the Nuremberg Trials.[118] The Geneva Conventions of 1949, as well as Additional Protocol I, designate certain "grave breaches"[119] as universal and extraditable offenses within the criminal jurisdiction of each state party and require states parties to search for alleged offenders, submit them for prosecution before their own courts, or alternatively, to extradite them to another state party.

Although the jurisdiction in respect of grave breaches of the Geneva Conventions of 1949 extends to neutral states, yet they have been reluctant to act.[120] Similarly, though it is generally agreeable by most authorities that war crimes may be punished by any state that obtains custody of alleged offenders, however, the practical effect of the universal jurisdiction has been quite rare.[121] Also, the attitude of combatants toward prosecutions is often the key impediment to successful invocation of the humanitarian law of international armed conflict as neither the states are willing to prosecute their own soldiers for war crimes nor of the opponent's for fear of retaliation, if the opponent is still holding their soldiers as prisoners.[122]

Another factor the international community has realized as responsible for non-prosecution of war criminals is the lack of political will or "inertia". For instance, in the Iran-Iraq War (1981–88) and the Soviet intervention in Afghanistan (1981–89), the unannounced policy of the combatants was that of unrestricted warfare. Both sides routinely perpetrated atrocities, and no war crimes trials were ever held. Such was also the case with regard to the first Gulf War (1991), with the only exception of their establishment of the Yugoslavia Tribunal for atrocities in

---

[117] G.A. Resolution 3074, U.N. GAOR, 28th Session, Supp. No. 30, at 78, U.N. Doc. A/9030 (1973).

[118] Ratner and Abrams, *supra* note 98, at 41-44. See Murphy, *supra* note 1, at 14.

[119] Geneva Conventions, *supra* note 25.

[120] Murphy, *supra* note 1, at 15.

[121] *Ibid.*

[122] Ratner and Abrams, *supra* note 98, at 91. See, Murphy, *Ibid.*

Bosnia perhaps because of wide publicity.[123] What happens in the matter of prosecution of war criminals in the Iraq War (2004) is yet to be seen. Although a special Iraqi Tribunal has started investigation against Saddam Hussein and accomplices, but the determination of crimes by the coalition forces and their commanders/bosses seems to be far from reality.

Trying war crimes becomes more difficult in the case of non-international conflicts. States generally resist extending the law of armed conflict to internal struggles for power because they prefer to deal with those who rebel against their authority solely under the national laws.[124] Common Article 3 of the Geneva Conventions of 1949 requires parties to any "armed conflict not of an international character" to apply, "as a minimum," certain standards to "persons taking no active part in the hostilities." But it is unclear that what level of conflict is necessary to trigger these protections.[125] The fact that violations of Common Article 3 do not give rise to grave breaches adds further to difficulties.[126]

Crimes against Humanity: The scope and content of crimes against humanity have been uncertain.[127] This is due to the fact that the development of the law on such crimes has been primarily through customary international law and not through the widely ratified multilateral treaties.[128] There was no authentic definition of crimes against humanity enjoying universal acceptance[129] except that the Charter of the Nuremberg Tribunal contained the charge of crimes against humanity, which has been described as "the birth of the modern notion of crimes against humanity",[130] and their mention in the Statutes of the Yugoslavia and Rwanda Tribunals.[131] However, on the entry into force of the ICC Statute, an authoritative definition has been found, since it is the product of deliberations stretching over several years and involving a great number of countries and numerous non-governmental organizations and private experts.[132]

The ICC definition of crimes against humanity is seen as a significant improvement. It is expected to resolve conflicting issues concerning the previously available definition.[133] For instance, according to the ICC definition, establishing the

---

[123] Murphy, *supra* note 1, at 15-16.
[124] Ratner and Abrams, *supra* note 98, at 92-93.
[125] *Ibid*, at 92.
[126] Murphy, *supra* note 1, at 16.
[127] Ratner and Abrams, *supra* note 98, at45-48.
[128] *Ibid.*, at 48-49.
[129] *Ibid.,* at 48-67.
[130] *Ibid.*, at 46.
[131] ICTY Statute, *supra* note 53, Article 5; and ICTR Statute, *supra* note 54, Article 3 have the mention of "crimes against humanity".
[132] ICC, *supra* note 23, Article 7. See, Murphy, *supra* note 1, at 17.
[133] For a full discussion of these issues, see Ratner and Abrams, *supra* note 98, at 48-67. Also see Murphy, *Ibid*, at 19.

crime against humanity would not require a connection between the crime and armed conflict, where this was a necessary condition in the case of the charge at Nuremberg.[134] Another key issue regarding crimes against humanity is how to distinguish the crime from, say, the crime of murder as found in national legal systems around the world. To this end, it has long been agreed that acts must involve more than isolated instances for them to qualify as crimes against humanity,[135] like they must also involve either atrocities on a large scale or a policy of acting in a preconceived and systematic way.[136] In requiring that the acts specified be "committed as part of a widespread or systematic attack directed against any civilian population, with knowledge of the attack," the ICC definition reflects the generally agreed limitations.[137] Still another issue has been whether the motive behind the crime should play any role in the definition of crimes against humanity, i.e., whether the perpetrator must have acted based on some character trait of the victim.[138] On this issue, there has been divergence of opinion between authorities. While some support the proposition that certain acts, such as murder, torture or deportation, are so atrocious that motive is irrelevant,[139] others argue that all crimes against humanity require the presence of a motive that identifies the victim with a particular racial, religious, political, social, or cultural attribute.[140] The Statute for the Yugoslavia Tribunal provides grounds for commission of the acts relevant only in the case of persecutions, and not for the other acts listed under the definition of crimes against humanity.[141] This is also the approach taken under the ICC Statute.[142]

Further, until recently, the majority view has been that a crime requires governmental involvement for its transformation into a crime against humanity.[143] However, the Statutes of the Yugoslavia or Rwanda Tribunals have not favoured this approach.[144] The reason for this deviation from the majority view could be that the Security Council recognized that many persons who committed crimes in Yugoslavia and Rwanda were not associated with a recognized state.[145] Similarly, the ICC Statute does not require the presence of state action for this purpose.[146]

---

134 *Ibid.*, at 56-57.
135 *Ibid.*, at 59.
136 *Ibid.*, at 57.
137 ICC, *supra* note 23, Article 7.1. See Ratner and Abrams, *supra* note 98, at 59-60. See also Murphy, *supra* note 1, at 19.
138 Ratner and Abrams, *Ibid.*, at 60.
139 *Ibid.*, at 63-64.
140 *Ibid.*
141 ICTY Statute, *supra* note 53, Article 5. See Murphy, *supra* note 1, at 20.
142 ICC, *supra* note 23, Article 7.1.h.
143 Ratner and Abrams, *supra* note 98, at 64-67.
144 ICTY Statute, *supra* note 53, Article 5; and ICTR Statute, *supra* note 54, Article 3.
145 Ratner and Abrams, *supra* note 98, at 66.
146 ICC, *supra* note 23, Article 7.2.a.

Terrorism: The world is suffering from the menace of terrorism resulting in killings and serious wounds. Until 1997, terrorist bombings, unlike other manifestations of terrorism, such as aircraft hijacking or sabotage, attacks on internationally protected persons, including diplomats, hostage taking, and the theft of nuclear material, were not covered by any multilateral treaty that required states parties to criminalize such activity under their domestic law. On December 15, 1997, the United Nations General Assembly adopted by consensus an International Convention for the Suppression of Terrorist Bombings. However, as stated above, the ICC Statute does not include any manifestations of terrorism within the court's jurisdiction. The 1994 ILC draft statute would have provided for such coverage,[147] but these provisions, as well as others that would have covered other international crimes including torture, were dropped and do not appear in the ICC Statute.[148]

Prosecuting and punishing acts of terrorism poses considerable obstacles. For various reasons neither the United Nations nor its specialized agencies have been able to agree on a definition of international terrorism.[149] No single convention on the legal control of terrorism could so far emerge. Rather, the United Nations has adopted a piecemeal approach to the problem through the adoption of separate conventions aimed at suppressing aircraft hijacking, unlawful acts against the safety of civil aviation, or of airports serving international civil aviation, attacks against internationally protected persons, including diplomats, the taking of hostages, unlawful acts against the safety of maritime navigation, the theft of nuclear material, the use of plastic explosives, terrorist bombing, and financing of terrorism. They establish a legal framework for states parties to cooperate toward punishment of the perpetrators of criminal acts dealt therein. They also create a system of universal jurisdiction over these crimes for states parties.[150] As the acts covered under these conventions are criminalized as terrorist acts, they are often loosely described as "antiterrorist" conventions.[151]

Thus, it can be said that these conventions deal with certain criminal acts and not "terrorism" as such.

Torture: In contrast to terrorism, torture, however, may qualify as a war crime or a crime against humanity, depending on the circumstances in which it is

---

[147] Report of the International Law Commission the work of its forty-sixth session, *Draft Statute for an International Criminal Court*, Article 20.e.

[148] Murphy, *supra* note 1, at 23.

[149] John F. Murphy, "Defining International Terrorism: A Way Out of the Quagmire", 19 *Israel Yearbook of Human Rights* 13, 14-18 (Yoram Dinstein ed., 1989). See also Murphy, *Ibid.*, at 24.

[150] Murphy, *Ibid.*, at 24-25.

[151] John F. Murphy, "The Future of Multilateralism and the Efforts to Combat International Terrorism", 25 *Columbian Journal of Transnational Law* 35 (1986), at 37-38. See also Murphy, *Ibid.*, at 24.

committed. It may also qualify as an independent crime outside of the context of armed conflict or crimes against humanity.[152] It is generally agreed that prohibitions against torture constitute *jus cogens* norms.[153]

There is a wide range of international legal instruments that implicitly or explicitly prohibit torture.[154] Nevertheless, prosecution of this crime also faces various impediments. Earlier, these instruments simply imposed obligations on states to refrain from and to take preventive measures against the torturous acts.[155] However, in 1975, United Nations General Assembly adopted the Declaration on the Protection of All Persons from Being Subjected to Torture and Other Cruel, Inhuman or Degrading Treatment or Punishment. The declaration defines "torture," and calls upon states to ensure that all acts so defined are criminal offenses under their criminal law, with the provision for redress and compensation for the victims. Later, in 1984, on the basis of this Declaration, the General Assembly adopted the Convention against Torture and Other Cruel, Inhuman or Degrading Treatment or Punishment.[156] The Convention aims to enhance the prospects for prosecution of those who engage in torture. Each state party is obliged to "ensure that all acts of torture are offenses under its criminal law,"[157] and that it is able to exercise jurisdiction over an alleged offender when it decides not to extradite him.[158] The choice of whether to extradite or prosecute is up to the state party where an alleged offender is found.[159] Each state party is also required to "ensure in its legal system that the victim of an act of torture obtains redress and has an enforceable right to fair and adequate compensation."[160]

---

[152] Ratner and Abrams, *supra* note 98, at 110.
[153] See Murphy, *supra* note 1, at 24.
[154] Richard Pierre Claude & Burns H. Weston, *Amnesty International, Torture as Policy, Human Rights in the World Community* 79 (2nd edition, 1992). See Murphy, *Ibid*, at 26.
[155] *Universal Declaration of Human Rights* (1948), Article 5.
[156] Convention Against Torture and Other Cruel, Inhuman or Degrading Treatment or Punishment, G.A. Res. 39/46, U.N. GAOR, 39th Session, Supp. No. 51, at 197, U.N. Doc. A/39/51 (1984).
[157] Torture Convention, *Ibid*, Article 4.1.
[158] *Ibid.*, Article 5.2.
[159] *Ibid.*, Article 7.2.
[160] *Ibid.*, Article, 14.1.

The definition[161] of the crime of torture worked out in the Convention is generally considered as an authoritative one.[162] However, it has certain ambiguities. The definition includes an illustrative list of purposes for which the severe pain is inflicted on the victim.[163] The perpetrator of the torture need not be a public official, but a public authority must have ordered or acquiesced in the action.[164] It is less clear what situations would precisely be covered under the Convention's required nexus to official conduct. Apart from that, the Convention does not address torture committed by a purely private group.[165] Further, as a justification of torture, the Convention does not permit exceptional circumstances to be invoked.[166]

Torture is not listed as a separate crime in the Statutes of the Yugoslavia and Rwanda Tribunals. Moreover, as noted above, the ICC Statute also does not include torture in the list of crimes over which the court has jurisdiction. The lack of prosecution for torture may be due in large part to the required nexus between the crime and official conduct.

6.6. Principle of Complementarity and ICC

As stated above,[167] prosecutions under the ICC Statute are complementary to the national prosecutions. This restricts the *proprio motu* powers (powers to initiate investigation on his own) of the ICC Prosecutor.[168] It may create a complex and potentially politically charged series of procedural hurdles that the Prosecutor might have to negotiate.[169] Where the Prosecutor may decide as to the existence of reasonable basis to proceed with an investigation, he has to so notify to all States Parties to the ICC and states that normally would exercise jurisdiction over the crime involved.[170] If any of these states responds that it is investigating or has

---

[161] *Ibid.*, Article 1. It defines the crime of "torture" as: Any act by which severe pain or suffering, whether physical or mental, is intentionally inflicted on a person for such purposes as obtaining from him or a third person information or a confession, punishing him for an act he or a third person has committed or is suspected of having committed, or intimidating or coercing him or a third person, or for any reason based on discrimination of any kind, when such pain or suffering is inflicted by or at the instigation of or with the consent or acquiescence of a public official or other person acting in an official capacity. It does not include pain or suffering arising only from, inherent in or incidental to lawful sanctions.
[162] Ratner and Abrams, *supra* note 98, at 111. See Murphy, *supra* note 1, at 26.
[163] Ratner and Abrams, *Ibid.*
[164] *Ibid.*
[165] *Ibid.*, at 112-13.
[166] Torture Convention, *supra* note 157, Article 2.2.
[167] See, *supra* note 62.
[168] John T. Holmes, "The Principle of Complementarity, see, Allison Marston Danner, Enhancing the Legitimacy and Accountability of Prosecutorial Discretion at the International Criminal Court", 97 *American Journal of International Law* 3, (2003), at 517.
[169] Danner, *Ibid.*
[170] ICC, *supra* note 23, Article 18.1.

investigated the offenders in respect of those crimes and requests the Prosecutor not to proceed, the Prosecutor "shall defer to the State's investigation."[171] The Prosecutor may, however, petition to the pre-trial chamber to find a case admissible in the face of a domestic investigation or prosecution if the state is unwilling or unable to investigate or prosecute.[172] These admissibility proceedings will have the effect of considerable delays in the investigations or prosecutions under the ICC Statute.[173] Prosecutor's functions in the ICC thus seem to be as a counterweight to state power,[174] a role not often played by prosecutors in domestic systems. At the same time, the ICC depends heavily on state support to discharge its mandate effectively. Reconciling this inherent conflict constitutes one of the primary challenges for the Court's Prosecutor,[175] which certainly would prove as impediment to the investigations and prosecutions under the ICC Statute.

7. Conclusions

Peace and security are the roots on which the civilized, prosperous, harmonious, fair and fearless tree of mankind can grow. The establishment of international peace and security has therefore been the main objective behind the creation of the United Nations, an organization with global representation. The Charter of the Organization has laid down the purposes of the UN, establishment of peace and security being the most basic among them. It has, at the same time, prescribed the principles to be applied in the carrying out of those purposes. However, for achieving the goal of the establishment of international peace and security, the true and impartial interpretation of Charter provisions and effective implementation thereof is a must. Criminal activities at any levels are the main factor, which destabilize society and leave behind the goal of establishing peace, by creating terror in the minds of people, and by causing a sense of insecurity. A variety of international crimes and sophisticated means of their commission have emerged. This challenge can only be met by having well-strengthened international criminal law. It is not that the efforts made so far by the international community toward containing the crimes and criminals are entirely ineffective or useless. However, keeping in view the frequency, the size and the degree of the menace of crime, special efforts are required to further strengthen international criminal law. One of the steps could be to look into the possibility of revising definitions of crimes in criminal law conventions in their respective fields and consolidating them in one instrument by identifying the principles of law commonly applicable to all crimes in the prevention and punishment thereof.

---

[171] *Ibid.*, Article 18.2.
[172] *Ibid.*, Article 17.1.
[173] Giuliano Turone, "Powers and Duties of the Prosecutor", in 2 *Rome Statute of the International Criminal Court* (2002), at 1137, 1142. See Danner, *supra* note 169.
[174] Danner, *Ibid.*, at 518.
[175] *Ibid.*

For the coverage of a wide range of serious crimes, it is necessary to bring the so far left out crimes likes aggression, terrorism and drug crimes to precise definitions acceptable to all nations. Thus, there is no denying that a lot is needed yet to be done as the process of creating preventive and combative measures always remaining evolving because of changing social conditions, due to new scientific and technological developments.

As has been discussed above, for a variety of reasons, states have been unwilling or unable to prosecute perpetrators of serious crimes. It remains to be seen whether the ICC proves to be a successful instrument for such prosecutions. Although the ICC Statute is widely ratified, certain provisions of it may result in undermining the effectiveness of the Court. They include: the consent regime for the exercise of jurisdiction by the Court; "opting out" of the Court's jurisdiction by states parties over war crimes for a limited period; referral of cases and deferral of proceedings by the Security Council, which may have the effect of direct interference by a political body in the functioning of a judicial body; and freedom of the Prosecutor to initiate investigation or prosecution on his own and the potential reaction of states.

Further, the custody of the alleged criminal for prosecution and evidence sufficient lead to a conviction, is a must. Where the criminal is outside the jurisdiction of the court, extradition laws are the most substantive of international laws to secure his presence before the court for prosecution. Presently, in most cases, extradition is considered subject to the discretion of the requested State. In this scenario, the most useful international campaign to help prosecute the criminals could be the conclusion of new, and the revision of old extradition treaties and mutual legal assistance treaties, adoption of tougher anti-crime policies, and intensive exchanges of information among police and intelligence agencies. However, if the world community is really serious in preventing and dealing effectively with the widespread criminality, it may have to put sincere efforts into having a comprehensive international extradition treaty creating explicit obligation to extradite a criminal. Wide-ranging international criminal justice reforms are thus required in defining the crimes, providing for more effective measures to counter them by ensuring the availability of criminals for prosecution, which could certainly help to minimize the criminal activities and could contribute to the goal of establishing international peace and security.

STATE RESPONSIBILITY AND INTERNATIONAL ENVIRONMENTAL LAW

M. Gandhi*

1. Introduction

State responsibility in international law refers to a regime of international law applicable to international wrongs or internationally wrongful acts.[1] However, international environmental harms are not only covered by the regime of State responsibility, but also by various liability regimes. As opposed to the regime of State responsibility, which deals with international wrongs, the liability regimes deal with activities not prohibited under international law. The rules of liability differ from sector to sector and are generally addressed in the international Agreements.[2] The International Law Commission has undertaken a possible codification of both State responsibility and the liability, having regard to the different nature of the legal regimes.[3]

From the point of view of States, judicial bodies, and arbitral tribunals, the State responsibility and liability are separate and distinct streams. Owing to their peculiarities, the International Law Commission had also treated them in its works separately.[4] However, academic writings on international environmental law attempt to bridge these regimes either by giving broader interpretation to best-known cases[5], or by prompting crystallization of new customary law, out of soft law

---

* Counsellor & Legal Adviser, Permanent Mission of India to the United Nations (New York). The views expressed herein are the personal views of the author and do not reflect the views of the Government of India

[1] To adopt the words of the ILC report: "There is an internationally wrongful act of a State, when conduct consisting of an action or omission is attributable to the State under international law; and that conduct constitutes a breach of an international obligation of the State".

[2] *See infra* note. 28.

[3] The State responsibility regime deals with secondary rules of international law, whereas the liability regime deals with primary rules of international law.

[4] The International law Commission felt that the two matters, Responsibility of States for internationally wrongful acts and International liability for injurious consequences arising out of certain acts not prohibited by international law, "in spite of certain appearances, are quite distinct, and would not be dealt with in one and the same draft". *The Work of the International Law Commission*, United Nations, New York, (6th edition, vol. I, 2004) at 198.

[5] *See* G. Handle, "State liability for accidental transnational environmental damage by private persons", 74 AJIL (1980) at 525. Horbach. N, "Liability versus responsibility under international Law", Ph. D Leiden cited in Richard S.J. Tol and Roda Verheyen, *State responsibility and compensation for Climate Change damages – a legal and economic assessment*, 32 Energy Policy 1109-1130 (2004). Arsanjani & Reisman, "The Quest for an International

***Bimal N. Patel (ed.),* India and International Law, 223-247.**

instruments, with a view to expanding the scope of State responsibility to include the environmental harm. Nonetheless, State practice in this field remains more supportive of the restricted view of State Responsibility[6] than the expanded view.

Considering the space constraints, an attempt has been made here to shed light on State responsibility related issues in today's international environmental law including the Indian approach in this regard.

2. State Responsibility in International Law

State responsibility is the principle by which States may be held accountable in interstate claims under international law. It presupposes a clear legal duty or obligation for States to comply with on the international plane. This obligation arises, in general, under treaty or customary law.

International judicial decisions and arbitral awards have outlined this obligation. It is expedient to discuss some of the pronouncements from the judicial and arbitral forums, which are relevant for identifying the contours of State responsibility in regard to environmental harm. The Arbitral decision of March 11, 1941, in the *Trial Smelter case*[7], is very significant in this regard, as it affirmed what may be called the obligation of good neighbourliness as a State responsibility in the following manner:

> [u]nder the principle of international law... no State has the right to use or permit the use of its territory in such a manner as to cause injury by fumes in or to the territory of another or the properties or persons therein, when the case is of serious consequence and the injury is established by clear and convincing evidence.

This decision is now widely considered to be part of general international law. State practice regularly confirms its acceptance.[8] This decision is also considered as

---

Liability regime for the protection of global commons", in K. C. Wellens (ed.) *International Law: Theory and Practice – Essays in Honour of Eric Suy* (The Hague: Nijhof, 1998) 46-98. The decisional materials are interpreted as supporting both fault based and strict liability. See Francisco Orrego Vicunna on "The evolving Law of State responsibility" in Edith Brown Weiss, *Environmental Change and International Law: New Challenges and Dimensions* (Tokyo: The United Nations University, 1992) available in http://unu.edu/unimpress/unupbooks/uu25ee0f.htm. International Environmental Law. at 55-56.

[6] Patricia Bernie & Alan Boyle, (ed.) *International Law and the Environment,* (2nd edition, Oxford, 2002) at 185.

[7] 3 R.I.A.A. 1905 (1949).

[8] International Law Association Report of the 60th Conference, Montreal (1982) at 163. See also Franz Zaver Perrez, "The Relationship between "Permanent Sovereignty" and the

having laid the foundation of international environmental law.[9] Another important statement of principle in regard to obligation of State, which is very often invoked in the context of environmental harm, is derived from the decision in *Corfu channel case* which ruled that States have duty "not to allow knowingly its territory to be used for acts contrary to rights of other States".[10]

A procedural rule of State responsibility derived from the award in the Lake *Lanoux* case[11]is important in this context. Although this rule is specifically applicable in regard to the utilization of shared natural resources it plays a significant role in matters of environmental dispute resolution. According to this, States have to conduct in good faith the consultations and negotiations designed to arrive at, through agreements, settlements of conflicting interests.

3. Claims based on State Responsibility

Under traditional international Law, to sustain a claim under State responsibility, a claimant needs to answer the following questions: Was there a duty under international law? Was the duty breached? Can responsibility be attributed to a State for the violation of international law?[12]

Moreover, under the scheme of State responsibility, only the State's own obligations are in focus. Private parties or companies are not in general bound by public international law[13], unless and otherwise those private acts are attributable to State.[14] These limiting factors have rendered the system of State responsibility into an inefficient, cumbersome tool that does not readily offer any help to remedy the environmental harm.

---

obligation not to cause transboundary environmental damage", 26 *Environmental Law* (1996) at 1200.

[9] Alexandre Kiss and Dinah Shelton, *International Environmental Law*, (3rd edition, Transnational, 2004) at 88.

[10] *Corfu Channel* (UK *v.* Albania), ICJ Reports 1949 at 22. In this Case, the Court said "every state's obligation not to allow knowing its territory to be used for acts contrary to the rights of other states".

[11] Lake Lanoux Arbitration (*Spain v. France*) 1957 ILR 101. According to Lammers the general international law derived from the award is: "a duty for the riparian states of an international water course conduct in good faith, consultations and negotiations to designed to arrive through agreements at settlements of conflicting interests". Lammers (1984); 517 cited in Nico Schrijver at 225.

[12] *See* Bernie, *supra* note 6 at 181 and at 188-189; See also M. Gandhi, "Towards a liability regime under Biosafety Protocol" in R.K. Dixit and C. Jayaraj, (ed.) *Dynamics of International Law in the New Millennium*, (New Delhi: ISIL, 2004) at 363.

[13] *See* Bernie, *supra* note 6 at 182.

[14] *Ibid.*

4. Evolution of Law of State Responsibility to Environmental Harm since the Stockholm Conference

The developments that took place in the field of the environment, since the Stockholm Conference, ushered in a process of assimilation of rules of State responsibility into international environmental law, in a gradual manner. Adoption of Principle 21 of the Stockholm Declaration marks an important phase of development of law in this regard. Principle 21 declares that State's have "responsibility to ensure the activities within their jurisdiction or control do not cause damage to the environment of other States or areas beyond the limits of national jurisdiction." The stipulation of rights and responsibilities of States[15], in equal terms under one principle brings out an idea that the "no harm principle" stipulated in principle 21 is severely limited by the States right to exploit their natural resources. In other words, this principle does not prohibit all kinds of transboundary harm. Its prohibition is limited only to significant or substantial transboundary harm.[16] According to this view, all the detrimental transboundary effects arising from the use of natural resources of a State cannot be prohibited under principle 21. The prohibition under this principle must be limited only to certain transboundary pollutions that met the following conditions: the harm from the pollution

- "must result from human activity"
- "must result from a physical consequences of a casual human activity"
- "must cross national boundaries", and
- " must be significant and substantial.[17]

This higher threshold is felt to be unhelpful to seek remedy for all cases of environmental harm as this threshold makes sure that only certain environmental harm which reached a certain degree of criticality is justiciable. Nonetheless, the

---

[15] Principle 21 of the Stockholm declaration says: "States have, in accordance with the Charter of the United Nations and the principles of international law, the sovereign right to exploit their own resources pursuant to their own environmental policies, and the responsibility to ensure that activities within their jurisdiction or control do not cause damage to the environment of other States or of areas beyond the limits of national jurisdiction."

[16] Gerog Dahm *et al*, 1Völkerrecht Public International Law] 445 (2nd edn., 1989); cited in Franz Xaver Perrez, "The Relationship between "Permanent Sovereignty" and the obligation not to cause Transboundary Environmental Damage", 26 *Environmental Law* (1996) at 1202. This linkage has been criticized as indicative of a swing in favour of a right to development. Some authors suggest that the two additional words: *and developmental*, appear in Principle 2 of Rio Declaration has been criticized as "skillfully masked step backwards", with its stronger emphasis on development which "upsets the delicate balance struck in Stockholm between the sovereign use of natural resources and the duty of care for the environment".

[17] *See* Xaver Perez, *supra* note16 at 1202.

evolution of this principle can certainly be treated as progress over the traditional rule of State responsibility in as much as it sets some ultimate limits beyond which a State causing transboundary pollution cannot cross.[18]

Twenty years after the Stockholm Conference, the ideas presented in principle 21 of the Stockholm Declaration underwent further changes during the United Nations Conference on Environment and Development held in Rio de Janeiro in 1992. The outcome document, the Rio Declaration, in principle 2, recognises that the "developmental policies of a State" can also be a balancing factor additional to the exploitation of natural resources, a balancing factor already recognized in principle 21 of the Stockholm Declaration in relation to the prohibition of singnificant harm. However this addition has been claimed to have weakened the traditional obligation of States: not to cause transfrontier damage.[20]

Following the UN Conference on Environment and Development another significant development took place in the international legal arena. The principle of prohibition of causing significant harm to others or to places outside of State territory as well as the duty to take into account and protect the right of other States, has been declared as a principle of international environmental law in the Advisory Opinion on the *Legality of the Threat or Use of Nuclear Weapons.*[21] Courts in national jurisdictions also took a similar view in a few other not so well-known cases.[22] Nonetheless, the judicial recognition given to this principle does not seem to have provided any great strength to the probable claimants of transboundary harm. On the other hand, the political process, which brought forth principle 21 of the Stockholm Declaration and principle 2 of the Rio Declaration, has provided a strong indication of States unwillingness to accept the "no harm" principle as an absolute principle. The conduct of States thus reveals a consistent pattern of a large majority of States treating the principle of no harm as a relative principle – relative

---

[18] C. Tomuschat, "Obligations Arising for States without or Against Their Will", 241 *Recueil des cours* (1993-V) at 195, 237 and 292.

[20] Xaver Perez, *supra* note 16, footnote 165

[21] *Legality of the Threat or Use of Nuclear Weapons, Advisory Opinion,* I.C.J. Reports 1996, at 226, paragraph 29. In the Advisory Opinion on the *Legality of the Threat or use of Nuclear Weapons* the court recognized the importance of the environment and said: "environment is not an abstraction but represents the living space the quality of life and the very health of human beings, including generations unborn. The existence of the general obligations of states to ensure that activities within their jurisdiction and control respect the environment of other states, or of areas beyond the national control, now part of the corpus of international law relating to the environment".

22 Cases concerning *Karin B. Zanoobia*, *The Jolly Rosso*, and the *Deep Sea Carrier* (Case of poisonous Ships) cited in Tullio Scovazzi, "State responsibility for environmental harm", 12 *Yeabook of International Environmental Law* (2001) at 47.

to the right of States to exploit natural resources and pursue their development policies.[23]

Academic writings are replete with commentaries on the evolution of international environmental law of State responsibility hinting at the emergence of stronger rules including the strict liability rule against a State for the pollution caused by it to the places outside the State territory. This view is built upon the soft law instruments which sprang out of the political process in the Stockholm and Rio conferences. However, these writings are not supported with state practice. For these reasons, some writers express skepticism about strict and absolute liability as a general principle of law.[23a] In reality, however, the application of international rules of State responsibility in the post-Rio scenario in the context of the environment remains dismally low for the following reasons: First, under the State responsibility regime, the notions of responsibility and fault are closely inter-related. The establishment of breach of a primary rule of international law by the source State is still a precondition for the right of the affected State to be compensated for the damage suffered.[24] Second, any successful claim under State responsibility required a proof from the claimant of intention of recklessness on the part of the State.[25] Third, in a case where breach cannot be established the source State will not be liable to repair any part of it. Lastly, the concept of State responsibility does not foresee any duty to compensate for damage due to activities, which are not prohibited by international law.[26]

The inability of the regime to cover all kinds of tranboundary environmental harms, and also the difficulties the claimant would have to encounter in proving a causal connection between the significant harm and damage have led States which suffered transboundary harm to prefer settling the claim through negotiation rather than by judicial settlement. For example, the Canadian claim relating to the damage caused by Cosmos 954 against the Soviet Union, was settled only *ex gratis* (without the Soviet Union accepting any legal liability for the damage caused), in spite of the fact that the act in question was covered under the 1972 Space Object Liability Convention, to which both Canada and Soviet Russia are parties.[29] Similarly, in the

[23] Lakshman Guruswamy, "International Environmental Law: Boundaries, Landmarks, and Realities", 10 *Nature Resources and Environment* (1995) at 43 and 46.
[23a] *See* Bernie, *supra* note 6 at 185.
[24] "Primary rules" establish the distinction between the lawful and unlawful activities. Their violation entails legal consequences, which are specified in "secondary rules". See First Report, Yearbook of International Law Commission (1980) paras. 20-25.
[25] *See* M. Gandhi, *supra* note 12; Bernie, *supra* note 6 at 182. See also, Scott Barret, *Environment and State: The Strategy of Environmental Treaty making* (Oxford, 2003) at 120-123.
[26] Thomas Gehring and Markus Jachtenfuchs, "Liability for transboundary environmental damage towards a general liability regime?" 4 *European Journal of International Law* (1993) at 93.
[29] Notes of 23rd January 1970 and 15th March 1979, 18 ILM (1979) 954, Canada – USSR. Protocol on settlement of Canada's Claim for Damages Caused by Cosmos;, 20 ILM (1982)

case of the *Chernobyl Nuclear accident,* which had caused huge loss to many countries in Europe, including France and United Kingdom, the affected countries were hesitant to make any claim due to their inability to prove direct injury, which is very essential to sustain a claim under State responsibility.[30] This has led to processing of claims concerning environmental damage in the national courts under civil liability provisions rather than by the international tribunal or Court[31]. Given the state practice, one cannot be very optimistic about the efficacy of the regime of State responsibility in providing remediation to transboundary environmental harm. This regime may be suitable only for certain limited situations. The present status of the law of State responsibility for the environmental harm is succinctly stated thus: "… as a general principle, covering all sources of transboundary harm…States are in general responsible for environmental damage only if it results from want of due diligence".[27]

The difficulties experienced by States in regard to the limited scope and application of rules of State responsibility gave rise to the development of special legal regimes of liability well suited to protect the environment from certain lawful, but hazardous activities such as oil pollution, nuclear damage, marine pollution damage – by shipping or off-shore oil exploitation, damage caused during the carriage of dangerous goods, and the acts that deplete the Ozone Layer, change in climate, depletion or acts that deplete fish stock, movement of waste across the boundaries.[28] These liability regimes are varied and employ different methodologies

---

689. The Canadian claim was based on the Convention on International Liability for Damage caused by Space objects, 29th March 1972, 24 UNT 23892389, TIAS No. 7762 and on general principle of international law.

[30] *See* Bernie, *supra* note 6, at 184 – 185.

[31] For example the Sandoz pollution to Rhine had been litigated in the national courts. See Tulio Scovazzi *op.cit.*, n.22. However, some national courts are inclined to take the view that the international environmental norms generally create rights and obligations for States only, not for individuals. See Daniel Bodansky and Jutta Brunnee, "The role of National Courts in the Field of International Environmental Law", 7 *Review of European Community & International Environmental Law*, 11-20 (1998) at 17. In this regard a number of decisions from the national courts from the Netherlands and United States Courts are cited in Andre Nollkaemper, "Compliance Control in International Environmental Law: Travesting the Limits of the National Legal Order", 13 *Yearbook of International Environmental Law* (2002) at 177-178.

[27] *See* Bernie, *supra* note 6, at 185

[28] The following are some of the important multilateral legal instruments dealing with liability provisions for the environmental harms: Convention on Third Party Liability in the field of Nuclear Energy, 1960; Vienna Convention on Civil Liability for Nuclear Damage, 1963; Convention Relating to Civil Liability in the field of Maritime Carriage of Nuclear Material, 1971; Brussels Supplementary Convention on Third Party Liability in the field of Nuclear Energy and amended by additional protocols adopted in 1964 and 1988; the Joint Protocol relating to the application of Vienna Convention and Paris Convention, 1992; International Convention on Civil Liability for Oil Pollution Damage, 1969; International Convention on the Establishment of an International Fund for Compensation for Oil Pollution, 1971; Convention on Civil Liability for Oil Pollution Damage resulting from

in accordance with the harm anticipated.[29] These regimes generally cover activities of private persons. Although these regimes do not replace the rules of general international law on State responsibility, they are successful in evolving new rules on civil liability, including holding the operator strictly liable for the hazardous acts, which resulted in harm or allocating the loss for different parties namely, the operator, international financial arrangement (such as oil Fund.) In certain cases responsibility of the State is supplemented as a last resort by creating a residual liability on the State that had jurisdiction and control over the activity.[30]

The evolution of new principles and adoption of new approaches through Agenda 21 had certainly enriched the liability conventions with new concepts like polluter pay, precautionary principle, intergenerational equity, prior information, consultation, early warning, and common but differentiated obligations.[31] Yet, the assessment of the efficacy of liability regimes proved to be very difficult as the liability related instruments were either very few[32] in number or many liability conventions have not come into force. Moreover, doubt has been raised, with regard to a number of instruments as to whether they can enter into force at all. A recent document which surveyed the efficacy of liability regimes states thus: "Work in this field has met with many failures: either because the negotiations were not concluded or because the adopted instruments did not enter into force". Nonetheless, claims have been made that some of the new principles have become

---

Exploration for and Exploitation of Seabed Mineral Resources; Kuwait Regional Conventions for cooperation on the Protection of the Marine Environment from Pollution, 1978; IMO Protocol to amend the International Convention on Civil Liability on 1992; Convention on Civil Liability for Damage caused During Carriage of Dangerous Goods by Road, Rail and Inland Navigation Vessels, 1989; International Convention on Liability and Compensation for Damage in connection with the Carriage of the Hazardous and Noxious Substances by Sea, 1996; and Basel Protocol on Liability and Compensation for damage resulting from Transboundary Movements of Hazardous Wastes and their Disposals, 1999; Convention on Liability for Damage Caused by Space Objects,1972; the Convention on Civil Liability for Damage resulting from Activities dangerous to the Environment, 1993; and the Convention on the Protection of Environment through Criminal Law, 1998; and the United Nations Frame work Convention on Climate Change.

[29] This includes, *inter alia*, obligation of percentage of pollution reduction according to the size of the industry, reduction of production of certain substances including particular chemicals, Prior informed consent procedures and EIA procedures etc.

[30] *See* Birnie, *supra* note 6 at 187; Tulio Seovazzi, *supra* note 22 at 59 – 61. For detailed study of compliance and control procedures in civil liability conventions, see Robin R. Churchill, "Facilitating (Transnational) Civil Liability Litigation for Environmental Damage by Means of Treaties: Progress, Problems, and Prospects", 12 *Yearbook of International Environmental Law* (2001) 3 – 41.

[31] Nico Schrijver, Chapter 8, and International Environmental Law: Sovereignty *v* the Environment.p. 220. *Sovereignty over Natural Resources: Balancing Rights and Duties* (Cambridge University Press, 1997).

[32] Liability and Redress, *UNEP Report of the workshop on liability and redress in the context of the convention on biological diversity*, UNEP Doc. UNEP/CBD/COP/6/INF/5 28 February 2002.

general principles of international law or customary international law,[33] although such claims are not readily acceptable to many writers, in the absence of State practice.[34]

5. State Responsibility and International Commons

State responsibility and liability for the damage caused to the international Commons has been the subject matter of intense debate in international law. The liability regimes evolved in relation to depletion of the ozone layer, the Framework Convention on Climate Change, and provisions concerning the prevention of pollution to the High Seas seek to address State responsibility, traditionally a bilateral issue, in a multilateral context linking the harming and the harmed States. It has added another dimension also as it seeks to address a situation where the perpetrators are many (States and individuals) and the victim is only the international community as a whole.[35]

Another problem arising in this case is that of the identification of the claimant and the quantification of the damage. In the absence of identification of a definite wrongdoer, and the quantification of loss, it would be difficult to get the remedy for the harm done to the global commons either under national law or under international law. Moreover, in the case of emission of greenhouse gases and

---

33 Alexandre Kiss and Dinah Shelton, *supra* note 9 at 46 & 54. Dupuy observed "the principle of information and consultation, which has manifested itself in the obligation of States to inform and consult one another prior to engaging in any activity or initiative that is likely to cause transboundary harm ... can be said to reside in the realm of customary international law". See Pierre–Marie Dupuy, "Soft Law and International Law of the Environment", 12, *Michigan Journal of International Law* (1991) at 420. Handle, citing recent state practices concludes that there is a general acceptance of a duty to prevent significant transboundary harm. G. Handle, "National Uses of Transbounary Air Resources - The International Entitlement is Reconsidered", 26 *Natural Resources Journal* (1986) at 436 – 438. Some writers assert that the precautionary principle is recognized as binding international law See Harold Hohmann, *Precautionary legal duties and principle of Modern International environmental Law, (USA:* Norwell, Kluwer, 1994) at 344.

34 *See* for detailed discussion of lacunae in the civil liability regimes Robin R. Churchill, "Facilitating (Transnational) Civil Liability Litigation for Environmental Damages by means of Treaties: Progress, problems, and Prospects", 12 *Yearbook of International Environmental Law* (2001) 3 – 41. There are many writers who are very critical of the Hohmann's assertion that the Precautionary Principle has become customary international law. See G. Handle, 'Environmental Security and Global Change: The Challenge to International Law", in Wilfred Lang and et. al. (eds.) *Environmental Protection and International Law* (1994) at 59 & 78. *See* also Ulrich Fastenrath' book review on Hohman's Book, 7 *Denver Journal of International Law* 4 (1996).

35 *See* Mahnouse H. Arsanjani and W. Michael Reisman, "The quest for an international liability Regime for the Protection of the Global Commons" in K. C. Wellens (ed.) *International Law: Theory and Practice – Essays in Honour of Eric Suy* (The Hague: Nijhoff, 1998) 475-482.

the depletion of the ozone layer, a number of States can be identified as causing harm to the global commons. States from which the pollution originates have to effect control on their nationals from causing significant harm. Without which the harm done to the global commons cannot be arrested and reversed. Therefore, concerted efforts on the part of States to control the pollution from their territory not to cause damage to the global commons becomes a pre requisite.

A number of liability conventions whose target is to protect the global commons from pollution, in general, impose liability on the operator or the State for harm caused by certain types of activity to the global commons. However, on a careful analysis one may easily find that the aim of these regimes is not to address the harm done to the global commons, but rather address measures that would avoid causing injury to States, their citizens and entities and their properties. As most of the activities, which cause harm to the global commons, are lawful, the State responsibility rules which are generally applicable to internationally wrongful acts could seldom be applied to fix the responsibility of States towards international commons. However, attempts have been made to conceive a legal regime applicable to global commons by liberally interpreting the decision in *Trial Smelter*, Principle 21 of the Stockholm Declaration and Principle 2 of the Rio Declaration, to forge a view that general international law imposes an obligation on States not to cause damage to areas beyond the limits of national jurisdiction including the international commons.[36] According to this view, a number of international conventions that focus on prevention of specific harm to the environment may converge at a point, from where emerged a general principle not to harm the environment, including the global commons.[37] Violation of this general principle has been equated by a few writers with breach of *erga omnes* obligation of State which is owed to a multitude of States and thus can be invoked by States jointly and individually[38]

It may be noted that the acceptability of such an obligation has been intensely debated in the International Law Commission and in the Sixth Committee of the UN General Assembly in the context of draft articles on State Responsibility adopted recently in the General Assembly[39], and also in the context of the work of the International Law Commission on the topic of International Liability for Injurious Consequences arising out of Acts not Prohibited by International Law.[40]

---

[36] *Ibid.*, 472.

[37] *Ibid.*, *See* also RSJ Tol and Verheyen *supra* note 5 at 1114– 118. *See* also Stephen McCaffrey *International Water Law for the 21st Century: The contribution of the UN Convention*, Paper delivered at the Stegner Center's Fourth Annual Symposium, University of Utah, College of Law Salt Lake City, 16 April 1999 at 16.

[38] *Ibid.*,1113. *See* also Weiss, *infra* note 46.

[39] The *Work of the International Law Commission, supra* note 4 at 204.

[40] *Ibid.*

It has been argued that the State Responsibility Articles 42 and 48 provide a possible way to make claims against States which cause harm to the international commons as they have violated the common obligations (obligation *erga omnes*) and multilateral treaties.[41] However, the linkage created between *erga omnes* (principle derives out of a dictum of the ICJ in *Barcelona Traction* case) and *jus congens,* (a treaty principle, that a treaty derogating from a preemptory norm is void as per Article 53 of the Vienna Convention) has been seriously questioned by publicists on the ground that both obligation *erga omnes* and *jus cogens* are unlinkable as they greatly differ in terms of their origin, and application.[42] Even those who believe that Articles 42 and 48 of the State Responsibility draft are a significant contribution to the progressive development of law, were not so certain about the value of these

---

[41] Article 42 of The responsibilities of States for internationally wrongful acts says:

> A State is entitled as an injured State to invoke the responsibility of another State if the obligation breached is owed to:
> (a) That State individually; or
> (b) A group of States including that State, or the international community as a whole, and the breach of the obligation:
> (i) Specifically affects that State; or
> (ii) Is of such a character as radically to change the position of all the other States to which the obligation is owed with respect to the further performance of the obligation.

Article 48 says:

> 1. Any State other than an injured State is entitled to invoke the responsibility of another State in accordance with paragraph 2 if:
> (a) The obligation breached is owed to a group of States including that State, and is established for the protection of a collective interest of the group; or
> (b) The obligation breached is owed to the international community as a whole.
>
> 2. Any State entitled to invoke responsibility under paragraph 1 may claim from the responsible State:
> (a) Cessation of the internationally wrongful act, and assurances and guarantees of non-repetition in accordance with article 30; and
> (b) Performance of the obligation of reparation in accordance with the preceding articles, in the interest of the injured State or of the beneficiaries of the obligation breached.
>
> 3. The requirements for the invocation of responsibility by an injured State under articles 43, 44 and 45 apply to an invocation of responsibility by a State entitled to do so under paragraph 1.

[42] G.Gaja, *Obligations* "*Erga Omnes*, International Crimes and *Jus Cogens*: A tentative Analysis of Three Related Concepts" in J. H. H. Weiler, Acassese, M. Spinedi, Walter de Gruyter (eds.) *International Crimes of States: A Critical Analysis of the ILC Draft Article 19 on State Responsibility* (Berlin, New York, 1989) at 149. *See* also Xue Hanquin, *below* note 47 at 174.

articles in conferring standing for a State[43], because of the fact that the notion of injury contemplated in these articles is different from the natural sense of injury as understood in today's legal parlance i.e., harm, material or moral suffered by the obligee or beneficiary of the obligation breached.[44] States themselves have expressed similar views in the Commission and in the Sixth Committee of the UN.[45] This point has been succinctly stated by Xue Hanqin thus:

> 'Invocation of State responsibility may involve such claims as that for compensation', filing and application before a competent tribunal, or even taking counter measures. For this, the injured State needs "cause". The commentary made it clear that the injured State must have specific right to make such a claim, conferred either by treaty or customary international law. The current wording of the article, however, is not clear on this point.[46]

Xue Hanqin emphasized thus: "Article 48 does not make it clear what kind of specific right a State should have to bring a claim on behalf of the international

---

[43] Citing ILC responsibility draft Tullio Scovazzi, says that where several States are responsible for the same internationally wrongful act, the responsibility of each State may be invoked in relation to the act. He concludes thus: "It is however doubtful if this provision is sufficient to address cases of gradual and cumulative pollution arising from numerous sources that are located in different States." See Tulio Scovazzi, *supra* note 22 at 61. In addition, on the basis of a rigorous analysis of ICJ decisions on *South West Africa, East Timor* and *Monetary Gold* cases, Iain Scobbie concludes that whether the jurisdiction title exists or not depends on the circumstances of the case but depends on the substantive content of the claim present. *See* Iain Scobbi, "The invocation of responsibility for the Breach of 'obligations under Premptory Norms of General International Law", 13 *EJIL* (2002) 1218 – 1220. Another writer says that "... the conditions for an *actio popularis* in international law remain, today as previously, thoroughly imprecise". *See* Pierre-Marie Dupuy, "A General stock taking of the connections between the Multilateral Dimension of Obligation and Codification of the Law of Responsibility", 13 *EJIL* (2002) at 1075.

[44] James Crawford, "The ILC Articles on Responsibility of States in internationally wrongful Acts: A Retrospect", 96 *AJIL* (2002) at 880-881.

[45] See the *First Report of the International Law Association (ILA) Study Group on the Law of State Responsibility* refers to India's reservation on the incorporation into draft articles of the concept of differentially injured States. In the context of plurality of injured States, India said: "Each injured State is entitled to recover by way of compensation only that much of the damage that itself suffered, and nor more". *See* statement by Dr. P.S. Rao, on Agenda item 162: Report of the International Law Commission on the work of its fifty-third session – State Responsibility, November 1, 2001. Poland also emphasized a need for elaboration in the framework of the definition of an injured State the notion of obligation *erga omnes,* which involves procedural issues of subjects, entitled to claim responsibility. See James Crawford, *supra* note 44.

[46] Remarks by Xue Hanqin, "The state of State Responsibility", *Proceedings of the 96th Annual meeting of the ASIL,* (Washington D.C., 13-16 March 2002) at 173. For a different view, *see* Weiss, "Invoking State responsibility in the Twenty First Century", 96 AJIL (2002) 798-816.

community against the defaulting State".[47] One may thus conveniently conclude that "…in the field of environmental protection there does not exist a widely recognized norm of international *erga omnes* character".[48]

ILC's preoccupation with the issue of harm to the global commons is not new. In one of the earlier draft articles on State Responsibility the ILC had included among International Crimes, "a serious breach of an international obligation of essential importance for safeguarding and preservation of the human environment, such as those prohibiting massive pollution of atmosphere or of the seas".[49] However, this move was not agreeable to many members in the International Law Commission, and the draft article was dropped.[50] Some isolated instances such as imposition of responsibility on Iraq for causing pollution to the sea by the destruction of oil wells during the Gulf War were considered by some writers as acknowledging State responsibility for the environment.[51] Never the less, this conclusion could be challenged on many grounds including that the responsibility fixed on Iraq in the instant case was for its violation of the law of war and not under the law of State responsibility.

6. The ILC and International Liability for Injurious Consequences Arising out of Acts not Prohibited by International Law

Besides its work on State responsibility, the International Law Commission has been working on another related topic: International Liability for Injurious Consequences arising out of Acts not Prohibited by International Law. This topic was placed on the agenda of the ILC in 1978. Since 1978 three special Rapporteurs have worked on this topic, namely, Quentin Baxter (1978-1984), Julio Barboza (1985-1996), and P.S. Rao, (1997 till date). Baxter had submitted five reports to the Commission, and his schematic outline was considered as a distinct contribution.[52] Mr. Barboza submitted 12 reports. However, the scope and content of the topic remained unclear, owing to such factors such as conceptual and theoretical

47 *Ibid., at* 173.
48 ILA Report, *infra* note 49 at para. 158.
49 Article 19.3 sub (d) of the Draft Articles on State Responsibly, *ILC Yearbook 1980* (vol. II, Part Two, 1980) at 30-34, and *ILC Yearbook 1985* (vol. II, Part Two, 1985) at 24-25.
50 Eric Wyler, "From 'State Crime' to Responsibility for 'Serious Breaches of Obligations under premptory Norms of General International Law'" 13 *European Journal of International Law* (2002) at 1148.
51 Operative Paragraph 16 of Security Council Resolution 687 (1991) adopted on 3rd April 1991 says: "Reaffirms that Iraq, without prejudice to the debts and obligations of Iraq … is liable under international law for any direct loss, damage, including environmental damage and the depletion of natural resources, or injury to foreign Governments, nationals and corporations, as a result of Iraq's unlawful invasion and occupation of Kuwait".
52 A/CN.4/487 pp.17-18.

difficulties, the question of the appropriateness of the title, and the relation of the subject to the topic of State responsibility.[53]

A Working Group of the ILC in 1992, therefore, considered some of the general issues relating to the scope, the approach to be taken, and possible direction of the future work on the topic. On the basis of the recommendations of the Working Group, the Commission took a number of decisions in July 1992.[54]

The Commission, however, to proceed with the work on the topic, in 1997 concentrated first on matters concerning prevention under the sub-title "Prevention of Transboundary Damage from Hazardous Activities". The concept of prevention conceived in the ILC draft articles also sprang from the neighborhood principle[55], which obligates a State to employ its best possible efforts to prevent transboundary damage.[56] In that connection, the duty of prevention is considered a due diligence obligation, and founded upon knowledge regarding operation of hazardous activities, materials used, the process of managing them, and the risk involved.[57] Prevention is considered imposing an obligation of conduct[58], and not obligation of result. By and large, the present special Rapporteur built these articles on the basis of conclusions, reached by earlier special Rapporteurs.

For example, Barboza's conclusions that a State engaging in activities involving risk of transboundary harm should rectify, consult and negotiate a mutually accepted regime governing such activity, and in that process, if the States so desired, they could even prohibit the activity[59], was readily accepted by the current Rapporteur, Dr. P.S.Rao. And also Barboza's caveat that there was no requirement of prior consent from the States likely to be affected to be comprised with, by the State interacting such activities in its territory[60], were fully taken into consideration. On the scope of due diligence, full credit was given to the views of Barboza and Baxter that the standard of due diligence that should be deemed applicable with regard to the principle of prevention was generally considered to be proportional to the degree of risk of transboundary harm, in a particular case.[61] The view that the standard of adequate protection should be determined with due regard

---

[53] A/CN.4/487. See *ILC Yearbook 1992*, (Vol. II, Part-I) at 61-62.
[54] A/CN.4/487.
[55] *Ibid.*
[56] *Ibid.*, paragraph 32
[57] *Ibid.*
[58] The obligation of conduct involves States obligation to take necessary legislative, administrative, and other action for improving its laws, decisions, and policies. The standard of obligation required to be assessed on the basis of, among other things the size of the operation, its location special climatic conditions, and material used in the activity etc.
[59] *Ibid.*, Paragraph 54.
[60] *Ibid.*
[61] *Ibid.*, Paragraph 55.

to the importance of the activity, and its economic viability, taking into account the means at the disposal of the acting State, and the standards applied in the affected State and regional and international practice[62], has been highlighted in the draft articles on prevention. Thus it is clear that the draft articles do not deal with every transboundary activity. They deal with activities, which have a risk of causing substantial or significant harm.[63] This necessitated the definition of risk also. In the absence of any perception of risk of a magnitude covered under the threshold by the State of origin of the pollution there appears to be no requirement for any preventive measures. Having regard to the impossibility of formulating a general rule of international law, fixing at a level at which the damage produced by transfrontier pollution can be discerned substantially in view of difference in permissible pollution in accordance with the technical standard of the industry and the level of pollution generally accepted in the region concerned, or even of the level of general damage caused by human influence on the environment,[64] the activities involving the risk of significant harm formed the threshold. The implication of this threshold is that to make harm significant, the harm must lead to a real detrimental effect on matters such as, human health, industry, property, environment, or agriculture in other States. Although the threshold is determined by factual and objective criteria, it nonetheless involves a value determination, which depends on the circumstances of a particular case and the period in which such determination is made.[65]

The contribution of the draft articles on Prevention of Transboundary harm from Hazardous Activities to international environmental law is important to assess the legal status of obligation of prevention in that field. Draft Article 3 says, "State shall take appropriate measures to prevent significant transboundary harm or at any event minimize the risk of." The Rapporteur himself has treated this only as a general principle.[66] Moreover the scope of these articles is very restrictive in the sense that they seek to impose duty on States to be implemented internally, as they do not cover harm to the environment outside the territory or other place under the jurisdiction or control of a State such as ships or platforms, high seas, or outer space.[67] The duty to prevent transboundary harm is not absolute but qualified. The State of origin is not under any obligation to guarantee that significant harm be

---

[62] *Ibid.*

[63] *Ibid.*, Paragraph 73.

[64] *See* text corresponding to footnotes 116 &117 in paragraph 87 of A/CN.4/487: First, the Commission had not yet made a final decision on its precise scope. Second, the Commission decided that the topic should be understood as comprising issues of both prevention and remedial measures. Third, the Commission decided that attention should be focused at first, drafting articles in respect of activities having risk of causing transboundary harm, it would then decide on the next stages of work.

[65] *See* the Rapporteur's commentary at 389.

[66] A/CN.4/489 paragraph 16.

[67] Lammers, *supra* note 11 at 9-10.

prevented, but only to take "all appropriate measures" to prevent such harm.[68] These articles also seem to have taken care of differential responsibility of States in the observance of a due diligence obligation as the commentary to Article 3 says: "The degree of care expected of a State with a well developed economy and human and material resources and with highly evolved systems and structures of governance is different from States which are not so well placed".[69] In addition most of the obligations in these articles are viewed as procedural in nature.[70]

In spite of the restrictive approach followed in these draft articles, States are unwilling to accept the prevention obligation in so far as that limits their basic right to develop.[71] Some of the provisions, more specifically, Articles 7 to 16 are viewed as either not in conformity with current requirements or inappropriate.[72] In any event these articles could be treated only as guidelines for the progressive legislative development.

The preceding analysis indicates that the draft articles on Liability of States for Injurious Consequences Arising from Acts not Prohibited by International Law have not met with the consensus,[73] and the draft articles recently finalized by the Commission on prohibition also not free from criticism. There is no indication that the reluctance of States has fundamentally changed and that they are now ready for a convention, imposing on them a general international liability for transnational environmental damage.[74]

7. The Status of State Responsibility and Liability in International Environmental Law

The law of State responsibility and liability appear to be, by and large, static in the core while a little dynamism can be seen in the peripheries. While resistance of States to the development of a general law of responsibility applicable to environmental harm appears to be stronger and consistent, their willingness to

---

[68] *See* Johan G. Lammers, "Prevention of Tansboundary harm from hazardous activities, the ILC draft articles", 14 *Hague Yearbook of International Law* (2001) at 9.

[69] *See* Report of the Law Commission on the work of its Fifty-Third Session, Official records of the General Assembly, Fifty Sixth Session, supplement No.10 (A/56/10) at 395.

[70] Lammers, *supra* note 11 at 17.

[71] Views of Malaysia and Indonesia as cited in Doc. A/CN.4/510 at 5.

[72] *Ibid.*, at 7.

[73] Liability and Redress, *UNEP Report of the workshop on Liability and Redress in the context of the convention on Biological Diversity*, 28 February 2002. Doc. UNEP/CBD/COP/6/INF/5. p. 14

[74] Thomas Gehring (*et.al*) *supra* note 26 at 107. *See* also Robert Rosenstock, "The ILC and State responsibility", 96 *AJIL* (2004) at 795. *See* also the Chair's observations in regard to the Report of the Workshop on Liability and Redress in the context of the Convention on Biological Diversity, which concurs with others stating, "The sole existence of such liability in customary international law is controversial, and there is strong resistance to its development." Doc. UNEP/CBD/COP/6/INF/5 at 14.

experiment with legally non-binding standards,[75] to protect the environment by adhering to Multilateral Environmental Agreements, (MEAs) appears to be stronger. As the nature of standards set in the MEA's, depends upon the purpose of the Agreement, accepting a particular principle in the context of the agreement becomes easier for the States than accepting a particular principle as part of general international law. For example, application of the precautionary principle in the context of the bio-safety protocol,[76] application of common but differentiated responsibility in the context of the Kyoto protocol are some instances which are indicative of the willingness of States to accept a particular principle in a particular instance. Moreover this becomes possible due to the concerted action by a number of countries[77]based on common interest and common philosophy[78], which provided them with new negotiating power.[79] Nonetheless, resistance to change has been, in general, the order of the day. Instances are not uncommon where States interpret certain accepted principles so differently, than what has been commonly understood, to suit their national interests.[80] This has led to a constant tension, in the sphere of environmental law, between the States that want to preserve the environment and the States which need to ensure continued development[81] or the right to development and exploit resources.[82] In this context, the developing countries either prefer to have lesser international obligations than the developed countries, or are inclined to have measures relating to environmental protection

---

[75] Monitoring data, control of private persons, report and evaluation.

[76] M. Gandhi, *supra* note 12 at 361-378.

[77] French Duncan, "Developing States and International Environmental Law: The Importance of Differentiated responsibilities", 49 *ICLQ* 35-60(2000).

[78] Developing countries wanted to fix more responsibility on developed countries on the basis of their past pollution leading to environmental degradation, their command over technological and financial resources etc. See *Ibid.* See International Environmental Law: Globalization Temptations? *Proceedings of the 93rd Annual Proceedings of the American Society of International Law*, 217-221 (24-27 March 1999).

[79] Linkage of environmental protection with development provided new negotiating power to the developing countries when their cooperation is indispensable to face a global challenge like ozone depletion and climate change. See Alexandre Kiss, "The Rio Declaration on Environment and Development" in Luigi Campiglio, Laura Pineschi, Domencio Sinicalco, Tullio Treves, (eds.) *The Environment After Rio: International Law and Economics*, (London: Graham & Trotman/Martinus Nijhoff, (1994) 64.

[80] The US position that the principle of common but differentiated responsibilities implies only the need to account for the present, practical differences rather than for the responsibility of the past has not been agreed by the developing countries. See Graham Mayeda, "Where should Johannesburg Take us – Ethical and Legal Approaches to Sustainable Development in the context of Environmental Law", 15 *Colorado Journal of International Law and Policy* 66 (2004); Jutta Brunnee, "Environmental Security in the Twenty First Century: New momentum for the development of International Environmental Law", 18 *Fordham International Law Journal* (1995) at 1742.

[81] *Ibid.*

[82] *Ibid.*

linked to financial or technical assistance.[83] In the case of fashioning national legislations the attitude of the developing countries is totally different from their attitudes toward international legal regimes. Developing countries would like to have stronger national regimes and are willing to employ new principles evolved in the context of sustainable development. This dualism contributes growth and development in national environment law and at the same time promotes the development of obligations under international environmental law in general, and State responsibility in international environmental law in particular. India is no exception to this trend. It is thus, opportune to see the Indian view on State responsibility and liability in environmental law.

8. Indian View on State Responsibility and International Environmental Law

India follows the dualistic concept of international law. The rules of International Law require to be specifically incorporated into national law, for the purpose of their implementation. Most of environmental legislations in India have been enacted immediately after the Stockholm Conference on Human Environment and are influenced by the outcome of the Conference. The 42nd amendment to the Constitution, which allowed incorporation of environmental concerns into directive principles of State policy, is also influenced by the Stockholm Conference.[84] To understand the Indian view on State responsibility to environment, one must necessarily know the policy of the Government on environment and development, which had existed prior to the Stockholm Conference.

The Indian aspiration to self-reliance and economic development through the five year planning process is well known. Its articulation on development issues, more particularly its demand for trade preference and removal of trade barriers by developed countries and transfer of 0.7percent of GNP from developed countries to the developing countries, during the North-South dialogue within the framework of the New International Economic Order stands testimony to Indian views on development in the context of international cooperation.[85] By and large, these views

---

[83] *Ibid.*

[84] The following are the significant administrative, legislative initiatives and directives to protect the environment: Wildlife Protection Act of 1972 and its amendment in 1991; Water (Prevention and Control) Act of 1974; Forest Conservation Act of 1980; Air (Prevention and Control) Act1981; followed by the notification of National Ambient Air Quality Standards in 1994; Environment Protection Act of 1986; National Forest Policy, 1988: Policy Statement for Abatement of Pollution and National Conservation Strategy; Policy Statement on Environment and Development, 1992; National River Conservation Plan. 1995; National Environmental Appellate Authority Act of 1997; Biodiversity Act of 2000; Energy Conservation Act of 2001; and Wildlife Conservation Strategy, 2002.

[85] *See* M.Gandhi, *Right to Development in International Law: Prospects and Reality*, Ph.D thesis, (University of Madras, 1991) pp. 362-363.

stand unaffected not withstanding global changes that had deviated from NIEO like discourses.[86]

The Indian policy on environmental protection is based on the inherent linkage between environment and development. In view of its perception of development being the main driving force in international interactions, it is not inclined to view environmental concerns in isolation from developmental imperatives.[87] Forging a balance between developmental and environmental imperatives has been in its national and international agenda for many years now. It believed that the right to development should be fulfilled so as to equitably meet the developmental and environmental needs of present and future generations.[87a] It expressed time and again that meeting the environmental objectives would place additional onerous burdens on developing countries. For this reason, it believed in the creation of a framework for assistance by the international community to complement and support the efforts of developing countries. The Indian perspective of State responsibility to the environment cannot be understood without understanding its views on environment.

India always believed that any protective measures on environment should proceed hand in hand with promotion of economic development. Even at a time when international concern over environment issues was yet to fully crystallize, the then Indian Prime Minister Mrs. Indira Gandhi, during the Stockholm Conference, 1972 emphasized that the environmental concerns cannot be viewed in isolation from developmental imperatives. She said: "Poverty is the greatest polluter". She made a point coherently thus: "The environment cannot be improved in conditions of poverty – how can we speak to those who live in villages and slums about keeping the oceans, the rivers, and the air clean, when their own lives are contaminated at the source".[88] This point was well taken by the Stockholm Conference on Human Environment, which confirmed the linkage of poverty and environment in a vicious spiral in which degradation of the environment increases poverty, while poverty increases environmental degradation.[89]

The linkage created between environment and development in the Stockholm Conference was further strengthened by the Earth Summit which adopted the Declaration of Rio and a comprehensive program of action to give effect to those

[86] See Duncan, *supra* note 77 at 49-53.
[87] Ministry of External Affairs, Government of India, *India and the United Nations*, (New Delhi).
[87a] Statement by Mr. K.R.Malkani, Indian delegation to 53rd session of the UN General Assembly on the agenda item "Environment and Sustainable Development" www.un.int/india/statements/html.
[88] Maurice F. Strong, "Hunger, Poverty, Population and Environment", *The Hunger Project Millennium Lecture*, 7 April 1999, Madras, India.
[89] *Ibid.*

principles: Agenda 21. India fully accepts Agenda 21. From Stockholm to Rio, India has campaigned for the shared concern of most developing countries. It expressed a concern that inadequate availability of funds for the financing of sustainable development remains the greatest impediment to alleviating the hunger, poverty, and environmental degradation, which continue to plague less developed countries. India has amplified and echoed this idea in all the international environmental negotiations, and in the multilateral forums including the U.N. General Assembly. For example, during the high level segment of the Seventh Session of the Commission on Sustainable Development, the Indian delegation[90], in its statement recalled the recognition of the 19th Special Session of the UN General Assembly in June 1977, the issue of unsustainable patterns of production and consumption, particularly in developed countries as the major cause of continuing deterioration of the global environment. Adding further, the Indian delegation said that the developed countries not only have the primary responsibility in taking a lead in this regard, but also required to assist developing countries technologically as well as financially.[91] India had always stressed the need for fulfillment of the obligation of developed countries to provide new environmentally sound technologies to the developing countries and also implement cutbacks of pollution or to take on additional obligations[92]regarding pollution reduction. India was also critical of developed countries over using limited natural resources to exhaustion and their heavy contribution to world pollution. It underscored the harmful nature of global freedom of trade which was responsible for a boom of export of harmful chemicals banned in producing countries, to poorer countries. It further emphasized that the right to development must be fulfilled so as to equitably meet developmental and environmental needs. The Indian view on the implementation of Agenda 21 has been succinctly stated in the following words:

> [I]t was also recognized that meeting the environmental objective in Agenda 21, would place additional, even onerous, burdens on developing countries. Therefore, we forged a balance between developmental and environmental imperatives and created a framework for assistance by the international community to complement and support the efforts of developing countries.[93]

The Government of India's priority had not changed even during the Johannesburg's Summit. It demanded in the summit that the rich world should show that it was serious about tackling poverty, and conserving the environment. It

---

[90] Statement by Mr. Viswanath Anand, Secretary Environment and Forest, 29 April 1998 at the High level segment at the Seventh Session of the Commission on Sustainable Development. www.un.int/india/statements.html.

[91] *Ibid.*

[92] Statement by Mr. Jayant Malhoutra, Member of Parliament, on Agenda item 101 Environment and Sustainable Development on 22 October 1999.

[93] Statement by Mr. K.R. Malkani, Member of Parliament in U.N. General Assembly on Agenda item 94: Environment and Sustainable Development, on 22 October 1998.

called upon the rich world to reduce its high consumption levels, and to increase development assistance,[93a] despite the fact that there was a recognition in official and non-governmental circles that India must and can find its own solutions to sustainable development. The following words of the then Prime Minister Mr. Atal Bihari Vajpayee echoes this conviction: "We cannot make the poor and the deprived wait any longer in their aspiration to live a better life. This is the first and foremost task in sustainable development, the ultimate ethical responsibility for those of us who have been voted into government by the poor".[94]

In the negotiating sessions of multi-lateral environmental agreements (MEAs) in the international forums, India always reiterated the above views. For example, disappointed with the final Montreal result, that contained only an undertaking on funding for ozone-friendly technology for the developing world, India avoided initially the signing of the Montreal Protocol.[95] India demanded $2 billion – an amount related to its cost of ozone friendly technology in the future as its price to join the 1987 Protocol during the 1990 negotiations. The developed nation's agreement to provide such assistance up to $240 million later proved to be sufficient attraction for China and India to become parties to the Protocol.

Although India has been party to a number of multilateral environmental conventions, which include the Framework Convention on Climate Change, the Convention on Biological Diversity, the Vienna Convention on the Protection of Ozone Layer, the Montreal Protocol on Substance that deplete the Ozone Layer, the Basel Convention on the Tranansboundary Movement of Hazardous Wastes, and the Convention to Combat Desertification and the Stockholm Convention on Persistent Organic Pollutants; these Conventions either do not have liability provisions or have rudimentary enabling provisions which await elaboration by further negotiations. It is, therefore, rather hypothetical, to spell out probable the Indian stand on State liability/responsibility to the environment. However, the development of a standard-setting process since the Stockholm Declaration of 1972, and the interpretation of the Supreme Court since its landmark decision in the *Oleum Gas leak case*[96] and the recently released Environmental Policy document[97] would be

---

[93a] *See* Statement by Mr. T.R.Balu, Minister of Environment and Forests, 4th PrePcom Meeting on the World Summit on Sustainable Development in Bali, 5 June 2002. *See* also statement of Mr.Yashwant Sinha, Minister for External Affairs in World summit on Sustainable Development, Johannesburg, South Africa, 4 September 2002.

[94] Statement by Prime Minister Mr. Atal Bihari Vajpayee, Delhi, February 2002, *quoted in Roads to the Summit, Reports from six countries on progress towards sustainable development, prepared* by Lead International and Panos London for the World Summit on Sustainable Development. www.Panon.Org.UK.

[95] James K. Sebenius, "The Law of the Sea Conference: Lessons for Negotiations to Control Global Warming" in Gunnar Sjosdett (ed.) *International Environmental Negotiation* (New Delhi, London: Sage, 1993) at 194.

[96] Also popularly known as *Sriram case* M.C.Mehta *v.* Union of India AIR 1987 SC 965.

of some help in identifying the Indian view on State responsibility to the environment. The statements made by the Government of India on the ILC reports concerning liability and the ILC draft articles on State responsibility also would serve as guidance for this purpose.

The Indian Supreme Court has been pro-active in the protection of the environment. It keeps abreast of all the developments of international environmental law, including the constituting principles of sustainable development. In one of its Constitutional decisions, it declared the right to a clean environment a fundamental right.[98] In *M.C.Mehta's* case[99], the Supreme Court laid down that "where an enterprise is engaged in hazardous, or inherently dangerous activity, and harm results to anyone on account of an accident in the operation of such hazardous or inherently dangerous activity, for example in escape of toxic gas, the enterprise is strictly and absolutely liable to compensate all those affected by the accident…" Further, the Court ruled that this ruling is an exception to the rule in *Rylands v. Fletcher*[100]. The factors such as "non-natural user" and "forerseability", which are of vital importance in tort cases, where generally the liability is fault-based, do not play any role when the case is one on strict liability. In other words, a harm resulting out of hazardous industry and operation would be covered under strict liability and cases of this nature will not be governed under ordinary tort law, where the liability for the harm is based on fault. This means, the victims of harm will be compensated without adducing any proof that the harm has resulted out of a fault/negligence of the hazardous operation. The Supreme Court reiterated this principle of strict liability in *Indian Council for Enviro Legal Action v. Union of India*[101], and held that "once the activity carried on is hazardous or inherently dangerous the person carrying on such activity is liable to make good the loss caused to any other person by his activity irrespective of the fact that whether he took reasonable care while carrying on his activity". The rule is premised upon the very nature of the activity carried out.

It may be seen from these decisions that the Supreme Court had applied not only an important principle of modern international law namely "polluter pays" but also invoked, where appropriate, some of the constituent principles of sustainable

---

[97] National Environment policy 2004. (Draft for comments: 21 August 2004) http://envfor.nic.in/nep.htm.

[98] In *Subhashkumar v State of Bihar,* AIR 1991 SC 420, the Supreme Court of India held that right to life is a fundamental right under the Article 21 of the Constitution and it includes the right of enjoyment of pollution-free water, and air for full enjoyment of life. In another case *Damodhar Rao v. The Special Officer Municipal Corporation of Hyderabad,* (AIR 1987 AP 171) The Andhra Pradesh High Court held that the right to live couldn't be enjoyable without protection and preservation of the environment.

[99] *M.C.Mehta v. Union of India* (1987) ISCC 395, popularly known as Oleum gas leak case.

[100] (1868) LR 3 HL 330.

[101] AIR 1996 SCW 1069.

development such as intergenerational equity, precautionary principle, obligation to cooperate to assistance, as interpretative tools in environmental related litigations.[102] Indian courts, as courts that apply common law have to acknowledge and apply the customary international law where the relevant customary international law is sufficiently certain. Another way of applying international legal principles through the municipal system is by expantial interpretation where the Supreme Court can relate the provisions of the international norms and conventions to which India is a party, in the absence of legislation, to the fundamental rights provisions of the Constitution of India.[103] These two modes did provide enormous scope for the Supreme Court to enrich the national environmental jurisprudence including the expansion of the ambit of the State responsibility to the environment.

As has been stated elsewhere India seemingly, had no occasion to negotiate on the issue of State responsibility to environment, although it became party to some of the Conventions which have liability provisions. Recently during the negotiations concerning the international liability provisions on the Bio-safety Protocol, India participated very actively. The stand taken by the Indian delegation during the negotiation was a middle line approach. India advocated for a due diligence obligation for States when a harm relating to the environment is caused during the transportation of a living modified organism outside the territory of the originating State. At the same time it supported strict liability for the harm done to the environment (within the territory) by the private operator. It also supported the idea of imposition of residual liability on states, i.e., State responsibility as a last

---

[102] *Vellore Citizens Welfare Forum v. Union of India.* AIR 1996 SC 2715. p.2720. In this case the Court held that the precautionary principle is one of the essential features of sustainable development. The Court interpreted the precautionary principle in the context of municipal law, in the following manner:

a) Environmental measures by the State government and the statutory authorities must anticipate, prevent and attack the causes of environmental degradation. b) When there are threats of serious and irreversible damage, lack of scientific certainty should not be used as a reason for postponing measures to prevent environmental degradation, and c) The "onus of proof" is on the actor or the developer/industrialist to show that his action is environmentally benign.

[103] *People's Union for Civil Liberties v. Union of India,* AIR 19971203, *Vishaka v. State of Rajasthan,* AIR 1997 SC 3011. In Vishaka's case the Court had used an international convention as a tool of interpretation. This trend attracted wider criticism. Although this approach results in lawmaking, something which is not distributed according to the judicial branch of the Government according to the Constitution, the use of international Conventions for construing the provisions of fundamental rights is unquestionable as every common law court is known to interpret the constitutional provisions in the same way India Court has done. See Dato Gopal Sri Ram, *Human Rights: Incorporating International Law into Present system,* paper presented at the conference on Constitutionalism, Human Rights and Good Governance at Kuala Lumpur on September 30, through October 1 2003. http://www.mlj.com.my/free/articles/gopalsriram.htm accessed on September 13, 2004.

resort covering the residual claims after the operator's responsibility and the insurer's responsibility had been sufficiently discharged.[104]

The Government of India's policy on the environment also employs a pragmatic approach in this regard. The National Environmental Policy (NEP) laid down 14 principles. Most of them are sustainable development related principles,[105] where legal liability also finds a place. Mention has been made in the Policy document of fault-based liability and strict liability. Thus, by implication the NEP subscribes to a liability scheme, which could combine fault-based and strict liability.

9. Conclusions

Over the years the concept of State responsibility in international environmental law has been evolved through hard and soft laws, predominantly built on the principle of "no harm", a general principle of State responsibility. Yet, the rules of State responsibility are inadequate to address all the issues of pollution. The chief difficulty with these rules is their inapplicability in most of the situations of transboundary pollution where several parties are responsible for pollution (combined progressive pollution) and where the establishment of a causal connection between pollution and significant harm arising out of pollution or damage cannot be established with a required standard of proof.

The multilateral environmental agreements fashioned for addressing international liability for certain kinds of pollution are so varied in nature that they are neither susceptible for generalization from which a general principle can be derived, nor put in practice by a great number of States leading to the creation of new norms. However, the soft law instruments have influenced the process of standard-setting by encouraging international cooperation which the traditional adversarial approach – "I win" "you lose" has failed to deliver. Well-informed legislature and proactive judiciary keep constantly internalizing these standards by infusing them in rulebooks and case laws. The contribution of Indian legislature and judiciary in evolving new national standards for environmental protection, therefore, is noteworthy.

However, in the international scene, the prevailing tension between the North and South on developmental issues keeps captive the development of environmental law, including State responsibility for environmental harm. India as an important member of G77 has always been championing the cause of developing countries by seeking a balance between the environment and development

---

104 See M. Gandhi. *Toward a liability regime under Biosafety Protocol, supra* note 12.

105 The sustainable development related principles are: intra-generational equity, inter-generational equity, right to development, environmental protection as an integral part of the development process, precautionary approach, polluter pays, equity, and public trust doctrine.

imperatives. The development priorities which are inherently linked to obligations of prevention of environmental pollution lead States to withhold their ratification from international environmental instruments, even after agreeing on the text.

At the national level, the scene is different. States are proactive in promulgating stringent environment laws, contrary to the reluctance they show towards accepting an internationally agreed standard. This duality of approach needs to be converged. Providing incentives to the States, which are willing to shoulder tougher environmental obligations, could work better than punitive measures imposed on the unwilling States. One such incentive is: setting equitable standards, on the basis of the principle of common but different obligation, for the developing countries, in vital areas of life threatening pollution such as that which affects climate change. Another possible way is, by a codification of the law of State responsibility through integration and unification of nationally accepted environmental standards on State responsibility and liability, which by nature are more stringent, legalistic, and free from development related expression. This could be done through a process modeled on the UNCITRAL model law on specific pollution and also through formulation of general principles comparable to the UNCITRAL code. This method could certainly help consolidation and codification of pure principles of environmental law acceptable to many developing countries as they are fit for instantaneous application.

INTERNATIONAL ENVIRONMENTAL LAW AND INDIA

A. David Ambrose*

1. Introduction

"Dualism" and "Monism" are the two concepts that are generally used to explain the nature of the relationship between international law and municipal law. In spite of this doctrinal division international law and municipal law supplement each other's growth. Sometimes certain principles of municipal law because of their uniform practice of many states may become rules (customary or general principles) of international law; thus municipal law contributes to the growth of international law. At times international (conventional/treaty) principles may diffuse into the municipal systems thus strengthening and reinforcing the municipal systems. In the case of India this has become very much true as far as the growth of environmental law (both international and municipal) is concerned. The developments that took place at international level towards the later part of the 20th century were to a greater extent instrumental in grooming Indian environmental jurisprudence. At the same time the national developments have greatly helped in defining some of the legal concepts of modern environmental law.

A great deal of law-making policy shift can be witnessed in the evolution of environmental law. Earlier environmental regulation was incidental to economic regulation especially natural resources exploitation. From this the focus shifted to a holistic approach to environmental protection within and beyond state borders. Based on this shift it is common to divide the development of environmental law into three stages.[1] The first pre-dates the 1972 Stockholm Conference and is characterized by piecemeal and reactive responses to particular problems of resource use and exploitation. The second stage is the Stockholm Conference era, starting immediately before the UN sponsored 1972 Stockholm Conference on Human Environment that provided a non-binding Declaration of Principles and Programme for Action and ending at the last decade of the last century. The development of environmental law, both international and domestic, was in this period simultaneous with concerns about environmental destruction highlighted especially in the 1960s. In fact the 1972 Stockholm Conference on the Human Environment stimulated hectic regional and global treaty-making activity. This

---

* Lecturer, Department of Legal Studies, University of Madras.

[1] See Francioni, F, 'Developments in Environmental Law from Sovereignty to Governance: The EC Environmental Policy', in Markesinis, B (ed), *The Gradual Convergence: Foreign Ideas, Foreign Influences, and English Law on the Eve of the 21st Century* (Oxford Clarendon Press, 1994), at 205.

Bimal N. Patel (ed.), **India and International Law, 249-264.**

period witnessed a fragmented and sectoral approach to environmental protection. The third stage that normally starts from the 1990s onwards usually referred to as the sustainable development era adopts a holistic approach to environmental protection. It mainly aimed at addressing the relationship between environment and development. Though no definite international law-making took place in this period due to the involvement of diversified interests, consensus regarding the conservation of biological diversity and preventing further adverse changes in the earth's climate emerged.

2. The Pre-Stockholm Era

Before the 1970s ecology and its protection were apparently considered as mythological vestige. The questions relating to environmental protection were addressed with the main focus on economic development. Economic development was insisted upon for the disapproval of "pollution of poverty."[2] Like many developing countries, India too felt that the major portion of environmental problems in developing countries was a result of underdevelopment and that once development (economic) took place, environmental problems would disappear. Therefore it was emphasized that any environmentally related action should not contradict the goals for development.[3]

India genuinely feared that the Western countries to stall the economic development of developing countries should not use environmental concerns. Bitten by the call for a New International Economic Order (NIEO) and drawn in to the North-South Dialogue, India apparently gave priority to economic development over environmental protection.

The late Prime Minister, Mrs. Indira Gandhi, told the UN Conference on Human Environment in Stockholm in 1972, "The rich countries may look upon development as the cause of environmental destruction, but to us it is one of the primary means of improving the environment of living, of providing food, water, sanitation and shelter, of making the deserts green and the mountains habitable." She further added: "when they themselves feel deprived how can we urge the preservation of animals. How can we speak to those who live in village and in slums about keeping the oceans, rivers and the air clean when their own lives are contaminated at the source? Environment cannot be improved in conditions of

---

[2] R. P. Anand, 'Development and Environment: The Case of Developing Countries" 20 *Indian Journal of International Law* 2 (1980) at 8.

[3] See the report of the Preparatory Committee for the UN Conference and Human Environment UN Doc. A (conf) 48/PC/13(1971) pp 13-27.

poverty."[4] She also lamented that century after century progress has become synonymous with an assault on nature.

3. Post-Stockholm Era

Proudly it should be noted that India was an active participant in the Stockholm Conference of June 1972 and is signatory to almost all international conventions on environment. Compelled by the domestic environmental concerns like that of the Bhopal gas tragedy, India started playing a vital role in consolidating international environmental law. Many non-binding environmental principles were made as binding legal principles. In fact the Stockholm Declaration and the UN General Assembly resolution[5] are just non-binding instruments. However, because of a large nation like India's state practice, many environmental principles are accorded customary law status in this period.

In response to the environmental developments that took place at international level after the UN Stockholm Declaration on Human Environment in 1972, the once "environmentally blind" Indian Constitution was made "environmentally sensitive" in the year 1976 by the 42nd Amendment.[6] For the first time the word "environment" found its due place in the Constitution after this Amendment. Moreover, in order to give definite shape to international environment treaties and conventions and to honour them, the Indian Government passed many key central acts on environment resulting in the swelling of environmental jurisprudence in India. The following Central Acts are given as examples. The Air Act 1981 was enacted by the Parliament based only on the 1972 Stockholm Conference. The Preamble to the Air (Prevention and Control of Pollution) Act 1981 (Air Act) says: "Whereas decisions were taken at the United Nations Conference on Human Environment in Stockholm in June, 1972, in which India participated to take appropriate steps for the preservation of the natural resources of the earth which among other things, include the preservation of the quality of the Air and Control of Air pollution". From the Preamble of the Environment (Protection) Act, 1986,[7] the supposed to be the omnibus legislation, it becomes clear that this Act is also passed in furtherance of government's commitment to honour

---

[4] Mrs. Indira Gandhi, *"The Unfinished Revolution address before the conference on the Human Environment"*, speech at the Stockholm.Conference, June 1972.

[5] GA Res 2977 (XXVII) of December 1972.

[6] The 42nd Amendment to the Constitution in 1976 inserted Art 48-A under Directive Principles of State Policy and Art 51 A (g) under Fundamental Duties. Art 48-A says that the state shall endeavour to protect and improve the environment and safeguard the forest and wild life of the country whereas Art 51A(g) speaks about citizen's duty to protect and improve the environment.

[7] The Preamble reads as follows: "Whereas decisions were taken at the United Nations Conference on Human Environment held at Stockholm in June, 1972, in which India participated to take appropriate steps for the protection and improvement of environment".

international agreements. The National Environment Tribunal Act, 1995, passed to mitigate the hardship caused by the Bhopal-like environmental catastrophes appears to be passed in response to the 1992 Rio Conference. The Tribunal Act's Preamble reads thus: "Whereas the decisions were taken at the United Nations Conference on Environment and Development held at Rio de Janeiro in June 1992, in which India participated, calling upon the states to develop national law regarding liability and compensation for the victims of pollution and other environmental damages".

It is pertinent to note that these central acts are passed taking recourse to Article 253 of the Indian Constitution which empowers the Parliament to make any law for the whole or any part of the territory of India for implementing any treaty, agreement or convention with any other country or countries or any decision made at any international conference, association or other body. This enables the courts to uphold the Parliament's power to enact these laws, even though these laws incidentally or otherwise touch upon entries of Concurrent or State Lists.

4. Era of Sustainable Development

The concerns about development and environment, their close linkage, have become a much discussed topic towards the end of twentieth century, as the shaping of the normative framework for international economic relations aimed to promote global development and stability needs to take into account the specific concerns about development and environment. The discussion on the relationship between the development and the environment resulted in the emergence of the concept of sustainable development. Sustainable development insists upon an integrated and holistic approach to the environmental concerns and places environmental concerns firmly within the context of growth. From the period starting from the 1990s a new approach to environmental issues has been employed. Modern environmental law has become synonyms with sustainable development. Accordingly a study of modern environmental law should necessarily include the study of sustainable development.

5. Sustainable Development

Sustainable development has emerged as a new paradigm in contemporary international law. It is conceived to encapsulate the specific concerns about development and environment and tries to balance the competing demands of development and environmental protection. Under modern international law sustainable development compendiously refers to the refined right to development.[8]

---

[8] See the separate opinion of Justice Weeramandry in the case concerning *Gabčikovo-Nagymaros Project* (Hungary/Slovakia), reprinted in 37 International Legal Material (1998) at 206.

Understanding this, the World Commission on Environment and Development (WCED) established by a resolution of the UN General Assembly and chaired by Mrs.Gro Harlem Brundtland, the Prime Minister of Norway in its Report[9] (generally known as Brundtland Report) called for the adoption, globally, of a strategy of sustainable development. The report also defined sustainable development as "development that meets the needs of the present without compromising the ability of future generations to meet their own needs."[10]

The Report underscored the linkage between development and environment and called for the adoption, globally, of a strategy of sustainable development. The general agreement that implementation of developmental plans or programmes should be carried out in a sustainable manner, was reflected in the recommendations of the WCED. The WCED, projecting the view that as environment and development go together, they have to be examined simultaneously in the present context, emphasized that sustainable development is vital to the well-being of humanity.

Sustainable development as a positive concept that aims to speak about good partnership by man with nature and especially ways and means for economic development without adverse impact on the capacity of natural resources to regenerate was enshrined in Agenda 21 of the Rio Declaration on Environment and Development. It also became a major focus in the World Summit on Sustainable Development in Johannesburg in 2002.

To the leaders from the industrialized North who state that things may have been much better if the domestic economics of the South had been managed efficiently, sustainable development signifies the growth and expansion of their economies within certain ecological limits so as to keep the planet healthy and habitable for the future generations. For the South which views the global environmental damage as the doing of the North, sustainable development means, to quote from the Report of the South Commission, "The need for compatibility between growth and the preservation of the environment and to warn against a narrow-minded and short-sighted approach to development and economic modernization".

The actual term "Sustainable development" was introduced in 1980 in The World Conservation Strategy (1980).[11] The concept emerged in the context of conservation of natural resources, but clearly contained within it wider implications in that it related to, "development". Therefore, sustainable development, which means that the goals of economic and other developments must be defined in terms

---

[9] *Our Common Future*, 1987 (Oxford, 1981).

[10] *Ibid.*, 43.

[11] Published in 1980 by the World Conservation Union, World Wild Life Fund and the United Nations Environment Programme.

of sustainability or keeping future generations in mind. Since then the concept of sustainable development has been elaborated and new dimensions of sustainable development have been highlighted. Professor Ben Boer in his study brings out the multi-dimensional character of the concept of sustainable development.[12] There he refers to a UK study that gives subsequent elaboration of the concept by Brundtland, which runs as follows:

> [T]here are many dimensions to sustainability. First, it requires the elimination of poverty and deprivation. Second, it requires the conservation and enhancement of the resources base which alone can ensure that the elimination of poverty is permanent. Third, it requires a broadening the Concept of development so that it covers not only economic growth but also social and cultural development. Fourth, and most important, it requires the unification of economics and ecology in decision making at all levels.[13]

The major premise of sustainable development according to Subrata Roy Chowdhury is two-dimensional. First, all human beings have the fundamental right to an environment adequate for their health and well-being. Second, states shall conserve and use the environment and natural resources for the benefit of present and future generations.[14]

The first part deals with the rights aspect while the second part deals with the duties side of the concept. The rights part of sustainable development i.e., right to environment, is not new to the international community. The right to environment had been asserted to be a human right for over a decade to this effect and much discussion has also taken place. And what is new in the concept of sustainable development is the duty part of it i.e. duty to conserve and use the environment and natural resources for the benefit of present and future generations, which is better known as "environmental duty". As early as in 1972 itself the Stockholm Declaration on Human Environment recognized this responsibility/duty. Principle I of the Declaration states:

> [M]an has the fundamental right to freedom, equality and adequate conditions of life, in an environment of a quality that permits a life of dignity and well

[12] Ben Boer, "Implementing Sustainability in Developing Countries" presented at the *Bangkok Conference on Environmental Law* (August, 1991).
[13] Pearce D.Markandya A.Barbier E.B., *Blueprint for a Green Economy* (London, 1989) p 175. (A Report for the United Kingdom Department of the Environment).
[14] Subrata Roy Chowdhury, "Intergenerational Equity" Substratum of The Right to Sustainable Development" in Subrata Roy Chowdhury, Erik M.G.Denters and Paul de Waart (eds.), *The Right to Development in International Law* (Martinus Nijhoff, 1992) at 234.

> being, and he bears a solemn responsibility to protect and improve the environment for present and future generation's.[15]

But the right to sustainable development converts this solemn responsibility into legal responsibility duty.

India's contribution to the development of sustainable development is immense and important. India actively participated in all the international negotiations on sustainable development. India became party to the Convention on Biological Diversity in 1994, was among the early signatories to the UN Convention to combat desertification. India had actively participated in the 22nd Special Session of the General Assembly and also at the Global Conference on Sustainable Development of Small Island Developing States held in Barbados in 1994. After ratifying the Kyoto Protocol on Climate Change, India earnestly appealed to countries that have not done so to accede to the Protocol. By continuously and strongly stressing certain important points, India helped the shaping of sustainable development concept. They are (1) international co-operation (2) financial assistance to developing countries, and (3) fair and equitable sharing of benefits arising out of utilization of revenues.

6. International Cooperation

India has consistently argued that strengthening of global co-operation is central to any effort to address global environmental problems.[16] Speaking on 4 September 2002 at the World Summit on Sustainable Development, Johannesburg, Mr. Yaswant Sinha Minister for External Affairs of India, categorically stated that India's commitment to sustainable development is second to none. He further said that sustainable development was conceived as a unifying philosophy. It was born out of combined idealism at Rio where the international community had pledged to act in a concerted manner for the future good of mankind and caring planet.[17]

To stress this he concluded with an invocation, quoting from the ancient Indian text Atharvaveda composed 3200 years ago in 1200 BC " O Mother Earth! You are the world for us and we are your children; let us speak in one accord; let us come together so that we live in peace and harmony".

---

[15] Declaration of United Nations Conference on the Human Environment (Stockholm) UN Doc A/Conf./48/Rev./ (1972). Reprinted in *Selected Documents on International Environmental Law* (Oceana, New York 1975) at 3.

[16] See the statement made in the Second Committee of UN by Honorable Mr.Prem Chand Gupta MP on November 14,2002; cf. Statements by Indian Delegates at UN Conference in New York 2002, p 95.

[17] *Ibid.,* 226.

Presently, preservation and exploitation involves a high degree of science and technology, and so technology becomes very important and decisive for the realization of the principle of sustainable development.[18] Hence international co-operation in training of personnel, facilitating their participation in relevant international programmes, supplying them with necessary equipment, advice for monitoring programmes and for the preparation of environmental assessments are necessary.[19]

This duty to co-operate in transferring technology is enshrined in Article 10 A of the Montreal Protocol of 1990.

> [E]ach party shall take every practicable step to ensure: (a) That the best available, environmentally safe substitutes and related technologies are expeditiously transferred to parties operating under Para 1 of art.5 (less-consuming developing countries) and (b) that the transferred referred to in sub-paragraph (a) occur under fair and most favourable conditions.[20]

7. Financial Assistance

The most hotly contested subject matter within environmental discussion is the question of financial co-operation because it is becoming obvious that the environment is being used as a potent weapon in the North-South political and economic battle. India for a long time stressed that to set right the global environmental wrongs, the industrialized nations responsible for damaging the earth's environment must pay for all incremental costs of steps the developing nations have to undertake.[21] This claim is the result of the fear that the environment is being used to slow down development in the South. Under these circumstances it may not be possible without recognising the duty to funding for the developing states to encourage the developing states to comply with the environmental control measures. This claim is now being recognized as the polluter pays principle, as a component of sustainable development.

India's stand along with other developing nations is that the developed countries must, since they earlier caused environmental damage for their development, bear the financial costs for the same and the developing nations are entitled to environmental compensation. This point is stressed by the proposal put forth by the World Bank, the UNDP and the UNEP for a "global environmental

---

[18] See Art 7(2) of WCED Legal Principles in this connection.

[19] See Art 202 of Law of the Sea Convention (1982).

[20] Annex 11 to the Report of 2nd meeting of the parties to the Montréal Protocol EPL (1990) 4/5 at 166.

[21] See the statement of Mr. Kamal Nath, Minster of State for Environment and Forests (India) In *The Hindu,* 31 October 1992 at 9.

facility". It emphasizes the need to mobilize additional resources to meet related costs for technical assistance and other supporting measures.

While endorsing the recommendations of the WCED, the former Prime Minister of India, the late Mr. Rajiv Gandhi and President Robert Mugabe of Zimbabwe clearly stated that "developing countries can only be expected to join in co-operative efforts to deal with such global risks as climate change and ozone depletion if they have access to the required additional financial and technological resources that these efforts requires".[22]

8. Equitable Sharing

India also supported a sustained claim for equitable sharing of benefits arising out of utilization of resources like genetic resources. Thus Dr Abid Hussein, Member of the Indian delegation while making a statement before the UN Second Committee on Environment and Sustainable Development: Implementation of Agenda 21 and the Programme for the Further Implementation of Agenda 21, submitted that, for India, a country rich in biodiversity and associated traditional knowledge, the decision to negotiate an international regime to protect and safeguard the fair and equitable share of benefits arising out of the utilization of genetic resources is particularly significant. Developing countries, have for a long time, been seeking equitable benefit-sharing and have argued in support of establishing *sui generic* systems for the protection of traditional knowledge as the provisions of TRIPS do not adequately address the concerns of developing countries. Further, he looked forward to the early commencement of work on an international regime that was agreed to at Johannesburg.[23]

9 Role of the Indian Judiciary

Unlike in the past, today treaties have become a major source of international law due to institutionalized law-making. Generally international law-making is now effected by the international institutions through negotiations and consensus. It may be true that because of the end of the Cold War polarized political differences could have subsided, however, other differences like social, cultural and economic ones still persist. These differences sometimes hamper the transformation of the generally agreed abstract policies into concrete binding legal principles for want of consensus. In other words different ideologies may slow down the process of "soft law" becoming "hard law". Unless in cases where domestic actions are warranted to implement international decisions incorporation of international law within the municipal system takes place, the development of international law may not be at

---

[22] Maurice F.Strong, "Eco'92 Critical Challenges and Global Solutions" in *Journal of International Affairs* (Winter 1991) at 282 & 289.

[23] *Supra* note 16 at 92

the desirable pace. Thus, positive state action becomes necessary for the shaping of the international legal principles. The state action could also be termed as state practice necessary to make treaty principles into customary law principles.

When the executive and the legislative fail, the only other state institution – the state judiciary can contribute to the state actions. In this fashion the municipal courts play a crucial role in swelling the content of international law. Professor Richard A. Falk in his book, *The Role of Domestic Courts in the International Legal Order*, observed that domestic courts could help to overcome structural weakness (politically weak central institutions) in the international legal system.[24] Moreover, when the domestic judiciary is independent and is free from executive interferences, the chances of domestic courts contributing to the growth of the international legal principles and its contents are more.

In spite of the fact that the concept of sustainable development has been accepted as a principle of contemporary international law, for its effective implementation the essential legal principles have to be culled out. In this regard, the judiciary in the vibrant democratic India, enjoying a great deal of independence and wielding power of judicial review, has played a vital role in shaping the normative principles of sustainable development. Thus, the Supreme Court of India has found out that inter-generational equity, use and conservation of natural resources, environmental protection, precautionary principle, polluter pays principle, obligation to assist and co-operate, eradication of poverty and financial assistance to the developing countries, are some of the principles that emerge out of the sustainable development concept.[25] The Indian judiciary, in order to strengthen and supplement the existing domestic environmental legal regime, has duly called in the principles of sustainable development and while doing so has indeed elaborated the concept of sustainable development.

10. Right to Environmental Protection

As seen already, one of the major premises of sustainable development is that all human beings have a fundamental right to an environment adequate for their health and well-being. Accordingly Article 1 of the "Legal Principles for the Environmental Protection and Sustainable Development" says: "All human beings have the fundamental right to an environment adequate for their health and well being."[26] The General Assembly resolution adopted without vote on the need to ensure a

---

[24] Richard A. Falk, *The Role of Domestic Courts in the International Legal Order* (Syracuse University Press, 1964), p. xi.

[25] *Vellore Citizens Welfare Forum v Union of India*, AIR 1996 SC 2715, p. 2720.

[26] Adopted by the World Commission on Environment and Development (WCED). Experts Group on Environment and Development during 18-20 June 1986 at Peace Palace. Cf. 29 *Journal of Indian Law Institute* 3 (1987) p 306.

healthy environment for the well-being of individuals[27] also emphasizes this right to environment.

The Indian judiciary has successfully expanded the scope of the fundamental right to life and personal liberty guaranteed in Article 21[28] of the Indian Constitution to include environmental protection. As a first step, the judiciary emphasized the importance of life, health and ecology to the people.[29] Thus, in *Damodhar Rao v. The Special Officer Municipal Corporation of Hyderabad*[30], the Andhra Pradesh High Court held that the right to live cannot be enjoyed without protection and preservation of the environment. The Kerala High Court, too, in *K.K.Hussain v Union of India*[31] has held that the right to sweet water and right to fresh air, the right to wholesome environment are attributes of the right to life, for these are the basic elements which sustain life itself. Reiterating this in *Subhashkumar v State of Bihar*[32], the Supreme Court held that the right to life is a fundamental right under Article 21 of the Constitution and it includes the right of enjoyment of pollution free water and air for full enjoyment of life. Thus, the judiciary being aware of the fact that the right to environment is a basic principle of sustainable development and has recognized the right to environment/environmental protection. Once it is found out that the right to environment is a fundamental right, that too under Article 21, then it becomes easier to enlarge the boundaries of environmental protection resulting in the development of environmental jurisprudence.

11. Development Not at the Cost of Environment

Another basic tenet of sustainable development is that development should not be at the cost of the environment. Thus, sustainable development makes it imperative that economic and industrial development must also accommodate environmental

---

[27] UN GA Res 45/94 of 10 December 1990.

[28] Art. 21that deals with the protection of life and personal liberty runs as follows:
"No person shall be deprived of his life or personal liberty except according to procedure established by law".

[29] The right to wholesome environment was recognised by the Supreme Court in *R.L and E.Kendra, Dehradun v State of U.P* AIR 1985 SC 652 at 656. Similarly in the *Ganga Pollution* case the Supreme Court through Justice K.N.Singh held that life, health and ecology have greater importance to the people than loss of revenue, unemployment etc. *M.C-Metha v Union of India* AIR 1988 SC 1037 at 1048.

[30] AIR 1987 AP 171 at 181. The Court said, "The enjoyment of life and its attainments and fulfillment by Art. 21 of the Constitution embrace the protection and preservation of nature's gift without which life cannot be enjoyed. The slow poisoning of the atmosphere by environmental pollution and spoliation should also be regarded as amounting to violation of Art 21 of the Constitution".

[31] AIR 1990 Ker 321.

[32] AIR 1991 SC 420.

protection. Development should not be at the cost of environment.[33] Thoughtless exploitation of natural resources would degrade the environment. For example, plants of asbestos, iron, coal, copper etc., constructed without environmental quality, emit smog, soot and toxic wastes that pollute the environment. The Indian Supreme Court's decision in *R.L and E.Kendra Dehradun v State of U.P*[34] also falls in this line. Here as a result of thoughtless mining of limestone, the Doon Valley in the Himalayan foothills lost its trees and forests there by accelerating soil erosion resulting in landslides and blockage of underground water channels which fed the many rivers and springs in the river valley. The Court, weighing environmental implications against the need for extraction of limestone for industrial purposes, ordered the closure of certain mines that caused environmental damage. While passing orders for the closure of Tanneries polluting the River Ganga, the Supreme Court observed that no doubt the leather industry brought the much needed foreign exchange, but it should not be allowed at the cost of the environment.[35] The Rio Declaration i.e. Agenda 21, by stating "to achieve sustainable development environmental protection shall constitute an integral part of the development process and cannot be considered in isolation"[36], also echoes similar views. The Supreme Court has now rejected the old notion that development and environmental protection cannot go together, and firmly believes that sustainable development has now come to be accepted as "a viable concept to eradicate poverty and improve the quality of human life while living within the carrying capacity of the supporting ecosystems."[37]

12. Intergenerational Equity and Public Trust Doctrine

Intergenerational equity emanating from the concept of sustainable development from environmental perspective can refer to two things. First, it refers to the relationship of human beings with the environment. We can use the natural resources on a sustainable basis or we can overexploit them, degrading the natural environment in a manner detrimental to posterity. Second, it refers to the relationship of human beings of the present generation to that of future generations.[38] Intergenerational equity imposes a duty on the present generation to

---

[33] See Art.7 Para 1 of the WCED Convention on Environmental Protection and Development which says that "State shall ensure that environment is treated as an integral part of the planning and implementation of developing activities".

[34] See *supra* note 29.

[35] Ganga Pollution case, *supra* note 29.

[36] See Principle 4 of Rio Declaration: Agenda 21 UN Conference on Environment and Development, Rio de Janeiro, 1992.

[37] *Vellore Citizens Welfare Forum v Union of India* , *supra note* 25 at 2720.

[38] Edith Brown Weiss, "Our Rights and Obligations to Future Generations or the Environment", 84 *American Journal of International Law* (1990) at198.

use the natural environment not in a manner which degrades the environment. In short, we hold the earth in trust for future generations.[39]

This theory of trust under intergenerational equity and sustainable development to some extent can be equated with the "public trust doctrine" that exists within the municipal systems.[40] The public trust doctrine is found to be part of our jurisprudence by the Supreme Court in *M.C.Metha v Kamal Nath.*[41] The Court further held that "The State is a trustee of all natural resources which are by nature meant for public use and enjoyment. Public at large is the beneficiary of the seashore, running waters, air, forests and ecologically fragile lands. The state as a trustee is under a legal duty to protect natural resources. These resources meant for public use cannot be converted into private ownership."[42] Thus, a duty to protect and preserve the environment is imposed on the state, the trustee.

13. Precautionary Principle

The Supreme Court in the *Vellore Citizens Welfare Forum* case[43] held that the precautionary principle is one of the essential features of the sustainable development. The "Precautionary Principle" in the context of municipal law, as held by the Court, means:

(1) Environmental measures by the state government and the statutory authorities must anticipate, prevent and attack the causes of environmental degradation.

(2) When there are threats of serious and irreversible damage, lack of scientific certainty should not be used as a reason for postponing measures to prevent environmental degradation.

(3) The "onus of proof" is on the actor or the developer/industrialist to show that his action is environmentally benign.[44]

14. Polluter – Pays Principle

The polluter pays principle is also held to be an essential feature of sustainable development by the Supreme Court.[45] The Supreme Court had the opportunity to

---

[39] *Ibid.*

[40] For detailed discussion on Public Trust Doctrine See David Ambrose, "Public Trust Doctrine as a Basis of Environmental Law" in 2 *Kerala University Journal of Legal Studies* 39-48 (2002).

[41] 1997 1 SCC at 413.

[42] *Ibid.*

[43] *Supra* note 25 at 2720.

[44] *Ibid.*

[45] *Ibid.*

introduce this legal principle in the *Sriram Gas Leak* case[46], where the Supreme Court evolved a new principle of strict liability for damages caused by hazardous or inherently dangerous activity resulting, for example, in escape of toxic gas. Reiterating this principle in the Indian Council for the *Enviro Legal Action v Union of India*[47], the Supreme Court held that once the activity carried on is hazardous or inherently dangerous, the person carrying out such activity is liable to make good the loss caused to any other person by his activity irrespective of the fact whether he took reasonable care while carrying out his activity. The rule is promised upon the very nature of the activity carried out.

The polluter-pays principle lays down that the financial cost of preventing or remedying damage caused by the pollution should lie with the undertakings which cause pollution and not with the Government. The Court further held that remediation of the damaged environment is part of the process of sustainable development and as such the polluter is liable to pay the cost to the sufferer as well as the cost of reversing the damaging ecology.[48]

15. Right to Compensation

The Supreme Court has innovatively expanded the remedial potential of Article 32[49] to award compensation or damage in all appropriate cases. The Court believed that the power of awarding compensation for violation of fundamental rights is within the scope of Article 32. The Court felt that this power is remedial in nature and provides relief against a breach of fundamental rights already committed.[50] Apart from this, the Supreme Court while compensating victims of pollution, also sought to apply the polluter pays principle.

The polluter-pays principle, according to the Supreme Court, means that the absolute liability for harm to the environment extends to compensate the victims of pollution in addition to the cost of restoring the environmental degradation.[51] Thus, the remedial power of the Supreme Court under Article 32 is also strengthened by the polluter pays principle of the sustainable development concept as far as environmental pollution cases are concerned.

---

[46] *M.C.Metha v Union of India* AIR 1987 SC 965.

[47] JT 1996 (2) SC 196: AIR 1996 SCW 1069.

[48] *Ibid.*

[49] The right to move the Supreme Court for the enforcement of fundamental right is guaranteed by Art.32 of the Indian Constitution. This right itself is a fundamental right. Further it confers power on the Supreme Court to issue appropriate directions or orders or writs including writs in the nature of *habeas corpus, mandamus,* prohibition, *quo-warranto* and *certiorari* for the enforcement of any of the fundamental rights guaranteed by the Constitution.

[50] *M.C.Metha v Union of India* AIR 1987 SC 1086.

[51] *Supra* note 25 and also *supra* note 46.

16. Conclusions

The basic customary law principle under which environmental concerns are addressed by traditional international law is that no state may, on its own territory, engage in, promote or tolerate any activities which give rise to significant damage on the territory of a neighboring state.

The elements and substance of customary international law regarding environmental protection can be generally summarized as follows:

1. Transfrontier environmental protection was as such considered as part of the law of state responsibility,
2. In order to fix the state responsibility or liability, the presence of material damage is a must,
3. And this damage must have come from a "tangible injury translatable into provable monetary damages" and be "established by clear and convincing evidence",
4. Since a state, under international law, is made internationally responsible for pollution done by it, the law had more flavour of "punitive effect" rather than "preventive or prohibitory effect",
5. The principle of the territorial integrity of foreign states forms the basic rule of customary international law applicable to transfrontier environmental protection,
6. As the principle of territorial integrity happens to be the basic rule of transfrontier environmental protection, states are barred from violating the territorial integrity of neighboring states. This proposition led to the application of the principle *sic utere tuo ut alienum non laedas* to matters of transfrontier environmental protection, and
7. Consequently, only acts or omissions of states done knowingly gave rise to international responsibility because such acts were considered as "abuse of rights" and acts unlawful *per se.* [52]

Thus, the classical international regime relating to environmental protection was based on the idea relating to delimitation of territories and jurisdiction. But under modern environmental law Mother Earth is considered as a single indivisible unit and is shared by the people of all the nations. Modern environmental law has many objectives that include the protection of and preservation against damage to plant and animal life, reaching goals ensuring continued economic growth and development and maintenance of an aesthetically acceptable and enjoyable environment. The success of international law depends upon the effective municipal implementation of the same. Accordingly, like human rights law, the interaction between international law and municipal law becomes very much evident in the field of environmental protection also. Environmental protection presupposes vigorous

---

52 A. David Ambrose, "Transfrontier Environmental Protection: New Challenges and International Response", V *Law and Social Problems* (1997-98) at 71.

national efforts based on sound international policy. Understanding this as far as environmental law is concerned, India has been a contributor as well as a consumer. It has used international environmental law to shape its domestic law and at the same time richly contributed to the content of it. The Executive actively participated in all the major international environmental negotiations and discussions from which the *opinio juris* part of customary international law can be made out and the Legislative incorporated the decisions taken at such international negotiations within the municipal system by enacting appropriate legislations thereby providing evidence of much needed state practice. The third limb of a government, the Judiciary, has also contributed to the development of international environmental law by adding legal content to it. It is of interest to note that the Supreme Court has held that sustainable development concept has been accepted as part of customary international law.[53] Conferment of customary law status to sustainable development is made with a purpose that once a principle is accepted as part of customary international law there would be no difficulty in accepting it as part of domestic law. In the words of the Court, "it is almost accepted proposition of law that the rules of customary international law which are not contrary to municipal law shall be deemed to have been incorporated in the domestic law and shall be followed by courts".[54]

If it is agreed that the supremacy of law and the sanctity of treaties which remain a *sine qua non* for the growth of law among nations,[55] then from the contributions made jointly or separately by Indian Executive, Legislative and Judiciary, it can safely be concluded that there is a symbiotic relationship between India (and its environmental jurisprudence) and international environmental law. India thus not only contributed to the development of ancient international law[56] but also to the development of modern international (environmental) law.

---

[53] *Vellore Citizen Welfare Forum* case, *supra* note 25 at 2720.

[54] *Ibid.*, at 2722.

[55] Nagandra Singh, *India and International Law* (Chand & Co, 1969) at 13.

[56] According to Singh the universality principle a distinct Indian contribution to the development of inter-state law dates back to two thousand years and it has given birth to several basic principles of international law; see Singh *ibid.* at 3.

THE LAW OF OUTER SPACE AND INDIA

C. Jayaraj*

1. Introduction

Ever since the erstwhile Soviet Union launched its Sputnik in 1957 into outer space humankind has witnessed tremendous progress in scientific and exploratory activities relating to outer space and celestial bodies. There is also an increasing realization that outer space and the celestial bodies are of immense use, which could be beneficially exploited for mankind's welfare. However, one ought to be conscious that when mankind is divided into states and nations, based on the fundamental principle of state sovereignty,[1] it is very difficult to have an orderly and unified exploration and exploitation for the benefit of humanity as a whole. No doubt while there is competition among scientifically and technologically advanced countries to explore and exploit the resources, the sheer immense nature of space has forced nations to work together and take joint and cooperative measures. There is a growing recognition that only a rule based system of exploration and exploitation of outer space and celestial bodies would make space activities meaningful and accountable. No sooner was the Soviet Sputnik launched into space than the international community began acting towards a regulatory framework by way of normative principles and institutional mechanisms.

Due to the constant deliberations within the United Nations Committee on Peaceful Uses of Outer Space (UNCOPUOS),[2] particularly within of its Legal Sub-Committee a corpus of a special regime of law known as international space law has become part of general international law.[3] However, even though space activities are

* Secretary-General, Indian Society of International Law, New Delhi; Advocate, Supreme Court of India.

[1] V. S. Vereshchetin, "On the Principle of State Sovereignty in International Space Law", *Annals of Air and Space Law* 429-436 (1977); Maurice Andem, *International Legal Problems in the Peaceful Exploration and Use of Outer Space*, 69-121 (University of Lapland, Faculty of Law, Rovaniemi 1992).

[2] See Nandasiri Jasentuliyana, "A Survey of Space Law as Developed by the United Nations", in N. Jasentuliyana (ed.) *Perspectives on International Law*, 349-384 (Kluwer Law International, The Hague, Boston, London: 1995) 349-384; On the establishment of UNCOPUOS, See Nandasiri Jasentuliyana, *International Space Law and the United Nations*, 23-32 (Kluwer Law International, The Hague: 1999).

[3] Manfred Lachs, considered as the father of International Space law, has provided an analysis of the theoretical and practical linkages of issues regarding the then emerging legal debates. See Manfred Lachs, "The International Law of Outer Space", III *Recueil des Cours* 1-115 (1964); For subsequent developments see Stephen Gorove, "International Space Law in Perspective", Vol. 181 *Recueil des Cours*, 349-409 (1983-III); Maurice Andem, *supra note* 1; Nandasiri Jasentuliyana (ed.), *Perspectives on International Law*, (Kluwer Law International,

***Bimal N. Patel (ed.),* India and International Law, 265-288.**

normally oriented towards national interests and carried out by states and their agencies it has become a field for other actors as well including private parties[4]. Though they started as sheer scientific activities, space activities have reached a stage where "with or without our cognizance, space law affects us all, particularly with the increasing privatization and commercialization of space applications".[5] Space communication or telecommunication by artificial earth satellites have had a tremendous impact on national and international mass communication systems. Emphasizing the importance of communication satellites President John F. Kennedy pointed out on the occasion of signing the Communications Satellite Act of 1962:

> [B]y enacting this legislation, Congress has taken a step of historic importance. It promises significant benefits to our people and to the whole world. Its purpose is to establish a commercial communications system utilizing space satellites which will serve our needs and those of other countries and contribute to world peace and understanding.... The benefits which a satellite system should make possible within a few years stem largely from a vastly increased capacity to exchange information cheaply and reliably with all parts of the world by telephone, telegraph, radio and television. The ultimate result will be encourage and facilitate world trade, education, entertainment, and many kinds of professional, political, and personal discourse which are essential to healthy human relationship and international understanding.[6]

London, The Hague, Boston: 1995) particularly Chapter IV, pp. 349-480; V. S. Mani, S. Bhatt and V. Balakista Reddy (ed.), *Recent Trends in International Space Law and Policy*, (Lancers Book, New Delhi: 1997); Chia-Jui Cheng (ed.), *The Use of Air Space and Outer Space for All Mankind in the 21st Century*, (Kluwer Law International, The Hague, London, Boston: 1995); Nandasiri Jasentuliyana (ed.), *International Space Law and the United Nations*, (Kluwer Law International, The Hague, London, Boston: 1999); Sir Robert Jennings & Arthur Watts (ed.), *Oppenheim's International Law*, 826-845 (9th ed., Vol. 1, Parts 2 & 4).

[4] Peter Malanczuk, "Actors: States, International Organizations, Private Entities" in Gabriel Lafferandere and Daphone Growither (ed.), *Outlook on Space Law Over the Next 30 years: Essays Published for the 30th Anniversary of the Outer Space Treaty*, 23-36 (Kluwer Law International, The Hague, London, Boston: 1997).

[5] Nandasiri Jasentuliyana, 1999 *supra* note 1. *See* also Ricky J Lee, "Reconciling International Space Law with Commercial Realities of the 21st Century", 4 *Singapore Journal of International and Comparative Law*, 194-251 (2000); Space Industry is worth of $ 90 billion in revenue which is growing at 20% annually, Message of U.N. Secretary General, *World Space Week*, 2001; See Tjaco T.Van Hout, "Resolving Outer Space Related Disputes", *UN/International Institute of Air and Space Law*, ST/SPACE/14, at 3.

[6] See Maurice Andem, *supra* note 1 at 236.

Today there are about 330 active satellites in the Geo-Stationery Orbit (GEO) and 350 active satellites outside the GEO.[7] This is a long way from the days of the "Early Bird" satellite which marked the arrival of the era of space-based telecommunication services in 1965. There are internationally sponsored satellite systems serving the field of telecommunications such as the International Telecommunications Satellite Organization (INTELSAT), the International Maritime Satellite Organization (INMARSAT), EUTELSAT, ARABSAT (Arab Corporation for Space Communications), INTERSPUTNIK (International System and Organization of Space Communications).[8] The satellite systems have made life much easier and more efficient in so far as they are instrumental in the fields of long distance communications, direct television, broadcasting, data networks, maritime communications, disaster relief communications, cellular phones etc. Events such as the Olympics are directly telecast to millions of households. The fields of education, medicine etc. have also benefited from the satellite systems. In view of this mass utility of space technology, the telecommunications industry is worth more than US$ 1 trillion annually.

Similarly, space technology and satellite systems have been employed for meteorological purposes. The use and importance of space technology for meteorology was emphasized as early 1969.

> [T]he importance of space technology for meteorology is that satellites provide an additional observing platform which, of course, can only be used if proper radio links can be established with earth stations in order to real-time telemetring of meteorological data. In addition to the use of satellites as an observing platform, satellites will provide new telecommunication systems for the collection, exchange and distribution of meteorological data. From the point of view of the observing system, satellites will contribute to a global observing system which would permit, on a truly world wide basis, the possibility of observing the whole atmosphere. Up to now, this was not possible because of the large uninhabited areas and the fact that two-thirds of the globe is covered by the ocean and, for these reasons, it was difficult to obtain meteorological observations.[9]

Under the auspices of the World Meteorological Organization (WMO) a global network of weather forecasting through satellites is in place, which is called the World Weather Watch Programme (WWWP). Such systems are designed to avoid duplication in preparing analyses and prognoses, while still providing each

---

[7] Nandasiri Jasentuliyana, "International Space Law, Challenges in the Twenty-First Century Keynote Address to the Space Law Conference 11-13 March 2001 Singapore", 5 *Singapore Journal of International and Comparative Law 1* 10-21 (2001) at 17.

[8] A.A. Cocca, "The Legal Aspects Relating to the Civilian Applications of Space Technology", in Nandasiri Jasentuliyana (ed.), *Perspectives on International Law*, pp. 411-440.

[9] Maurice Andem, p. 304, 305

meteorological service with the data and background information it requires to carry out its responsibility.[10] There are also regional systems such as EUMETSAT, which is serving Europe.

Remote sensing of earth resources is the latest field where satellites are used for purposes of exploration and exploitation of earth resources, which are available within and above the surface of the earth. Remote sensing is described as, 'a technique of measuring information about a subject of interest without being in direct contact with it'.[11] The technique relies on detecting electro magnetic radiation, which is either reflected or emitted by the subject. This technique is used to study earth's environment and mineral resources.[12] The images produced by remote sensing satellites have led to appreciable commercial activities with attendant legal issues.[13]

The remote sensing technology is used in the following areas:

> [I]nventory of rice field and yield estimate, natural resources mapping and monitoring, forestry, mining, plantations, mangrove forest inventory; coral reef mapping, forest fire detection and monitoring. Also, drought monitoring, flood monitoring and flood susceptibility assessment, aquaculture, fishing vessel monitoring, identification of potential fishing zones, urban planning, utilities, enhancement (power supply, mobile telephone network, infrastructure development) and land taxation, etc.[14]

The present paper seeks to locate the policy and institutional aspects of Indian space activities within the context of the existing international space laws and argues for a legally binding domestic regulatory framework in the light of its obligations under various international legal instruments. It is, however, proposed first to analyze the existing international treaty and normative framework, which internationally governs the space activities. It is also essential to recapture the basic principles in this regard since they form the basis of a State Party's obligations domestically and internationally. Moreover, India has been an active participant in the deliberations in the UNCOPUOS contributing significantly to the progressive development of international space law. An overview of India's space activities and institutions will also be discussed to show that such activities have legal consequences for India. Finally, a basic structure of a possible legal framework is also produced.

---

[10] *Ibid* at 310.

[11] *Ibid.*

[12] *Ibid.*

[13] K.R. Sridhara Murthi, "Commercial Availability of High Quality Remote Sensing Imageries: Legal Issues", *5 Singapore Journal of International and Comparative Law* (2001) pp. 149-150.

[14] Emmanuel Nabet, "Legal Aspects of the Use and Applications of Remote Sensing in South East Asia", 5 *Singapore Journal of International and Comparative Law* (2001), 156-164.

2. International Space Law: Binding Norms

The present day international space law is composed of five legally binding multilateral treaties and four normative declarations of the United Nations General Assembly. The multilateral treaties that form the basic layer of international space law are: Treaty on Principles Governing the Activities of States in the Exploration and the Use of Outer Space, including the Moon and Other Celestial Bodies (Outer Space Treaty, 1967)[15]; Agreement on the Rescue of Astronauts, Return of Astronauts and the Return of Objects Launched into Outer Space (Rescue Agreement, 1968)[16]; Convention on International Liability for Damage Caused by Space Objects (Liability Convention, 1972)[17]; Convention on Registration of Objects Launched into Outer Space (Registration Convention, 1975)[18]; Agreement Governing the Activities of States on the Moon and Other Celestial Bodies (Moon Agreement, 1979)[19]. In what follows an overview of these treaties is provided bringing out the basic principles, which are binding upon the State Parties. While the paper attempts to argue that a corpus of legal and normative standards are in place, international space law however adequate is not satisfactory to meet all challenges of emerging activities in space. For instance, the international community is yet to agree on basic issues such as the definition and limitation of outer space, the definition of launching state, the definition of space object, the definition and limitations of Geo-Stationery Orbit.

2.1. Multilateral Treaties

i. Outer Space Treaty (OST)[20]

The Outer Space Treaty (OST) is the founding legal framework[21] for outer space activities, to which the status of *'Magna Carta'* has been attributed.[22] It is a transformation of the 1963 Declaration of Legal Principles Governing the Activities of States in the Exploration and Use of Outer Space.[23] The OST contains several

---

[15] 27 January 1967, 610 U.N.T.S. 205.
[16] 22 April 1968, 672 U.N.T.S. 119.
[17] 29 March 1972, 961 U.N.T.S. 187.
[18] 14 January 1975, 1023 U.N.T.S. 15.
[19] 18 December 1979, 1363 U.N.T.S. 3.
[20] As of November 2003, 98 states have ratified the OST and 27 states have signed it. For the text of the OST see *United Nations Treaties And Principles on Outer Space*, UN DOC. ST/SPACE/11, (United Nations: New York, 2002) 3-8.
[21] Vladimir Kopal, *Introduction to the United Nations Treaties and Principles on Outer Space, Proceedings, UNI Republic of Korea Workshop on Space Law, United Nations Treaties on Outer Space: Actions at the National Level*, ST/SPACE/22, p. 12.
[22] Damodar Wadegoankar, *Orbit of Space Law*, (Stevens & Sons Ltd, and N.M. Tripathi Ltd, London, Bombay: 1994) p. 3.
[23] Resolution 1962, (XVIII) adopted unanimously on 13 December, 1963.

principles most of which formed the foundation for subsequent independent multilateral treaties for the operationalisation of such principles. OST guarantees the principles of freedom in the exploration and use of outer space, freedom of scientific investigation and international cooperation in such investigation.[24] It emphasizes upon a declaratory, fundamental and binding legal tenet that the realm of outer space including moon and other celestial bodies would be out of national appropriation. In other words, it ensures the concept of *res communes* in relation to outer space.[25] Further, it ensures that all space activities should be conducted in accordance with international law including the Charter of the United Nations and such activities should be in the interest of maintaining international peace and security and promoting international cooperation and understanding.[26] There is a prohibitory mandate that no nuclear or other weapons of mass destruction should be placed in outer space and that the Moon and other celestial bodies shall be used by all state parties exclusively for peaceful purposes and that no act should be carried out with a military intention.[27] OST declares that astronauts shall be the envoys of mankind and that they are entitled to all possible assistance.[28] It provides for international responsibility for national activities in outer space notwithstanding whether such activities were carried out by governmental or non-governmental entities.[29] The launching state is made internationally liable for damage caused by space objects launched by it.[30] OST provides for registration of space objects and for retaining jurisdiction and control over such registered objects and over any personnel by virtue of such registration.[31]

ii. The Rescue Agreement (1968)

The Rescue Agreement[32] is the extension and further elaboration of the principles contained in Article V of OST which states:

> [S]tates Parties to the Treaty shall regard astronauts as envoys of mankind in outer space and shall render to them all possible assistance in the event of accident, distress, or emergency landing on the territory of another State Party or on the high seas. When astronauts make such landing, they shall be safely and promptly returned to the State of registry of their space vehicle ...In carrying out activities in outer space and on celestial bodies, the astronauts of one State Party shall render all possible assistance to

---

24 Article I of OST.
25 Article II of OST.
26 Article III of OST.
27 Article IV of OST.
28 Article V of OST.
29 Article VI of OST.
30 Article VII of OST.
31 Article VIII of OST.
32 Opened for signature on April 2002, 1968 and entered into force on December 2 of the same year. As of November 2003, 88 ratification and 25 signatures have been made.

> the astronauts of other States Parties …States Parties to the Treaty shall immediately inform the other States Parties to the Treaty or the Secretary General of the United Nations of any phenomena they discover in outer space, including the Moon and other celestial bodies, which could constitute a danger to the life or health of astronauts.

It is considered to represent the interface between the principle of humanity and international cooperation,[33] besides providing a binding framework establishing the obligation of mutual cooperation for rescuing and returning astronauts and space objects to the state of registry. The Rescue Agreement addresses the issues of obligations relating to rescue and return of astronauts, artificial space objects and their component parts, and the inter-relationship with the Liability Convention. It defines the circumstances under which an astronaut is considered to be in distress. It also provides for the duty to notify firstly, the launching authority or in case of inability to so notify to make immediately a public announcement by all appropriate means of communication upon the discovery or receipt of information about astronauts in distress. Further, the UN Secretary General should also be notified, enabling him to disseminate such information. Similarly, the duty to notify and the duty to return the space objects are also obligatory on the state, which discovers such objects. Even though the Rescue Agreement is considered to be transitional in nature the principles contained in the Rescue Agreement are very much binding as they are relevant. These could be improved by the international community in the light of the increased space activities.[34]

iii. Liability Convention (1972)

The Liability Convention[35] elaborates the principles of Article VII of the 1967 OST which states

> [E]ach State Party to the Treaty that launches or procures the launching of an object into outer space, including the Moon and other celestial bodies, and each State Party from whose territory or facility an object is launched, is internationally liable for damage to another State Party to the Treaty or to its natural or juridical persons by such object or its component parts on the Earth, in air space or in outer space, including the Moon and other celestial bodies.

---

[33] For a contemporary view on the Rescue Agreement see V.S. Mani, "The Agreement on the Rescue of Astronauts, the Return of Astronauts and the Return of Objects Launched into Outer Space, 1968", *Paper Presented to the UN/Republic of Korea Workshop on Space Law*, ST/SPACE/22, pp. 35-48.

[34] *Ibid.*

[35] Adopted on 1971 entered into force on September 1972. As of 2002, 82 ratifications and 26 signatures have been made.

It may be noted that the Liability Convention faced some controversial debate during its deliberations and continues to engage debate on its application.[36] The Liability Convention defines the notion of 'damage' to cover loss of life, personal injury or other impairment of health; loss or damage to property of states or of persons or of the properties of international organizations. The criteria for the launching state[37] are also provided as follows:

(i) A state which launches or procures launching of space objects;
(ii) A state from whose territory or facility a space object is launched.

It is interesting to note that two different levels of liability regime have been provided by the Convention. Firstly, the launching State is absolutely liable if the damage was caused by the space object on the surface of the earth or to an aircraft in flight. If damage is caused to space objects of other States by the space objects of the launching State, then the latter is liable upon proof that the damage has been caused by persons under its control. This is subject to the condition that the damage occurs elsewhere than on the surface of the Earth.[38] It may be noted that there could be more than one launching State with regard to a launch and with regard to a single space object in view of the composite nature of the definition. In view of this possibility the Liability Convention provides joint and several liability. A notable point of this Liability Convention is that the damages caused to nationals of the launching State are not covered. In other words the claimant victim of the damages should be a foreign national.[39] It addresses the issue of competency for making claims, to whom such a claim is to be made, the time frame within which such claim is to be made as well as the dispensation of the traditional notion of prior exhaustion of local remedy. An important aspect of the Liability Convention is the applicable law with regard to the claim for damages. In this regard it categorically states that the compensation to be paid as damages should be determined in accordance with international law and the principles of justice and equity.[40] Another noteworthy feature of the Liability Convention is that it provides for a Claims Commission to settle the compensation dispute in the event diplomatic negotiations under Article IX fail and for composition of the Commission and appointment of the Chairman.

---

[36] Ricky J. Lee, "The Convention on International Liability for Damage Caused by Space Objects and the Domestic Regulatory Reporters to its Implications", *United Nations/Republic of Korea Workshop on Space Law*, ST/SPACE/22, pp. 105-126; Also Armel Kerrest, "The Liability Convention and Liability for Space Activities", *Proceedings, United Nations/National Institute of Air and Space Workshop*, ST/SPACE/14, pp. 25-30.

[37] The concept and criteria of 'Launching State' continues to be discussed within the Legal Sub-Committee of UNCOPUOS, see *Report of Legal Sub-Committee on its Thirty Ninth Session*, 27 March to April 6, 2000, A/AC. 105/738, p. 11. For further development in this regard see A/AC. 105/826, pp. 24-27.

[38] Article III of the Liability Convention.

[39] Article VII of the Liability Convention.

[40] Article XII of the Liability Convention.

iv. The Registration Convention

The Registration Convention[41] elaborates the first principle of Article VIII of the OST which states

> [A] State Party to the Treaty on whose registry an object launched into outer space is carried shall retain jurisdiction and control over such object, and over any personnel thereof, while in outer space or on a celestial body. Ownership of objects launched into outer space, including objects landed or constructed on a celestial body, and of their component parts, is not affected by their presence in outer space or on a celestial body or by their return to the Earth. Such objects or components parts found beyond the limits of the State Party to the Treaty on whose registry they are carried shall be returned to that State Party, which shall, upon request, furnish identifying data prior to their return.

The purpose of the Registration Convention is primarily to make the identification of the launching State in case of causing damage due to launching of space objects. It was felt that the earlier space treaties left a gap regarding the identification process and with the advent of this Convention, it has become easier, quicker to identify the State in view of the public and reliable registration system. In the words of Prof. Diederiks–Verschoor , "(1) a well ordered, complete and informative register would minimize the likelihood and even the suspicion of weapons of mass destruction being tentatively put into orbit and (2) it is not possible to identify a space craft that has caused damage without an international system of registration".[42]

The Convention makes it obligatory for the launching State to register the space object in its national registry, and when it is done it becomes the State of Registry for purposes of attribution of liability and in that capacity should provide the Secretary General with specific information on the space object for inclusion in the UN register. The launching State definition has been incorporated into it from the Liability Convention with precisely the same criteria. Under this Convention it is possible for launching States, if there are more than one, to determine who ought to be the State of Registry. Doubts about its efficiency have been raised with regard to ramifications of the concepts of 'Launching State' and 'Space Objects'.[43] Notwithstanding such a situation, the Registration Convention is considered to be an important link in the chain of space law treaties.[44] It is also viewed that this

---

[41] Entered into force on September 15, 1976. As of November 2003, 44 ratifications and 4 signatures have been made.

[42] Cited in Yun Zhao, "Revisiting the 1975 Registration Convention: Time for Revision", UN/Republic of Korea Workshop on Space Law, n. 21, pp. 127-134 at p. 127. For a comment on the objectives of this convention see Sushma Malik, "Editorial Comment: The Registration of Space Objects", 9 *Indian Journal of International Law* 412-416 (1969).

[43] Yun Zhao, at 128.

[44] *Ibid* at 134.

Convention could play an important role in the context of States being engaged in space activities, especially when their telecommunication industries/ systems are dependant on satellites.[45]

v. The Moon Treaty (1979)

The Agreement Governing the Activities of States on the Moon and Other Celestial Bodies was concluded in 1979.[46] A striking aspect of this agreement is that it did not, unlike the earlier UN Space Treaties, require acceptance by the USA, the then Soviet Union and the United Kingdom. The Moon Agreement has been a controversial instrument, which has resulted in States not forthcoming to sign or ratify it, notwithstanding its comprehensive nature and reflection of the principles of the 1967 OST. Its important aspect is that it incorporates the concept *res communes* as well as the concept 'Common Heritage of Mankind', The Moon and its natural resources are declared to be the common heritage of mankind, in paragraph 5 of Article 11.

> [S]tates Parties to these Agreement hereby undertake to establish an international regime, including appropriate procedures, to govern the exploitation of the natural resources of the Moon as such exploitation is about to become feasible. This provision shall be implemented in accordance with article 18 of this Agreement.

The establishment of an international regime as envisaged above is not likely to occur in the near future in view of the lukewarm support to the Moon Agreement by States. Moreover, it is also suggested that the incorporation of the concept of "equitable sharing" with regard to the benefits of space resources has not encouraged many states to become parties to the Moon Agreement. It is regretful that even though the UN General Assembly adopted the Moon Agreement by consensus, it has not drawn much support to make it enforceable.[47]

The substantive legal aspects of the Moon Agreement include

(1) The Moon shall be used exclusively for peaceful purposes;[48]

---

[45] See H. Peter van Fenama, "The Registration Convention", *Proceedings, United Nations/International Institute of Air and Space Law Workshop on Capacity Building in Space Law*, UN ST/SPACE, 14, p. 35.

[46] General Assembly Resolution 34/68. For the text see 18 *International Legal Materials* (1979) 1434; Entered into force on July 11, 1984. As of May 2004, 10 ratifications and 5 signatures have been made. For a comment see Carl Q. Christol, "The Moon Treaty Enters into Force", 79 *American Journal of International Law*, 163-168 (1985).

[47] For a brief comment on the controversies regarding the Moon Agreement, see Vladimir Kopal, *supra* note 21, p. 15, 16.

[48] Article 3 of the Moon Agreement.

(2) The exploration and use of the Moon shall be carried out for the benefit and in the interests of all countries;[49]
(3) The Secretary-General of the UN, as well as the public and international scientific community should be uniformed of the activities concerning the exploration of the Moon, to the extent possible;[50]
(4) Freedom of Scientific Investigation on the Moon, to be on the basis of the non-discrimination and equality of all concerned;[51] and
(5) Environmental balance must be preserved.[52]

The Moon Agreement further provides for operational rights and duties such as the landing on and launching from the Moon of space objects; [53] and establishment of manned and unmanned stations on Moon.[54] Other legal provisions relate to jurisdiction over space objects and personnel, international responsibility for national activities on the Moon, and obligations of a State Party to assure itself that other States Parties conduct their activities in accordance with the Moon Agreement.

2.2. General Assembly Resolutions

In addition to the multilateral treaties as stated above, the United Nations General Assembly has adopted a series of resolutions containing normative principles seeking to regulate space activities which were not covered by the treaties, such as Principles Governing the Use by States of Artificial Earth Satellites for International Direct Television Broadcasting, (The DBS Principles, 1982)[55]; Principles Relating to Remote Sensing of the Earth from Outer Space (The Remote Sensing Principles, 1986[56]); Principles Relevant to the Use of Nuclear Power Sources in Outer Space (the NPS Principles)[57] (1992); and Declaration on International Cooperation in the Exploration and Use of Outer Space for the Benefit and in the Interest of All States (1996)[58]. It is but natural to wonder why having successfully made binding conventions, the international community opted for the method of adopting resolutions by the United Nations General Assembly, on the matter covered by these resolutions. These resolutions were perhaps the consequences of the failure of the 1979 Moon Treaty to be widely acceptable and the conflicts which it had witnessed during its making. The legal status of the General Assembly resolutions

[49] Article 4 of the Moon Agreement.
[50] Article 5 of the Moon Agreement.
[51] Article 6 of the Moon Agreement.
[52] Article 7 of the Moon Agreement.
[53] Article 8 of the Moon Agreement.
[54] Article 9 of the Moon Agreement.
[55] Resolution 37/92 of December 10, 1982.
[56] Resolution 41/65 of December 3, 1986.
[57] Resolution 45/68 of December 14, 1992.
[58] Resolution 51/22 of December 13, 1996.

regarding space activities has been of considerable interest in the past. Could be it argued that they are part of state practice and therefore evidence of custom? It has been suggested that General Assembly resolutions on space activities have given birth to instant customs.[59] The DBS principles[60] mainly lay down that international direct television broadcasting by satellites should be carried out in a manner compatible with sovereign rights of States and with the right of everyone to seek and impart information and ideas; that access to satellite broadcasting technology should be available to all States and particularly with special consideration to developing countries and their development interests; and that activities in this regard should take place in accordance with international law. The Remote Sensing Principles similarly emphasize that remote sensing should be carried out for the benefit of the whole of mankind, taking note of the needs of developing countries and that such activities should be conducted in accordance with international law. Most importantly, the sensed State should have access to the data collected from its territory at a non-discriminatory basis and on reasonable cost.

3. India's Space Policies, Institutions and Role in Law-Making

3.1. Space Policy

India has come of age in space technology and converting its skills in this area for the socio-economic development of the nation. This has rescued India emerging as a truly space-faring nation. It is to be noted that India's space policy is part of its general policy on science. Speaking for the nation, the first Prime Minister of India, Pandit Jawaharlal Nehru stated in 1958:

> [S]cience alone could solve the problem of hunger and poverty, insanitation and illiteracy, of superstition and deadening custom and tradition, of vast resources running to waste, of a rich country inherited by starving people.[61]

While articulating India's commitment to international co-operation in space explorations, the then Prime Minister stated in a message to the UN Secretary General in 1968:

---

[59] Bin Cheng, "United Nations Resolutions on Outer Space: 'Instant' International Customary Law", *Indian Journal of International Law*, 23-48 (1965).

[60] It was the first ever occasion where UNCOPUOS failed to adopt a resolution by consensus. Within the UN General Assembly the resolution was adopted by voting and thereby dividing the states. For the legal significance of these principles see C.Q. Christol, "Prospects for an International Legal Regime for Direct Television Broadcasting", 34 *International and Comparative Law Quarterly* (1985) at 142.

[61] See Rajiv Lochan, "India's Space Programme and its Policy Dimensions", *Proceedings, United Nations/International Institute of Air and Space Law*, ST/SPACE/14, pp. 240-284 at p. 246.

> [T]he peaceful uses of outer space, particularly in the fields of telecommunications and meteorology, promise to confer great benefits to developing nations ... India looks forward to expanding areas or international collaboration and would take initiatives as she has at the United Nations sponsored International Rocket Launching Station in Trivandrum and at the Experimental Satellite Communication Earth Station.

Dr. Vikram Sarabhai (considered as the father of the Indian space programme) drew up a strategy for the space programme in India in the early sixties and stated:

> [T]here are some who question the relevance of space activities in a developing nation. To us, there is no ambiguity of purpose. We do not have the fantasy of competing with the economically advanced nations in the explorations of the moon or planets or manned space flights. But we are convinced that if we are to play a meaningful role nationally and in the comity of nations, we must be second to none in the application of advanced technologies to problems of man and society, which we find in our country. And we note that the application of sophisticated technologies and the methods of analysis to our problems is not to be confused with embarking on grandiose schemes whose primary impact is for show rather than for progress measured in hard economic and social terms.[62]

One may infer from the above that India's vision on its space program was comprehensive and people-oriented. Further, the objectives of the space program were clearly stated in the introduction to the decade plans of 1970-80, including the need for becoming self-reliant as follows:

> The principal objectives of the space program in India are to develop indigenous competence in designing and building sophisticated hardware involved in space technology including rockets and satellites for scientific research and practical applications, the use of these systems for providing point to point communications and a National TV hook up through a direct broadcast synchronous satellite and the application of satellites for meteorology and for remote sensing of earth resources.[63]

3.2. Organizational Structure

The space efforts started in the sixties with the investigation of the ionosphere by establishing the Thumba Equatorial Rocket Launching Station near Trivandrum. The most important organization, the Indian Space Research Organization (ISRO), was established in 1969 under the Department of Atomic Energy. However, having

---

[62] See V. Balakista Reddy, "Space Law and Space Policy in India", in V.S.Mani et.al., (ed.), *Recent Trends in International Space Law and Policy*, (115-151), at 151.

[63] See K.R. Sridhara Murthy, Kasturi Rangan, Mukund Rao, M.Y.S. Prasad and Madhavan Nair, "Indian Space Endeavour – A Historical Perspective", *Paper Presented to the 51st International Astronautical Congress*, 2-6 October 2000, Rio de Janeiro, pp. 3-4.

realized the need for an independent department, the Government of India established the Department of Space (DoS) in 1972, along with a Space Commission. The DoS is directly under the Prime Minister of India, since its inception. The Space Commission comprising scientists and administrators formulates the functional policies and the technical strategies to realize the felt needs of the Indian space program. The DoS is responsible for implementing the policies framed by the Space Commission. In turn, ISRO is responsible for implementing the programmes at the field level. An impressive array of institutions has been established in India under the supervision of ISRO to carry out research on various aspects of space science and also to carry out launching, tracking activities.[64]

3.3. Indian Satellite System

India has made laudable achievements in using space technology in the fields of telecommunications and remote sensing. There are two types of satellite systems currently in operation, namely INSAT and IRS.

(i) Indian National Satellite System (INSAT)

This system is in the service of telecommunications, television broadcasting and meteorology, including disaster warning. Under this series, India has launched 15 satellites from 1982 to 2002. However, at present only five satellites are operating in the series, namely, INSAT-2C, INSAT-2DT, INSAT-2E, INSAT-3B and INSAT-3C. [65]

(ii) Indian Remote Sensing Satellite (IRS)

The IRS forms an operationally maintained and updated civilian series of remote sensing satellites offering earth observation data, which would be useful for many developmental activities. At present, India has the largest constellation of remotesensing satellites in space, which include IRS-lC, IRS-lD, IRS-P3, IRS-P4 (Oceansat) and TES (Technology Experiment Satellites)[66]. On October 17, 2003, India launched its RESOURCESAT and put it in its precise orbit of 821 kilometers above the earth. The RESOURCESAT is the world's most sophisticated remote sensing spacecraft since it is equipped with the finest earth observing cameras.[67] RESOURCESAT will be helpful in determining the health of crops, locating

---

[64] For a complete list of the institutional network that India has created, see Annual Report 2003-2004, Department of Space, Government of India, pp. 8-13.

[65] Annual Report 2003-2004, pp. 14-18. ISRO and DOS have about 17000 scientific and other employees under ISRO so far 30 satellites have been launched.

[66] T.S. Subramanian, "A Remote-Sensing Success", *Frontline*, 129-131 (7 November 2003) at 130.

[67] *Ibid.*

groundwater availability, surveying the spread of lakes and ponds or their shrinkage, assessing the severity of droughts, real-time monitoring of floods, mapping wasteland, studying the destruction of forests, detecting the death of coral reefs, and landslip-prone areas.

(iii) Integrated Mission for Sustainable Development

Moreover, the remote sensing data are integrated with other relevant data through a common program called Integrated Mission for Sustainable Development, in order to derive comprehensive developmental plans with the participation of local communities. The space data are also used in support of disaster management in India. For instance, in areas of flood monitoring, drought assessment and land slide hazard, etc. A remarkable benefit for an average citizen in India from space research and data is the concept of telemedicine.[68] The telemedicine facilitates expert medical consultations to reach rural and remote areas by connecting hospitals and health centers in those locations with super specialty hospitals in major towns and cities. For instance, a telemedicine project has been implemented in far-flung areas like the Andaman and Nicobar Islands, by connecting them with a super specialty hospital at Chennai.

3.4. New Policy Initiatives

i. Satcom Policy

The Government of India formulated and approved a Satcom policy in the form of "Norms, guidelines and procedures for implementation of policy framework for satellite communications in India" in January 2000. Major features of the policy are:

a. Authorize INSAT capacity to be leased to non-government (Indian and foreign) parties.
b. Allow commercial activities on INSAT system.
c. Allow Indian parties to provide services including TV up-linking through Indian satellites.
d. Enable establishment of "Indian Satellite Systems" and networks by Indian private parties.
e. Enable operations from Indian soil using foreign satellites, under certain conditions (enabling Indian participation in such ventures).

---

68 For a brief conceptual and technical account, see, Annual Report, 2002-2003, Department of Space, Government of India, pp. 22-23.

ii. Remote Sensing Data Policy

The Government of India has approved and adopted a Comprehensive Remote Sensing Data Policy (RSDP) for acquisition and distribution of satellite remote sensing data from Indian and foreign satellites for civilian users in India. It is a policy that sets guidelines for satellite data acquisition and distribution in the country as well as for licensing the IRS capacities to other countries. Permission from the government will be required for operating remote sensing satellites from India and for distribution of satellite images in India. RSDP streamlines the distribution of high-resolution data to government users and private users involved in developmental activities, including academia and foreign users. RSDP would help in regulating the process of image distribution so that Indian users are not denied access to valuable satellite-based imageries, which can be used in the development of natural resources.

iii. Industrial Participation Policy

ISRO and the Department of Space are in the process of developing an "Industry Participation Policy". The thrust areas of the proposed policy are:

a. ISRO will realize higher levels of aggregates in system/stage level supply from the industry.
b. ISRO will encourage the industry to invest in the future production facilities.
c. The production level of supply quantities will be committed to the industry by ISRO on a long-term basis.
d. ISRO will evolve suitable guidelines for the deputation of ISRO experts to work in industry.
e. ISRO will develop adequate provisions to safeguard its own intellectual property rights, as well as the IPR of joint developments.
f. ISRO will consider incentives to encourage commercial development of space systems and support services, including to a certain extent the financial support in the form of Venture Capital.

iv. Commercialization Policy

The Antrix Corporation is the marketing wing of the Department of Space. The Corporation makes commercially available the data collected from its remote sensing satellites. Its tie up with Space Imaging, USA is a growing business. The company also supplies various IRS specific hardware and software items. It has successfully executed several export orders received from major spacecraft/satellite manufacturers for spacecraft/satellite systems, assemblies and components.

The corporation also intends to use commercially the Polar Satellite Launch Vehicle (PSLV) for launch services. For instance, PSLV was used to launch the Korean satellite KITSAT-3 and a German satellite. In view of this commercial use of its space products and services, India is earning a good amount of valuable foreign exchange.[69] The present policy also aims at playing an active market role globally. It was reported recently that Antrix Corporation and the Malaysian company have entered into an agreement that ISRO would be building and launching satellites for Malaysia.[70]

v. Citizen's Charter of Department of Space[71]

The Department of Space (DoS) has the primary objective of promoting development and application of space science and technology to assist in all-round development of the nation. With this end in view, DoS has evolved the following programmes:

a. INSAT programme for telecommunications, broadcasting, meteorology, developmental education, etc.
b. Remote Sensing programme for application of satellite imagery for various developmental purposes;
c. Research and development in space sciences and technology for sub serving the end of applying them for national development; and
d. Launch Vehicle Programme having indigenous capability for launching spacecraft.

The DoS is committed to provide national space infrastructure for the telecommunication needs of the country; provide satellite services required for weather forecasting, monitoring etc.; provide satellite imagery required for the developmental and security needs of the country; provide satellite imagery and specific products and services required for application of space science and technology for developmental purposes to the central government, state governments, quasi-governmental organizations, NGOs and the private sector; and promote research and development in space sciences and technology. While implementing the above objectives, the DoS will provide required transponders and facilities out of its own capacity as well as by hiring additional capacity, if need be; register Indian Satellite System for public and private sectors; and provide its products and services in a prompt and efficient manner to all the users/clients.

---

[69] Antrix Corporation earned about Rs. 300 million over years.
[70] *Hindustan Times*, New Delhi, 21 December 2004.
[71] For the text see Annual Report 2002-03, *supra* note 68 at 4.

4. Should India Enact Space Legislation?

4.1. India's Policy and Practice Regarding Outer Space Law

India has actively contributed to the progressive development of space law within the General Assembly and UNCOPUOS and its Legal Sub Committees.[72] At the early stages of debates on international space law, India's views were expressed as follows:

> [O]uter space was a new field and there were no vested interests to prevent the international community from embarking on a regime of co-operation rather than conflict. The problems of outer space were fortunately not those of modifying an existing regime but of fashioning a new pattern of international behaviour.[73]

Basing itself on such perspective India has satisfactorily discharged its task toward creating a viable international legal framework to regulate space activities. It had even submitted a draft of the Liability Convention for the consideration of the Legal Sub-Committee of UNCOPUOS.[74] It is a party to four out of the five UN treaties on outer space law, namely, Treaty on Principles Governing the Activities of States in the Exploration and Use of Outer Space, including the Moon and Other Celestial Bodies; Agreement on the Rescue of Astronauts, the Return of Astronauts and the Return of Objects Launched into Outer Space; Convention on International Liability for Damage Caused by Space Objects; and Convention on Registration of Objects Launched into Outer Space. However, India is not a party to the Agreement Governing the Activities of States on the Moon and Other Celestial Bodies, whereas it has merely signed it. India is a party to all the Principles adopted by the General Assembly.

Further, India has been actively participating in formulating the legal principles relating to the current issues of space law, such as, Use of Nuclear Power Sources in Outer Space; definition and delimitation of outer space; character and utilization of geostationary orbit; the concept of "launching State" etc. It has also taken up the issue of space debris.[75]

---

[72] See V. Balakista Reddy, "India's Contribution to the United Nations Committee on Peaceful uses of Outer Space", in V.S. Mani et. al (ed.), *Recent Trends in International Space Law and Policy*, pp. 153-188.

[73] Statement by Krishna Rao, UN. Doc. A/AC. 105/e.2SR. 29-37, p. 78.

[74] India has been a member of UNCOPUOS from the beginning. For India's draft on Liability Convention see A/AC.105/C.2/L.32/Rev.2.

[75] Along with Brazil, India is actively involved in the deliberations regarding the problems of space debris.

4.2. Legal Consequences of India's Space Activities

India as a State Party to four of the five outer space treaties is obliged, under general international law, to carry out the obligations arising out of these treaties. India has ratified all the space treaties except the Moon Treaty and such ratifications express India's consent to be bound by the treaties. [76] These treaties have already entered into force for India in view of her ratifications and thus are binding on India with respect to her entire territory.[77] Any breach of an enforceable multilateral treaty would entail international responsibility for the State Party.[78] On the consequence of any such breach, the Permanent Court of International Justice said that, 'it is a principle of international law, and even a greater conception of law, that any breach of engagement involves an obligation to make reparation.'[79]

India does not have a domestic law to address the consequences of its international and domestic obligations with regard to the Outer Space Treaties. India is already in the process of privatization and globalization of its economy and to some extent ISRO itself is planning to privatize some of its activities. The Antrix Corporation, the commercial wing of ISRO, is already engaged in trade and commerce in space products and space services. This entails legal issues such as encumbrances of being a launching State liability, and compensation for damage caused by space objects, registration and insurance of space objects, procedures and forums for settlement of claims, etc. It is surprising that though India is an active and advanced space-faring nation, it has not put in place a law regulating space activities by Indian nationals and corporations within Indian territory. However, by a combination of policy declarations, norms, guidelines and administrative directives, as we saw earlier, the Government of India seeks to administer the whole range of space activities, including the commercial aspects.

The objectives of the Indian domestic legislation should be able to secure compliance with the international obligations of India with respect to special operational regimes of the various multilateral treaties on space. It should also give expression in its preamble to India's contemporary policies such as privatization/ commercialization of space products and services and commercial launch services, institutions and procedures. Further, it should create necessary structures with general powers, policy-making and providing operational scope, besides providing for licensing of space operations, liability regime, registration, insurance, dispute settlement etc. In other words, the Indian legislation should be comprehensive enough to address all issues relating to space activities. There is no need to enact a

---

[76] See Article 14 of the Vienna Convention on Law of Treaties, 1969.
[77] Article 29 of the Vienna Convention on Law of the Treaties.
[78] See Generally Malcolm N. Shaw, *International Law*, (4th edition, Cambridge University Press: 1997), Chapter –14. Also see Gregory Tunkin, *International Law*, (Progress Publishers, Moscow: 1986), Chapter-9.
[79] *Ibid.*, at 542.

separate legislation to give effect to each international space treaty to which India is a State Party.

4.3. National Space Legislations

The importance and need for domestic legislations on space was emphasized by the Third United Nations Conference on the Exploration and Peaceful Uses of Outer Space (UNISPACE-III) in 1999 "the need for effective laws and policies on space activities, not just on an international level but also on the national level is becoming clear to the increasing number of States now actively involved in the field of space".[80] The American Astronautical Society, in 2001 observed:

> [T]he accessibility and integration into our daily lives of numerous commercial applications in space, include satellite telephony, direct-to-home television, high speed internet connectivity, telemedicine, distance learning, remote sensing of the Earth, global positioning and navigation and materials processing are a testament to that fee. Yet for private entities investors to expand their business models and to reach for the next new application, they will need to see predictable, transparent and flexible international and domestic legal frameworks within which they may operate their businesses and protect their investments.[81]

Although the above view advocates the interests of the private investments and their protection, the basic truth about space activities and uses of outer spaces are ultimately serving the interests of people rather than states. Therefore, even a State like India which is investing governmental funds i.e. public funds is accountable to people and the only way to be accountable to people is to conduct its space activities under the rule of law.

Several countries that are States Parties to the outer space treaties have made domestic legislation in accordance with their international obligations arising from them.[82] They are: Argentina, Australia, Brazil, Canada, Chile, France, Germany, Italy, Japan, Norway, Russian Federation, South Africa, Spain, Sweden, Ukraine, United Kingdom of Great Britain and Northern Ireland, and United States of America. There is no uniformity in the form and content of these legislations nor in their scope and application. It is, perhaps, due to the fact that each country has made its law to regulate its current space activities and as one could guess these activities are different from country to country. While some of them have made a comprehensive law, others have made separate and independent legislation to implement

---

[80] Cited in Joanne Irena Gobrynowicz, "Foreword, The Journal of Space Law: New Century", 29 *Journal of Space Law* 1 & 2 (2003) VI.
[81] *Ibid.*
[82] For the various domestic legislations on Space see website of the Office for Outer Space Affairs, at http://www.oosa.unvienna.org/spacelaw/national/index.html.

obligations under individual space treaties. Some of these national legislations are intended to give United Nations Treaties on Outer Space the force of law in those countries.[83] Several others such as Argentina, Brazil, Canada, Chile, France, Japan, South Africa, Russian Federation and Ukraine have enacted legislations to create national space agencies.[84] Argentina and Spain have also established separate national registries to register the space objects. Australia, Russian Federation, Sweden, Ukraine, the United Kingdom and United States of America have enacted more comprehensive laws on space activities.[85]

4.4. Implementation of International Law in India

Even though India is under an obligation to carry out the obligations under space treaties, a treaty as a matter of general practice in India, does not *ipso facto* become enforceable law in India. India does not have a law made by Parliament to implement international law, but the Indian Constitution in Article 51 states:[86]

> "The State shall endeavour to: … (c) foster respect for international law and treaty obligations."

Interpreting Article 51, M. K. Nawaz states that *Pacta Sunt Servanda* is a rule of international law which India is committed to uphold under Article 51 (c) of the constitution.[87] The Indian constitution also provides for the implementation of treaties within the territory of India in Article 253.

> [N]otwithstanding anything in the foregoing provisions of this chapter, Parliament has power to make any law for the whole or any part of the territory of India for implementing any treaty, agreement or convention with any other country or countries or any decision made at any international conference association or other body.[88]

India seems to follow what was observed by Lord Atkin:

---

[83] See *Space Law Update*, Vol. 1, Issue 2, May 2004, p. 2.

[84] *Ibid.*

[85] *Ibid.*

[86] On scope and extent of this article see C.H. Alexandrowicz, "International Law in India", 1 *International Comparative Law Quarterly*, (1952) at 291, also P. Chandrasekhara Rao, *The Indian Constitution and International Law*, (Taxmann, Delhi: 1993) pp. 5-7.

[87] M.K. Nawaz, *The Changing Law of Nations*, Calcutta, (Eastern Book House, New Delhi: 2000) at 12.

[88] For an interpretation of Article 253 see judgements of the Indian Supreme Court in *Maganbhai v. Union of India*, AIR 1969, SC, 783. Also Promod Nair, "The Application of International Law by Domestic Courts. An Indian Perspective", XXI *Delhi Law Review* (1999) at 214; V.S. Mani, "Implementation of International Law in India", *Asian Yearbook of International Law* (1994); Rajeev Dhawan, "Treaties and People: Indian Reflections", 31 *Journal of Indian Law Institute* 1 (1997).

> There is a well established rule that making of a treaty is an executive act, while the performance of its obligations, if they entail alteration of this existing domestic law, requires legislative action… the stipulations of a treaty duly ratified do not …. by virtue of the treaty alone, have the force of law. If the national executive, the government of the day, decide to incur the obligations of a treaty which involve alleviation of law, they have to turn the risk of obtaining the assent of Parliament.[89]

The Indian Supreme Court has held earlier that a rule of international law is not enforceable within India unless it is made part of the municipal law.[90] This trend has been changed to the effect that Indian courts are said to have power to implement the provisions of international human rights covenants to which India is a party in the absence of a domestic law in the given context.[91]

Answering the question whether customary international law is part of municipal law, the Indian Supreme Court held:

> [I]t is almost an accepted proposition of law that the rules of customary international law which are not contrary to the municipal law shall be deemed to have been incorporated in the domestic law and shall be followed by the Court of Law.[92]

It may, however, be noted that the recent trend of reading international law to do justice in the absence of a domestic law is confined only to human rights, environmental rights of individuals. It is arguable whether this legal position could be applied to the space treaties some of which are very sophisticated and needs unusual scientific and technical input to make domestic law in order to implement international obligations of India with regard to its space activities.

The basic features of Indian law should address the following aspects:

a. **Definition Clause:** This must provide for the definitions of various concepts and terms of art, such as astronaut, space object, launching, launching state, registration, state of registration, license, licensing authority etc.

---

[89] (1937) AC 326, cited in Promod Nair, *Ibid.*

[90] *Maganbhai v. Union of India*, AIR 1969, SC 783; *Ram Narayan Agarwal v. State of UP*, AIR 1983 UP SC 862.

[91] See *Vishaka v. State of Rajasthan*, JT 1997 (7) SC 392. Also *D.K. Basu v. State of West Bengal*, AIR 1997, SC 610.

[92] *Vellore Citizens Welfare Forum v. Union of India*, (1996) 5 SCC 647. It is said that this judgement was given by referring to earlier cases such as *ADM Jabalpur v. Shivakant Shukla*, AIR 1976 SC 1207; *Jolly Verghese v. Bank of Cochin*, AIR 1980 SC 470; *Gramaphone Company v. Birendra*, AIR 1984 SC 667. See Pramod Nair, at 227.

b. **Scope and Applicability:** The Act should define its scope and applicability as to the persons i.e., both natural and legal. It should also clarify whether it is applicable to government as a person / operator for the purposes of the act. It should also enumerate the permissible and non-permissible space activities. Then the issue of jurisdiction under the act could be made clear.
c. **Creation of a National Space Authority:** India should create a statutory national space authority, which would discharge the statutory functions. Most of the national space legislations of other space-faring nations provide for this. For instance, the Space Commission which is currently serving as the policy-making body should be made the National Space Authority under the Act which would be statutorily responsible for regulating the entire range of space activities both with reference to India's proclaimed policies and India's obligations under international space regimes. The Act should specifically provide for the functions, powers and the composition of the Authority. India has a legal tradition of creating statutory bodies for scientific research and commercial activities by Parliamentary enactments.
d. **Licensing:** The Act should provide for the activities for which license could be granted and the conditions attached thereto. It should also designate a licensing authority with necessary powers to make rules for licensing.
e. **Registration of Space Objects:** The Act should provide for carrying out the obligations of the Registration Agreement. It should provide for the creation of a designated Central Registry wherein all space objects and their components would be registered.
f. **Rescue Operations:** The Act should provide for rules and procedures for Rescue and Return of astronauts and space objects if and when they are found on the territory of India and to carry out obligations arising from the Rescue Agreement.
g. **Liability Regime:** The Act should provide for a liability regime for damage caused by space objects launched from India and under its registration. It should also provide for third party liability, indemnity etc. This act should specifically state that damage caused to Indian nationals would also be covered. This is required in view of the Liability Agreement, 1972, which specifically excludes the nationals of state of registry from the scope of the international liability regime.
h. **Insurance Regime:** The Act should provide for insuring the space objects and the safety of personnel.
i. **Dispute Settlement Mechanism:** The Act should provide for creation of a National Space Disputes Redressal Commission (NSDRC) in order to render justice in disputes relating to space activities. India should follow its own tradition of creating various claims tribunals under various Statutes such as Motor Vehicles Act, Railway Accidents Claims Tribunal Act, Consumer Protection Act, etc.
j. Intellectual property rights regarding data collection and determination should be properly addressed.

5. Conclusions

India is a democratic Republic, which believes in the rule of law as a basic structure of its constitution. The country is expected to be governed in the name of its people, in accordance with the preamble of the constitution. India's space research and explorations have paid enormous dividends to the public. The space research and its practical application have resulted in providing a modern and affordable telecommunication system, internet connectivity, radio and television broadcasting, in addition to contributing to the spreading of education, telemedicine etc. Space operations are carried out of public funds. It is noteworthy that India has declared that its entire range of space research is for peaceful purposes and not for military purposes. It employs several thousand scientists and civilians. The space organizations such as Indian Space Research Organization and its scientists enjoy enormous public esteem in view of their excellent contribution to India's reputation as a space-faring nation. Under such circumstances India could do better if it enacts a domestic law on its space activities subject to such constitutionally permissible restrictions and national security interests. Before ending, it may be pointed out that enacting a comprehensive domestic space legislation for India, given the range of activities, is undoubtedly a tedious task. Neither scientists nor lawyers alone can confidently discharge the task in this regard. What is needed is a working group comprising space scientists and expert international lawyers to make draft legislation for the consideration of the government.

INTERNATIONAL COURT OF JUSTICE AND INDIA

Bimal N. Patel*

1. Introduction

This essay examines how India has contributed to the development of jurisprudence and to the functioning of the International Court of Justice (hereinafter referred either as ICJ or the Court). It analyses India's contribution to the advisory jurisdiction of the Court, looks at the contentious cases in which India was involved as a party, and considers the general attitude of India towards the Court.

The literature on India and the ICJ is very limited, though the few contributions Indian authors have made thus far have been important.[1] What little has been produced focuses more on cases in which India was involved rather than on the general functioning of the ICJ. There are few direct references to ICJ judgments in the domestic case law of India – though the same can be said of many other Member States of the United Nations (UN). The lack of literature can be explained in part by the small number of cases before the ICJ in which India has been either an applicant or a respondent. That in turn can be attributed to the importance India has attached to settling international disputes through negotiation rather than litigation, which it has tended to regard as an option of last resort. This attitude can also find reflection in President Nagendra Singh's *The Role and Record of the International Court of Justice*.[2] He advocates that recourse to the ICJ is a normal and natural step in the face of any dispute not resolved by negotiation.[3]

Should we look at the contribution of India as an isolated product of thinking or was it inspired and influenced by contemporary theories and phenomena

---

* Staff member, Organization for the Prohibition of Chemical Weapons, The Hague, the Netherlands. The views are expressed in the personal capacity of the author.

[1] Anand, R.P., *International Courts and Contemporary Conflicts*, (Popular Press, 1974); ______ The International Court of Justice and Impartiality between Nations In XII *The Indian Yearbook of International Affairs* (1963), World Rule of Law Booklet Series, No. 26; ________*Compulsory Jurisdiction of the International Court of Justice*, (Asia Publishing House, London: 1961); J. N. Singh, International Justice, (Harnam Publications, New Delhi: 1991); Ramesh Thakur, (ed.) Past Imperfect, Future Uncertain, (MacMillan Press Ltd., New York: 1998); Nagendra Singh, The Role and Record of the International Court of Justice (Martinus Nijhoff, Dordrecht, 1989).

[2] Judge Nagendra Singh served as Judge *ad hoc* and a member of the Court from 1973 to 1988, including as the President from 1985 to 1988.

[3] Nagendra Singh, *supra* note 1 at 83.

***Bimal N. Patel (ed.),* India and International Law, 289-318.**

elsewhere? What has been the exact influence and the judicial legacy? The pursuit of these issues seems an indispensable exercise when we discuss the contribution of India to the functioning of the ICJ and the jurisprudence.

2. India as a Party in the Contentious Cases: A Short Description

India has appeared before the ICJ as the respondent in three cases, namely, the *Right of Passage over Indian Territory*[4], the *Trial of Pakistani Prisoners of War*[5], and the *Aerial Incident of 10 August 1999*[6]. In each of these it has challenged the jurisdiction of the Court. The *Trial of Pakistani Prisoners of War* case was removed from the General List of the Court. The *Aerial Incident of 10 August 1999* case was discontinued because of the lack of jurisdiction of the ICJ. The ICJ rejected the preliminary objections of

---

[4] Portugal instituted proceedings against India on 22 December 1955. The case lasted for 4 years, 3 months and 21 days and the final judgment was delivered on 12 April 1960. The Portugese possessions in India included the two enclaves of Dadra and Nagar-Aveli which, in mid-1954, passed under an autonomous local administration. Portugal claimed that it had a right to passage to those enclaves and between one enclave and the other to the extent necessary for the exercise of its sovereignty and subject to the regulation and control of India; it also claimed that, in July 1954, contrary to the practice previously followed, India had prevented it from exercising that right and that that situation should be redressed. A first judgment, delivered on 26 November 1957, related to the jurisdiction of the Court, which had been challenged by India. The Court rejected four of the preliminary objections raised by India and joined the other two to the merits. In a second Judgment, delivered on 12 April 1960, after rejecting the two remaining preliminary objections the Court gave its decision on the claims of Portugal, which India maintained were unfounded. The Court found that Portugal had in 1954 the right of passage claimed by it that such right did not extend to armed forces, armed police, arms and ammunition, and that India had not acted contrary to the obligations imposed on it by the existence of that right. Source: *the International Court of Justice* (1986), p. 92.

[5] Pakistan instituted proceedings against India concerning 195 Pakistani prisoners of war on 11 May 1973, whom, according to Pakistan, India proposed to hand over to Bangladesh, which was said to intend trying them for acts of genocide and crimes against humanity. India stated that there was no legal basis for the Court's jurisdiction in the matter and that Pakistan's application was without legal effect. The case lasted for 7 months and 4 days. The case was removed from the General List on 15 December 1973. Pakistan having also filed a request for the indication of interim measures of protection, the Court held public sittings to hear observations on this subject; India was not represented at the hearings. In July 1973, Pakistan asked the Court to postpone further consideration of its request in order to facilitate negotiations. Before any written pleadings had been filed, Pakistan informed the Court that negotiations had taken place, and requested the Court to record discontinuance of the proceedings. Accordingly, the case was removed from the list by an order of 15 December 1973. Source: *the International Court of Justice* (1986), p. 98.

[6] Pakistan instituted proceedings before the Court against India in respect of a dispute concerning the destruction on 10 August 1999 of a Pakistani aircraft. India raised preliminary objections to the jurisdiction of the Court. The Court declared, by a vote of fourteen to two, that it had no jurisdiction to adjudicate upon the dispute brought by Pakistan.

India in the *Right of Passage over Indian Territory* case and handed down its judgment on the merits. India has also brought a fourth case to the ICJ - the ICAO appeal.[7] In this case, the ICJ found that it had jurisdiction to deal with the case lodged by India. Three of the four cases concerned disputes between India and Pakistan; the exception was the *Right of Passage over Indian Territory* case, which was brought by Portugal.

2.1. Basis of jurisdiction

All four cases were brought before the ICJ through a unilateral application under Article 40 of the ICJ Statute. Portugal invoked Article 36(2) of the Statute in the *Right of Passage over Indian Territory* case Pakistan invoked Article IX of the Genocide Convention and Article 36(1) of the Statute in the *Trial of Pakistani Prisoners of War* case, and Pakistan invoked Article 36(1) and (2) of the Statute, the General Act of 1928 and declarations of the Pakistan and India accepting the jurisdiction of the ICJ in the *Aerial Incident of 10 August 1999* case. While India, in its sole case as an applicant, invoked Article 84 of the Convention on International Civil Aviation of 7 December 1944, Article II of the International Air Services Transit Agreement of 7 December 1944, and Articles 36 and 37 of the Statute.

3. The Position of India on the Legal Rules and Principles in the Contentious Cases

How have the cases concerning India contributed to the clarification of legal principles and rules and the emergence of new ones, and how have they affected practices followed by the ICJ or by member States of the UN. The following section examines what was the position of India concerning the elements of political motives in the contentious cases; its standpoint on reciprocity, mutuality and equality before the Court; emphasis on the *prima facie* jurisdiction and consent for the purposes of interim measures of protection and its views on the compulsory jurisdiction of the Court.

---

[7] The case lasted for nearly eleven months and 12 days (from 30 August 1971 to 18 August 1972). In February 1971, following an incident involving the diversion to Pakistan of an Indian aircraft, India suspended overflights of its territory by Pakistan civil aircraft. Pakistan took the view that this action was in breach of the 1944 Convention on International Civil Aviation and the International Air Services Transit Agreement and complained to the Council of the International Civil Aviation Organization. India raised preliminary objections to the jurisdiction of the Council, but these were rejected and India appealed to the Court. During the ensuring written and oral proceedings before the Court, Pakistan contended, *inter alia,* that the Court was not competent to hear the appeal. In its judgment of 18 august 1972, the Court found that it was competent to hear the appeal and that the Council had jurisdiction to deal with Pakistan's case. Source: *the International Court of Justice* (1986) at 98.

3.1. Political Motives

India has been quite sensitive to the political use of any legal instrument in the proceedings of the Court. India has vehemently objected whenever the opposing party had relied on political connections of the legal disputes. For example, India made it clear that the *Trial of Pakistani Prisoners of War* case could have been instituted against another state, namely, Bangladesh, which was not yet a Member State of the UN. Since India had nothing to do with the crimes or trials that were at the centre of the case, "it could not be made a party to the application and request for interim measures just in order to enable the respondent to seek extraneous political advantages."[8] It also alleged that Pakistan had had political motives in bringing the case and had thus "shown utter disregard for the object and purpose of the Genocide Convention."

3.2. Principles of Reciprocity and Equality

The contribution of India has enabled a clarification of the legal principle of reciprocity, mutuality and equality through its pleadings in the *Right of Passage over Indian Territory* case. India argued that the Portuguese application had been filed before the lapse of brief period. In the normal course of events, the UN Secretary-General would have, in compliance with Article 36 (4), transmitted copies of the Portuguese declaration to the other parties to the Statute. By doing this, Portugal violated equality, mutuality, and reciprocity to which India was entitled under the optional clause and under the express condition of reciprocity contained in its own declaration of 1940; and consequently, the conditions did not yet exist to entitle Portugal to file the application. This argument led the Court to clarify and reinforce its jurisprudence of Article 36 (4) of the Statute which has two parts, one the deposition of the declaration, a mandatory requirement; and transmission of the declaration to the States, an administrative/procedural obligation of the UN Secretary-General. In other words, the Indian argument necessitated that the Court clarify an important point of law - namely, whether it is necessary that some time must elapse between depositing of the declaration with the UN Secretary-General under Article 36(4) of the Statute and filing of an application against some state. The ruling of the Court reaffirmed that "as soon as a State Party to the Statute deposits a declaration with the UN Secretary-General, it may invoke the compulsory jurisdiction against any other State party to the Statute, and every other State is likewise bound by its acceptance of the jurisdiction. It is immaterial whether those other states know that the declaration has been deposited."[9] The ICJ clarified that there is no additional requirement that the information transmitted by the UN Secretary-General must reach the parties to the Statue or that some period must elapse subsequent to the deposit of declaration before it can become effective.

---

[8] Pleadings, Oral Arguments and Documents, *Trial of Pakistani Prisoners of War*, p. 152.

[9] Case concerning *Right of Passage over Indian Territory* (Preliminary Objections), Judgment of November 26th, 1957: I.C.J. Reports 1957, p. 145-147.

Although the Indian argument of an entitlement to expect a reasonable degree of certainty in regard to the obligations imposed on them by the declarations of other states was put aside by the Court, this clarification of the Court had useful effects as far as similar situations were concerned. Furthermore, several Member States following the judgment of the Court in this matter modified the content of their declaration accepting the compulsory jurisdiction of the Court.[10]

3.2.1 Reciprocity

India has consistently mentioned in its declaration accepting compulsory jurisdiction that it has accepted the jurisdiction only on condition of reciprocity. This shows India's general attitude towards international law wherein it believes that rules of law ought to reciprocally bind the parties. India invoked this clause in the *Right of Passage over Indian Territory* case. India argued that Portugal violated India's reciprocal right by filing an application against on 22 December 1955, before India knew, or had any means of knowing, the terms of the conditions of the Portuguese Declaration. Furthermore, Portugal violated India's reciprocal right, with respect to the third condition in the Portuguese Declaration which reserved to itself the right at any time to exclude from the scope of Portugal's acceptance of compulsory jurisdiction any given category or categories of dispute by mere notification to the UN Secretary-General. In view of India, the instantaneous filing of the application was inconsistent with India's right to reciprocity and was wholly incompatible both with the terms of the optional clause and with the express conditions of India's own declaration.

The above position of India has helped to understand that the relation created between states by adherence to the clause is a consensual relation involving reciprocal rights and obligations. Therefore, in its view, it was "essential to the operation of this consensual relation that the contractual nexus between any two states should only become effective in law when the action of the UN Secretary-General under Article 36(4) of the Statute has had its appropriate effects with respect to other states which have previously adhered to the optional clause."[11] This principle is of particular importance with respect to a state against which the state making the declaration already intends to file an application. Although India offered a set of lengthy arguments on this principle, its arguments were far from convincing to the Court, as is clear from the Court's rejection of India's arguments.

---

[10] Pleadings, Oral Arguments and Documents, *Right of Passage over Indian Territory*, p. 111.

[11] Case concerning *Right of Passage over Indian Territory* (Preliminary Objections), Judgment of November 26th, 1957: I.C.J. Reports 1957, p. 141-5.

3.2.2. Equality

India has shown determination to uphold the principle of equality of states, in fact, as well as in law, before the ICJ. Thus, India holds that a correct procedure should be followed to ensure equality to all states before the ICJ. In the *Right of Passage over Indian Territory* case, its arguments showed that the principle that states have a right to be in a position of complete equality before the Court in regard to access to the Court and to the Court jurisdiction is fundamental. In the words of India's chief counsel, "the principle of equality finds particular expression in Article 35 (2) of the Statute, which expressly provides that the conditions laid down by the Security Council under which states not parties to the Statute may have access to the ICJ shall in no case place the parties in a position of inequality before the ICJ."[12] It also finds particular expression in Article 36 (2) of the Statute, which provides equality only in relation to any other state accepting the same obligation. In the view of India, the purpose of transmission by the UN Secretary-General of declarations under optional clause to the Court and all Member States is to protect the interests of all other parties to the Statute and with this end in view to ensure that all states that have accepted the optional clause have equal knowledge of the scope both of their obligations and rights under the optional clause. Thus, India considered the lack of sufficient elapse of time period between depositing the declaration and the filing of the case in the Court as a manifest infringement of the principle of equality.

3.3. Necessity for Jurisdiction and Consent of State for the Judgment on Interim Measures

As far as the issue of interim measures is concerned, Indian position shows that the question of interim measures of protection does not arise in the face of the patent and manifest lack of jurisdiction, and more so where the Court is not properly seized of the matter.[13] This was apparent in the Indian argument in the *Trial of Pakistani Prisoners of War* case. India argued that "there is an inextricable link between an application and a request for interim measures which can only follow the application. The request cannot go beyond the scope of the application. The request must be founded on the application and the application alone, and the state making an application is not entitled to urge any point, particularly regarding jurisdiction, beyond what is contained in its application."[14]To prove its point further, it relied upon case law of the ICJ in the *Fisheries Jurisdiction* case, where it was argued that "when the absolute absence of jurisdiction is so patent and manifest at the threshold of the institution of proceedings, the question of summoning the parties for a hearing to determine its jurisdiction does not arise…the only proper

---

12 Pleadings, Oral Arguments and Documents, *Right of Passage over Indian Territory*, pp. 210-213.

13 Pleadings, Oral Arguments and Documents, *Trial of Pakistani Prisoners of War*, p. 131.

14 *Ibid.*, p. 140.

action for the ICJ to take…is to remove the application from the list by an administrative order."[15]

3.4. Consent of State

India declined to give consent to the ICJ in the *Trial of Pakistani Prisoners of War* case. India had made reservation under Article IX of the 1948 Genocide Convention, according to which India declared that, for the submission of any dispute in terms of this Article to the jurisdiction of the ICJ, the consent of all the parties to the dispute is required in each case.[16] India, accordingly, presuming that the application and request of Pakistan which were submitted to India sought the consent of India, regretted that it cannot give consent and informed the Court that it cannot be in proper seisin of the case[17] and cannot proceed with it. It was also of the opinion that there was no legal basis whatsoever for the jurisdiction of the Court. It provides that any dispute relating to the interpretation or application of the treaty in question may be referred to the Court; however, the consent of the respondent is required to perfect the jurisdiction of the Court in any concrete case.

India submitted a written statement elaborating its position declining the consent through its letter dated 28 May 1973. It detailed its reasoning for refusing the consent to the jurisdiction of the Court. India made it clear that its views did not constitute preliminary objections within the meaning of Article 67 of the Rules of the Court, despite Pakistan's assertion to the contrary. It made clear that its views are those of a sovereign state that refuses to give its consent to frivolous and vexatious proceedings instituted against it for interim measures for an ulterior purpose and to seek extraneous political advantages against the object and purpose of the Genocide Convention[18] and the Statute and Rules of the Court.

3.5. Compulsory Jurisdiction of the ICJ

India has accepted the compulsory jurisdiction of the Court and has made eleven separate reservations in its current declaration which has been in effect since 1974. Each of the revisions to the original declaration shows the new ways and ingenious reservations of India to avoid the Court as far as possible in a concrete case. Which

---

15 Fisheries Jurisdiction (Federal Republic of Germany *v.* Iceland), Interim Protection, Order of 17 August 1972, I.C.J. Reports 1972, p.33.

16 Pleadings, Oral Arguments and Documents, *Trial of Pakistani Prisoners of War*, p.132.

17 The case-law suggests that the Court in interpreting the relevant texts has reached the conclusion that it allows a unilateral seisin. Once the court has been validly seized, both parties are bound by the procedural consequences which the statute and the rules make applicable to the method of seisin employed. Maritime Delimitation and Territorial Questions between Qatar and Bahrain, Jurisdiction and Admissibility, Judgment, I.C.J. Reports 1995, p. 23.

18 Pleadings, Oral Arguments and Documents, *Trial of Pakistani Prisoners of War*, p. 124.

are the factors and how has the Indian position on compulsory jurisdiction evolved over time? An evolution of India's acceptance of compulsory jurisdiction dating back from the Permanent Court of International Justice is annexed at the end of this chapter.

The first significant revision of the declaration by India was made in the wake of the ICJ judgment in the *Right of Passage over Indian Territory* case. As mentioned above, India was unaware of the deposit of the declaration of Portugal and immediate filing of the case in the Court which had long-term implications for the equilibrium of the compulsory jurisdiction. Not only India, but several other states also made significant changes in their declaration subsequent to this judgment.[19]Bulgaria, Cyprus, Hungary, Israel, Malta, Mauritius, New Zealand, Philippines, Poland, Somalia, Spain and the United Kingdom introduced changes to their reservations to the compulsory jurisdiction, subsequent to this judgment. India made a change on 14 September 1959 according to which disputes in respect of which any other party to a dispute has accepted the compulsory jurisdiction of the Court exclusively for or in relation to the purposes of such dispute; or where the acceptance of the Court's compulsory jurisdiction on behalf of a party to the dispute was deposited or ratified less than 12 months prior to the filing of the application bringing the dispute before the Court.

There is one particular aspect of India's reservation, namely, its reservation for the Commonwealth countries. A close reading of India's 1959 and 1974 Commonwealth reservations gives the impression that the reservation is made against a particular state – *ratione personae*, properly so described[20]. There may be an argument about whether this reservation may somehow defeat the purposes which it hoped to achieve by means of the purposes of Article 36 (2) and (6) of the Statute.

---

[19] As Rosenne says, "Since that decision (Right of Passage over Indian Territory), several states previously bound by compulsory jurisdiction have made new declarations containing stipulations designed to counteract the two novel features of the declaration of Portugal and of the decision upholding it in the Right of Passage over Indian Territory case – the unexpected and unknown deposit of a declaration very shortly after a state became a party to the Statute and the equally sudden introduction of proceedings by that state before the respondent could have known that the declaration had been deposited". Shabtai Rosenne, *The Law and Practice of the International Court* (3rd ed., 1997), p. 799.

[20] India modified its reservation in 1959 reading *disputes with the government of any state which, on the date of this declaration, is a member of the Commonwealth of Nations.* This reservation omitted *all of which disputes shall be settled in such manner as the parties have agreed or shall agree* which were contained in previous declarations. In 1974, India modified again the reservation reading *disputes with the government of any state which is or has been a member of the Commonwealth of Nations.* Dissenting opinion of Judge Al-Khasawneh, Aerial Incident, paragraph 9 In the Case Concerning the *Aerial Incident of 10 August 1999* (Pakistan *v.* India), Judgment, I. C. J. Reports 2000, p. 50.

British India accepted the compulsory jurisdiction of the Permanent Court of International Justice on 19 September 1929 with a number of reservations. The declaration was revised on 28 February 1940. The revised declaration of 1940 continued to be in force after the formation of the ICJ under Article 36 (5) of the Statute. It was the *Right of Passage over Indian Territory* case which awakened the Indian government to make an appropriate change to the declaration. India withdrew the previous declaration and a new declaration under Article 36 (2) on 9 January 1956 was submitted which was terminable immediately without any notice, and contained apart from others, the most sweeping reservation on the American lines (Connally reservation - under this reservation, the USA has excluded disputes with regard to matters which are essentially within the domestic jurisdiction of the USA as determined by the USA). India excluded disputes in regard to matters which are essentially within the domestic jurisdiction of India as determined by India. Such a reservation leaves very little scope for a case to be brought before the Court without the will of the country making it and is in fact against the very spirit of the compulsory jurisdiction of the Court. Realizing this fact, it seems, India in its 14 September 1959 declaration withdrew the most objectionable part of this reservation by which it was India and not the Court which had the authority to decide whether a matter was or was not within the domestic jurisdiction of India. The new declaration, which has again been made terminable on notice, applies only to disputes arising after 26 January 1950 with regard to situations or facts subsequent to that date.

In the *Right of Passage over Indian Territory* case, the declaration of Portugal had a reservation according to which it had the right to exclude from the scope of its declaration, at any time during its validity, any given category or categories of disputes, by notifying the UN Secretary-General and with effect from the moment of such notification. India maintained that this condition gave Portugal the right by making at any time a notification to that effect, to withdraw from the jurisdiction of the Court a dispute which had been submitted to it prior to such notification. It argued that the notification had retroactive effect and asserted this to be incompatible with the principle and notion of compulsory jurisdiction as established in Article 36 of the Statute. The Court rejected India's argument and its rejection enabled it to draw a conclusion that when an application has been regularly filed in a particular case while the declarations of both states were current, the subsequent lapse of one of the declarations, whether by the expiry of a fixed period or by denunciation under the terms of the declaration does not deprive the Court of jurisdiction over the case. On the other hand, the prior lapse of a declaration by however brief a period, suffices to prevent the establishment of the Court's jurisdiction by means of an application based upon the expired declaration. As Anand explains, this is an important clarification which this case brought to bear in the subsequent cases.[21]

---

[21] Anand, *supra* note 54 at 176.

Several Indian scholars have shown hesitation towards the advocacy of the acceptance of unqualified compulsory jurisdiction. For example, Anand says the maxim *calculate the limits of the possible* should be observed. He is cautious in showing optimism that the acceptance of the jurisdiction of the Court in essentially legal disputes is the first step towards the establishment of the rule of law in international society. Anand outlines the factors which keep Member States away from accepting the unqualified compulsory jurisdiction. Some of the most important are: the absence of any machinery for the execution of the Court's judgments, the fact that not all conflicts of interests are capable of being terminated by judicial techniques within the existing legal framework, the alleged insufficiency and the uncertainty of the rules of international law to deal with all situations arising between the states and the lack of confidence in the impartiality of its judgments. He predicted optimism in the late 1950s that the ICJ will gain the confidence of the legal community and that it will play an ever more useful role when world tension eases to some extent and states are more willing to entrust the solution of their differences to impartial judgment. Although the ICJ has gained significant confidence, particularly since the 1990s, and more and more states are bringing their disputes to the Court, it would be difficult to imagine whether this trend will have positive spill-over effect on India's reservations to the compulsory jurisdiction.

It is no doubt that the practice of attaching more and more reservations and exclusions has reduced the usefulness of the optional clause system and thus of the Court itself.

3.6. Preference for Diplomatic Negotiations

As mentioned above in the introduction, India has shown consistently and strongly advocated its preference for the negotiation in all types of disputes. This position has been reinforced in its pleadings at the Court in all four cases involving India.

For example, one of its objections to the Court in the *Right of Passage over Indian Territory* case was that Portugal filed its application when the diplomatic negotiations had not yet reached the point at which they could no longer be profitably pursued. It contended that it is a rule of customary international law that the filing of a unilateral application must be preceded by a full trial of diplomatic negotiations. It held that "The reason why customary law requires a state to undertake negotiations and continue them until they can no longer profitably be pursued is that states which accept the system of compulsory jurisdiction of the Court do not wish to be brought before the Court without first having made every reasonable effort to obtain a settlement through the diplomatic resources available to them, or to be obliged to appear before the Court in cases except those in which settlement by negotiation is not possible. It is for this reason that many treaties of compulsory jurisdiction and arbitration contain an express condition that there should be previous negotiations."[22] The ruling of the ICJ on this point of India in the *Right of Passage over Indian Territory* case shows that it is not essential to have diplomatic means fully exhausted and that only the failure in reaching diplomatic settlement will enable any institution of the proceedings in the Court.

This preference for diplomatic negotiations and the predictable attitude of India during the *Trial of Pakistani Prisoners of War* case helped Pakistan to remain engaged in the diplomatic dialogue. Hoping that diplomatic negotiations would result in the resolution of the dispute, Pakistan requested the Court to discontinue the proceedings in this case

Judge Nagendra Singh said, "When a state is reduced to desperation but is still not in a position to use force or otherwise prepared to do so, it may resort to the Court as a last resort, whenever the character of the dispute – whether close to it or distant or whether vital or peripheral."[23] In the *ICAO Appeal* case, India, having been left with no alternative by the deliberations of the ICAO Council, took recourse to the Court. This move also furnished an interlude which ultimately helped to resolve the dispute to the satisfaction of both parties.

4. ICJ Advisory Proceedings

India has been active in promoting recourse to the Court, especially through the advisory proceedings, as can be seen through its participation in the general debates in the Sixth Committee of the General Assembly and voting records on the General Assembly resolutions requesting the Court to deliver advisory opinions. It has also been active in filing written submissions in the advisory proceedings. It has filed written statements in eight advisory proceedings, starting from 1948,[24]and presented oral statement in one advisory proceeding. If participation is measured in terms of written and oral statements, India has been the most active state in Asia followed by China which has submitted written statements in seven proceedings and none in oral hearings. India ranks fourth, after the USA, UK and France, in terms of submission of written submissions in the advisory proceedings. It should be noted that India has never challenged the Court's jurisdiction to entertain the request of the requesting organ in any of the advisory proceedings.

India filed its written statements in the advisory proceedings concerning the *Conditions of Admission of a State to Membership in the UN*, *Reparations for Injuries*, *International Status of South-West Africa*, *Voting Procedures on Questions Relating to Reports and Petitions concerning the Territory of South-West Africa*, *Constitution of the Maritime Safety*

[22] Pleadings, Oral Arguments and Documents, *Right of Passage over Indian Territory*, p. 117.

[23] Nagendra Singh, *supra* note 1 at 226.

[24] India submitted its written observation in the advisory opinion concerning *Conditions of Admission of a State to Membership in the United Nations (Article 4 of the Charter)* through a letter dated 28 January 1948.

Committee, *Legal Consequences for States of the Continued Presence of South Africa in Namibia*, *Legality of the Use by a State of Nuclear Weapons in Armed Conflict*, *Legality of the Threat or Use of Nuclear Weapons* advisory proceedings. It presented an oral statement in the advisory opinion concerning the *Legal Consequences for States of the Continued Presence of South Africa in Namibia.*

While India has been active in filing written statements, it has been an original proponent of only one resolution which requested the advisory opinion, namely *International Status of South-West Africa.* The other original proponents were Denmark, Norway, Syria and Thailand of Resolution 338 (IV) of 6 December 1949. In the advisory proceedings concerning *Voting Procedure on Questions relating to Reports and Petitions concerning the territory of South-West Africa*, India, along with Mexico, Norway, Syria and the US submitted the formal proposal (Resolution 904 (IX) of 23 November 1954). It should be noted that the Hyderabad question (1949) and the question of Kashmir (1949) were mooted in the Security Council for the advisory opinions of the Court, but no formal request emanated from the Security Council.

In the *Nuclear Weapons* advisory opinion, India did not participate in the oral hearings despite its staunch support and advocacy for the elimination of nuclear weapons. As Mani argues its "physical presence before the Court might have given an added weight to the cause of nuclear disarmament. By not participating at the hearings, India lost an opportunity formally to address the international community on such an important aspect of its foreign policy. Or, was the decision on non-participation deliberates, reflecting a desire to assume a low profile on the issue?"[25] Mani's observation needs some analysis. As mentioned above, India made oral statement only in one advisory proceeding, namely, the *Legal Consequences for States of the Continued Presence of South Africa in Namibia* where it strongly condemned the illegal presence of South Africa in Namibia. In those advisory proceedings where India filed written statements and refrained from making oral statements, the opinions rendered by the Court were more or less reflective of the Indian position. Although whether the physical presence of India would have decisive effects on the Court's consideration of the matter is a subject of separate scrutiny, one thing is clear, the physical absence definitely reflects India's low profile in the subject, particularly, seen in the context of the subsequent nuclear explosion in 1998. In the same way, India's lack of written or oral submission in the *Wall* advisory proceedings in 2004 also leads to believe that the Indian decision was influenced by foreign policy interests, namely, the growing relations with Israel without revoking the historical support for the cause of Palestine.

In view of the conspicuous absence in filing oral statements, it becomes interesting to see why India did not file written or oral submissions in some of the important landmark advisory proceedings which concerned the broad objectives of

---

[25] V. S. Mani, "The Nuclear Weapons and the World Court" In 37 *Indian Journal of International Law* (1997), p. 167.

development of international law. India participated in eight advisory proceedings, but one would have firmly expected its active participation in the *Competence of the General Assembly for the Admission of a State to the UN, Certain Expenses*[26], *Reservation to the Genocide Convention, Application of Article VI, Section 22 of the Convention on the Privileges and Immunities of the UN and Difference Relating to Immunity from Legal Process of a Special Rapporteur of the Commission on Human Rights opinions.* These advisory opinions have significantly contributed to the codification and progressive development of international law in the matters dealt with by the opinions. The advisory opinions concerning *Western Sahara, WHO-Egypt Agreement, Interpretation of Peace Treaties, Application of Article VI, Section 22 of the Convention on the Privileges and Immunities of the UN, Applicability of the Obligation to Arbitrate under section 21 of the UN HQ Agreement of 25 June 1947* could be considered as having no significant foreign policy interest. In the *Admissibility of hearing* advisory proceedings, India did not consider it necessary to submit any written statement, in view of the fact that its views in the matter were already indicated in the relevant records of the tenth Session of the General Assembly. India did not file any submissions in the five advisory proceedings that dealt with the administrative law matters either.[27] Thus, the brief examination of records shows that India actively participates in the Court's advisory proceedings when the outcome of the opinion or proceedings themselves may have potential impacts on India's national interests, in particular, the foreign policy.

As far as the use of substantive laws in the written submissions of states is concerned, India has shown heavy reliance on the general principles of international law. This is partially led by India's firm belief that the general principles of law are principles expressing legal ideas common to the legal systems of civilized states which the Court is authorized to apply in Article 38 of the Statute.

4.1. India's Position on the Legal Rules and Principles in the Advisory Proceedings

What contribution has India made towards the substantive law and procedures dealing with the advisory opinion rendered by the Court? Has India's position contributed to the clarification of legal principles and rules involved in the advisory opinion? The following section analyses India's position in each of the advisory proceedings where she has filed a written statement.

[26] It is known that although the issue involved the interpretation of Article 17(2) of the UN Charter, the obligations of the members was the real matter of dispute.

[27] *Effect of Awards of Compensation made by the UNAT; Judgments of Administrative Tribunal of ILO upon Complaints Made against UNESCO; Application for Review of UNAT Judgment No. 158; Application for Review of UNAT Judgment No. 273* and *Application for Review of UNAT Judgment No. 333.*

In the advisory opinion concerning, the *Reparation for Injuries,*[28] India submitted that "if it is established that the United Nations, as an Organization, is competent legally to bring an international claim against the responsible State for reparation of damage caused to the victim, the Government of India consider that the only way to deal satisfactorily with the rights of the State of which the victim is a national and of the United Nations of which he was agent is to make the State as well as the United Nations parties to the proceedings in order that the rights of both may be worked out in the same proceedings."[29]

In the advisory proceedings of the *Admission of a State to UN Membership*,[30] India suggested it adheres to the view that the Members of the United Nations are entitled to take into consideration only those points which are specified in Article 4 of the Charter and that it is wrong to import extraneous considerations into this matter, consequently, India forwarded that the ICJ should negatively answer the question contained in the resolution.[31]

---

[28] The question referred by the General Assembly Resolution of 3 December 1948 to the Court: (1) In the event of an agent of the United Nations in the performance of his duties suffering injury in circumstances involving the responsibility of a State, has the United Nations, as an Organization, the capacity to bring an international cliam against the responsible *de jure* or *de facto* government with a view to obtaining the reparation due in respect of the damage caused (a) to the United Nations, (b) to the victim or to persons entitled through him? (2) In the event of an affirmative reply on point 1(b), how is action by the United Nations to be reconciled with such rights as may be possessed by the State of which the victim is a national? This is one of the most quoted advisory opinions of the ICJ and is considered to be one of the most important judicial pronouncements. If statistics are any significant indication of the most-quoted advisory opinion of the Court in its case law then, the Court up to 31 December 2000, has quoted directly or indirectly this advisory opinion six times in the advisory opinion and three times in its contentious cases. One would agree that this advisory opinion in several respects has significantly aided the international organizations law. Source: Bimal N. Patel, *The World Court Reference Guide* (Kluwer Law International, 2002).

[29] Letter from the Deputy Secretary to the Government of India to the Registrar of the International Court of Justice dated 28 December 1948.

[30] UN General Assembly Resolution 296(IV) of 22 November 1949: Can the admission of a State to membership in the United Nations, pursuant to Article 4, paragraph 2, of the Charter, be effected by a decision of the General Assembly when the Security Council has made no recommendation for admission by reason of the candidate failing to obtain the requisite majority or of the negative vote of a permanent Member upon a resolution so to recommend?

[31] Letter from the Joint Secretary to the Government of India, Ministry of External Affairs and Commonwealth Relations, to the Registrar of the Court of 28 January 1948.

4.1.1. Advisory opinion - *IMO Safety Committee*[32]

In this advisory proceeding, India submitted a lengthy written statement covering among others the legal points concerning the nationality of the ship, protection of ships, the standards to be applied to ascertain the "largest ship-owning nations", the term "ship-owning" nations, ownership by nationals as a criterion and the object behind the provision on the functions of the maritime safety committee

Regarding the nationality of the ships, India suggested that the ICJ should base its opinion in the light of international practice and through the reasoned application of the generally accepted principles of international law. It cited Article 5 of the Geneva Convention of the High Seas of 1958 as one of such principles which reads that each state is free to fix conditions for the grant of its nationality to ships, for the registration of ships in its territory, and for the right to fly its flag. India argued that the registration of ships and the need to fly the flag of the country where the ship is registered are considered essential for the maintenance of order on the open sea, since it is easy to enforce the rule that a vessel not sailing under the maritime flag of a State enjoys no protection whatsoever.[33]

On the question of protection of vessels, India relied on the case-law of *Noim Molvan v. Attorney-General for Palestine* in which it was established that a vessel not sailing under the flag of any State has no right to protection just as a vessel sailing under the flags of two different States is deprived of any protection whatever.[34] India contended that Article 6 of the Geneva Convention on the High Seas of 1958 rules has now become part of the treaty law.

One can also say that the Indian position is based on general principles of law as it substantially used these principles to justify its position. For example, it used in establishing the relationship between a ship and the state whose flag it flies a principle propounded by the majority in the *Lotus* judgment, according to which "a corollary of the principle of the freedom of the seas is that a ship on the high seas is assimilated to the territory of the state the flag of which it flies, for, just as in its own territory, that state exercises its authority upon it, and no other state may do so … By virtue of the principle of the freedom of the seas, a ship is placed in the same position as national territory."[35]

---

[32] Resolution of the Assembly of Inter-Governmental Maritime Consultative Organization of 19 January 1959: Is the Maritime Safety Committee of the Inter-Governmental Maritime Consultative Organization, which was elected on 15 January 1959, constituted in accordance with the Convention for the Establishment of the Organization?

[33] Pleadings, Oral Arguments and Documents, *Composition of the Maritime Safety Committee of the Inter-Governmental Maritime Consultative Organization*, p. 253.

[34] *Ibid.*, at 254.

[35] *Ibid.*, at 256.

India argued that it is the law of the flag unconnected with the ownership of the vessel which provides the necessary authority to the master of a ship to deal with the cargo during the voyage and the manner in which he should execute it. India argued that "the term has been used to convey the idea of jurisdiction and authority over the ship and not that of ownership of the ship in its literal sense."[36] To ascertain the nationality of the ship, one has to look to the flag and the registry of the ship. Another major argument India forwarded was that the intention for the inclusion of Article 28(a) of the Convention seems to be to restrict membership of the maritime safety committee to nations having the powers to enforce rules and regulations for maritime safety; this certainly could be done only under the law of the flag state and under no other. India took strong exception and considered that the test of ownership which could change at will of shareholders at a moment's notice is totally unsuited with reference to the question of formulation and enforcement of maritime safety rules.[37] India considered that the economic success of ship-owning and ship-operating business depends upon a reasonably reliable forecast of the laws and regulations which will apply to the ship. The law as to the nationality of the ship must be definitely known in advance. India argued that the election which took place on 15 January 1959 to elect the members of the IMCO Maritime Safety Committee was not in accordance with the Convention and Liberia and Panama should have been elected. The ICJ ruled by nine votes to five that the Maritime Safety Committee of the Inter-Governmental Maritime Consultative Organization, which was elected on 15 January 1959, was not constituted in accordance with the Convention for the Establishment of the Organization. Belgium, France, Switzerland, Italy, Denmark, UK, Norway and the Netherlands stated that the Council was duly elected, whereas, India, Liberia, Panama and the USA stated that the Council was not duly elected.

4.1.2. Advisory opinion - *Voting Procedures*[38]

The Indian statement in this advisory proceeding displayed it's active advocacy for holding up the principle of absolute sovereignty. It articulated the relationship between the principle of sovereignty and voting methods. According to India, a world where national sovereignty is so widely stressed, the principle of unanimity as opposed to the more convenient doctrine of a majority decision has a natural appeal. India forwarded that "the UN Charter has not accepted the principle of

---

[36] *Ibid.,* at 258.

[37] *Ibid.,* p. 259.

[38] UN General Assembly Resolution 904 (IX) of 23 November 1954 : Is the following rule on the voting procedure to be followed by the General Assembly a correct interpretation of the advisory opinion of the International Court of Justice of 11 July 1950:
"Decisions of the General Assembly on questions relating to reports and petitions concerning the Territory of South-West Africa shall be regarded as important questions within the meaning of Article 18, paragraph 2, of the Charter of the United Nations'?"
that the said rule is the correct interpretation of the Advisory Opinion of July 11th, 1950.

unanimity except in the Security Council and believed that the results of the rule of unanimity in international conferences have not been reassuring. It has proved to be highly dilatory in some cases and intolerably obstructive in others."[39] It is interesting to note that these two arguments of India were more heavily grounded in the writers' opinion than in treaty or customary international law or the general principles of law. The Indian position was vindicated when the Court unanimously confirmed that the decisions of the General Assembly on questions relating to reports and petitions concerning the Territory of South-West Africa shall be regarded as important questions within the meaning of Article 18, paragraph 2, of the Charter of the United Nations is the correct interpretation of the Advisory Opinion of July 11th, 1950.

4.1.3. Advisory opinion - *International Status of South-West Africa*[40]

In its written statement for this advisory proceeding, India did not make any particular pronouncement but its submission attempted to provide a detailed interpretation of the resolution of the League mandate. It submitted that a reservation made during the discussions of a multilateral treaty does not affect the operation of the treaty unless reservation has also been made at the time of the signature of the treaty and duly attached to the signature and recorded in a process-verbal or unless reservation is attached to the ratification. A reservation is the refusal of an offer. But an offer is not made in the case of a multilateral treaty until the treaty is offered for signature. Therefore, a reservation made previous to the making of an offer cannot have any legal effect. It argued that the Union of South Africa having not renewed its reservation at the time of signing of the UN Charter or at the time of its ratification under Article 110 of the Charter (which, at any rate, does not provide for a limited ratification), "cannot derive any advantage from the reservation made during the drafting of the Charter."[41] The subsequent codification by the Vienna Convention on the Law of Treaties lends support to this position of India which was pronounced back in the 1960s. Furthermore, the Vienna Convention on the Law of Treaties has formulated the principle on this aspect in Article 19 which provides that a State may, when signing, ratifying, accepting, approving or acceding to a treaty formulate a reservation. The position of India was well reflected in the final opinion of the Court.

---

[39] Pleadings, Oral Arguments and Documents, *Voting Procedures on Questions Relating to Reports and Petitions Concerning the Territory of South-West Africa*, p. 77.

[40] UN General Assembly Resolution of 6 December 1949: What is the international status of the Territory of South-West Africa and what the international obligations of the Union of South Africa arising therefrom.

[41] Written statement of India in the advisory proceedings concerning the *International Status of South-West Africa*, p. 150.

4.1.4. Advisory Opinion - Namibia[42]

India advocated three basic principles in its oral statement. In the view of India, the inalienable right of the colonial people to self-determination and independence, the non-acquisition of territory by threat or use of force or any other form of aggression, the non-recognition of the fruits of aggression or illegal occupation of territory, and the duty to fulfil international obligations in good faith, are the foundations of international legal order. India explained that these principles have universal value and are therefore in the interest of the international community of states as a whole. India emphasized that the Court should recognize and apply these principles in its opinion so that the principles strengthen and promote the rule of law in international relations.

4.1.5. Advisory Opinion - World Health Organization Request on the Question of *Use of Nuclear Weapons in Armed Conflicts*[43]

India submitted its one and half page statement on the last date of filing of the statement, i.e. 20 July 1995. In its statement, India strongly advocated the elimination of nuclear weapons and outlawing of the use of these weapons as a first step. India argued that based on the understanding that the international community has agreed that the use of nuclear weapons constitutes a crime against humanity and violation of the Charter, the use of nuclear weapons has already been generally accepted as illegal. It also considered that the use of nuclear weapons is a violation of international humanitarian law. It invited the Court to confirm the generally accepted view among nations that the use of nuclear weapons is illegal. In this proceeding, India, arguing the importance of the question for the future well-being of the international community, advocated that the Court should give its considerate opinion on the question posed by the WHO.

4.1.6. Advisory Opinion - UN General Assembly Request on the Question of the *Use or Threat of Use of Nuclear Weapons*[44]

India submitted a seven-page statement on the last date of filing of the written statement, i.e. 20 July 1995. India argued that "the use of force is prohibited by Article 2(4) of the UN Charter and the prohibition is so comprehensive and

---

[42] What are the legal consequences for States of the continued presence of South Africa in Namibia (South West Africa) notwithstanding Security Council Resolution 276 (1970)? Security Council Resolution 276 (1970) of 29 July 1970.

[43] World Health Assembly Resolution WHA 46.40 of 14 May 1993: In view of the health and environmental effects, would the use of nuclear weapons by a State in war or other armed conflict be a breach of its obligations under international law including the WHO Constitution?

[44] UN General Assembly Resolution 49/75K of 15 December 1994: Is the threat or use of nuclear weapons in any circumstances permitted under international law?

fundamental as to be regarded as a *jus cogens* or an obligation of an absolute character, on the basis of this principle it is clear that any use of nuclear weapons as a measure of use of force to promote national policy objectives would be unlawful."[45] The qualification that the use of force to promote national policy objectives is prohibited lends support to the argument that in case of a survival crisis, a state may resort to the use of force including nuclear weapons. Is it possible that the lack of argument of a categorical denial to use nuclear weapons in any circumstances enabled the ICJ to find support of its argument in the Indian position?

India reinforced its position in this advisory proceeding that the right of self-defence is to be regarded as a provisional measure or a remedy and hence as soon as other means or measures become available, the resort to self-defence through use of force has to cease. It advocated that the use of nuclear weapons in any armed conflict as a first attack would be unlawful under international law. This legal argument derives support from India's political position on this issue. In its view, nuclear weapons could not be used by way of reprisal against another state if that state did not commit any wrongful act of *delict* involving use of force. Second, when a state commits such a wrongful act or *delict*, the use of force by way of reprisal would have to be proportionate and as such if the wrongful act did not involve the use of nuclear weapons, the reprisal could also not involve the use of nuclear weapons. Even where a wrongful act involves use of a nuclear weapon the reprisal action cannot involve use of a nuclear weapon without violating certain fundamental principles of humanitarian law. In this sense, prohibition of the use of a nuclear weapon in an armed conflict is an absolute one, compliance with which is not dependent on corresponding compliance by others but is a requisite in all circumstances. But India was a little hesitant when it argued that the use of nuclear weapons by way of reprisal or retaliation, *appears* to be unlawful. One can note a lack of categorical denial of the use of nuclear weapons in this position of India.

It emphasized that the use of nuclear weapons in an armed conflict is unlawful being contrary to the conventional as well as customary international law. In its view, if peace is the ultimate objective there can be no doubt that disarmament must be given priority and has to take precedence over deterrence. India went to the extent of arguing that "since the production and manufacture of nuclear weapons can only be with the objective of their use, it must follow that if the use of such weapons itself is illegal under international law, then their production and manufacture cannot under any circumstances be considered as permitted."[46] In a nutshell, in the view of India, the use of nuclear weapons which is otherwise contrary to international law could only be effectively prevented by eliminating

---

[45] Written statement of India in the advisory proceedings concerning the *Legality of the Threat or Use of Nuclear Weapons*, p. 1.
[46] Written statement of India in the advisory proceedings concerning the *Legality of the Threat or Use of Nuclear Weapons*, p. 6.

completely their production, manufacture and by ensuring the dismantling of existing nuclear weapons. India submitted that the threat or use of nuclear weapons, in any circumstance, whether as a means or method of warfare or otherwise, is illegal or unlawful under international law.

All in all, the Indian argument neither fully justified that use of nuclear weapons in armed conflict would be illegal or that use of nuclear weapons in a survival case is legal. In the author's view, the ICJ's opinion in some respects was in balance with what India argued. In view of the subsequent nuclear testing in 1998, the Indian position, retrospectively viewed, is not surprising. In this respect, Falk summarizes in an apt manner that "ever since India exploded a nuclear device in May 1974, the Indian relationship to nuclear weaponry has been ambivalent and controversial."[47] His analysis is quite correct because India has maintained a dual posture of staking its claims as a threshold nuclear weapons state, and claiming its upgrading of geopolitical status that follows therefrom, on the one hand and strong advocacy for complete nuclear disarmament as a moral and political imperative for all countries. The Indian government, regardless of its political leadership, has for several decades sustained this dual posture: a virtual member of the exclusive club of nuclear weapons states and a leading critic of nuclearism and advocate of comprehensive denuclearization.

The decision of the ICJ gives strong support on the basis of international law to the abiding Indian view that nuclear weapons states are under an obligation to move prudently, but insistently, toward the implementation of nuclear disarmament. The ICJ opinion apparently has not any discernible impact on the policy of India with respect to the role assigned to nuclear weapons and with regard to the duty to seek nuclear disarmament through self-restraint. The opinion underlined an offer to India of an important instrument with which to support its central contention that nuclear armament abolition is the proper legal path for international society. It also offered support to advocates of the Comprehensive Test Ban Treaty who contend that the end of testing is a step on the path to nuclear disarmament and this path now enjoys a prescriptive status in international law.

India following the advisory opinion strongly advocated for the phased program for the complete elimination of nuclear weapons at the Non-Aligned Movement (NAM). The NAM also urged nuclear weapons states to commence negotiations on a legally binding international instrument to provide unconditional assurances to all non-nuclear weapons states against the use or threat of nuclear weapons.[48] The Indian position was vindicated in a number of respects. First, the ICJ accepted that it should comply with the request for an advisory opinion from

---

[47] Richard Falk, "Nuclear Weapons, International Law and the World Court: A Historic Encounter" In 37 *Indian Journal of International Law* (1997) at 149.

[48] Yogesh K. Tyagi, "Judicial Statesmanship without Political Courage: The ICJ Advisory Opinion on Nuclear Weapons" In 37 *Indian Journal of International Law* (1997), at 198.

the General Assembly despite strong arguments against from nuclear weapons states. The final opinion of the ICJ seemed to endorse the strongly held Indian view which insists upon a time-bound program for nuclear disarmament. The Court in this opinion seemed to recognize a state of legal vacuum or *non liquet* governing the status of nuclear deterrence in international law. In this regard, the views expressed by some judges that accord with the Indian position must be noted: that the ICJ is not justified in expressing the existence of *non liquet* in any legal matter particularly given the wide range of principles which are available for application (Judges Weeramantry, Shahabuddeen and Koroma).[49]

5. Indian Position on the Role and Functioning of the Court

In this Section, an attempt is made to examine India's approach on the judicial settlement of international disputes, its general attitude towards the functioning of the ICJ and the Indian representation in the membership of the ICJ.

5.1. Preferred Means of Dispute Settlement

It is interesting to note that the Indian Constitution makes it the duty of the government to foster respect for international law and encourage settlement of international disputes by arbitration. (Part IV, Directive principles, Article 51 of the Constitution of India). India has taken a principled position and consistently followed the practice of resolving legal disputes or questions through negotiations than adjudication. It has preferred negotiation which does not involve an element of compulsion to any third party binding judgment such as is involved in arbitration and adjudication. In fact, the observation of Professor Wright that (commenting on new nations of Asia and Africa) "the Orient has preferred government by good men applying institutions of justice to the facts rather than government by law that is government by magistrates bound by rules making for certainty and predictability in decisions" is very much applicable in the case of India.[50] The Indian attitude of preferring less adjudication is not a typical of India, in fact, the Asian-African states have preferred negotiations assisted by conciliatory measures in their conflicts.

Has there been any marked change in this basic posture of India? In the last decade, the preference for diplomatic solutions or negotiations is also imbibed in India's general lack of pro-active support for the establishment of international courts and tribunals.

---

[49] P. Sreenivasa Rao, "Advisory Opinion of ICJ on Nuclear Weapons" In 37 *Indian Journal of International Law* (1997), p. 224.

[50] Quincy Wright, The Influence of the New Nations of Asia and Africa upon International Law In *Foreign Affairs Reports*, (New Delhi, March 1958), p. 38.

The scholastic community explains the advantages of these preferred means of India for the settlement of disputes. Anand cites an example of the Canal Water dispute of 1950 between India and Pakistan where India strongly advocated a resolution tribunal consisting of judges from the two countries and failing to find a solution for a part of the dispute, to be submitted to arbitration or to the ICJ. Anand argues that "rarely have such disputes, such as Kashmir, affecting such vital interests of the states, been submitted to any judicial procedure. Such matters may be decided by negotiation or conciliation or mediation, but they cannot be decided by a judicial tribunal. It can be confidently stated that any country in India's position would have behaved in the same way as she has done."[51] Thus, scholars also indicate the preference for other peaceful means to adjudication.

In one of the earliest reports on India and the UN, Report of a study group set up by the Indian Council of World Affairs, New York, 1957, the conclusion was drawn that India's policy is one of caution and of eagerness to safeguard India's sovereignty when it comes to accepting any additional legal obligations in the international field. This conclusion is still more or less valid even today.

5.2. Role of the Court in the Contemporary World

Is India pro-actively interested in the overall functioning of the Court? The following two examples are indicative of its interest. The leaders of the Indian delegations at the UN General Assembly annual sessions have made very few reference in their speeches regarding the role and importance of the ICJ and those few references are related to a particular case or opinion.[52] Furthermore, India did not provide its comments on the General Assembly resolution on the review of the role of the Court. The UN Secretary-General prepared the questionnaire pursuant to Resolution 2723 of the General Assembly which among others contained the aspects of (1) the role of the ICJ within the framework of the UN (2) organization of the ICJ (3) jurisdiction of the ICJ (4) procedures and methods of Work of the ICJ: (5) future action by the General Assembly. These two sporadic examples can give some indication that India is not so pro-active as one would have expected of it.

---

[51] R. P. Anand, *Compulsory Jurisdiction of the International Court of Justice*, (Indian School of International Studies, Jawaharlal Nehru University, 1961) at 256.

[52] The website of the Permanent Mission of India to the UN, New York, reproduces the text of landmark speeches by the leaders of the Indian delegation to the UN GA annual session. Reference to the ICJ is found in six speeches, namely, (8th Session 448th Plenary Meeting, 28th September,1953 ; Eleventh Session 611th Plenary Meeting, 6th December, 1956; 12th Session 703rd Plenary Meeting, 8th October, 1957; Fourteenth Session 823rd Plenary Meeting, 6th October, 1959; 26th Session 1940th Plenary Meeting, 27th September, 1971; Address by H. E. Mr I. K. Gujaral, Prime Minister of the Republic of India to the 52nd Session of the UN General Assembly, 24th September 1997.

5.3. Representation on the Bench of the Court

What is India's record as far as its representation on the Bench of the Court is concerned? The available records shows that India has never made any reference regarding the composition of the ICJ Bench in its speeches at the UN General Assembly except when India advocated the case of China's representation in various organs of the UN including the ICJ.[53]

Three Indian nationals have been elected as a member of the ICJ, namely, Sir Benegal Rau, Dr Nagendra Singh and Justice R. S. Pathak. In addition, Justice Chagla, Nagendra Singh and Reddy have served as *ad hoc* judges in the *Right of Passage over Indian Territory*, *ICAO Appeal*, and the *Aerial Incident of 10 August 1999* cases, respectively. It is interesting to observe that all of these Judges including the *ad hoc* judges have served the Indian government in various capacities before joining the Court.[54] Sir Benegal Rau (1952-1953) and Dr. Nagendra Singh (1972) were elected during the time when India was holding a non-permanent membership in the Security Council.[55] Dr. Pathak was elected upon the death of Judge Nagendra Singh. Although India was not a member of the Security Council in 1988 during the time of the election, following the tradition of the ICJ, a judge from the same nationality as the preceding judge who died during the service of the ICJ, was elected.[56]

---

[53] Statement of V. K. Krishna Menon, 8th Session, 448th Plenary Meeting of the UN General Assembly, 28th September,1953.

[54] Judge Benegal Rau was the first Indian judge ever to sit on the bench of the ICJ, he was Prime Minister of Kashmir, he participated in two contentious cases and gave one dissenting opinion in the *Rights of US Nationals in Morocco* case. Judge Nagendra Singh was Secretary to the President of India prior to his election as a member of the Court. He participated in 15 contentious cases and six advisory opinions and appended six declarations and ten separate opinions. Judge Pathak was the Chief Justice of India prior to his election as a member of the Court. He participated in five contentious cases and one advisory opinion. He appended no opinion.

[55] Sir Benegal Rau was elected in 1951 while Judge Nagendra Singh was elected in 1972 and assumed the functions in the following years respectively.

[56] Sir Benegal Rau was nominated as a candidate in October 1948 and December 1951. He was elected on 6 December 1951 at the triennial election along with Judges Armond-Ugon, Golunsky, Klaestad and Hackworth. Following the death of Sir Benegal Rau, India nominated Radha Binod Pal during the supplementary election in 1954 and in triennial election in 1957[56], however, he was not elected. Dr. Nagendra Singh was nominated first in 27 October 1969 for the triennial election of judge starting office from 6 February 1970. However, he was elected on 6 February 1973, following the expiry of the term of Sir Muhammad Zafrulla Khan on 5 February 1973. Sir Zafrulla Khan was not nominated for re-election at this stage. Dr. Pathak was elected on 18 April 1989 at the supplementary election caused by the vacancy following the death of Judge Nagendra Singh. The other Asian candidates were Messrs S. Kraichitti, D. Patel and M. C. W. Pinto. His term of office expired

5.4. Views of the Indian Academicians on the Functioning of the Court and its Members

Indian writers have held in high esteem the independence, impartiality and objectivity[57] of the judges and have never challenged it in slightest, and have believed that the judges are custodians of international law and justice.[58] All official positions of India speak highly of the judges and the ICJ even in the fierce arguments of the South-West Africa cases.[59] The fact that the national judges and the *ad hoc* judges usually give judgment in favour of their country or friendly countries, especially on important issues, is not a healthy trend and it certainly reflects on the degree of their objectivity. The position of *ad hoc* judges is more invidious as standing somewhere between independent judges and representative of the parties. They have to give a solemn declaration to act as judges, but they are probably expected by their countries to defend their interests and are chosen because their past opinions indicate that they will. In this regard, it can be observed that Judge *ad hoc* Nagendra Singh rendered an individual separate opinion in the *Trial of Pakistani Prisoners of War* - interim measures of protection phase - and Judge *ad hoc* Reddy supported the Court's rejection of its jurisdiction in the *Aerial Incident 10 August of 1999* and issued an individual opinion. Judge *ad hoc* Chagla issued a dissenting opinion in the *Right of Passage over Indian Territory* case – preliminary objection and merits phases.

---

on 5 December 1991. Justice Pathak was nominated for the second term at the triennial election but was unsuccessful.

[57] Mani, reflecting on the weakness in favour of one's own country, says that the fact can hardly be denied that it is very difficult for a man to resist the affiliations of the people and the country with which his interests are so much bound up. As a committee of the Permanent Court itself, consisting of Judges Loder, Moore and Anzilotti said: "...of all influences to which men are subject none is more powerful, more persuasive, or more subtle, than the tie of allegiance that binds them to the lands of their homes and kindred and to the great sources of honours and preferments for which they are so ready to spend their fortunes and to risk their lives. This fact, known to all the world, the Statute frankly recognizes and deals with." P.C.I.J Series E, No. 4, p. 75.

[58] Anand succinctly justifies that the Court's criticism regarding the possible partiality and political motivation is unfounded. Although, he refrains from giving a categorical denial to the criticism, as he mentions that *although impartiality is a characteristic which is universally prized in a judicial tribunal, it must never be forgotten that the impartiality of atribunal is always relative, never absolute.* However, in his final analysis, he shows even more optimism and holds a view that *distrust of the competence and impartiality of the International Court of Justice is* scarcely the reason why Governments do not submit their cases to the tribunal. Anand In *International Courts and Contemporary Conflicts* at 193.

[59] It should be noted that there was no judge from India on the bench whenever India presented its written statement during any of the advisory proceedings.

5.5. Records on the Declarations and Opinions of Indian Members of the ICJ

Sir Benegal Rau appended only one opinion, namely, joint dissenting opinion in the *Rights of US Nationals in Morocco* (France *v.* USA). Judge Nagendra Singh appended declarations in *Fisheries Jurisdiction* (UK *v.* Iceland – merits); *Fisheries Jurisdiction* (Federal Republic of Germany *v.* Iceland – merits); *Nuclear Tests* (Australia *v.* France - interim measures of protection); *Nuclear Tests* (New Zealand *v.* France - interim measures of protection) as well as to two advisory opinions *Application for Review of UNAT Judgment No. 158* and *Western Sahara.* Judge Nagendra Singh also appended an individual opinion in *Trial of Pakistani Prisoners of War* during interim measures of protection ruling (Pakistan *v.* India); *Aegean Sea Continental Shelf* during interim measures of protection ruling (Greece *v.* Turkey); *Continental Shelf* (Libya/Malta – intervention); *Military and Paramilitary Activities in and against Nicaragua* (intervention, preliminary objections and merits – Nicaragua *v.* USA); and in one advisory opinion *Application for Review of UNAT Judgment No. 273.* Judge Nagendra Singh appended a dissenting opinion in the *Appeal Relating to the Jurisdiction of the ICAO Council* (India *v.* Pakistan). Judge Pathak did not append any opinion in the two contentious cases in which he participated (*Land, Maritime and Island Frontier Dispute*, El Salvador/Honduras; and *Arbitral Award of 31 July 1989*, Guinea Bissau v. Senegal). In both cases, he voted with the majority.

6. Conclusions

Based on the above analysis, the author proposes the following ideas, primarily with a view to have enhanced contribution of India towards the role and functioning of the ICJ in the future.

It is observed that the Indian position and attitude towards the Court, like any other sovereign state, is guided by the considerations of the national interest. It is proposed that there is more scope for India, in line with her overall influence in international relations, to guide the development of international law by way of increased activeness in its overall functioning of the Court. One way of doing this is to submit written statements and participate in the oral proceedings of all advisory proceedings, particularly when such proceedings may have impact on the broad objectives of development of international law. It has been observed that the pro-active approach in the past has helped in achieving some of the important long-term objectives to bring the rule of law in the world. For example, the ICJ judgment in the *Right of Passage over Indian Territory* case proved helpful in decolonizing the territory and strengthening India's territorial sovereignty. India's active participation in the debates of the UN General Assembly and the advisory proceedings concerning the South-West Africa helped the entity in achieving full sovereignty and to make Namibia a sovereign and independent state a reality. Cases and opinions concerning South-West Africa basically involved the question of legal obligation of the government of South Africa to fulfil the *sacred trust of civilization.* India fully defended this cause. One can draw a conclusion that India has found that ICJ could be a key effective international platform to resolve the legacy of colonization and achieve independence of erstwhile colonies.

The Indian position in the advisory proceedings concerning the broad issues of development or where interpretation of international law was concerned shows that it has high faith in the impartiality, objectivity and capability of the ICJ. Despite the post-adjudicative phase uncertainty in the compliance of the judgment of the ICJ, the Indian stand in the contentious cases does not enable to think about the futility of the judicial process. India has respected the judgments of the ICJ which reached the merit stage.

India, during the negotiations of the current and future treaties, should consistently advocate attaching a jurisdictional clause to every multilateral treaty conferring jurisdiction, at least, primarily, upon the ICJ. Furthermore, India can favourably look into the idea of national court or tribunal seeking guidance from the ICJ.[60] Last but not the least, Judge Nagendra Singh advocated for the use of advisory opinion in case of inter-state disputes, to obtain – if not actual settlement of the dispute – at least a legal basis for such settlement. This position which has found support among number of Indian scholars is another meritorious proposal.

[60] The USA passed a resolution on 17 December 1982 for the possibility of an advisory opinion of the ICJ upon request by a national court or tribunal which is duly authorized by national legislation to make such a request, regarding any question of international law of which such court or tribunal has jurisdiction.

ANNEX

Compulsory jurisdiction of India: An evolution

A. Current declaration effective since 15 September 1974

1. I have the honour to declare, on behalf of the Government of the Republic of India, that they accept, in conformity with paragraph 2 of Article 36 of the Statute of the Court, until such time as notice may be given to terminate such acceptance, as compulsory *ipso facto* and without special agreement, and on the basis and condition of reciprocity, the jurisdiction of the International Court of Justice over all disputes other than:

1) disputes in regard to which the parties to the dispute have agreed or shall agree to have recourse to some other method or methods of settlement;
2) disputes with the government of any State which is or has been a Member of the Commonwealth of Nations;
3) disputes in regard to matters which are essentially within the domestic jurisdiction of the Republic of India;
4) disputes relating to or connected with facts or situations of hostilities, armed conflicts, individual or collective actions taken in self-defence, resistance to aggression, fulfillment of obligations imposed by international bodies, and other similar or related acts, measures or situations in which India, has been or may in future be involved;
5) disputes with regard to which any other party to a dispute has accepted the compulsory jurisdiction of the International Court of Justice exclusively for or in relation to the purposes of such dispute; or where the acceptance of the Court's compulsory jurisdiction on behalf of a party to the dispute was deposited or ratified less than 12 months prior to the filing of the application bringing the dispute before the Court;
6) disputes where the jurisdiction of the Court is or may be founded on the basis of a treaty concluded under the auspices of the League of Nations, unless the Government of India specifically agree to jurisdiction in each case;
7) disputes concerning the interpretation or application of a multilateral treaty unless all the parties to the treaty are also parties to the case before the Court or Government of India specially agree to jurisdiction;
8) disputes with the Government of any State with which, on the date of an application to bring a dispute before the Court, the Government of India has no diplomatic relations or which has not been recognized by the Government of India;
9) disputes with non-sovereign States or territories;
10) disputes with India concerning or relating to:

a) the status of its territory or the modification or delimitation of its frontiers or any other matter concerning boundaries;
b) the territorial sea, the continental shelf and the margins, the exclusive fishery zone, the exclusive economic zone, and other zones of national maritime jurisdiction including for the regulation and control of marine pollution and the conduct of scientific research by foreign vessels;
c) the condition and status of its islands, bays and gulfs and that of the bays and gulfs that for historical reasons belong to it;
d) the airspace superjacent to its land and maritime territory; and
e) the determination and delimitation of its maritime boundaries.

11) disputes prior to the date of this declaration, including any dispute the foundations, reasons, facts, causes, origins, definitions, allegations or bases of which existed prior to this date, even if they are submitted or brought to the knowledge of the Court hereafter.

2. This declaration revokes and replaces the previous declaration made by the Government of India on 14 September 1959.

New Delhi, 15 September 1974 (signed by Swaran Singh, Minister for External Affairs)

B. India's declaration of 14 September 1959[61]

I have the honour, by direction of the President of India, to declare on behalf of the Government of the Republic of India that they accept, in conformity with paragraph 2 of Article 36 of the Statute of the Court, until such time as notice may be given to terminate such acceptance, as compulsory *ipso facto* and without special agreement, and on the basis and without special agreement, and on the basis and condition of reciprocity[62], the jurisdiction of the International Court of Justice over all disputes arising after 26 January 1950 with regard to situations or facts subsequent to that date, other than:

(1) Disputes, in regard to which the Parties to the dispute have agreed or shall agree to have recourse to some other method or methods of settlement;

[61] India's reservation is quite broad in substance. There is no doubt that, over a period of time, the ever expanding scope of reservations is going to impair the efficacy of the compulsory jurisdiction.

[62] Over the period of time, the principle of reciprocity has become an inherent part of the compulsory jurisdiction. As Rosenne says, one might infer that the inclusion of a specific reference to reciprocity or to the principle of reciprocity in an acceptance of the compulsory jurisdiction is not necessary. Shabtai Rosenne, *The Law and Practice of International Court (1920-1996)* (3rd ed., 1997) at 766.

(2) Disputes with the government of an State which, on the date of this declaration, is a member of the Commonwealth of Nations;[63]
(3) Disputes in regard to matters which are essentially within the jurisdiction of the Republic of India;
(4) Disputes concerning any question relating to or arising out of belligerent or military occupation or the discharge of any functions pursuant to any recommendation or decision of an organ of the United Nations, in accordance with which the Government of India have accepted obligations;
(5) Disputes in respect of which any other party to a dispute has accepted the compulsory jurisdiction of the International Court of Justice exclusively for or in relation to the purposes of such dispute; or where the acceptance of the Court's compulsory jurisdiction on behalf of a party to the dispute was deposited or ratified less than 12 months prior to the filing of the application bringing the dispute before the Court; and
(6) Disputes with the Government of any State with which, on the date of an application to bring a dispute before the Court, the Government of India has no diplomatic relations. (New York, 14 September 1959, signed C.S.Jha)

C. India's declaration of 7 January 1956[64]

I have the honour by direction of the President of India, to declare on behalf of the Government of India that, in pursuance of paragraph 2 of Article 36 of the Statute of the International Court Justice, the Government of India recognize as compulsory *ipso facto* and without special agreement, on condition of reciprocity and only till such time as notice may be given to terminate this Declaration, the jurisdiction of the International Court of Justice in all disputes arising after the 26th January 1950 with regard to situations or facts subsequent to that date concerning:

(a) the interpretation of a treaty;
(b) any question of international law;
(c) the existence of any facts which if established would constitute a breach of an interantiaonl obligation; or
(d) the nature or extent of the reparations to be made for the breach of an international obligation.

---

[63] India modified this reservation in 1974 which now reads *disputes with the government of any State which is or has been a Member of the Commonwealth of Nations. ICJ Yearbook 1996-1997*, p. 99.
[64] By a letter dated 7 January 1956, addressed to the UN Secretary-General and received on 9 January 1956, the Government of India gave notice of the termination of the declaration of 28 February 1940, deposited with the Secretary-General of the League of Nations on 7 March 1940, accepting as compulsory the jurisdiction of the PCIJ which, by virtue of Article 36 (5) of the ICJ Statute, constituted an acceptance of the compulsory jurisdiction of that Court. By an instrument dated 7 January 1956, deposited with the Secretary-General on 9 January 1956, the Government of India accepted the compulsory jurisdiction of the ICJ.

But excluding the following: -

(i) disputes in regard to which the parties to the dispute have agreed or shall agree to have recourse to some other method of peaceful settlement;
(ii) disputes with the Government of any country which on the date of thi Declaration is a member of the Commonwealth of Nations, all of which disputes shall be settled in such manner as the parties have agreed or shall agree;
(iii) disputes in regard to matters which are essentially within the domestic jurisdiction of India as determined by the Government of India; and
(iv) disputes arising out of or having reference to any hostilities, war, state of war or belligerent or military occupation in which the Government of India are or have been involved (signed Arthur S. Lall, Permanent Representative of India to the United Nations)

D. India's declaration of 28 February 1940 prior to independence[65]

(Signed on 28 February 1940, deposited with the Secretary-General of the League of Nations on 7 March 1940)

Reciprocity. 5 Years (as from February 28th, 1940), and thereafter until notice of termination is given. For all disputes after February 5th, 1930, with regard to situations or facts subsequent to that date, other than:

Disputes in regard to which the Parties to the dispute have agreed or shall agree to have recourse to some other method of peaceful settlement;

Disputes with the government of any other Member of the League which is a Member of the British Commonwealth of Nations, all of which disputes shall be settled in such manner as the Parties have agreed or shall agree;

Disputes with regard to questions which by international fall exclusively within the jurisdiction of India;

Disputes arising out of event occurring at a time when the Government of India were involved in hostilities.

The right is reserved to suspend judicial proceedings under certain conditions in the case of disputes under consideration by the Council.

---

[65] This declaration replaced that of 9 September 1929, in respect of which a reservation was formulated on 27 September 1939, and notice of termination was given on 28 February 1940. See PCIJ Series E, No. 16, p. 341.

INTERNATIONAL COMMERCIAL ARBITRATION AND ENFORCEMENT OF FOREIGN AWARDS IN INDIA

Amal K. Ganguli*

1. Law of Arbitration in India

Ever since the East India Company came to be vested with the powers to frame regulations by the British Parliament, the techniques of resolution of disputes by arbitration have received legal recognition in India. It was as early as in 1772 that arbitration was introduced in India. The East India Company framed several regulations which were then applicable only to the three metropolises i.e., Bengal, Bombay and Madras. For instance, the Bengal Regulation 1 of 1772, Bombay Regulation 1 of 1799 and Madras Regulation 1 of 1802. These regulations empowered the courts to submit matters in dispute in a suit to the decision of an arbitrator mutually agreed to by the parties. But if the parties could not agree to the appointment of an arbitrator or if their nominated arbitrator refused to act in the matter and if the parties could not agree upon the appointment of another arbitrator, the court could appoint an arbitrator. The Code of Civil Procedure, 1859, for the first time, recognized reference to arbitration without intervention of courts. Sections 312-327 of the Code also dealt with arbitration in suits, filing in court, the agreements to refer to arbitration and for filing of awards. India, as is apparent, was equipped with arbitration laws much before the international community took serious note of India.

India had an ancient system of informal adjudication of disputes by the elders of the society called the Panchayat. Their jurisdiction writ large on almost every aspect of human life and was not limited only to disputes arising out of commercial transactions between members of society. With the advent of the court systems more and more disputes were relegated to formal adjudication. However, the spirit of informal adjudication of disputes by a chosen adjudicator eventually led to a formal recognition of arbitration by law. Since arbitration is a mechanism for alternative dispute resolution, the Indian laws recognize arbitration agreements by which parties could bind themselves not to litigate in court, but seek their remedy outside courts. Even though Section 28 of the Indian Contract Act, 1872 makes void any such agreement by which anyone is prohibited to approach the courts for relief, arbitration agreements are an exception to this law. This has become a part of the fundamental law of the country.

---

* Senior Advocate, Supreme Court of India.

Bimal N. Patel (ed.), **India and International Law, 319-343.**

Tracing the history of arbitration as a method of resolution of disputes in England, Holdsworth said "The practice of arbitration therefore, comes, so to speak, naturally to primitive bodies of law; and after courts have been established by the State and a recourse to them has become a natural method of settling disputes, the practice continues because the parties to a dispute want to settle them with less formality and expense than is involved in recourse to courts."[1] Whatever be the motive[2] for the continued support to the alternative techniques of resolution of disputes particularly arising out of trade, commerce and intercourse in the domestic sector, it will be inappropriate to describe international commercial arbitration as an alternative dispute resolution mechanism in the realm of international trade and commerce, for, the law does not provide for an established mechanism for resolution of such disputes. In the absence of international commercial arbitrations, the parties to an international commercial contract would be compelled to initiate proceedings in the domestic fora of their respective countries and then seek enforcement of such decisions by initiating fresh round of litigation on the self same subject matter in the country of enforcement.[3]

2. Protocol on Arbitration Clauses

After the First World War, with the increase in importance of international trade and use of international commercial arbitration, the International Chamber of Commerce (ICC) promoted an international convention for removal of impediments to the enforceability of the arbitral clauses in commercial contracts. The early efforts in codifying international arbitration concepts enveloped around the need for enforcing the arbitral clause. A serious effort was made under the auspices of the League of Nations, which resulted in the conclusion of a treaty on 24 September 1923, called the Protocol on Arbitration Clauses.

Article 3 of the Protocol, which dealt with the execution of the awards, required the Member States to execute the arbitral award in case (1) the award has been rendered in accordance with the provisions of the national laws of the executing State; and (2) the award has been rendered in the territory of the executing State. Thus, Article 3 ensured the execution of only 'domestic awards'.

---

[1] *History of English Law* (vol. XIV, 1964) at 187.

[2] "The move towards alternative techniques in business disputes and the development of ADR programs was mainly fueled by a desire to reduce the sometimes enormous transaction cost of litigation (not only in direct legal cost but also in executive time and energies diverted from core business, disruption of business, and harm to business relationships) and to reach more constructive outcomes, to find 'business solutions' to 'business problems." Christian Buhring–Uhle, *Arbitration & Mediation in International Business* (1996) at 266.

[3] Sections 13 & 14 of 1908 Code of Civil Procedure provides for enforceability of foreign judgments and decrees. And sub-sections (5) and (6) of Section 2 of the Code defines 'foreign court' and 'foreign judgment' respectively.

The Protocol therefore failed to subserve its objective and this proved to be the biggest pitfall in the development of international arbitration.

3. International Convention on the Execution of Foreign Arbitral Awards, 1927

The problem faced by the Protocol gave birth to the International Convention on the Execution of Foreign Arbitral Awards (hereinafter called, 'the Geneva Convention'), which was concluded on 26 September 1927. The purpose was to ensure enforcement of foreign arbitral awards, that is, awards rendered in a State other than the one where it is sought to be enforced. The Convention supplemented the Protocol. According to the Convention, each member State was required to recognize as binding and to enforce, in accordance with the rules of the procedure of its territory, arbitration award made in another contracting State pursuant to an agreement covered by the Protocol. India became a signatory to the Convention and ratified the Protocol on 23 October 1937.

4. India's Position on the Arbitration Protocol and Geneva Convention

To abide by its international obligation under the Protocol and the Geneva Convention, India enacted the Arbitration (Protocol and Convention) Act, 1937 with the following objects:

> [T]he Government of India have had for sometime under consideration the question of India's adherence to the Geneva Protocol on Arbitration Clauses (1923) and the International Convention on the Execution of Foreign Arbitral Awards (1927). The object of these instruments is to meet the widely expressed desire of the commercial world that arbitration agreements should be ensured of effective recognition and protection. A large number of countries including many of first class commercial and industrial importance, e.g., the United Kingdom, France, Germany, the Netherlands have adhered to these instruments.

After consulting local Governments, High Courts and commercial bodies, a majority of whom were found to be in favour of India's accession to these Instruments, the case was placed before the Commerce Department, Standing Advisory Committee of the legislature, who recommended that India should adhere to the Instruments. These have accordingly been signed at Geneva on behalf of India, subject to reservations limiting India's obligations under the Instruments to commercial contracts and excluding the Indian States from the scope of the Instruments.'

India, thus, fulfilled its international obligations under the Protocol and the Geneva Convention to ensure recognition and enforceability of the arbitration clauses and foreign awards. It is rather significant that India was one of the early countries to not only sign and ratify the Protocol and Convention but also to legislate and introduce laws in tune with the same; much before many of the developed countries. Thus, consistent with the general principles of law, India became a part both to the Protocol and Geneva Convention which recognized adjudication of dispute through arbitration as a valid and legal adjudication that bind the parties and enforceable in any of the convention countries.

In the meantime with a view to consolidate the law relating to arbitration, the Arbitration Act, 1940, came to be enacted. The provisions of the Act applied to all arbitrations held in India. It made no distinction between arbitration proceedings, which could be appropriately termed as 'domestic' in contradistinction, to 'international commercial arbitration'. The Act defined the expression 'arbitration agreement' to mean a written agreement to submit present or future dispute to arbitration, whether an arbitrator is named therein or not. The expression 'award' was defined to mean an arbitration award. The Act *inter alia* provided for reference to arbitration by the parties themselves without the intervention of the Court. Though not expressly provided for, it is implied in the statute that the Act applied to awards, which may be 'domestic' or 'international' but not to 'foreign' awards. An international award is not synonymous with a foreign award. The Act did not define as to what constitutes an international arbitration. But it was obvious that when one of the contracting parties to arbitration was a national or resident of a country other than India, an arbitration between them held in India, though an international arbitration would be dealt with under the Act. Even if the seat of arbitration happened to be outside India but if the arbitration agreement was governed by the Indian law, such awards have also been held to be governed by the Indian Arbitration Act.[4]

5. Implementation of the Arbitration Protocol and Geneva Convention

The main objective of the Geneva Protocol of 1923 was to ensure that the arbitration clauses in international commercial transactions were recognized and enforced internationally and, in the process, to help the parties to such transactions to seek resolution of their disputes by arbitration rather than litigating through

---

[4] *ONGC vs. Western Co. of North America* (1987) 1 SCC 496. The contracting parties in this case had agreed that the reference to arbitration in case of any difference or disputes arising out of the contract would be governed by the Indian Arbitration Act. Arbitration proceedings were held, as well as the awards were made in London. The Supreme Court held that since the contracting parties agreed that the arbitration agreement be governed by the Indian law, the Indian courts had exclusive jurisdiction to determine the validity and enforceability of the awards. It was only with regard to the 'foreign awards' that the enforcement thereof in India was governed by the Arbitration (Protocol & Convention) Act, 1937.

courts. The other objective of the Protocol was to ensure that awards made in such international arbitration proceedings are enforced within the territory of the countries in which they were made. The Protocol however, contained two important limitations that severely restricted its scope and effect. The first limitation was that it applied to only such arbitration agreements made between parties who are 'subject respectively to the jurisdiction of different contracting states'.[5] The other limitation was that even the contracting States could wriggle out of the Protocol by availing themselves of the 'commercial reservation'.[6] In order to comply with these conditions the parties suffered what is known as '*double-exequatur*'. A successful party, before seeking enforcement of an award in another country, was often required to first initiate legal proceedings in the court of the country, where the arbitration had taken place, for a declaration that the award had become final and enforceable in that country. To overcome these and many other impediments in the enforcement of international commercial arbitration awards, further efforts were continued amongst others by the International Chambers of Commerce (ICC).

With the introduction of the Arbitration (Protocol and Convention) Act, 1937, in respect of the awards not rendered in India, the courts did recognize, respect and enforce such awards. In *Francesco Corsi v. Gorakhram*[7], the Bombay High Court, dealt with the question whether the Protocol Act, a pre constitutional law, had any force in India after her independence. The Court was of the opinion that India being signatory to the Protocol on Arbitration Clauses and to the Convention on the Execution of Foreign Arbitral Awards, the obligations undertaken thereunder continue to bind India even after India was constituted a Dominion and thereafter. This decision is particularly interesting in view of the decision of an English court in *Dalimia Cement Ltd. v. National Bank of Pakistan*,[8] wherein the question was whether India and Pakistan were parties to the Convention set out in Schedule II to the English Arbitration Act, 1950 and whether the awards passed in these countries were 'foreign awards' within the meaning of Section 35(1)(d) of the Act. It was held that since no formal Order in Council was issued with respect to India and Pakistan, the awards made under the substantive law of India were not 'foreign awards' for the purpose of enforcement under Part II of the Arbitration Act, 1950. Thus, while the Indian Court's interpretation of the Convention favoured enforcement of foreign awards, the restrictive approach of the English Courts, did not and at times, slowed down the progress of international arbitration.

In *Transocean Shipping Agency (P) Ltd. v. Black Sea Shipping*,[9] the Supreme Court brushed aside the technical objections and permitted enforcement of a foreign

---

[5] Art. I (first part) Geneva Protocol, 1923.
[6] Art. I (second part) Geneva Protocol, 1923.
[7] AIR 1960 Bombay SCR 91.
[8] 1975 (1) QB 9.
[9] (1998) 2 SCC 281.

award made in Ukraine though at the time of making of the award, there was no independent notification issued by India recognizing Ukraine as a reciprocal territory under the Foreign Awards Act, 1961. The Supreme Court, however, relying upon the notification issued in 1972 recognizing USSR as a reciprocal territory, held that subsequent break-up of USSR in 1991-92 and Ukraine becoming an independent republic are not sufficient to deny Ukraine the status of a reciprocal territory especially so when Ukraine continues to be a signatory to the New York Convention. The 1972 notification would continue to operate in the territories then forming part of the USSR, including the territory of Ukraine.

In *Mury Exportation v. D. Khaitan & Sons Ltd.*,[10] the Calcutta High Court made it clear that Arbitration Act, 1940 would not be applicable to arbitrations held under the rules of the International Chamber of Commerce (ICC) where the Arbitration (Protocol and Convention) Act, 1937 applied.

The issue of *'finality'* of a foreign award as a condition for its enforcement in India came up for consideration before the Bombay High Court in *Se Se Oil v. Gorakhram Gokalchand.*[11] It was contended that unless and until an award was made a *rule of the court* and was enforceable as a judgment, it was not final within the meaning of Section 7(1)(d) of the Protocol Act, 1937. Negativing the contention, the Court held that:

> [A]n award would be final within the meaning of sub-section (d) of Section 7(1) of the Act even if it is not made a rule of court. What is made enforceable under the provisions of the Act is the award and not the decree making award a rule of court… It appears to me that the word 'final' as used in sub-clause (d) of section 7(1) was not meant to refer to an award which is made a rule of court. The award which is made a rule of Court would according to the laws of the particular country in which it was made always be executable as a decree.'

In *Union Nationale des Cooperatives Agricles de Cereales vs. Robert Catterall & Co. Ltd.*[12], the agreement was made in Paris, the proper law was Danish law, and the seat of award was Copenhagen. Proceedings were initiated in England for enforcement of the award. For enforcement of a foreign award, English laws required that it should be a final award in the country in which it was made. Under the Danish law, an award is final only when an order from a Danish court is obtained for the enforcement of the award, which, admittedly, was not done. The issue was whether the award could be enforced in England even though it was not final under the Danish law. The court held that there was a difference between finality and enforcement of awards and that the award was final even though it could not have

---

[10] AIR 1956 Calcutta SC 644.
[11] (1962) 64 Bombay LR 113.
[12] 1959 (2) QB 44.

been immediately enforced in Denmark. Since the award was final, it was held that under the English law, it could be enforced.

Though the Geneva Convention of 1937 considerably widened the scope of the Protocol by ensuring recognition and enforcement of the Protocol Awards not merely in the States in which such awards are not made but also within the territory of the contracting States, in its actual operation many more problems were encountered. One of the major impediments that came in the way of enforcement of the Protocol awards was the requirement of the Geneva Convention that the party relying upon an award on claiming its enforcement must supply, in particular – 'Documentary and other evidence to prove that the award has become final in the sense defined in Article I (d) in the country in which it was made.'[13] Article I (d) of the Convention required that to obtain recognition and enforcement of an award in the territories of any High Contracting Party to which the Convention applies, it shall be necessary that 'the award has become final in the country in which it has been made, in the sense that it will not be considered as such if it is open to opposition, appeal or *pourvoi en cassation* (in the countries where such forms of procedure exist) or if it is proved that any proceedings for the purpose of contesting the validity of the award are pending.[14]

6. Shortcomings of the Geneva Convention

The actual working of the Geneva Convention over a period of time raised certain problematic issues which prompted the nations to once again consider a revision of the basic concepts. The instrument was found to be lacking the required thrust for speedy enforcement of foreign arbitral awards and the requirements of international trade. One of the dominating reasons which prompted the nations to look for an alternative was, that the beneficiary of the award was required to show to the court, before which the matter came for enforcement, that the award has become 'final' in the country in which it was made. Thus the party opposing the enforcement of the award could effectively prevent its execution on the ground that the award was the subject-matter of litigation in the country where it was rendered. Furthermore, different interpretations given by each member-State to the provisions of the Geneva Convention lead to ambiguities that virtually threatened the system of enforcement of 'foreign' awards to a grinding halt. It was realized that further clarity in the arbitration concepts and uniformity in the rules of interpretation were urgently required.

---

[13] Art. 4 (2).
[14] Art. 1 (d).

7. Birth of the New York Convention

To give a further impetus to international arbitrations and to alleviate the shortcomings of the Geneva Convention, the International Chamber of Commerce (ICC) issued a draft convention in 1953 on International Arbitral Awards. The United Nations Economic and Social Council (ECOSOC), to whom the ICC draft was presented, prepared another draft in 1953. A Conference was held to conclude a convention on the recognition and enforcement of foreign arbitral awards which ultimately adopted the International Convention on the Recognition and Enforcement of the Arbitral Awards (hereinafter called, 'the New York Convention') on 10 June 1958. India became a signatory to this Convention as well.

8. Working of the New York Convention

The New York Convention not only made considerable improvement upon the Geneva Protocol of 1923 and the Convention of 1927 and replaced them between the States that are parties to both the Conventions and the Protocol, but also gave much wider effect to the international arbitration agreements and to foreign arbitral awards by providing for their recognition and enforcement in countries which are neither the seat of the arbitration nor when the contracting parties are 'subject to the jurisdiction of' one of the contracting States. All the same, in the actual operation of the Convention, a number of practical difficulties have been encountered by almost all the nations.

Except for the provisions contained in Article II (3) the principle objective of the Convention, as is evident from its long title, was recognition and enforcement of foreign arbitral awards. Only Article II (3) dealt with a stage anterior to the arbitration proceeding itself. This provision of the Convention mandates that the 'court of a Contracting State, when seized of an action in a matter in respect of which the parties have made an agreement' in writing to submit to arbitration all or any differences which have arisen or which may arise between them, 'shall, at the request of one of the parties, refer the parties to arbitration, unless it finds that the said agreement is null and void, inoperative and incapable of being performed'.

Though the New York Convention, unlike the Geneva Convention, did not limit its application to arbitral awards made in a territory of one of the contracting parties to which the Convention applied and between persons who are subject to the jurisdiction of one of the contracting parties yet, at the stage of drafting of the Convention the dichotomy between the common law and civil law in certain spheres greatly influenced its terms. Article I itself is a prominent example of such influence. Article I has two clear and distinctive parts. The first part reflects the influence of the common law, which provides that the Convention shall apply to the foreign arbitral awards made in the territory of a State, other than the State where the recognition and enforcement of such awards are sought. The second part of the Article, which reflects the influence of civil law, provides that the Convention 'shall apply to arbitral awards not considered as domestic awards in the State where their recognition and enforcement are sought'. It is this dichotomy of the two sets of legal principles that led to serious divergence of views in the interpretation of the provisions of the Convention by the national courts.

The plain language employed in Article I of the Convention suggests that the two sentences contained therein are independent of each other. The first sentence is rather unqualified and it recognized any award made in the territory of a State, other than the State where the recognition and enforcement of such awards are sought, to be 'foreign award.' The second sentence clearly indicates that the conditions laid down therein are independent of the first one as it employs the expression '*shall also apply to*'. The second sentence however, subjects enforcement of arbitral awards to the condition that such awards are 'not considered as domestic awards' in the State where the recognition and enforcement are sought. The question is, whether in spite of the clear language employed in the two sentences in Article I of the Convention, the second sentence, by implication, limit the operation of the first sentence. If it does, then the further question is, whether in order that an arbitral award could be enforced in the territory of a State, it should satisfy both the conditions. The questions are not capable of easy answers as is evident from various judicial pronouncements. The issue is further complicated by reason of the provisions contained in Article V (1) of the Convention. Article V requires the party, against whom recognition and enforcement of an award is sought and who wishes that enforcement of such award be refused, to furnish proof that 'the award has not yet become *binding* on the parties or has been set aside or suspended by a competent authority of a country in which or under the law of which the award was made.' This provision undoubtedly recognizes that the court of the country in which, or under the law of which, the award is made has the jurisdiction to set aside or suspend the award and that such country is different from the country where the recognition and enforcement of the award is sought. Evidently, it is only in respect of a domestic award rendered in accordance with the law of the country that the courts of that country will have jurisdiction to set aside such awards and not in respect of 'foreign awards' within the meaning of Article I of the Convention. If that be the correct legal position, the provisions contained in Article V(1)(*e*) undoubtedly create difficulties and contradicts the scope of Article 1 of the Convention. Many courts have thus attempted to harmonise these provisions by judicial interpretation, which naturally have not shown uniformity in the application of the Convention.

It is now well settled that in the realm of international arbitration, there are at least four distinct possibilities of different laws being applicable at different stages. Firstly, the law governing the contract i.e. the proper of the underlying contract. Secondly, the proper law of the arbitration agreement. Thirdly, the proper law of reference that governs the actual arbitration proceedings, and lastly, the curial law, i.e. the law of the country that applies during the conduct of the arbitration proceedings. Justice Potter of the English Commercial Court, has succinctly summarised the law thus:[15]

(1) The proper law of the underlying contract, i.e., the law governing the contract which creates the substantive rights and obligations of the parties out of which the dispute has arisen.
(2) The proper law of the arbitration agreement, i.e., the law governing rights and obligations of the parties arising from their agreement to arbitrate and, in particular, their obligation to submit their disputes to arbitration and to honour an award. This includes *inter alia* questions as to the validity of the arbitration agreement, the validity of the notice of arbitration, the constitution of the tribunal and the question whether an award lies within the jurisdiction of the arbitrator.
(3) The proper law of the reference i.e., the law governing the contract which regulates the individual reference to arbitration. This is an agreement subsidiary to be but separate from the arbitration agreement itself, coming into effect by the giving of a notice of arbitration from which point a new set of mutual obligations in relation to the conduct of the reference arise upon the lines canvassed in the *Bremer Vulkan Schiffbau Und Maschinenfabrik v. South India Shipping Corpn.*[16] (Llyod's Rep. At p.263) and developed by Mr. Justice Mustill (as he then was) in *Black Clawson International Ltd. v. Papiewerke Waldhor Aschaffenburg A.G.*[17] The law governs the question of whether by reason of subsequent circumstance the parties have been discharged (whether by repudiation or frustration) from their obligation to continue with reference of the individual dispute, while leaving intact the continuous agreement to refer future disputes pursuant to the arbitration agreement.
(4) The curial law, i.e., the law governing the arbitration proceedings themselves, the manner in which the reference is to be conducted. It governs the procedural powers and duties of the arbitrators, questions of evidence and the determination of the proper law of the contract.

These propositions have since received judicial recognition in most countries including in India when the Indian Supreme Court quoted them with approval in *Sumitomo Heavy Industries Ltd. v. Ongc Ltd.*[18]

9. Position of India on the New York Convention

India, true to the spirit of the New York Convention, enacted the Foreign Awards (Recognition and Enforcement) Act, 1961. The earlier 1937 statute was repealed. It was an Act enacted to give effect to the New York Convention. The Act provided for the filing and enforcement of foreign awards in courts in India in accordance

[15] 1994 (1) Lloyd's Law Reports 45.
[16] 1981 (1) Lloyd's Rep 253.
[17] 1981 (2) Lloyd's Rep 446.
[18] (1998) 1 SCC 305 at p. 310.

with the Convention. Since all countries were not signatories to both the Geneva Convention and the New York Convention and since India is a signatory to both, foreign awards are recognized by India under both the Conventions. Any party could approach the courts in India for enforcement of the 'foreign awards' under either of the Conventions.

10. What is a Foreign Award?

The New York Convention though does not define the expression "foreign arbitral awards", article I thereof specifies the arbitral awards which could be treated as such. We have already noticed the respective scope of the two parts of Article I of the Convention. In a ONGC's case[19] the question before the court was whether an award made in London in respect of disputes arising between an Indian Company – Oil and Natural Gas Commission (ONGC) and an American Company – Western Company of North America which were to be adjudicated upon in accordance with the Indian Arbitration Act, 1940, was an arbitration to which the provisions of the Convention would apply or whether the award was a 'domestic' award to be dealt with under the Indian Arbitration Act, 1940 and in respect of which the Indian courts alone had jurisdiction. The disputes between the parties had been referred to two arbitrators who also appointed an umpire. The arbitrators entered into a reference in London, which was the agreed venue as per the arbitration clause. On October 1, 1985 the arbitrators informed the umpire that they were unable to agree on the matters outstanding in the reference. Consequently, the umpire entered upon the arbitration and straight away made non-speaking awards on 17 October 1985 without affording any hearing to the parties. On 5 November 1985, the Western Company requested the umpire to authorise an advocate in India to file the award in an appropriate court in India. The umpire duly authorised the advocate pursuant to which the award was filed in the High Court of Bombay on 22 November 1985. On 28 November 1985, the umpire rendered a supplementary award, which was also filed in the High Court of Bombay. Simultaneously, the Western Company also lodged a plaint in the United States district court seeking an order confirming the two awards and for a judgment against ONGC in respect of the amounts mentioned in the awards. In the meantime, on 20 January 1986 ONGC filed an application under Sections 30 and 33 of the Indian Arbitration Act, 1940 for setting aside the award rendered by the umpire. A learned Single Judge of the High Court initially granted an *ex parte* interim order restraining the Western Company from proceeding further with the action initiated in the United States court, but later vacated the order, which gave rise to the proceedings before the Supreme Court.

The Court though did not refer to the provisions of Article I of the Convention, it, in effect, gave recognition to the latter part of Article I attaching no

---

[19] *Oil and Natural Gas Commission v. Western Company of North America* (1987) 1 SCC 496.

importance to the first part of the Article which determined its applicability to an award depending entirely upon the seat of arbitration. If the seat of arbitration had been the criteria, the arbitration proceedings having been held in London, the award in question would be 'foreign award' to which the Convention would apply. The Court held that since the arbitration proceedings were governed by the Indian Arbitration Act, 1940, the validity of the awards and their enforceability were to be determined by the Indian courts applying the provisions of the said Act. It was held that serious incongruities would arise if the American Court were to decide upon the prayer for confirmation of the award at the instance of the Western Company in as much as, in deciding the said question, the American Court would undoubtedly follow its own laws and not the Indian Arbitration Act, which governed the arbitration proceedings as agreed to between the parties. Whereas the courts in India may possibly reach an opposite conclusion following the provisions of the Indian law.

Though it was not necessary, yet, the Court repelled the contention of the Western Company that the American Court still had jurisdiction to confirm the award and declare them to be enforceable in view of the provisions contained in Article V (1)(*e*) of the New York Convention, which provided that recognition and enforcement of the award will be refused if the award 'has not yet become binding on the parties or has been set aside or suspended by a competent authority of the country in which or under the law of which that award was made.' It was held that since the binding effect of the award would have to be determined in accordance with the Indian law, the awards could not be held to be binding since under the Indian law 'till an award is transformed into a judgment and decree under Section 17 of the Arbitration Act, it is altogether lifeless from the point of view of its enforceability. Life is infused into the award in the sense of its becoming enforceable only after it is made a rule of the court upon the judgment and decree in terms of the award being passed.' Thus, according to the Court, the anomaly would be, 'the American Court would have therefore enforced an award which is a lifeless award in the country of its origin, and under the law of the country of its origin which law governs the award by choice and consent.'

It is well settled that the parties to an arbitration agreement have the liberty and the right to make a choice expressly or by necessary implication, of the proper law or substantive law that will govern their contractual relationship as well as the proper law of the arbitration agreement including the procedural law governing the arbitral reference. In the absence of any express choice however, a presumption, though rebuttable, arises that the laws of a country where the arbitration proceedings are held, would be the proper law of the arbitration agreement and of the reference.

In *NTPC's* case[20] the Indian Company entered into two agreements with a foreign company – M/s Singer Company. The contracts *inter alia* provided that 'the laws applicable to this contract shall be the laws in force in India. The courts of Delhi shall have exclusive jurisdiction in all matters arising under this contract,' and the arbitration clause provided that 'the arbitration shall be conducted by three arbitrators, one each to be nominated by the owner and the contractor and the third to be named by the President of the International Chambers of Commerce (ICC), Paris. Save as above, all rules of conciliation and arbitration of the International Chambers of Commerce (ICC) shall apply to such arbitrations. The arbitration shall be conducted at such places as the arbitrators may determine.'

The disputes between the parties were referred to an arbitral tribunal constituted by the Court of ICC in terms of its rules of arbitration and London was chosen to be the place of arbitration. The award was also made in London. NTPC invoked the provisions of the Indian Arbitration Act, in a proceedings initiated before the Delhi High Court for setting aside the award made in London. The High Court rejected the application as not maintainable. The award having been rendered at London, was a 'foreign award' within the ambit of the Foreign Awards (Recognition and Enforcement) Act, 1961 and hence, the High Court had no jurisdiction to entertain the application filed under Sections 14, 30, 33 of the Arbitration Act, 1940.

On appeal, the Supreme Court reversed the decision of the High Court holding *inter alia* that 'an award is 'foreign' not merely because it is made in the territory of a foreign State, but because it is made in such a territory on an arbitration agreement not governed by the law of India. An award made on an arbitration agreement governed by the law of India, though rendered outside India, is attracted by the saving clause in Section 9 of the Foreign Awards Act and is, therefore, not treated in India as a 'foreign award'. Invoking the provisions of Section 9 of the Foreign Awards Act which declared that the provisions of the Act would not apply 'to any award made on arbitration agreement governed by the laws of India', it was held that the award though made in London necessarily fell within the purview of the Arbitration Act, 1940. The arbitration agreement being governed by the Indian law, as in the case of any other domestic award, the awards were amenable to the jurisdiction of the Indian courts and controlled by the Indian system of law 'except that the proceedings held abroad and leading to the award were in certain respects amenable to be controlled by the public policy and the mandatory requirements of the law of the place of arbitration and the competent courts of that place.'

This decision of the court clearly signifies that the court treated the two conditions in Article I as cumulative conditions required to be satisfied in every

---

[20] *National Thermal Power Corporation v. Singer Company and Others* (1992) 3 SCC 551.

case before the provisions of the Convention are held to be applicable to an award. The criticism that the provisions of Section 9 of the Foreign Awards (Recognition and Enforcement) Act, 1961 are not in conformity with the Convention is not valid in as much as the second part of the Article I clearly envisages that the Convention would be apply only to such arbitral awards which are 'not considered as domestic awards' in the States where their recognition and enforcement are sought. Under the Indian law, an award made on an arbitration agreement governed by the law of India, is considered as a 'domestic' award irrespective of the seat of arbitration. Thus, Section 9 (b) was clearly in consonance with the latter part of Article I of the Convention.

The rule that arbitral proceedings are governed by the law of the seat of the arbitration[21] has also its limitation and may, at times, lead to unintended consequences. In the *NTPC's* case the parties agreed for settlement of their disputes in accordance with the ICC Rules. There was no agreement between the parties with regard to the seat of arbitration. However, in terms of Article 12 of those Rules, the ICC Court chose London to be the place of arbitration and, for that matter, the ICC Court could have chosen any other place. Could it be said that the parties had 'contemplated', even in the remotest sense of the term, that the award be governed by the law of that country where the arbitration is held, of which, the parties had no information or knowledge? Satisfaction of the cumulative conditions in Article I as a prerequisite for the application of the Convention to an arbitral award may be a better interpretation of Article I.

The decision of the House of Lords in *Hiscox v. Outhwaite*[22] is an interesting example of the Convention being made applicable to an award under totally fortuitous circumstances based only upon the criterion of the place where the award is 'made'. In that case the parties, who were members of Lloyd's Syndicates, referred their disputes to arbitration by Mr. R.A. MacCrindle, QC, as sole arbitrator. The arbitration agreement was governed by English law and it provided that the arbitration shall take place in London. The arbitration was conducted by stages. The arbitrator signed and dated the awards with the inscription 'dated at Paris, France', and his signature was witnessed by his secretary. When Mr. MacCrindle was in practice at the English Bar, he was in chambers at 4 Essex Court, Temple, London. He remained a 'door tenant' of those chambers and had the services of their clerk. On 20 November 1990, the clerk informed Mr. Hiscox's solicitors by fax that the award could be taken up at those chambers on payment of the charges due. Shortly afterwards, they collected the award. On 10 December

---

[21] Rule 57(2): 'In general, and subject to the mandatory rule of the law of the seat of the arbitration, the law chosen by the parties governs arbitral proceedings; in the absence of agreement, arbitral proceedings are governed by the law of the seat of the arbitration'. (Quoted from L. Collins ed., *Dicey and Morris on the Conflict of Laws*, 13th ed., Sweet & Maxwell, London (vol. 1, 2000) at 592.).

[22] 1992 (1) AC 562.

1990, Mr. Hiscox initiated three proceedings before the High Court, *viz.* (1) for leave to appeal to the High Court under Section 1 (3) (b) of the Arbitration Act, 1975; (2) for an order directing Mr. MacCrindle to state further reasons for this award; and (3) for seeking remission of the award pursuant to Section 22 of the Arbitration Act, 1950. Mr. Outhwaite then took a preliminary objection that the award being a Convention award in terms of the Arbitration Act, 1975 the High Court was disabled from adjudicating upon those proceedings. J. Hirst held that it was not a Convention award, as it was 'made' in London, though dated in Paris. Section 7 (1) of the Arbitration Act, 1975, defined 'Convention award' as meaning . . . 'an award made in pursuance of an arbitration agreement in the territory of a State, other than the United Kingdom, which is a party to the New York Convention.'

On appeal by the respondent, the Court of Appeal held that the award was 'made' in Paris, and thus, by definition, a Convention award and hence the High Court was deprived of its jurisdiction to entertain the applications moved by Mr. Hiscox. The appeal was, however, dismissed on the ground that by reason of his conduct, the respondent was estopped from objecting to the jurisdiction of the High Court. In his dissenting note on the first question, Lord Donaldson of Lymington, M.R., however, observed, 'I also accept that if the place of signature, or of the last signature, on the award is the crucial test, an award may become, or fail to become, a Convention award almost by caprice and contrary to the expectations and, it may be, the wishes of the parties.'[23]

On further appeal to the House of Lords, the appellant contended that by virtue of the place of signature being Paris, the award was 'made' in Paris and was therefore a Convention award. Lord Oliver of Ayemerton, speaking for the Court, held, "I do not, for my part, consider that it can be seriously open to doubt that Mr. MacCrindle had 'declared his final mind' when he signed the award in Paris. Whilst, therefore, I find it anomalous and regrettable that the fortuitous circumstance of signature in Paris should stamp what was clearly intended to be an award subject to all the procedural regulations of an English Arbitration, with the character of a Convention award."[24]

11. When Does an Award Become 'Final' or 'Binding'?

Article 1(2)(d) of the Geneva Convention requires that an arbitral award, in order that it be recognised and enforced in the State where the award is relied upon, not only have to be made in the territory of one of the contracting parties to which the Convention applies and between persons who are subject to the jurisdiction of one of the contracting parties but also that the award must "become final" in the

---

[23] *Ibid.*,at 569F.

[24] *Ibid.*,at 594-5.

country in which it had been made. Clause (d) further explains that the award must become final", 'in the sense that it will not be considered as such if it is open to opposition, appeal or *pourvoi nen cessation* . . . or if it is proved that any proceedings for the purpose of contesting the validity of the award is pending.' This provision contradicts the very concept of a "foreign award" and impliedly accepts jurisdiction of courts in more than one country over the very same award. The question of recognition and enforcement of an arbitral award in a Convention country would arise only if it is a Convention award or a foreign award. If the arbitral award is a Convention award, it could not be the subject matter of proceedings in a country in which it has been made, and hence the question of its becoming 'final' in that country would also not arise. The expression 'became final' itself became the subject matters of diverse judicial opinions.

In recognition of the Geneva Convention, the English Arbitration Act, 1950 provided in Section 37 thereof, that for enforcement of a foreign award, it must have 'become final in the country in which it was made.' In *Union Internationale des Co-operatives Agricoles de Cereales*,[25] by an agreement dated 31 August 1956 made in Paris, the appellant agreed to sell a certain quantity of wheat seed to the respondent. The arbitration clause in the agreement provided that '[a]ll differences arising out of the present contract will be judged by the Arbitration Chamber of Copenhagen which will settle without appeal with the powers of an amicable arbitrator.' The disputes between the parties were referred to the Copenhagen Chamber of Arbitration. The rules regulating the procedure for arbitration *inter alia* provided that the 'awards made by the Committee . . . shall be final. An award can only be appealed against to the appeal court attached to the Committee.' By an order dated 6 October 1958, the Committee awarded to the respondent a sum of £183,000/-. The Arbitration Committee refused the appellant's application for leave to appeal and notified that the award dated 6 October 1958 was final. As per Danish law, the award could not be enforced in Denmark without the order of a Danish court. The respondent, invoking the provisions of the Arbitration Act, 1950, sought enforcement of the award in England. The appellant claimed that the award was a foreign award, and that since it did not become final in the country in which it was made, it was not enforceable in England. The Court of Appeal held that for the purposes of Section 37(1)(d) of the Arbitration Act, 1950, the award must be treated as having become final according to the relevant law of Denmark and hence was enforceable in the same way as an English award. Lord Evershed, M.R., speaking for the Court, observed:

> [T]his award is, to my way of thinking, final according to the bargain made and according to the law of Denmark, so far as it is concerned with the problem with which we are presented. It is no doubt not enforceable

---

[25] *Union Internationale des Co-operatives Agricoles de Cereales v. Robert Calterall & Co. Ltd.* 1959 (2) QB 44.

> directly in Denmark or anywhere else; but it is, I think, final within the contemplation of this Section.

In order to overcome the difficulties placed in the interpretation of the expression 'became final', the New York Convention used, in Article V (1)(*e*), the expression 'the award has not yet become binding on the parties.'

In *ONGC v. Western Co. of North America*,[26] the Supreme Court, construing the expression 'not yet become binding', held that:

> The expression postulates that the Convention has visualised an award which becomes binding at a point of time later than the making of the award. In other words, the provision has in its contemplation, the fact that an award in some cases may become binding on the mere making of it and in some case become binding only at a later stage. If this was not so there was no point in using the expression not yet become binding.

Although judicial interpretations vary as to when does an award 'become binding' on the parties, the predominant view appears to be, that the question would have to be determined in the light of the law applicable to the award, and that law, as indicated in the latter part of Article V(1)(*e*), would be of the country in which or under the law of which the award is made. Considering the divergence in the judicial opinion on the interpretation of the conditions in Article V (1)(*e*), the Supreme Court concluded:

> (1) That the enforceability must be determined *as per the law applicable to the award.* (emphasis in the original)
> (2) French, German and Italian courts have taken the view that the enforceability as per the law of the country which governs the award is essential (sic) precondition for asserting that it has become binding under Article V(1)(*e*).[27]

In the context of the Indian Arbitration Act, 1940, it was held that till an award is transformed into a judgment and decree in terms of the award under Section 17 of the Act, the award was not enforceable. It became enforceable only after it becomes a rule of the court. This position has undergone a sea change after the coming into force of the Arbitration and Conciliation Act of 1996. Section 35 declares that the arbitral award shall be final and binding on the parties and persons claiming under them respectively. Section 36, which deals with the enforcement of arbitral awards, provides that '[w]here the time for making an application to set aside the arbitral award under S. 34 has expired, or such application having been made, it has been refused, the award shall be enforced under the Code of Civil

---

[26] (1987) 1 SCC 496 at 511.
[27] *Ibid.*,at 514.

Procedure, 1908 (5 of 1908) in the same manner as if it were a decree of the Court'. The requirement of a judgment or a decree passed in terms of the award as a pre-condition to its enforceability has thus been altered and now an arbitral award is final and binding on the parties and is *per se* enforceable as a decree of the court.

12. 'Public Policy' under Article V (2)(*b*) of the New York Convention

The first part of Article V requires the party against whom recognition and enforcement of a foreign award is invoked, must furnish proof of certain conditions mentioned therein in order that the competent authority, may refuse to do so. The second part of the Article provides that it is for the competent authority, in the country in which such recognition and enforcement is sought, to refuse such enforcement of an arbitral award if it 'finds' that . . . 'the recognition and enforcement of the award would be contrary to the public policy of that country." This provision was a clear departure from the Geneva Convention, which provided that for recognition and enforcement of an arbitral award, it shall be necessary to establish that the recognition and enforcement of the award is not contrary to public policy or "to the principles of the law of the country in which it is sought to be relied upon.'

The New York Convention therefore relieved the added condition for recognition and enforcement of an arbitral award of being in conformity with the 'principles of the law of the country' in which it is sought to be enforced. All the same, difficulties continued to be encountered in the interpretation of the words 'public policy' under Article V(2)(*b*) of the New York Convention. The English Arbitration Act, 1975 enacted for giving effect to the New York Convention also used the expression 'public policy' without any further qualification. It has, however, been an accepted position in that country that the said expression would only mean English public policy.

In France, there exists a distinction between international public policy and national public policy. Under the French Code of Civil Procedure, an international arbitral award may be set aside if recognition and enforcement thereof is contrary to international public policy, which is less restrictive in its approach than national public policy which concerns domestic considerations. Noticing the changes brought about in the New York Convention, in suppression of the Geneva Convention, American courts have adopted a restrictive approach while considering the defence of public policy. It has been held that 'enforcement of foreign arbitral awards may be denied on that basis only where enforcement would violate the forum state's most basic notions of morality and justice.'[28]

---

[28] *Parsons & Whittemore Overseas Co. Inc. v. Societe Generale de l'Industrie du Papier (Rakta) and Bank of America* 508 F.2d 969.

Construing the said expression 'public policy', the Supreme Court of India has held:[29]

> 'Article V (2) (b) of the New York Convention of 1958 and Section 7 (1) (b) (ii) of the Foreign Awards Act, do not postulate refusal of recognition and enforcement of a foreign award on the ground that it is contrary to the law of the country of enforcement and the ground of challenge is confined to the recognition and enforcement being contrary to the public policy of the country in which the award is set to be enforced. Here is nothing to indicate that the expression 'public policy' in Article V (2) (b) of the New York Convention and Section 7 (1) (b) (ii) of the Foreign Awards Act, is not used in the same sense in which it was used in Article I (c) of the Geneva Convention of 1927 and Section 7 (1) of the Protocol and Convention Act, of 1937. This would mean that 'public policy' in Section 7 (1) (b) (ii) has been used in a narrower sense and in order to attract to bar of public policy the enforcement of the award must invoke something more than the violation of the law of India. Since the Foreign Awards Act is concerned with recognition and enforcement of foreign awards which are governed by the principles of private international law, the expression 'public policy' in Section 7 (1) (b) (ii) of the Foreign Awards Act must necessarily be construed in the sense the doctrine of public policy is applied in the field of private international law. Applying the said criteria it must be held that the enforcement of a foreign award would be refused on the ground that it is contrary to public policy if such enforcement would be contrary to (i) fundamental policy of Indian law; or (ii) the interests of India; or (iii) justice or morality.'

13. UNCITRAL Model Law and the New Act

Unlike the trade related laws, UNCITRAL neither considered nor suggested framing of any international substantive law of arbitration. In contrast to the UNCITRAL Model Law relating to Procurement of Goods, Construction and Services (1995), International Credit Transfer (1994) and the Electronic Commerce (1996), the UNCITRAL Model Law on International Commercial Arbitration adopted in 1985 suggested uniformity in the law of arbitral procedures and international commercial arbitration practices. After the recommendation of the UN General Assembly, almost all the member countries started considering the possibilities of adoption of legislative measures on the lines suggested by UNCITRAL. In India, the Ministry of Law and Justice, Government of India prepared a draft bill. After a brief public debate, primarily organised by the associations of Indian trade and industry, like FICCI and its related organ ICA, the Arbitration and Conciliation Bill, 1995, was introduced in the Parliament but the bill could not be passed as an Act. On 16 January 1996, when the Parliament was not in session, the President, in exercise of the powers conferred by clause (1) of

---

[29] *Renusagar Power Co. Ltd. v. General Electric Co.* (1994) 1 SCC 644 at 682.

article 123[30] of the Constitution, promulgated the Arbitration and Conciliation Ordinance, 1996 (8 of 1996). The ordinance repealed the Arbitration Act, 1940 with immediate effect and brought into force a new regime of law relating to arbitration on the lines proposed in the Arbitration and Conciliation Bill, 1995. The ordinance, however, could not be replaced by an Act as the Parliament failed to enact a law to that effect. Since the life of the ordinance was limited to only six weeks from the re-assembly of the legislature and since in the meanwhile Parliament session was prorogued, in order that the law of arbitration continue to exist, on 26 March 1996 the President promulgated another ordinance called the Arbitration and Conciliation (Second) Ordinance, 1996 (11 of 1996). Even the second ordinance could not be replaced by an Act of Parliament. On 21 June 1996, the President promulgated yet another ordinance – the Arbitration and Conciliation (Third) Ordinance, 1996 (29 of 1996). Finally, the Parliament passed the Arbitration and Conciliation Act, 1996 (26 of 1996) on 16 August 1996 repealing, *inter alia*, the Arbitration and Conciliation (Third) Ordinance, 1996.

The Act has two parts. The provisions contained in Part I apply to all arbitrations 'where the place of arbitration is in India.' Such arbitrations could be both domestic as well as international commercial arbitrations. Section 11 of the Act provides for the appointment of arbitrators in respect of both domestic as well as international commercial arbitrations. Section 28 mandates that where the place of arbitration is in India, in a domestic arbitration, the arbitral tribunal shall decide the dispute between the parties in accordance with the substantive law for the time being in force in India, and that in respect of international commercial arbitration – (i) the arbitral tribunals shall decide the dispute in accordance with the rule of law designated by the parties as applicable to the substance of the dispute; (ii) any designation by the parties of the law and legal system of a given country shall be construed, unless otherwise expressed, as directly referring to the substantive law of the country and not to its conflict of laws rules; (iii) failing any designation of the law by the parties, the arbitral tribunal shall apply the rules of the law it considers to be appropriate given all the circumstances surrounding the dispute. In all cases, the law requires that the arbitral tribunal shall decide in accordance with the terms of the contract and shall take into account the usages of the trade applicable to the transaction. Section 34 provides the grounds for setting aside arbitral awards. The grounds are the same as contained in Article 34 of the UNCITRAL Model Laws. Section 35 declares that the arbitral award to be final and binding on the parties and Section 36 provides that the award shall be enforced as if it were a decree of the court. Part II of the Act contains provisions for the recognition and enforcement of foreign awards, and also incorporates both the Geneva and the New York Conventions. Sections 44 to 51 appearing under Chapter I deal with the New York

[30] Power of President to promulgate Ordinances during recess of Parliament - (1) If at any time, except when both Houses of Parliament are in session, the President is satisfied that circumstances exist which render it necessary for him to take immediate action, he may promulgate such Ordinance as the circumstances appear to him to require.

Convention awards and re-incorporate the provisions of the Foreign Awards (Recognition and Enforcement) Act of 1961, except that Sections 4(1), 5, 9 and 11 of the said Act which have been omitted and do not find any place in the new Act.

Sections 53 to 59 of Chapter II deal with the Geneva Convention awards. In *Fuerst Dey Lawson Ltd. v. Jindal Exports Ltd.*,[31] the Supreme Court held that a foreign award passed even before the coming into force of the 1996 Act could enforced under the new Act, since the Ordinance promulgated by the President had already come into force with effect from 25 January 1996. Construing the provisions of Sections 47 to 49 of the Act, the Court held that a party holding a foreign award can apply for its enforcement, but the Court before taking further effective steps for the execution of the award has to proceed in accordance with Sections 47 to 49. It held further that:

> In one proceeding there may be different stages. In the first stage the court may have to decide about the enforceability of the award having regard to the requirement of the said provisions. Once a court decides that the foreign award is enforceable, it can proceed to take further effective steps for execution of the same. There arises no question of making foreign award a rule of court/decree again. If the object and purpose can be served in the same proceedings, in our view, there is no need to take two separate proceedings resulting in multiplicity of litigation.'[32]

Section 9 of the Act enacts the provisions of Article 9 of the Model Law on the court's power to grant interim measures of protection. Since the said provision appears in Part I of the Act, the jurisdiction of the courts in India to order for interim measures of protection should naturally be referable to arbitral proceedings as are held or contemplated to be held in India irrespective of the fact whether such arbitration is domestic arbitration or international commercial arbitration.

In *Bhatia International v. Bulk Trading S.A.*,[33] the Supreme Court, by a curious process of interpretation of Sections 2 (7), 2 (1)(e) and (f), 2 (2), 2 (7), 9, 17, 28 and 36, held that the courts in India will have the power and jurisdiction to order interim measures of protection to the parties under Section 9 of the Act even in respect of arbitrations held outside India unless the parties by agreement excluded the provisions of any of the provisions of the Act. The appellant in that case was an Indian company that had entered into a contract with the respondent, a foreign company. The contract provided that arbitration would be as per the rules of the International Chamber of Commerce. Disputes having arisen between the parties, the respondent foreign company requested the ICC for initiation of arbitral proceedings. The parties agreed that the arbitration be held in Paris, France. ICC

---

[31] (2001) 6 SCC 356.
[32] *Ibid.*,at 371.
[33] (2002) 4 SCC 105.

appointed a sole arbitrator to enter upon the reference. In the meantime, the respondent filed an application under Section 9 of the Act before the Third Additional Session Judge, Indore, in the State of Madhya Pradesh, praying *inter alia* for an interim order of injunction against the opposite parties from alienating, transferring or creating third-party rights, disposing off, dealing with and/or selling their business assets and properties. The appellant raised objections as regards the maintainability of the said application since Section 9 contained in Part I of the Act did not apply to arbitration, where the place of arbitration is not in India. The Additional District Judge, however, held that the application was maintainable and that the Court at Indore had jurisdiction to entertain the same. The appellant filed a writ petition before the High Court of Madhya Pradesh, which was also dismissed. On appeal, the Supreme Court cited the following reasons as the necessary consequences that would follow if the Court were to hold that Section 9 would not apply to arbitrations which are not held in India:

> (a) Amount to holding that the legislature has left a lacuna in the said Act. There would be a lacuna as neither Part I or II would apply to arbitrations held in a country which is not a signatory to the New York Convention or the Geneva Convention (hereinafter called "a non-convention country'). It would mean that there is no law, in India, governing such arbitrations.
> (b) Lead to an anomalous situation, inasmuch as Part I would apply to Jammu and Kashmir in all international commercial arbitrations but Part I would not apply to the rest of India if the arbitration takes place out of India.
> (c) Lead to a conflict between sub-section (2) of Section 2 on one hand and sub-sections (4) and (5) of Section 2 on the other. Further, sub-section (2) of Section 2 would also be in conflict with Section I which provides that the Act extends to the whole of India.
> (d) Leave a party remediless inasmuch as in international commercial arbitrations which take place out of India the party would not be able to apply for interim relief in India even though the properties and assets are in India. Thus a party may not be able to get any interim relief at all. [34]

Interpreting the provisions of Section 9, the Court held that:

> [U]nder Section 9 a party could apply to the court (a) before, (b) during arbitral proceedings or (c) after the making of the arbitral award but before it is enforced in accordance with Section 36. The words 'in accordance with Section 36' can only go with the words 'after the making of the arbitral award.' It is clear that the words 'in accordance with Section 36' can have no reference to an application made 'before' or 'during the arbitral proceedings'. Thus it is clear that an application for interim measure can be made to the courts in India, whether or not the arbitration takes place in

[34] *Ibid.*,at 115.

> India, before or during arbitral proceedings. Once an award is passed, then that award itself can be executed. Sections 49 and 58 provide that awards covered by Part II are deemed to be a decree of the court. Thus, 'foreign awards' which are enforceable in India, are deemed to be decrees. A domestic award has to be enforced under the provisions of the Civil Procedure Code. All that Section 36 provides is that an enforcement of a domestic award is to take place after the time to make an application to set aside the award has expired or such an application has been refused. Section 9 does suggest that once an award is made, an application for interim measure can only be made if the award is a 'domestic award' as defined in Section 2 (7) of the said Act. Thus, where the legislature wanted to restrict the applicability of Section 9, it has done so specifically.'[35]

Finally, the Court held that the provisions of Part I would apply to all arbitration proceedings, and that when such proceedings are held in India, the provisions of Part I would compulsorily apply and the parties would be free to deviate only to the extent permitted by the derogable provisions of Part I. In international commercial arbitration held outside India, the provisions of Part I would also apply unless the parties by agreement, express or implied, exclude all or any of its provisions.

In contrast, a learned Single Judge of the Supreme Court,[36] exercising the delegated powers of the Chief Justice of India in a proceeding under Section 11(4) of the Act for the appointment of an arbitrator in respect of arbitral proceedings to be held in New York, held that the said proceedings was not maintainable since Section 11 is placed in Part I of the Act, and sub section (2) of Section 2 thereof provided that '[t]his part shall apply where the place of arbitration is in India.' The Supreme Court by a decision of a Constitution Bench[37] has clarified that the decision regarding appointment of arbitrators by the Chief Justice of India or his designate under Section 11 of the Act does not act as a tribunal, and that the order passed in such proceedings is not an adjudicatory order.

In *Owners and Parties Interested in the Vessel M.V. 'Baltic Confidence' v. State Trading Corporation of India*,[38] the Supreme Court relegated the parties to arbitration in accordance with the arbitration clause contained in a Charter Party agreement, which was applicable to the disputes between the endorsee of the Bill of Lading and the owners and charterers of the ship concerned in accordance with the mandate of Section 45 of the Act, which is based on Article II (3) of the New York Convention. The second respondent in that case, the charterer of the ship, had on 8 May 1997 entered into a Time Charter Party agreement with the appellants. Five bills of lading, all dated 26 May 1997, were issued by the appellants whereunder the second respondent agreed to carry on board the vessel M.V. Baltic Confidence

---

[35] *Ibid.*,at 122.
[36] *Shrijee Traco India (P) Ltd. v. Paperline International Inc.* (2003) 9 SCC 79.
[37] *Konkan Railways Corporation v. Rani Construction Ltd.* (2002) 2 SCC 388.
[38] (2001) 7 SCC 473.

11,433.510 metric tonnes of Canadian yellow peas from the port of Vancouver in Canada to the port of Calcutta. The first respondent, the State Trading Corporation of India (STC), was the holder and endorsee of each of the said bills of lading and also the owner of the said stock of peas. STC filed a suit in the High Court of Calcutta in its admiralty jurisdiction, against the appellant and the second respondent alleging negligence and breach of contract of carriage which resulted in short delivery and damage to the goods. The appellants and the second respondent filed an application under Section 45 of the Act for stay of the said proceedings and for referring the disputes to arbitration in the terms of Clause 62 of the Charter Party agreement. The application was rejected by the Single Judge, which was confirmed by the Division Bench, holding *inter alia* that the arbitration clause in the Charter Party agreement was not applicable to the disputes arising from the Bill of Lading, and hence the application under Section 45 was not maintainable. On further appeal to the Supreme Court, it was held that while incorporating the conditions of the Charter Party Agreement in the bills of lading, specific reference had been made to the arbitration clause by the use of the expression 'including the law and arbitration clause'. On a fair reading of Clause 62 of the Charter Party Agreement and the conditions of the Bill of Lading, there was no manifest inconsistency and insensibility, and hence the High Court was not justified in refusing to relegate the parties to arbitral proceedings, staying the suit filed by STC. This and many other cases decided under the new Act amply bear out that the courts in India have fully encouraged international arbitrations and enforcement of the foreign awards.

14. Conclusions

India not only responded in positive terms to the need for speedy and effective resolution of disputes arising out of international commercial transactions and respected every single united move of the world of nations being a signatory to all the international Protocol and Conventions and ratifying them at the earliest, but also took appropriate legislative measures to give full effect to the same. In the same spirit, India has adopted the UNCITRAL Model Law with a view to bring about an uniformity in the law and practise of international commercial arbitrations and also to provide for enforcement of the foreign arbitral awards and enacted a consolidated law- the Arbitration and Conciliation ACT, 1996. With the statutory recognition of institutional arbitrations, India is for now the ideal venue for conduct of all international arbitrations particularly those involving Asian countries. The institutions like Indian Council of Arbitration (ICA), (ICADR), etc. are the counterparts of the European institutions like International Court of Arbitration (ICC), International Council for Commercial Arbitration (ICCA), London Court of International Arbitration (LCIA). The Law Commission of India in its 176th Report has suggested a number of legislative reforms. In fact, in the Arbitration and Conciliation (Amendment) Bill 2003, international arbitration awards have been given a special status by limiting the scope of the expression 'public policy of India' to mean '(i) fundamental policy of India, or (ii) interests of India, (iii) justice or morality' which perfectly match the concept under the private international law. Large number of arbitration awards that came up for enforcement in the Indian courts received due recognition and are executed with expedition. Many proceedings initiated in the domestic courts are stayed and the parties are relegated to arbitrations if the contracts between them provide for such arbitrations. A large number of ICC awards have already been enforced. India could certainly boast of its well-developed legal regime, jurisprudence and its experts, both legal and technical, comparable to the best in the world. India could therefore be the natural choice for the men of commerce for the seat of international arbitrations.

INDIA'S POSITION ON MULTILATERAL TREATIES DEPOSITED WITH THE UN SECRETARY-GENERAL STATUS AS OF 31 DECEMBER 2004

Leeladhara Bhandary M.*

Sl. No.	Name of the Convention	Date and Place of Adoption	Entry into Force	Registration	Status		Application	Date of Definitive Signature (S) Ratification (R) Accession (A) Succession (d) Acceptance (a) Consent to be bound (P)	Date of Signature
					Signatories	Parties			
1	UN Charter & ICJ Statute	26 Jun 1945, San Francisco	24 Oct 1945		191			30 Oct 1945 (R)	
2	Amendment to Articles 23, 27 and 61 of UN Charter	17 Feb 1963, New York	31 Aug 1965	1 March 1966		107		10 Sep 1964 (R)	
3	Amendment to Article 109 of UN Charter	20 Dec 1965, New York	12 Jun 1968	12 Jun 1968		93		11 Jul 1966 (R)	
4	Amendment to Article 61 of the UN Charter	20 Dec 1971, New York	24 Sep 1973	24 Sep 1973		106		5 Jan 1973 (R)	
5	Convention on the Privileges and Immunities of the UNs	13 Feb 1946, New York	17 Sep 1946	14 Dec 1946		148		13 May 1948 (A)	
6	Convention on the Privileges and Immunities of the Specialized Agencies	21 Nov 1947, New York	2 Dec 1948	16 Aug 1949		110		10 Feb 1949 (A)	

* Reseach Officer, Indian Society of International Law, New Delhi, India

Bimal N. Patel (ed.), **India and International Law, 345-362.**

7	Annex I-ILO to the Convention on the Privileges and Immunities of the Specialized Agencies	10 Jul 1948, San Francisco		16 Aug 1949			10 Feb 1949		
8	Annex II-Food and Agriculture Organisation of the UN to the Convention on the Privileges and Immunities of the Specialized Agencies	29 Nov 1948, Washington		16 Aug 1949			10 Feb 1949		
9	Revised text of Annex II-Food and Agriculture Organisation of the UN to the Convention on the Privileges and Immunities of the Specialized Agencies	20 Nov 1959, Rome		2 Aug 1960			12 Apr 1963		
10	Annex III- ICAO to the Convention on the Privileges and Immunities of the Specialized Agencies	21 Jun 1948, Geneva		16 Aug 1949			10 Feb 1949		
11	Annex IV- UNESCO to the Convention on the Privileges and Immunities of the Specialized Agencies	7 Feb 1949		16 Aug 1949			10 Feb 1949		
12	Annex V- IMF to the Convention on the Privileges and Immunities of the Specialized Agencies	11 Apr 1949, Washington		16 Aug 1949			19 Oct 1949		
13	Annex VI- IBRD to the Convention on the Privileges and Immunities of the Specialized Agencies	19 Apr 1949, Washington		16 Aug 1949			19 Oct 1949		
14	Annex VII- WHO to the Convention on the Privileges and Immunities of the Specialized Agencies	17 Jul 1948, Geneva		16 Aug 1949			10 Feb 1949		
15	Second Revised text of Annex VII- WHO to the Convention on the Privileges and Immunities of the Specialized Agencies	27 May 1957, Geneva		22 Aug 1957			31 Jul 1958		

16	Annex VIII- Universal Postal Union to the Convention on the Privileges and Immunities of the Specialized Agencies	25 May 1949, Geneva		16 Aug 1949			19 Oct 1949		
17	Annex IX- ITU to the Convention on the Privileges and Immunities of the Specialized Agencies	6 Oct 1950, Geneva	16 Jan 1951				3 Jun 1955		
18	Annex XI-World Meteorological Organisation to the Convention on the Privileges and Immunities of the Specialized Agencies	17 Apr 1951, Paris	29 Dec 1951				9 Mar 1955		
19	Annex XIII- International Finance Corporation to the Convention on the Privileges and Immunities of the Specialized Agencies	2 Apr 1959, Washington		22 Apr 1959			3 Aug 1961		
20	Vienna convention on Diplomatic Relations	18 Apr 1961, Vienna	24 Apr 1964	24 June 1964	60	182		15 Oct 1965 (A)	
21	Optional Protocol to the Vienna Convention on Diplomatic Relations, Concerning Acquisition of Nationality	18 Apr 1961, Vienna	24 Apr 1964	24 June 1964	18	50		15 Oct 1965 (A)	
22	Optional Protocol to the Vienna Convention on Diplomatic Relations, Concerning the Compulsory Settlement of disputes	18 Apr 1961, Vienna	24 Apr 1964	24 Jun 1964	29	62		15 Oct 1965 (A)	
23	Vienna Convention on Consular Relations	24 Apr 1963, Vienna	19 Mar 1967	8 Jun 1967	48	166		28 Nov 1977 (A)	
24	Optional Protocol to the Vienna Convention on Consular Relations concerning Acquisition of Nationality	24 Apr 1963, Vienna	19 Mar 1967	8 Jun 1967	18	39		28 Nov 1977 (A)	

25	Optional Protocol to the Vienna Convention on Consular Relations Concerning the Compulsory Settlement of disputes	24 Apr 1963, Vienna	19 Mar 1967	8 Jun 1967	38	46		28 Nov 1977 (A)	
26	Convention on the Prevention and Punishment of the Crime of Genocide	9 Dec 1948, New York	12 Jan 1951	12 Jan 1951	41	136		27 Aug 1959 (R)	29 Nov 1949
27	International Convention on the Elimination of All Forms of Racial Discrimination	7 Mar 1966, New York	4 Jan 1969	12 Mar 1969	84	170		3 Dec 1968 (R)	2 Mar 1967
28	International Covenant on Economic, Social and Cultural Rights	16 Dec 1966, New York	3 Jan 1976	3 Jan 1976	66	151		10 Apr 1979 (A)	
29	International Covenant on Civil and Political Rights	16 Dec 1966, New York	23 Mar 1976	23 Mar 1976	67	154		10 Apr 1979 (A)	
30	Convention on the Non-Applicability of Statutory Limitations to War Crimes and Crimes Against Humanity	26 Nov 1968, New York	11 Nov 1970	11 Nov 1970	9	48		12 Jan 1971 (A)	
31	International Convention on the Suppression and Punishment of the Crime of Apartheid	30 Nov 1973, New York	18 Jul 1976	18 Jul 1976	31	101		22 Sep 1977 (A)	
32	Convention on the Elimination of All Forms of Discrimination Against Women	18 Dec 1979, New York	3 Sep 1981	3 Sep 1981	98	179		9 Jul 1993 (R)	30 Jul 1980
33	Convention Against Torture and Other Cruel, Inhuman or Degrading Treatment or Punishment	10 Dec 1984, New York	26 Jun 1987	26 Jun 1987	74	139			14 Oct 1997
34	International Convention Against Apartheid in Sports	10 Dec 1985, New York	3 Apr 1988	3 Apr 1988	72	58		12 Sep 1990 (A)	

35	Convention on the Rights of the Child	20 Nov 1989, New York	2 Sep 1990	2 Sep, 1990	140	192		11 Dec 1992 (A)	
36	Optional Protocol to the Convention on the Rights of the Child on the involvement of Children in armed conflict	25 May 2000, New York	12 Feb 2002	12 Feb 2002	117	91			15 Nov 2004
37	Optional Protocol to the Convention on the Rights of the Child on the sale of children, child prostitution and child pornography	25 May 2000, New York	18 Jan 2002	18 Jan 2002	110	89			15 Nov 2004
38	Protocol Amending the Agreements, Conventions and Protocols on Narcotic Drugs, Concluded at the Hague on 23 Jan. 1912, at Geneva November 1931 and at Geneva on 26 June 1936	11 Dec 1946, Lake Success, New York	11 Dec 1946	3 Feb 1948	24	63		11 Dec 1946 (S)	
39	Agreement Concerning the Suppression of the Manufacture of, International Trade In, and Use Of, Prepared Opium	11 Feb 1925, Geneva and 11 Dec 1946 Lake Success	27 Oct 1947						11 Dec 1946
40	Agreement Concerning the Suppression of the Manufacture of, International Trade In, and Use Of, Prepared Opium	11 Feb 1925, Geneva	28 Jul 1926	28 Jul 1926				17 Feb 1926 (R)	
41	International Opium Convention	19 Feb 1925, Geneva	25 Sept 1928	25 Sept 1928					17 Feb 1926
42	Convention for Limiting the Manufacture and Regulating the Distribution of Narcotic Drugs	13 Jul 1931, Geneva and 11 Dec 1946, Lake Success, New York	21 Nov 1947						11 Dec 1946
43	Agreement Concerning the Suppression of Opium Smoking	27 Nov 1931, Bangkok and 11 Dec 1946, Lake Success, New York	27 Oct 1947						11 Dec 1946

44	Agreement Concerning the Suppression of Opium Smoking	27 Nov 1931, Bangkok	22 Apr 1937	22 Apr 1937				4 Dec 1935 (R)	
45	Convention for the Suppression of the Illicit Traffic in Dangerous Drugs	26 Jun 1936, Geneva and 11 Dec 1946, Lake Success, New York	10 Oct 1947						11 Dec 1946
46	Convention of 1936 for the Suppression of the Illicit Traffic in Dangerous Drugs	26 Jun 1936, Geneva	26 Oct 1939	26 Oct 1939				4 Aug 1937 (R)	
47	Protocol Bringing under International Control Drugs Outside the Scope of the Convention of 13 July 1931 for Limiting the Manufacture and Regulating the Distribution of Narcotic Drugs, as amended by the Protocol signed at Lake Success, New York, on 11 December 1946	19 Nov 1948, Paris	1 Dec 1949	1 Dec 1949	39	88		10 Nov 1950 (a)	19 Nov 1948
48	Protocol for Limiting and Regulating the Cultivation of the Poppy Plant, the Production of, International and Wholesale Trade, and Use of Opium	23 Jun 1953, New York	8 Mar 1963	8 Mar 1963	33	51		30 Apr 1954 (R)	23 Jun 1953
49	Single Convention on Narcotic Drugs, 1961	30 Mar 1961, New York	13 Dec 1964	13 Dec 1964	61	149		13 Dec 1964 (R)	30 Mar 1961
50	Convention on Psychotropic Substances	21 Feb 1971, Vienna	16 Aug 1976	16 Aug 1976	34	175		23 Apr 1975 (A)	
51	Protocol Amending the Single Convention on Narcotic Drugs, 1961	25 Mar 1972, Geneva	8 Aug 1975	8 Aug 1975	54	121		14 Dec 1978 (A)	

52	Single Convention on Narcotic Drugs, 1961, as amended by the Protocol Amending the Single Convention on Narcotic Drugs, 1961	8 Aug 1975, New York	3 Aug 1975	8 Aug 1975		176		14 Dec 1978 (Participation in the Convention by virtue of ratification, accession or succession to the Protocol of 25 March 1972 or to the 1961 Convention after the entry into force of the Protocol)	
53	UN Convention Against Illicit Traffic in Narcotic Drugs and Psychotropic Substances	20 Dec 1988, Vienna	11 Nov 1990	11 Nov 1990	87	171		27 Mar 1990 (A)	
54	Protocol Signed at Lake Success, New York, on 12 November 1947, to Amend the Convention for the Suppression of the Traffic in Women and Children, Concluded at Geneva on 30 September 1921, and the Convention for the Suppression if the Traffic in Women of Full Age, concluded at Geneva on 11 October 1933	12 Nov 1947, Lake Success, New York	12 Nov 1947	24 Apr 1950	8	42		12 Nov 1947 (S)	
55	International Convention for the Suppression of the Traffic in Women and Children, Concluded at Geneva on 30 September 1921, as Amended by the Protocol Signed at Lake Success, New York, on 12 November 1947	12 Nov 1947, Lake Success, New York	24 Apr 1950	24 Apr 1950		45		12 Nov 1947 (Definitive Signature of the Protocol, Acceptance of the Protocol, Succession to the Protocol)	
56	Protocol Amending the International Agreement for the Suppression of the White Slave Traffic, Signed at Paris on 18 May 1904, and the International Convention for the Suppression of the White Slave Traffic, Signed at Paris on 4 May 1910	4 May 1949, Lake Success, New York	4 May 1949	4 May 1949	13	33		28 Dec 1949 (a)	12 May 1949

57	International Agreement for the Suppression of the White Slave Traffic, Signed at Paris on 18 May 1904, Amended by the Protocol Signed at Lake Success, New York, 4 May 1949	4 May 1949, Lake Success, New York	21 Jun 1951	21 Jun 1951				28 Dec 1949 (Definitive Signature of the Protocol, Succession to the Agreement and the Protocol, Acceptance of the Protocol)	
58	International Convention for the Suppression of the White Slave Traffic, Signed at Paris on 4 May 1910, Amended by the Protocol Signed at Lake Success, New York, 4 May 1949	4 May 1949, Lake Success, New York	14 Aug 1951	14 Aug 1951		53		28 Dec 1949 (Definitive signature of the Protocol, Acceptance of the Protocol, Succession to the Convention and the Protocol	
59	Convention for the Suppression of the Traffic in persons and of the Exploitation of the Prostitution of Others	21 Mar 1950, Lake Success, New York	25 Jul 1951	25 Jul 1951	24	78		9 Jan. 1953 (R)	9 May 1950
60	Final Protocol to the Convention for the Suppression of the Traffic in Persons and of the Exploitation of the Prostitution of Others	21 Mar 1950, Lake Success, New York	25 Jul 1951	25 Jul 1951	26	38		9 Jan. 1953 (R)	9 May 1950
61	Protocol to Amend the Convention for the Suppression of the Circulation of, and Traffic in, Obscene Publications, Concluded at Geneva on 12 September 1923	12 Nov 1947, Lake Success, New York	12 Nov 1947	2 Feb 1950	6	34		12 Nov 1947 (S)	
62	Convention for the Suppression of the Circulation of, and Traffic in, Obscene Publications, Concluded at Geneva on 12 September 1923 and Amended by the Protocol Signed	12 Nov 1947, Lake Success, New York	2 Feb 1950	2 Feb 1950		54		12 Nov 1947 (Definitive signature of the Protocol, Acceptance of the Protocol, Succession to the Convention and the Protocol)	

63	Protocol Amending the Agreement for the Suppression of the Circulation of Obscene Publications, signed at Paris, on 4 May 1910	4 May 1949, Lake Success, New York	4 May 1949	4 May 1949	15	35		28 Dec 1949 (a)	12 May 1949
64	Agreement for the Suppression of the Circulation of Obscene Publications, signed at Paris on 4 May 1910, Amended by the Protocol signed at Lake Success, New York, 4 May 1949	4 May 1949, New York	1 Mar 1950	1 Mar 1950		55		28 Dec 1949 (Definitive signature of the Protocol, Acceptance of the Protocol, Succession to the Agreement and the Protocol)	
65	Constitution of the WHO	22 Jul 1946, New York	7 Apr 1948	7 Apr 1948	59	190		12 Jan 1948 (a)	22 Jul 1946
66	Amendments to articles 24 and 25 of the Constitution of the WHO	28 May 1959, Geneva	25 Oct 1960	25 Oct 1960	59	190		23 Feb 1960 (a)	
67	Amendment to article 7 of the Constitution of the WHO	20 May 1965, Geneva	Not yet in Force			90		10 May 1966 (a)	
68	Amendments to articles 24 and 25 of the Constitution of the WHO	23 May 1967, Geneva	21 May 1975	21 May 1975	59	190		16 Mar 1971 (a)	
69	Amendments to articles 24 and 25 of the Constitution of the WHO	17 May 1976, Geneva	20 Jan 1984	20 Jan 1984	59	190		23 Jan 1978 (a)	
70	Amendment to article 74 of the Constitution of the WHO	18 May 1978, Geneva	Not yet in Force			91		2 Oct 2003 (a)	
71	Amendments to articles 24 and 25 of the Constitution of the WHO	12 May 1986, Geneva	11 Jul 1994	11 Jul 1994	59	190		12 Dec 1988 (a)	
72	Amendments to articles 24 and 25 of the Constitution of the WHO	16 May 1998, Geneva	Not yet in Force			116		2 Oct 2003 (a)	

73	Final Act of the International Health Conference, Arrangement concluded by the Governments represented at the Conference and Protocol Concerning the Office International D'Hygiene Publique	22 Jul 1946, New York	20 Oct 1947	20 Oct 1947	42	55		12 Jan 1948 (a)	22 Jul 1946
74	WHO Framework Convention on Tobacco Control	21 May 2003, Geneva	27 Feb 2005		168	49		5 Feb 2004 (R)	10 Sep 2003
75	Agreement establishing the African Development Bank done at Khartoum on 4 August 1963, as amended by resolution 05-79 adopted by the Board of Governors on 17 May 1979	7 May 1982, Lusaka	7 May 1982	7 May 1982	24	74		6 Dec 1983 (A)	25 Oct 1983 Signature by non-regional members under Section 3 (c) (i) of resolution 07-79
76	Agreement Establishing the Asian Development Bank	4 Dec 1965, Manila	22 Aug 1966	22 Aug 1966	30	46		20 Jul 1966 (R)	4 Dec 1965
77	Agreement Establishing the International Fund for Agricultural Development	13 Jun 1976, Rome	30 Nov 1977	30 Nov 1977	77	160		28 Mar 1977 (R)	21 Jan 1977
78	Constitution of the United Nations Industrial Development Organisation	8 Apr 1979, Vienna	21 Jun 1985	21 Jun 1985				21 Jan 1980 (R)	16 Nov 1979
79	Charter of the Asian and Pacific Development Centre	1 Apr 1982, Bangkok	1 Jul 1983	1 Jul 1983	3	17		25 Apr 1983 (S)	
80	Agreement to Establish the South Centre	1 Sep 1994, Geneva	30 Jul 1995	30 Jul 1995	39	32		13 Dec 1994 (R)	30 Sep 1994
81	International Convention to Facilitate the Importation of Commercial Samples and Advertising Material	7 Nov 1952, Geneva	20 Nov 1955	20 Nov 1955	6	63		3 Aug 1954 (A)	

82	Convention Concerning Customs Facilities for Touring	4 Jun 1954, New York	11 Sep 1957	11 Sep 1957	32	75		5 May 1958 (R)	30 Dec 1954
83	Additional Protocol to the Convention Concerning Customs Facilities for Touring, relating to the Importation of Tourist Publicity Documents and Material	4 Jun 1954, New York	28 Jun 1956	11 Sep 1957	25	70		15 Feb 1957 (A)	
84	Customs Convention on the Temporary Importation of Private Road Vehicles	4 Jun 1954, New York	15 Dec 1957	15 Dec 1957	32	77		5 May 1958 (R)	4 June 1954
85	Convention on Road Traffic	19 Sep 1949, Geneva	26 Mar 1952	26 Mar 1952	19	90		9 Mar 1962 (R)	19 Sep 1949
86	Protocol Concerning Countries or Territories at Present Occupied	19 Sep 1949, Geneva	26 Mar 1952	26 Mar 1952	17	19			19 Sep 1949
87	Protocol on Road Signs and Signals	19 Sep 1949, Geneva	20 Dec 1953	20 Dec 1953	14	37			29 Dec 1949
88	Convention on Road Signs and Signals	8 Nov 1968, Vienna	6 Jun 1978	6 Jun 1978	35	52		10 Mar 1980 (A)	
89	Intergovernmental Agreement on the Asian Highway Network	18 Nov 2003, Bangkok	Not Yet in Force		24	6			27 Apr 2004
90	Convention on the International Maritime Organisation (IMO)	6 Mar 1948, Geneva	17 Mar 1958	17 Mar 1958	24	164		6 Jan 1959 (a)	6 Mar 1948
91	Amendments to articles 17 and 18 of the Convention on the IMO	15 Sep 1964, London	6 Oct 1967	6 Oct 1967		164		17 Mar 1965 (a)	
92	Amendment to article 28 of the Convention on the IMO	28 Sep 1965, London	3 Nov 1968	3 Nov 1968		164		13 Oct 1966 (a)	
93	Amendments to articles 10, 16, 17, 18, 20, 28, 31 and 32 of the Convention on IMO	17 Oct 1974, London	1 Apr 1978	1 Apr 1978		164		16 Jan 1976 (a)	

94	Amendments to the title and substantive provisions of the Convention on the IMO	14 Nov 1975 and 9 Nov 1977, London	22 May 1982	22 May 1982		164		1 May 1978 (a)	
95	Amendments to the Convention on the IMO relating to the institutionalization of the Committee on Technical Co-operation in the Convention	17 Nov 1977, London	10 Nov 1984	10 Nov 1984		164		22 Jan 1979 (a)	
96	Amendments to articles 17, 18, 20 and 51 of the Convention on the IMO	15 Nov 1979, London	10 Nov 1984	10 Nov 1984		164		5 May 1980 (a)	
97	Amendments to the Convention on the IMO (institutionalization of the Facilitation Committee)	7 Nov 1991, London	Not yet in Force			87		31 Oct 1995 (a)	
98	Amendments to the Convention on the IMO	4 Nov 1993, London	7 Nov 2002	7 Nov 2002		164		28 Nov 1995 (a)	
99	Convention on a Code of Conduct for Liner Conference	6 Apr 1974, Geneva	6 Oct 1983	6 Oct 1983	22	78		14 Feb 1978 (R)	27 Jun 1975
100	Protocol Amending the International Convention Relating to Economic Statistics, Signed at Geneva on 14 December 1928	9 Dec 1948, Paris	9 Dec 1948	9 Dec 1948	8	19		14 Mar 1949 (a)	9 Dec 1948
101	International Convention Relating to Economic Statistics, Signed at Geneva on 14 December 1928, amended by the Protocol signed at Paris	9 Dec 1948, Paris	9 Oct 1950	9 Oct 1950		25		14 Mar 1949 (Definitive Signature or Acceptance of the Protocol	
102	International Convention for the Protection of Performers, Producers of Phonograms and Broadcasting Organizations	26 Oct 1961, Rome	18 May 1964	18 May 1964	26	79			26 Oct 1961
103	Convention for the Protection of Producers of Phonograms against Unauthorized Duplication of their Phonograms	29 Oct 1971, Geneva	18 Apr 1973	18 Apr 1973	32	73		1 Nov 1974 (R)	29 Oct 1971

104	International Agreement for the Establishment of the University for Peace	5 Dec 1980, New York	7 Apr 1981	7 Apr 1981		36		3 Dec 1981 (S)	
105	Statute of the International Centre for Genetic Engineering and Biotechnology	13 Sep 1983, Madrid	3 Feb 1994	3 Feb 1994	45	50		9 Jul 1985 (R)	13 Sep 1983
106	Protocol of the Reconvened Plenipotentiary Meeting on the Establishment of the International Centre for Genetic Engineering and Biotechnology	4 Apr 1984, Vienna	3 Feb 1994	3 Feb 1994	7	33		4 Apr 1984 (S)	
107	Convention on the Political Rights of women	31 Mar 1953, New York	7 Jul 1954	7 Jul 1954	47	118		1 Nov 1961 (R)	29 Apr 1953
108	Convention on the Nationality of Married Women	20 Feb 1957, New York	11 Aug 1958	11 Aug 1958	29	72			15 May 1957
109	Protocol Amending the Slavery Convention signed at Geneva on 25 Sep 1926	7 Dec 1953, New York	7 Dec 1953	7 Dec 1953	11	59		12 Mar 1954 (S)	
110	Slavery Convention, signed at Geneva on 25 September 1926 and Amended by the Protocol	7 Dec 1953, New York	7 Jul 1955	7 Jul 1955		95		12 Mar 1954 (Definitive signature or participation in the Convention and the Protocol)	
111	Supplementary Convention on the Abolition of Slavery, The Slave Trade, and Institutions and Practices similar to Slavery	7 Sep 1956, Geneva	30 Apr 1957	30 Apr 1957	35	119		23 Jun 1960 (R)	7 Sep 1956
112	International Convention against the Taking of Hostages	17 Dec 1979, New York	3 Jun 1983	3 Jun 1983	39	145		7 Sep 1994 (A)	
113	Convention on the Prevention and Punishment of Crimes against Internationally Protected Person, Including Diplomatic Agents	14 Dec 1973, New York	20 Feb 1977	20 Feb 1977	25	153		11 Apr 1978 (A)	
114	International Convention for the Suppression of Terrorist Bombings	15 Dec 1997, New York	23 May 2001	23 May 2001	58	132		22 Sep 1999 (R)	17 Sep 1999

115	International Convention for the Suppression of the Financing of Terrorism	9 Dec 1999, New York	10 Apr 2002	10 Apr 2002	132	132		22 Apr 2003 (R)	8 Sep 2000
116	UN's Convention Against Transnational Organized Crime	15 Nov 2000, New York	29 Sep 2003	29 Sep 2003	147	97			12 Dec 2002
117	Protocol to prevent, Suppress and Punish Trafficking in Persons, Especially Women and Children, Supplementing the UN's Convention against Transnational Organized Crime	15 Nov 2000, New York	25 Dec 2003	25 Dec 2003	117	77			12 Dec 2002
118	Protocol against the Smuggling of Migrants by Land Sea and Air, Supplementing the UN's Convention against Transnational Organized Crime	15 Nov 2000, New York	28 Jan, 2004		112	65			12 Dec 2002
119	Protocol Against the Illicit Manufacturing of and Trafficking in Firearms, Their Parts and Components and Ammunition, supplementing the UN's Convention against Transnational Organized Crime	31 May 2001, New York	Not Yet in Force		52	31			12 Dec 2002
120	Agreement Establishing the Asian Coconut Community	12 Dec 1968, Bangkok	30 Jul 1969	30 Jul 1969	6	11		18 Jun 1969 (R)	12 Dec 1968
121	Agreement Establishing the International Pepper Community	16 Apr 1971, Bangkok	29 Mar 1972	29 Mar 1972	3	5		29 Mar 1972 (R)	21 Apr 1971
122	Agreement Establishing the Asian Rice Trade Fund	16 Mar 1973, Bangkok	1 Dec 1974	1 Dec 1974	5	4		28 Nov 1974 (a)	29 Jun 1973
123	Agreement Establishing the International Tea Promotion Association	31 Mar 1977, Geneva	23 Feb 1979	23 Feb 1979	6	8		1 Nov 1977 (R)	20 Jul 1977
124	Agreement Establishing the Common Fund for Commodities	27 Jun 1980, Geneva	19 Jun 1989	19 Jun 1989	115	110		22 Dec 1981 (a\)	18 Sep 1981
125	Terms of Reference of the International Copper Study Group	24 Feb 1989, Geneva	23 Jan 1992	23 Jan 1992		23		30 Jul 1997 (Definitive Acceptance)	

126	International Sugar Agreement, 1992	20 Mar 1992, Geneva	Provisionally on 20 Jan 1993	20 Jan 1993	22	49	19 Jan 1993 (n)	20 Jan 1993 (R)	31 Dec 1992
127	International Tropical Timber Agreement, 1994	26 Jan 1994, Geneva	Provisionally on 1 Jan 1997	1 Jan 1997	49	60		17 Oct 1996 (R)	17 Sep 1996
128	Grains Trade Convention, 1995	7 Dec 1994, London	1 Jul 1995	1 Jul 1995	15	27		27 Jun 1995 (R)	22 Jun 1995
129	International Coffee Agreement, 2001	28 Sep 2000, London	Provisionally on 1 Oct 2001	1 Oct 2001	35	60		10 Sep 2001 (R)	10 Aug 2001
130	Agreement Establishing the Terms of Reference of the International Jute Study Group, 2001	13 Mar 2001	Not Yet in Force			4		25 Apr 2002 (Definitive Acceptance)	
131	United Nations Convention on the Law of the Sea	10 Dec 1982, Montego Bay	16 Nov 1994	16 Nov 1994	157	147		29 Jun 1995 (R)	10 Dec 1982
132	Agreement relating to the implementation of Part XI of the UN's Convention on the Law of the Sea of 10 December 1982	28 Jul 1994, New York	Provisionally on 16 Nov 1994	16 Nov 1994	79	119	16 Nov 1994	29 Jun 1995 (R)	29 Jul 1994
133	Agreement for the Implementation of the Provisions of the United Nations Convention on the Law of the Sea of 10 December 1982 relating to the Conservation and Management of Straddling Fish Stocks and Highly Migratory Fish Stocks	4 Aug 1995, New York	11 Dec 2001	11 Dec 2001	59	52		19 Aug 2003 (A)	
134	Convention on the Recognition and Enforcement of Foreign Arbitral Awards	10 Jun 1958, New York	7 Jun 1959	7 Jun 1959	24	135		13 Jul 1960 (R)	10 Jun 1958
135	Convention on Registration of Objects Launched into outer Space	12 Nov 1974, New York	15 Sep 1976	15 Sep 1976	25	45		18 Jan 1982 (A)	
136	Agreement Governing the Activities of States on the Moon and Other Celestial Bodies	5 Dec 1979, New York	11 Jul 1984	11 Jul 1984	11	11			18 Jan 1982
137	Constitution of the Asia-Pacific Telecommunity	27 Mar 1976, Bangkok	25 Feb 1979	25 Feb 1979	18	35		26 Nov 1976 (R)	28 Oct 1976

138	Amendment to article 11, Paragraph 2 (a), of the Constitution of the Asia-Pacific Telecommunity	13 Nov 1981, Bangkok	2 Jan 1985	2 Jan1985		19		15 Jul 1983 (R)	
139	Agreement Establishing the Asia-Pacific Institute for Broadcasting Development	12 Aug 1977, Kuala Lumpur	6 Mar 1981	6 Mar 1981	14	26		25 Feb 1986 (R)	20 May 1980
140	Tampere Convention on the Provision of Telecommunication Resources for Disaster Mitigation and Relief Operations	18 Jun 1998, Tampere	8 Jan 2005		60	30		29 Nov 1999 (R)	29 Nov 1999
141	Convention on the Prohibition of Military or any other Hostile Use of Environmental Modification Techniques	10 Dec 1976, New York	5 Oct 1978	5 Oct 1978	48	69		15 Dec 1978 (R)	15 Dec 1977
142	Convention on Prohibitions or Restrictions on the Use of Certain Conventional Weapons which may be deemed to be Excessively Injurious or to have Indiscriminate Effects (with Protocols I, II and III)	10 Oct 1980, Geneva	2 Dec 1983	2 Dec 1983	50	97		1 Mar 1984 (R)	15 May 1981
143	Additional Protocol to the Convention on Prohibitions or Restrictions on the Use of Certain Conventional Weapons which may be deemed to be Excessively Injurious or to have Indiscriminate Effects (with Protocol IV, entitled Protocol on Blinding Laser Weapons)	13 Oct 1995, Vienna	30 Jul 1998	30 Jul 1998		79		2 Sep 1999 (P)	
144	Protocol on Prohibitions or Restrictions on the Use of Mines, Booby-Traps and Other Devices as amended on 3 May 1996 (Protocol II as amended on 3 May 1996) annexed to the Convention on Prohibitions or Restrictions on the Use of Certain Conventional Weapons which may be deemed to be Excessively Injurious or to have Indiscriminate Effects	3 May 1996, Geneva	3 Dec 1998	3 Dec 1998		80		2 Sep 1999 (P)	

145	Convention on the Prohibition of the Development, Production, Stockpiling and Use of Chemical Weapons and on their Destruction	3 Sep 1992, Geneva	29 Apr 1997	29 Apr 1997	165	167		3 Sep 1996 (R)	14 Jan 1993
146	Vienna Convention for the Protection of the Ozone Layer	22 Mar 1985, Vienna	22 Sep 1988	22 Sep 1988	28	189		18 Mar 1991 (A)	
147	Montreal Protocol on Substances that Deplete the Ozone Layer	16 Sep 1987, Montreal	1 Jan 1989	1 Jan 1989	46	188		19 Jun 1992 (A)	
148	Amendment to the Montreal Protocol on Substances that Deplete the Ozone Layer	29 Jun 1990, London	10 Aug 1992	10 Aug 1992		175		19 Jun 1992 (A)	
149	Amendment to the Montreal Protocol on Substances that Deplete the Ozone Layer	25 Nov 1992, Copenhagen	14 Jun 1994	14 Jun 1994		164		3 Mar 2003 (A)	
150	Amendment to the Montreal Protocol on Substances that Deplete the Ozone Layer adopted by the Ninth Meeting of the Parties	17 Sep 1997, Montreal	10 Nov 1999	10 Nov 1999		124		3 Mar 2003 (A)	
151	Amendment to the Montreal Protocol on Substances that Deplete the Ozone Layer	3 Dec 1999, Beijing	25 Feb 2002	25 Feb 2002		86		3 Mar 2003 (A)	
152	Basal Convention on the Control of Transboundary Movements of Hazardous Wastes and Their Disposal	22 Mar 1989, Basel	5 May 1992	5 May 1992	53	163		24 Jun 1992 (R)	15 Mar 1990
153	United Nations Framework Convention on Climate Change	9 May 1992, New York	21 Mar 1994	21 Mar 1994	165	189		1 Nov 1993 (R)	10 Jun 1992
154	Kyoto Protocol to the United Nations Framework Convention on Climate Change	11 Dec 1997, Kyoto	16 Feb 2005		84	133		26 Aug 2002 (A)	
155	Convention on Biological Diversity	5 Jun 1992 Rio de Janeiro	29 Dec 1993	29 Dec 1993	168	188		18 Feb 1994	5 Jun 1992

156	Cartagena Protocol on Biosafety to the Convention on Biological Diversity	29 Jan 2000, Montreal	11 Sep 2003	11 Sep 2003	103	111		17 Jan 2003 (R)	23 Jan 2001
157	United Nations Convention to Combat Desertification in those Countries Experiencing Serious Drought And/Or Desertification, Particularly in Africa	14 Oct 1994, Paris	26 Dec 1996	26 Dec 1996	115	191		17 Dec 1996 (R)	14 Oct 1994
158	Stockholm Convention on Persistent Organic Pollutants	22 May 2001, Stockholm	17 May 2004	17 May 2004	151	89			14 May 2002
159	Multilateral Convention for the Avoidance of Double Taxation of Copyright Royalties	13 Dec 1979, Madrid	Not Yet In Force		3	7		31 Jan 1983 (A)	
160	Convention and Statute on the Regime of Navigable Waterways of International Concern	20 Apr 1921, Barcelona	31 Oct 1922	8 Oct 1921				26 Mar 1956 (Denunciation)	
161	Additional Protocol to the Convention on the Regime of Navigable Waterways of International Concern	20 Apr 1921, Barcelona	31 Oct 1922	8 Oct 1921				26 Mar 1956 (Denunciation)	
162	Convention Establishing an International Relief Union	12 Jul 1927, Geneva	27 Dec 1932	27 Dec 1932				9 Nov 1950 (Notification of withdrawal from the International Relief Union)	

HUMAN RIGHTS PROVISIONS IN THE UN DOCUMENTS AND IN THE CONSTITUTION AND LAWS OF INDIA*

No.	Provisions in UN Documents	Provisions in the Constitution of India and/or Central Act, if any
(1)	(2)	(3)
1.	All human beings are born free and equal in dignity and rights and should act in a spirit of brotherhood. (*Universal Declaration of Human Rights* 1948, art. 1)	Preamble and Article 51A (e)
2.	Prohibition of discrimination on grounds of race, colour, sex, language, religion, political or other opinion; national or social origin, property, birth or other status; special measures taken for purpose of securing advancement of certain social or ethnic groups requiring such protection not to be deemed social discrimination. (*Universal Declaration of Human Rights*, Article 2; *Declaration of the Rights of the Child*, 1959, principle 1; *International Convention on the Elimination of All Forms of Racial Discrimination*, 1966, Articles 1(4), 2 and 5; *International Covenant on Civil and Political Rights*, 1966, Articles 24 and 26; and *International Covenant on Economic, Social and Cultural Rights*, 1966 Article 2(2).)	Articles 15, 16 and 17; Protection of Civil Rights Act, 1955; Untouchability (Offences) Act, 1955/ Protection of Civil Rights Act 1955 (1976).**
3.	Right to life, liberty and security of person; deprivation of liberty to be only on such grounds and in accordance with such procedure as may be established by law; right to seek pardon or commutation of sentence of death; sentence of death not to be imposed for crimes committed by persons below 18 years of age and not to be carried out	Article 21; Indian Penal Code, 1860, section 54; Code of Criminal Procedure 1973, sections 416, 432-434.

* Reproduced from Subhash C. Kashyap, *Human Rights and Parliament,* Metropolitan, New Delhi, 1978 with necessary updates.

** The Untouchability (Offences) Act, 1955 was amended to be named Protection of Civil Rights Act 1955 with effect from 19 November 1976.

Bimal N. Patel (ed.), **India and International Law, 363-379.**

	woman. (*Universal Declaration of Human Rights,* Article 3; *International Covenant on Civil and Political Rights,* Articles 6 and 9)	
4.	Freedom from slavery or servitude, and cruel, inhuman or degrading treatment; prohibition of slave trade, of traffic in women and children, and of forced or compulsory labour. (*Universal Declaration of Human Rights,* Articles 4 and 5; *Declaration of the Rights of the Child,* principle 9; *International Covenant on Civil and Political Rights,* Articles 7 and 8; *Declaration on Elimination of Discrimination against Women,* 1967, Article 8; *Supplementary Convention on the Abolition of Slavery, the Slave Trade, and Institutions and Practices Similar to Slavery,* 1956; *Convention Concerning the Abolition of Forced Labour,* 1957.	Articles 17, 23 and 51A (e); Indian Penal Code, section 370; Untouchability (Offences) Act, 1955/Protection of Civil Rights Act 1955 (1976); Suppression of Immoral Traffic in Women and Girls Act 1956; Bonded Labour System (Abolition) Act, 1976.
5.	Equality before the law and equal protection of law; equality before the law in the enjoyment of the right of access to any place or service intended for use by general public, such as transport, hotels, restaurant, cafes, theatres and parks; equality of opportunity and treatment in respect of employment and occupation. (*Universal Declaration of Human Rights,* Articles 6 and 7; *Discrimination (Employment and Occupation) Convention,* 1958, Article 2; *International Convention on Elimination of All Forms of Racial Discrimination,* Article 5; and *International Covenant on Civil and Political Rights,* Article 26).	Articles 14, 15, 16 and 39A; Protection of Civil Rights Act, 1955.
6.	Right to an effective remedy to protect fundamental rights granted by Constitution or law. (*Universal Declaration of Human Rights,* Article 8; *International Covenant on Civil and Political Rights,* Article 2(3)).	Articles 32, 39A, 226 and 227.
7.	Protection against arbitrary arrest, detention or exile (*Universal Declaration of Human Rights,* Article 9; and *International Covenant on Civil and Political Rights,* Articles 6(1) and 9).	Article 22; Code of Criminal Procedure, sections 49, 50, 56, 57.

8.	Right to a fair and public hearing by a competent, independent and impartial tribunal in determination of rights and obligations and of any criminal charge against an individual (*Universal Declaration of Human Rights,* Article 10; *International Covenant on Elimination of All Forms of Racial Discrimination,* Article 5 (a); and *International Covenant on Civil and Political Rights,* Article 14(1)).	Article 50; Part V, Chapter IV; Part IV, Chapters V and VI; Code of Criminal Procedure, sections 55. 303, 304, 310, 327, 461, 479 etc.
9.	Right to be presumed innocent until proved guilty; prohibition of retroactive penal laws and of double jeopardy (*Universal Declaration of Human Rights,* Article 11; and *International Covenant on Civil and Political Rights,* Articles 14(1) and (2) and 15(1)).	Articles 20 and 22; Code of Criminal Procedure, section 300.
10.	Right to certain minimum guarantees in determination of criminal charge against an individual; procedure in case of juvenile persons to be such as takes account of their age and promotes their rehabilitation; right to one's conviction and sentence being reviewed by a higher tribunal. (*International Covenant on Civil and Political Rights,* Article 14(3), (4) and (5)).	Code of Criminal Procedure, 1973; Probation of Offenders Act, 1958.
11.	Protection against arbitrary interference with privacy, family, home or correspondence, and against unlawful attacks on honour and reputation (*Universal Declaration of Human Rights,* Article 12; *International Covenant on Civil and Political Rights,* Article 17).	Article 21 (as interpreted in *Kharak Singh's Case,* AIR 1963 SC 1295); Indian Penal Code, 1860, sections 441, 447, 499-503.
12.	Right to freedom of movement and residence within a State; right to leave any country, including one's own, and to return to one's country (*Universal Declaration of Human Rights,* Article 13; and *International Covenant on Civil and Political Rights,* Article 12).	Article 19(1) (d) and (e) and Article 21 as interpreted in the Passport Case (*Satwant Singh vs. Regional Passport Officer, New Delhi,* AIR 1967 SC 1836).

13.	Right to nationality; prohibition against arbitrary deprivation of nationality and right to change it; Right of the child to a name and a nationality from birth; Women to have the same rights as men to acquire, change or retain their nationality; marriage to an alien not to automatically affect nationality of wife (*Universal Declaration of Human Rights,* Article 15; *Declaration of the Rights of the Child,* principle 3; *Declaration of Elimination of Discrimination against Women,* Article 5).	Citizenship Act, 1955.
14.	Right to marriage and to found a family; marriage with free and full consent of intending spouses; family to be protected by society and State; equality of rights and responsibilities of spouses as to marriage, during marriage, and at its dissolution; Prohibition of Child marriage and betrothal of young girls before puberty; specification of a minimum age for marriage, compulsory registration of marriages (*Universal Declaration of Human Rights,* Article 16; *Declaration on Elimination of Discrimination against Women,* Article 6 (2) and (3); *International Covenant on Elimination of All Forms of Racial Discrimination,* Article 5; *International Covenant on Economic, Social and Cultural Rights,* Article 10(1)).	Hindu Widows' Remarriage Act, 1856; Indian Christian Marriage Act, 1909; Parsi Marriage and Divorce Act, 1936; Dissolution of Muslim Marriages Act, 1939; Arya Marriage Validation Act, 1937; Special Marriage Act, 1954; Hindu Marriage Act, 1955; Dowry Prohibition Act, 1961; Foreign Marriage Act, 1969; Child Marriage Restraint Act, 1929; Indian Penal Code, ss. 366, 493-498.
15.	Right to own property, and protection from arbitrary deprivation; Women to be ensured equal rights with men in civil law and in particular the right to acquire, administer, enjoy, dispose of, and inherit property (*Universal Declaration of Human Rights,* Article 17; and *Declaration on Elimination of Discrimination against Women,* Article 6(1) (a)).	Article 300A; Requisitioning and Acquisition of Immovable Property Act, 1952; Married Women's Property Act, 1874; Married Women's Property (Extension) Act, 1959; and Hindu Succession Act, 1956.

16.	Right to freedom of thought, conscience and religion including freedom to manifest religion in teaching, practice, worship and observance; right of ethnic, religious or linguistic minorities to profess and practice their own religion (*Universal Declaration of Human Rights,* Article 18; and *International Covenant on Civil and Political Rights,* Articles 18 and 27).	Articles 19, 25, 26, 29 and 30; Indian Penal Code, ss. 295-298.
17	Right to freedom of opinion and expression, Right to freedom of peaceful assembly and association, prohibition against compulsion to belong to an association (*Universal Declaration of Human Rights,* Articles 19 and 20; and *International Covenant on Civil and Political Rights,* Articles 19 and 21).	Article 19(1) (a), (b) and (c); the Trade Unions Act, 1926.
18	Right to take part in government of one's country right of equal access to public services; expression of people's will in free, universal and equal suffrage by periodic elections to be the basis of Government; Right of Women, on equal terms with men, to vote and to stand for elections, to hold public office, and to exercise public functions (*Universal Declaration of Human Rights,* Article 21; *Convention on Political Rights of Women 1953,* Articles I, II and III; *Declaration on Elimination of Discrimination against Women,* Article 4; *International Covenant on Civil and Political Rights,* Articles 1 and 25; *International Covenant on Economic, Social and Cultural Rights,* Article 1).	Preamble, Articles 16, 55, 56, 58, 62, 66, 67, 83, 84, 172, 173, 326; Representation of the People Act, 1950; Representation of the People Act, 1951; Representation of the People (Miscellaneous Provisions) Act, 1956; Presidential and Vice-Presidential Elections Act, 1952; Union Territories (Direct Election to the House of the People) Act, 1965; Parliament (Prevention of Disqualifications) Act, 1959.
19.	Right to social security, to realisation of economic, social and cultural rights indispensable to one's dignity and development of personality (*Universal Declaration of Human Rights,* Article 18; and *International Covenant on Economic, Social and Cultural Rights,* Article 9).	Preamble

20.	Right to work, to free choice of employment, to just and favourable conditions of work, and to protection against unemployment; Right to equal remuneration for men and women for work of equal value; Right to just and favourable remuneration; Right to form and join trade unions for protection of one's interests. (*Universal Declaration of Human Rights,* Article 23; *Convention concerning Equal Remuneration for Men and Women Workers for works of Equal Value,* Article 2; *International Covenant on Civil and Political Rights,* Article 22(1) and (2); *International Covenant on Economic, Social and Cultural Rights,* Articles 7 and 8(1) (a)).	Articles 16, 19, 39, 41, 42, 43 and 43A; Workmen's Compensation Act, 1923; Trade Unions Act, 1926; Industrial Employment (Standing Orders) Act, 1946; Mica Mines Labour Welfare Fund Act, 1946; Coal Mines Labour Welfare Fund Act, 1947; Industrial Disputes Act, 1947; the Factories Act, 1948; the Dock Workers (Regulation of Employment) Act, 1948; Employees State Insurance Act, 1948; Minimum Wages Act, 1948; Mines Act ,1952; The Employees Provident Funds and Miscellaneous Provisions Act, 1952; Apprentices Act, 1961; Motor Transport Workers Act, 1961; Iron Ore Mines Labour Welfare Cess Act, 1961; Equal Remuneration Act, 1976; The Payment of Wages Act, 1936.
21.	Right to rest and leisure, including limitation of working hours and periodic holidays with pay (*Universal Declaration of Human Rights,* Article 24; *International Covenant on Civil and Political Rights,* Article 7).	Article 43; Weekly Holidays Act, 1942; the Coal Mines Labour Welfare Act, 1947; Industrial Employment (Standing Orders) Act, 1946.
22.	Right to an adequate standard of living and right to security in the event of unemployment, sickness, disability, widowhood, old age or other lack of livelihood; Maternity and Child Welfare – Prevention of dismissal of Women on account of marriage or maternity leave and necessary social services; Protection of children and young persons from economic and social exploitation; child not to be admitted to employment before an appropriate minimum age and not to be caused or permitted to engage in any occupation or employment interfering with his physical, mental and moral development; Duty of society and public authorities to extend particular care to children without a family and to those without adequate means of support; special treatment, education and care to be given to a physically, mentally or socially handicapped child (*Universal Declaration of Human Rights,* Article 25;	Articles 24, 39, 41, 42 and 47; Children (Pledging of Labour) Act, 1933; Employment of Children Act, 1938; Mines-Maternity Benefit Act, 1941; Employees State Insurance Act, 1948; Plantations Labour Act, 1951; Orphanages and other Charitable Homes (Supervision and Control) Act, 1960; Children Act, 1960; Maternity Benefit Act, 1961; Personal Injuries (Compensation Insurance) Act, 1963; the Factories Act, 1948; Workmen's Compensation Act, 1923; Mica Mines Labour Welfare Fund Act, 1947; Coal Mines Provident Fund and Miscellaneous Provisions Act, 1948; Employment of Children Act, 1938; the Mines Act, 1952; the Apprentices Act, 1961; Dock Workers (Regulation of Employment) Act, 1948; Local Authorities Pensions and Gratuities Act, 1919; Employers' Liability Act, 1938.

	on Elimination of Discrimination against Women, Article 10; *International Covenant on Economic, Social and Cultural Rights,* Articles 10 and 11 (1)).	
23.	Right to education – elementary education to be free and compulsory; technical, professional and higher education to be made available on merit; Education for full development of human personality, strengthening of respect for human rights and to further activities of U.N. for maintenance of peace; Prior right of parents to choose the kind of education for their children; freedom of individuals and bodies to establish direct educational institutions subject to certain requirements; Girls and Women to be ensured equal rights with men in education (*Universal Declaration of Human Rights,* Article 26; *Declaration of the Rights of the Child,* principle 7; *Declaration on Elimination of Discrimination against Women,* Article 9; *International Covenant on Economic, Social and Cultural Rights,* Articles 13 and 14).	Articles 15, 21A, 28, 30, 45, 46, 51 and 51A(k); Delhi Primary Education Act, 1960.
24.	Right to freely participate in the cultural life of the community; to enjoy arts and to share in scientific advancement and its benefits; Right to protection of moral and material interests resulting to an author from his scientific, literary or artistic production; Right of ethnic, religious or linguistic minorities to enjoy their own culture and to use their own language (*Universal Declaration of Human Rights,* Article 27; *International Covenant on Civil and Political Rights,* Articles 2(1) and 27).	Articles 29 and 39; Designs Act, 1911; Copy-right Act, 1957; Patents Act, 1970.
25.	Duties of everyone to community, Limitations in exercise of rights and freedoms only for securing due recognition and respect for rights and freedoms of others and for morality; public order and general Welfare (*Universal Declaration of Human Rights,* Article 29; *International Covenant on Civil and Political Rights,* Articles 12, 18, 19, 21 and 22).	Articles 19(2) to (6), 23(2), 25(1), 26(1), 31C, 33 and 51A.

ANNEX II

List of Court Cases in Environmental Matters

1. *Buffalo Traders' Welfare Association vs. Maneka Gandhi,* (18.05.94), 1994 Supp (3) SCC 448: Slaughter House Idgah, Delhi

2. *Akhil Bharat Goseva Sangh vs. State of Andhra Pradesh,* (25.10.94), 1995 Supp (1) SCC: Establishment of abattoir at Rudraram, Andhra Pradesh

3. *M.C. Mehta vs. Union of India,* (3.12.93), 1994 Supp (3) SCC 717: Air Pollution caused by industries in Uttar Pradesh

4. *M.C. Mehta vs. Union of India,* (30.12.96), 1997 (1) Scale 61: Preservation of Taj

5. *M.C. Mehta vs. Union of India,* (9.5.96), 1996 (4) Scale (SP) 70: Lead free petrol in metropolitan cities

6. *M.C. Mehta vs. Union of India,* (29.3.96), 1996 (4) Scale (SP) 10: Pollution by stone crushers

7. *M.C. Mehta vs. Union of India,* (13.3.96), 1996 (4) Scale (SP) 4: Pollution of Agra due to diesel generating sets

8. *S. Jagannathan vs. Union of India,* (9.5.95), 1995 (5) Scale 208 (1): Pollution by aqua farms in coastal States and Union Territories

9. *S. Jagannathan vs. Union of India,* (9.5.95), 1995 (3) Scale 737: Pollution of coastal areas by aqua farms

10. *Vellore Citizens Welfare Forum vs. Union of India,* (28.8.96), 1996 AIR (SC) 2715: Right to clean environment

11. *M.C. Mehta vs. Union of India,* (30.12.96), 1997 (1) Scale 61: Compensation to workmen in case of closure of air polluting industry

12. *M.C. Mehta vs. Union of India,* (15.7.96), 1996 (5) Scale (SP) 14(1): Entitlement to wages to workers during closure of industry pending installation of pollution control devices

13. *S. Jagannanth vs. Union of India,* (11.12.96), 1997(2) SCC 87: Coastal pollution due to shrimp farming

14. *Indian Council for Enviro-Legal Action vs. Union of India,* (18.4.96), 1996 (5) SCC 281: Non-compliance of notification issued by Government on coastal pollution

15. *Indian Council for Enviro-Legal Action vs. Union of India,* (13.2.96), 1996 AIR (SC) 1446: Damages for damage caused by industrial pollution

16. *Ajay Singh Rawat vs. Union of India,* (9.3.95), 1995(3) SCC 266: Degradation of the natural lake of Nainital

17. *M.C. Mehta vs. Union of India,* (11.10.96), 1996(7) Scale 579: Protection of lakes around Delhi by banning construction activities around such lakes

18. *Pradeep Krishen vs. Union of India,* (10.5.96), 1996 AIR (SC) 2040: Declaration of Sanctuaries/ National Parks – Failure to protect these parks

19. *Pradeep D. Prabhu vs. State of Maharashtra,* (07.03.95), 1995 Supp (3) SCC 450: Housing – Forest Land

20. *T.N. Godavarman Thirzumulkpad vs. Union of India,* (12.12.96), 1996: Non Forest Activities – Running Saw Mills

21. *M.C. Mehta vs. Union of India,* (07.08.96), 1996: Ganga Action Plan

22. *F.B. Taraporawal vs. Bayer India Ltd.,* (09.09.96), 1996: Right to life – threat by hazardous industries

23. *M.C. Mehta vs. Union of India,* (15.03.96), 1996: Hazardous industries in West Bengal

24. *M.C. Mehta vs. Union of India,* (15.03.96), 1996: Hazardous industries in Delhi

25. *Indian Council for Enviro-Legal Action vs. Union of India,* (13.2.96), 1996 AIR (SC) 1446: 1996: Industrial Pollution

26. *Indian Council for Enviro-Legal Action vs. Union of India,* (13.2.96), 1996 AIR (SC) 1446: 1996: Industrial Pollution – Establishment of industries

27. *Indian Council for Enviro-Legal Action vs. Union of India,* (13.2.96), 1996 AIR (SC) 1446: 1996: Industrial Pollution – Damage to the environment by Hazardous Activities

28. *Indian Council for Enviro-Legal Action vs. Union of India,* (13.2.96), 1996 AIR (SC) 1446: 1996: Industrial Pollution – Environment audit

29. *Indian Council for Enviro-Legal Action vs. Union of India,* (13.2.96), 1996 AIR (SC) 1446: 1996: Industrial Pollution – Damage to Environment caused by Hazardous activities

30. *Indian Council for Enviro-Legal Action vs. Union of India,* (16.7.96), 1996 AIR (SC) 1446: 1996: Industrial Pollution – Compensation for pollution

31. *M.C. Mehta vs. Union of India,* (28.2.96): Industrial Pollution – pollution by hazardous industry in Delhi

32. *M.C. Mehta vs. Union of India,* (14.2.96), 1996: Industrial Pollution – pollution by hazardous industry in Delhi

33. *M.C. Mehta vs. Union of India,* (23.2.96), 1996: Industrial Pollution – foundries

34. *Vellore Citizens Welfare Forum vs. Union of India,* (19.2.96), 1996: Industrial Pollution – Pollution by tanneries

35. *M.C. Mehta vs. Union of India,* (08.07.96), 1996: Industrial Pollution – Hazardous industries

36. *M.C. Mehta vs. Union of India,* (13.3.96), 1996: Industrial Pollution in Delhi – Revocation of hazardous industries

37. *D.P. Bhattacharya vs. West Bengal Pollution Control Board,* (21.03.96), 1996: Industrial Pollution – hazardous industries and residential area

38. *M.C. Mehta vs. Union of India,* (24.4.96), 1996: Industrial Pollution – Hazardous industries removal

39. *M.C. Mehta vs. Union of India,* (26.04.96), 1996: Industrial Pollution – West Bengal

40. *Indian Council for Enviro-Legal Action vs. Union of India,* (10.5.96): Industrial Pollution – Andhra Pradesh

41. *M.C. Mehta vs. Union of India,* (06.02.96), 1996: Industrial Pollution – Direction to Pollution Control Board

42. *M.C. Mehta vs. Union of India,* (02.02.96), 1996: Industrial Pollution – Direction to Pollution Control Board

43. *F.M. Yamuna vs. Central Pollution Control Board,* (14.03.96): Industrial Pollution at Sonepat

44. *Hariram Patidar vs. Madhya Pradesh Pollution Control Board,* (18.03.96), 1996: Industrial Pollution in Madhya Pradesh

45. *M. C. Mehta vs. Union of India,* (14.03.96), 1996: Industrial Pollution – Pollution at Delhi (CETP)

46. *M.C. Mehta vs. Union of India,* (29.03.96), 1996: Industrial Pollution – Pollution in Bihar and West Bengal

47. *World Saviors vs. Union of India,* (13.03.96): Industrial Pollution – Installation of APCs

48. *M.C. Mehta vs. Union of India,* (10.05.96), 1996: Industrial Pollution – Hazardous industries in Tamil Nadu

49. *Vellore Citizens Welfare Forum vs. Union of India,* (28.8.96): Industrial Pollution – Hazardous industries in Delhi

50. *Textile Processors Association vs. Chief Secretary, State of Gujarat,* (04.01.96), 1996: Industrial Pollution – Direction for closures

51. *M.C. Mehta vs. Union of India,* (09.05.96), 1996: Air Pollution – Lead free petrol in metropolitan cities

52. *M.C. Mehta vs. Union of India,* (07.08.96), 1996: Mathura Refinery – setting up of Hospital

53. *Wasim Ahmed Saeed vs. Union of India,* (06.08.96), 1996: Monuments – preservation

54. *M.C. Mehta vs. Union of India,* (24.03.95), 1995: Industrial Pollution in Delhi

55. *M.C. Mehta vs. Union of India,* (30.01.96), 1997: Pollution – Burden of proof

56. *Rorokola Shramik Sangh vs. Union of India,* (04.04.96), 1996: Pollution – Equipment to control

57. *M.C. Mehta vs. Union of India,* (04.04.96), 1996: Pollution – Taj

58. *Vellore Citizens Welfare Forum vs. Union of India,* (26.04.96), 1996: Industrial Pollution – Tannery industries in Tamil Nadu

59. *Vellore Citizens Welfare Forum vs. Union of India,* (06.05.96), 1996: Industrial Pollution – Tannery industries in Tamil Nadu

60. *Vellore Citizens Welfare Forum vs. Union of India,* (09.04.96), 1996: Industrial Pollution – Tannery industries in Tamil Nadu

61. *M.C. Mehta vs. Union of India,* (12.01.96), 1996: Pollution by stone crushers

62. *M.C. Mehta vs. Union of India,* (10.05.96), 1996: Pollution by stone crushers (Haryana)

63. *M.C. Mehta vs. Union of India,* 1996: Pollution in Agra

64. *M.C. Mehta vs. Union of India,* (13.03.96), 1996: Pollution in Agra

65. *M.C. Mehta vs. Union of India,* (13.03.96), 1996: Pollution in Agra

66. *M.C. Mehta vs. Union of India,* (23.02.96), 1996: Pollution in Agra

67. *M.C. Mehta vs. Union of India,* (10.04.96), 1996: Pollution – Mathura refinery

68. *M.C. Mehta vs. Union of India,* (02.02.96), 1996: Pollution in Agra

69. *M.C. Mehta vs. Union of India,* (01.03.96), 1996: Pollution in Delhi – construction of CETPs

70. *M.C. Mehta vs. Union of India,* (30.12.96), 1997: Doctrines Precautionary Principle – Polluter pays principle

71. *M.C. Mehta vs. Union of India,* (15.03.96), 1996: Preservation of Taj Mahal

72. *Indian Council for Enviro-Legal Action vs. Union of India,* (09.03.95), 1995: Coastal regulation zone – Restriction/prohibition

73. *Indian Council for Enviro-Legal Action vs. Union of India,* (12.12.94), 1995: Protection of coastal areas

74. *M.C. Mehta vs. Union of India,* (30.12.96), 1997: Service Law – Wages – Quantum of – Deterinination of Shifting of Air Polluting Industries

75. *M.C. Mehta vs. Union of India,* (30.12.96), 1997: Relocation of air polluting industries

76. *M.C. Mehta vs. Union of India,* (30.12.96), 1996: Service Law – Wages – Quantum of – Deterinination of - Shifting of Air pollution industries

77. *M.C. Mehta vs. Union of India,* (26.07.96), 1996: Protection of Ridge Area – Removal of encroachments

78. *M.C. Mehta vs. Union of India,* (30.08.96), 1996: Protection of Ridge Area – Removal of encroachments

79. *M.C. Mehta vs. Union of India,* (12.07.96), 1996: Ridge Area – Badkhal lake and Surajkund

80. *M.C. Mehta vs. Union of India,* (03.04.96), 1996: Ridge area

81. *M.C. Mehta vs. Union of India,* (12.03.96), 1996: Ridge area – pollution in Delhi

82. *M.C. Mehta vs. Union of India,* (20.04.96), 1996: Ridge area – Depletion of Ridge forests in Delhi

83. *M.C. Mehta vs. Union of India,* (24.07.96), 1996: Ridge area – Restoration

84. *M.C. Mehta vs. Union of India,* (24.04.96), 1996: Ridge area – Depletion of Ridge forests in Delhi

85. *M.C. Mehta vs. Union of India,* (13.03.96), 1996: Ridge area – Depletion of Ridge forests in Delhi

86. *M.C. Mehta vs. Union of India,* (09.04.96), 1996: Ridge area – Depletion of Ridge forests in Delhi

87. *Virender Gaur vs. State of Haryana,* (24.11.94), 1995: Environment Right of hygienic environment

88. *Hawrah Ganatantrik Nagarik Samity vs. State of West Bengal,* (01.09.95): Litigation concerning local issues

89. *M.C. Mehta vs. Union of India,* (13.12.96), 1996: River Pollution – Encroachment on river bed

90. *M.C. Mehta vs. Union of India,* (19.02.96), 1996: Taj Mahal– Safety

91. *M.C. Mehta vs. Union of India,* (06.08.96), 1996: Sewage treatment Plant – Construction

92. *S. Jagannath vs. Union of India,* (11.12.96), 1997: Shrimps culture

93. *Buffalo Traders Welfare Association vs. Union of India,* (19.02.1996): Slaughter house

94. *Buffalo Traders Welfare Association vs. Maneka Gandhi,* (30.11.1996): Slaughter house in Delhi

95. *M.C. Mehta vs. Union of India,* (30.12.96), 1996: Taj Mahal – preservation

96. *M.C. Mehta vs. Union of India,* (30.12.96), 1997: Taj Mahal Preservation – NEERI and Varadharajan Reports

97. *News Item Hindustan Times A.Q.F.M. Yamuna vs. Central Pollution Control Board,* (29.08.96), 1996: Taj Mahal – Plantation of trees around the Taj Mahal

98. *M.C. Mehta vs. Union of India,* (07.08.96), 1996: Pollution by Mathura Refinery – setting up of Hospital

99. *Vellore Citizens Welfare Forum vs. Union of India,* (08.08.95), 1995: Pollution by tanneries in Tamil Nadu

100. *Vellore Citizens Welfare Forum vs. Union of India,* (08.08.95), 1995: Pollution by tanneries in Tamil Nadu

101. *M.C. Mehta vs. Union of India,* (07.05.96), 1996: Depletion of underground water

102. *M.C. Mehta vs. Union of India,* (14.02.96), 1996: Vehicular Pollution – Delhi

103. *Indian Council for Enviro-Legal Action vs. Union of India,* (10.11.95), 1995: Claim of damages

104. *Vineet Kumar Mathur vs. Union of India,* (08.11.95), 1996: Contempt of Court – Apology – Disobedience

105. *M.C. Mehta vs. Union of India,* (19.12.96), 1997: Water Pollution – tanneries in Calcutta

106. *Rural Litigation and entitlement Kendra and others Versus State of Uttar Pradesh and others* and Writ petition no. 8821 of 1983 *Devaki Nandan Pandey Versus Union of India and others* Writ Petitions nos. 8209 and 8821 of 1983: Environmental protection

107. *Vishakha and others vs. State of Rajasthan and others* writ petitions (crl.) Nos. 666-70 of 1992: Enforcement of the fundamental rights of working women

108. *Dr. B.I. Wadehra versus Union of India and others* writ petition (c) no. 286 of 1994, decided on March 1, 1996: Distribution of Polythene Bags, Door to door collection of garbage and its disposal

109. *M.C. Mehta vs. Kamal Nath and Others,* (1997) 1 SCC 388 W.P.(c) No. 182 of 1996, decided on December 13, 1996: Ecology – Public Trust doctrine

110. *T.N. Godavarman Thirumulkpad vs. Union of India and Others,* (1997) 2 SCC 267, W.P.(C) No. 202 of 1995 with No. 171 of 1996 decided on December 12, 1996: Ecology – Protection and conservation of forests

111. *M.C. Mehta vs. Union of India and Others,* (1997) 2 SCC 353 W.P.(C) No. 13381 of 1984, decided on December 30, 1996: Degradation of Taj Mahal, a monument of international repute

112. *M.C. Mehta vs. Union of India and Others,* (1997) 2 SCC 411 W.P.(C) No. 3727 of 1985, decided on December 19, 1996: Poisonous effluent into Ganga River polluting fend and river

113. *T.N. Godavarman Thirumulkpad vs. Union of India and Others,* (1997) 3 SCC 312, W.P.(C) No. 202 of 1995 with Nos. 171 and 897 of 1996 decided on March 4, 1997: Protection and conservation of forests

114. *State of Orissa vs. Duti Sahu and Others,* (1997) 3 SCC 501 Civil Appeal No. 316 of 1997, decided on January 13, 1997: Restrictions on reservation of forests

115. *Animal and Environment Legal Defence Fund vs. Union of India and Others,* (1997) 3 SCC 549 W.P. (C) No. 785 of 1996, decided on March 5, 1997: Ecology – Fishing activity in reservoirs within National Park area – Claim of tribals formerly residing in National Park area

116. *Akhil Bharat Goseva Sangh and Others vs. State of A.P. and Others,* (1997) 3 SCC 707, C.A. No. 3968 of 1994 with Nos. 3964-67 of 1994 and I.PL, No.5, decided on March 12, 1997: Environment Control and Pollution – Mechanised slaughterhouse

117. *M.C. Mehta vs. Union of India and Others,* (1997) 3 SCC 715 I.A. No. 29 in W.P.(C) No. 4677 of 1985, decided on October 11, 1996: Banning of construction activities

118. *T.N. Godavarman Thirumulkpad vs. Union of India,* (1997) 7 SCC 440, W.P.(C) No. 202 of 1995 with IAs.. Ecology Protection and conservation of forests

119. *M.C. Mehta vs. Union of India,* (1997) 8 SCC 770 W.P.(C) No. 13029 of 1985, decided on November 20, 1997: Management and control of traffic in the National Capital Region

120. *M.C. Mehta vs. Union of India,* (1997) 11 SCC 312 I.A. No. 32 in W.P.(C) No. 4677 of 1985, decided on December 10, 1996: Regulation and control of ground water management and development

121. *M.C. Mehta vs. Union of India,* (1998) 1 SCC 363 W.P.(C) No. 13029 of 1995, decided on December 10, 1997: Remover of hoardings

122. *T.N. Godavarman Thirumulkpad vs. Union of India and Others* with I.A. No. 13 in W.P.(C) No. 171 of 1996 *Environment Awareness Forum vs. State of J&K and Others* IAs.: Illegal mining activity

123. *M.C. Mehta vs. Union of India and Others,* (1998) 2 SCC 435 W.P.(C) No. 13029 of 1985, decided on January 7, 1998: Environment Pollution (Prevention and Control)

124. *M.C. Mehta vs. Union of India,* (1998) SCC 720 IAs. Nos. 38, 44-47 and 49-51 in W.P.(C) No. 13382 of 1984, decided on March 24, 1998: Environmental impact on Taj Mahal

125. *M.C. Mehta vs. Union of India,* (1998) 6 SCC 60 W.P.(C) No. 13029 of 1985 with Nos. 939 of 1996 and 95 of 1997, decided on May 12, 1998: Chaotic traffic conditions and vehicular pollution in Delhi

126. *M.C. Mehta vs. Union of India,* (1998) 6 SCC 60 W.P.(C) No. 13029 of 1985 with Nos. 939 of 1996, decided on July 28, 1998: Vehicular Pollution in Delhi

127. *M.C. Mehta vs. Union of India and Others,* (1998) 8 SCC 206 W.P.(C) No. 13029 of 1985, decided on September 22, 1998: Environmental Protection and Pollution Control

128. *M.C. Mehta vs. Union of India and Others,* (1998) 8 SCC 648 W.P.(C) No. 13029 of 1985 with W.P. (C) No. 9300 of 1982 decided on February 16, 1996: Environmental Pollution and Control – Supply of lead-free petrol

129. *M.C. Mehta vs. Union of India and Others,* (1998) 9 SCC 93 I.A. No. 38 in W.P.(C) No. 13381 of 1984, decided on March 17, 1997: Ecology – Taj Mahal Protection

130. *M.C. Mehta vs. Union of India and Others,* (1998) 9 SCC 381 W.P.(C) No. 13381 of 1984, with I.A. No. 39 of 1987, decided on January 19, 1998: Automatic Monitoring Equipments

131. *M.C. Mehta vs. Union of India and Others,* (1998) 9 SCC 448 I.A. No. 86 of W.P.(C) No. 3727 of 1985 with I.A. No. 88 in W.P. (C) No. 4677 of 1985, decided on December 16, 1997: Common Effluent Treatment Plant

132. *M.C. Mehta vs. Union of India and Others,* (1998) 9 SCC 589 W.P.(C) No. 13029 of 1985 with Nos. 9300 of 1982, 939, 95 of 1996, and IAs. Nos. 7 to 10 in W.P. (C) No. 13029 of 1985, decided on November 18, 1997: Protection and improvement of environment

133. *T.N. Godavarman Thirumulkpad vs. Union of India and Others,* (1998) 9 SCC 632 I.A. No. 225 of 1995 in W.P.(C) No. 202 of 1995 with IAs Nos. 71, 79, 104, 105, 107, 108, 113, 121, 166, 260, 261, decided on December 16, 1997: Protection and conservation of forests – Utilisation/disposal of illegally felled timber

134. *T.N. Godavarman Thirumulkpad vs. Union of India and Others,* (1998) 9 SCC 632 I.As. Nos. 254-257 & 276 in W.P. (C) No. 202 of 1995 with I.A. No. 227 in W.P. No. 202 of 1995, decided on February 23, 1998: Ecology – PIL Protection and conservation of forests

135. *A.P. Pollution Control Board vs. Prof. M.V. Nayudu (Retd) and Others,* (1999) 2 SCC 718, C.A. Nos. 368-371 of 1999 with Nos. 372 and 373 of 1999, decided on January 27, 1999: Interference in environmental matters

136. *Environment Awareness Forum vs. State of J&K and Others,* (1999) 1 SCC 210, IAs Nos. 12, 14, 15, 13 & 16 and Contempt Petition (C) No. 539 of 1996 in W.P. (C) No. 171 of 1996, decided on May 5, 1998: Forests – Conservation and protection – Katha

137. *M.C. Mehta vs. Union of India and Others,* (1999) 1 SCC 413 W.P.(C) No. 13029 of 1985, decided on December 1, 1998: Traffic management and pollution control in NCT, Delhi